BILLY THE KID

The famous full-length tintype of Billy the Kid taken at Fort Sumner sometime in 1880. It is often reversed, placing the Kid's revolver on his left side. *Courtesy of Lincoln County Heritage Trust.*

BILLY THE KID
His Life and Legend

Jon Tuska

A revised and expanded edition of
Billy the Kid: A Bio-Bibliography

Greenwood Press
Westport, Connecticut • London

Library of Congress Cataloging-in-Publication Data

Tuska, Jon.
    Billy the Kid: his life and legend / Jon Tuska.
        p. cm.
    Rev. and expanded ed. of: Billy the Kid, a bio-bibliography.   1983.
    Includes index.
    ISBN 0–313–28589–6 (alk. paper)
      1. Billy, the Kid. 2. Outlaws—Southwest, New—Biography.
  3. Southwest, New—Biography. 4. Billy, the Kid—Bibliography.
  I. Tuska, Jon. Billy the Kid, a bio-bibliography. II. Title.
  F786.B54T87   1994
  364.1′552′092—dc20   93–40176

British Library Cataloguing in Publication Data is available.

Library of Congress Catalog Card Number: 93–40176
ISBN: 0–313–28589–6

First published in 1994

Greenwood Press, 88 Post Road West, Westport, CT 06881
An imprint of Greenwood Publishing Group, Inc.

Printed in the United States of America

The paper used in this book complies with the
Permanent Paper Standard issued by the National
Information Standards Organization (Z39.48–1984).

10 9 8 7 6 5 4 3 2 1

For
Loren D. Estleman
La vérité ici n'a piont votre air d'improvisation.
Quel dommage!

CONTENTS

ILLUSTRATIONS

PREFACE TO THE SECOND EDITION

No book I have written has generated so much correspondence from interested or curious readers as this one. Students in high school have written term papers based on it and on more than one occasion I have been made a mentor and have been interviewed over the telephone by students in order to incorporate my comments into what they intended to write. A newspaper in Paris telephoned me long distance in an effort to locate the progeny of Billy the Kid. Fortunately perhaps for them they are all now dead. I was an expert witness in what I thought a ridiculous lawsuit between Morgan Creek Productions which produced YOUNG GUNS (20th-Fox, 1988) and M-G-M/Pathé in which the former asserted that the latter had been guilty of copyright infringement in producing the "The Young Riders" for the ABC television network. I was quite firmly in M-G-M/Pathé's camp that such an assertion was patently absurd. Some mention of this lawsuit is made at further length in the analysis of the two Morgan Creek films about Billy the Kid and his gang. To this must also be added the observation that more has been written by historians about Billy the Kid and the Lincoln County War and more films have been made about him in the decade since the first edition of this handbook appeared than in the previous two decades combined. I have included discussions of all these new arrivals in the appropriate chapters following the life of the historical Billy the Kid who, without all this media attention in the more than a century since his passing, would have remained an obscure New Mexican horse thief and minor participant in a mercantile war in which he found himself clearly on the losing side. Just why he should have been singled out in the fashion he has been by the media (and become the obsession of otherwise sane historians as well) is addressed in the chapter on The Legend of Billy the Kid.

However, I should begin by telling the reader how this book came to be written in the first place. Sometime in 1981 I was telephoned by Harrison Engel, producer, at the time of the Academy Awards. He was at work producing a new special for the ABC network on the "real" West and he wanted my suggestion as to an appropriate film clip showing Billy the Kid that he could feature in the program.

"How are you treating the Kid?" I asked him.

"Why, as a hero, of course," he replied. "How is it you ask?"

"For one thing, because it will tell me what kind of film clip to suggest."

"Are you implying that the Kid wasn't a hero?"

"No. I would state outright that the Kid wasn't a hero."

He assured me that he would get a research expert on the matter right away, that, since the special was to deal with the contrast between the legends and the realities of the Old West, if the Kid was not a hero, he would be presented as he was. In short, this television special was going to embody that worthy principle of German historian Leopold von Ranke, to reconstruct the past "*wie es eigentlich gewesen war*," as it really had been.[1]

I should have known better. When the special was aired, the viewer was informed that Billy the Kid's real name was William S. Bonney, that he was a savage killer who had killed twenty-one men by the time Sheriff Pat Garrett gunned him down, and that he had killed his first man at the age of fourteen. There is not a shred of historical truth in this image.

Shortly thereafter I received a letter dated 1 April 1981 from Leon C. Metz who wrote what remains the best biography to be had on the man who killed the Kid, PAT GARRETT: THE STORY OF A WESTERN LAWMAN (University of Oklahoma Press, 1974). "I came to find out, and to my surprise," he wrote, "that a definitive biography of Billy the Kid has yet to be written. Were I a smarter man I would have begun work on that biography soon after GARRETT and published it for this year, the centennial of the Kid's death."

When Marilyn Brownstein of Greenwood Press proposed that I write a book on Billy the Kid for their bio-bibliography series, after some consideration I thought the opportunity such a book would present would be welcome for two different, if related, reasons. First, I could provide the interested reader with a concise, reliable biography of Billy the Kid against the background of the Lincoln County War. Second, after presenting the uses to which the Kid's life and legend have been put by historians, authors of Western fiction, and filmmakers, I felt I could provide a more effective methodology for dealing with the Kid's popular legend than those so far employed in connection with it and possibly also, at least by extension, a methodology for dealing with other popular Western legends.

It ought, however, also be stated at this point what this book is not. It has not been my intention to repeat and then to correct all of the erroneous data about the Kid which have appeared in various publications over the years since his death on 14 July 1881. Much of the essential groundwork in this area has already been done, and done splendidly, by the late Ramon F. Adams in four books: A FITTING DEATH FOR BILLY THE KID (University of Oklahoma Press, 1960), BURS UNDER THE SADDLE: A SECOND LOOK AT BOOKS AND HISTORIES OF THE WEST (University of Oklahoma Press, 1964), SIX-GUNS AND SADDLE

LEATHER: A BIBLIOGRAPHY OF BOOKS AND PAMPHLETS ON WEST-
ERN OUTLAWS AND GUNMEN (University of Oklahoma Press, 1969), and
MORE BURS UNDER THE SADDLE (University of Oklahoma Press, 1979). Nor
has it been my intention to fill in the gaps which occur in the items listed by J. C.
Dykes in his book, BILLY THE KID: THE BIBLIOGRAPHY OF A LEGEND
(University of New Mexico Press, 1952), covering the years 1881–1952, and then
to bring his listing up to date. It is enough to note that Dykes included 437 items
in his bibliography and that items pertaining in some way to the Kid continue to
multiply at the rate of approximately 100 per decade and in the last decade, as stated
above, more so than previously.

In the chapters I have devoted to the uses to which the Kid and his legend have
been put in history—divided into three groups: fantasy books and firsthand accounts, the more reliable biographies of the Kid and others connected with him and
the events of his life, and general histories—as well as in fiction and film, I have
confined myself to *significant* appearances, which is to say appearances which have
some special relevance to the manner in which the Kid or his legend or both have
been interpreted. What this has meant in practice when it comes to films which
feature the Kid is that I have emphasized those films in which he is characterized
and portrayed by an actor, as opposed to those films where he might be mentioned
only by name. In detailing these appearances by the Kid in fiction and film, I have
made only a minimal effort in the text to correct errors of fact or distortions of
history since the reader should be in quite as able a position as I am to do this having
first read the biography of the Kid and then the critical survey of certain legendary
aspects in the chapter on Billy and the Historians. This chapter begins, in fact, with
an intensive analysis of Pat Garrett's book, THE AUTHENTIC LIFE OF BILLY
THE KID (1882), because Garrett's reasons for causing this book to be written are
of the utmost importance in understanding all later historical, as well as fictional
and cinematic, appearances of the legend. In a sense it might be claimed that the
legend of Billy the Kid was first derived from this "biography" and, whatever its
subsequent manifestations, I have serious doubts if the Kid would be known at all
today, much less be the familiar historical personality he has become, had this book
not been published. It is also generally the case that if a screenwriter, a novelist, or
a historian begins by accepting the Garrett account as an irrefutable *Urtext*, granting
it the same infallibility evangelical scholars grant the Bible when they insist that
each word and concept in it be taken literally as the Word of God, the fall into error
and fantasy is inevitable and assured. In addition to the fantasies which had their
origin in the Garrett book, ghosted by his friend Ash Upson, a wholly additional
set of fantasies was propagated by Walter Noble Burns in THE SAGA OF BILLY
THE KID (Doubleday, 1926) which also required outlining. For this second edition
yet one more set has had to be added outlining Robert M. Utley's fantasies about
the Kid in the three books he wrote in the interim since the first edition of BILLY
THE KID. Two of Utley's books touch upon the Kid indirectly as a participant in
the Lincoln County War and the third actually purports to be a biography of him.

So, no less than in recent fictional and cinematic treatments, the legend has proved equally alive and strong among historians.

In writing about the early life of the Kid, I am indebted, as any historian dealing with this subject must be, to Robert N. Mullin's THE BOYHOOD OF BILLY THE KID (Texas Western Press, 1967); just as it is not really possible to write accurately on the Lincoln County War without acknowledging an even greater debt to Colonel Maurice Garland Fulton's HISTORY OF THE LINCOLN COUNTY WAR (University of Arizona Press, 1969) edited by Robert N. Mullin. Another source on which I have relied in fashioning my own historical narrative is William A. Keleher's VIOLENCE IN LINCOLN COUNTY: 1869–1881 (University of New Mexico Press, 1957). To these the last decade has also seen the completion of what is, except for its coverage of the circumstances of the Kid's last days and his death, an exhaustive and generally reliable account in Frederick Nolan's long-awaited THE LINCOLN COUNTY WAR: A DOCUMENTARY HISTORY (University of Oklahoma Press, 1992). Nolan is perhaps the only historian since Colonel Fulton, William A. Keleher, and Robert N. Mullin to write about the broad subject of the Lincoln County War who has also retained the scientific historian's determination to arrive impartially at a truthful reconstruction, as opposed to the partisanship which has characterized so much of what has been published in the last decade. When these or other sources pertaining specifically to the Kid are quoted in the biography chapter, the endnotes are usually page citations. However, other documents cited not found in these books are provided with citations including locations in archives or other depositories of official records. The conversations reproduced in the text based on interviews conducted by Colonel Fulton or others, however, can only be cited as to archival source and in these cases the notes will indicate that archival source, e.g., the Fulton Papers, and complete information as to the physical *loca* of these various collections has been provided in Appendix A. For this second edition notes are provided for citations in all the chapters, not just for those to be found in the biography chapter.

Of course, even after one has assembled all of the relevant documents and devised a chronology—and the chronology I have used can be found in Appendix B and has been amended in view of subsequent research from what it was in the first edition—there is still the matter of historical interpretation. Where possible, I have tried to avoid attributing motives to any of the personalities involved. If this proved impracticable, or where I have differed from others, I have made note of my reasons for maintaining a particular interpretation. However, this is probably as suitable a place as any to mention that psychological dimensions are too often absent in virtually all of the accounts provided of the Lincoln County War, its participants, and above all in connection with the Kid. Why, once he had shot his way out of jail in Lincoln with a rope hanging over his head, did he not leave the Territory as had so many others who had found themselves on the wrong side of the Lincoln County War or of the law? He seems in those last weeks of his life to have achieved a serenity he had never known prior to that. He seems to have had no more interest in settling past scores. Yet, he did not leave. When asked, he would say he couldn't go to *viejo mejico* because he had no money, but he had never really had money at any time prior to those final days. Did he ignore unpleasant realities, as has been suggested, or was there some deeper motivation behind behavior so foolhardy that even Pat Garrett had trouble believing the Kid was hiding out near Fort Sumner? It is one of the conundrums of the Kid's personality that no one has been able to unravel. It is one with which I am still left despite now the years of study and research I have given the subject.

Finally, I should conclude these remarks with a confession. My first knowledge of Billy the Kid came to me when I was three years old by way of a phonograph recording, "The Ballad of Billy the Kid" (Capitol 25070), sung and narrated by Tex Ritter. I really believed that Billy the Kid had killed twenty-one men and that "Pat Garrett must make twenty-two." I believed it because Tex Ritter said so. No less, almost three decades later I believed Sam Peckinpah when he insisted to me that he was telling the "real fucking story" of the Kid in his film, PAT GARRETT AND BILLY THE KID (M-G-M, 1973). It was not until I happened to pick up a copy of Ramon F. Adams' A FITTING DEATH FOR BILLY THE KID that I realized that it was impossible to write film history, or literary history, or cultural history without knowing first the historical reality and by this standard to survey the varying degrees of deviation. "The recently published accounts of Billy the Kid are getting closer and closer to the truth," Adams concluded in his Epilogue, "but the truth has been a long time coming. And if in this critical examination of existing works on Billy the Kid I have awakened even one future author to the fact that writing biography or history is more than following his predecessors' footsteps blindly, I shall be amply repaid."[2] I trust I have been so awakened.

ACKNOWLEDGMENTS

It was American historian Frederick Jackson Turner who wrote in his essay "The Significance of the Frontier" that "history, both objective and subjective, is ever *becoming*, never completed."[1] A number of writers, scholars, historians, archivists, and readers have helped with this second edition to further the accuracy of the portrait provided in the chapter on "The Life and Death of Billy the Kid" as well as with the other chapters in this book. This list is not exhaustive but it is at least a beginning. Charles Johnston of Los Angeles has sent my way copies of everything published about Billy the Kid that he has encountered or provided notice when there was to be some televised treatment of the Kid or his legend. Nora Henn, indefatigable Historian and Custodian of the Collection of the Lincoln County Historical Society, has been unstinting in her uncovering of obscure details about which I inquired and she also read over the first edition for errors. Ret. Col. Francis C. Kajencki of El Paso who wrote the article "Alexander Grzelachowski: Pioneer Merchant of Puerto de Luna, New Mexico" published in ARIZONA AND THE WEST (Autumn, 1984) brought to my attention an error I made with regard to the statement that Grzelachowski operated a brothel in conjunction with his store and saloon in Puerto de Luna. I am sure both he and that merchant and gentleman's descendant, Charles Grzelachowski of Fort Worth, will be pleased to note that the offending reference has been removed from this text as something that cannot be documented and therefore ought not be stated. Karl Thiede as so often before has been immensely helpful in providing me with information about all the films in which the Kid has appeared as a character and Francis M. Nevins, Jr., provided me with a videotape of a Billy the Kid picture Karl and I did not know existed.

The late St. George Cooke of Guadalajara, Mexico lived long enough to see his first novel accepted for publication, THE TREASURE OF RODOLFO FIERRO (Doubleday, 1990). He was a longtime researcher into the life and times of the Kid and supplied me with a copy of his "Little Known Facts About Billy the Kid" which was privately printed. He also worked out an elaborate chronology in conjunction with the late Robert N. Mullin and I have consulted both it and the one appended to Frederick Nolan's recent book on the Lincoln County War cited above in updating and expanding the chronology which appears in this volume. Fred Nolan has also corresponded with me and I am pleased that his many, many years of untiring research should have given us all such a grand dividend. Nolan read the first two chapters of this edition in manuscript and offered his suggestions, for which I am profoundly grateful. St. George Cooke came very close to tracing the lives of the Kid's three children. He started with an admission from Vital Records in Santa Fe that it has the records but will not release them save to family members and went on from there. Dick Kreck of the *Colorado Springs Gazette Telegraph* came close enough to identify one of the mothers. Historian Eve Ball refused to name the other in print, although she had known her. Since now both mothers and all three children are deceased and since their names could not possibly shed any light on their father's life and death, it is just as well to let them keep their secret.

Donald R. Lavash of Santa Fe and author of SHERIFF WILLIAM BRADY: TRAGIC HERO OF THE LINCOLN COUNTY WAR (Sunstone Press, 1986) and I disagree on whether or not the word "hero" is aptly applied to Major Brady. However, in his somewhat detailed correspondence with me, he assisted in highlighting several of the points which appear in "Utley Fantasies" in the chapter on Billy and the Historians. Both he and Katherine Dorman, archivist at the State Records Center and Archives in Santa Fe, have added to my knowledge of the Kid's activities.

Gary Miller of the Lincoln County Heritage Trust was extremely helpful during my visit to Lincoln and even supplied me with a copy of Sheriff Brady's inventory on the contents of the McSween home and the Tunstall store prior to the five-day battle. Linda Suzanne Kopfer of West Linn, Oregon and Carolyn Duncan of Tulsa, Oklahoma also kept me abreast of articles published in various magazines about the Kid and his legend. David T. Alexander of Tampa, Florida, helped me with the citations for the Billy the Kid stories by Ray Nafziger which appeared in MAVER-ICKS.

Based on the vast number of letters I have received over the last ten years about the Kid, I would have to say that, while for the most part male historians have written about him, female readers in general have shown the greatest interest in him and his life. Even among students from whom I have heard, the females are by far in the majority. The Kid would no doubt be pleased.

BILLY THE KID

1

THE LIFE AND DEATH OF
BILLY THE KID

I

Although there has been much speculation about it, the truth of the matter is that it cannot be said with documentary certitude where the man known later in life as Billy the Kid was born. He himself between 17 and 19 June 1880 in Fort Sumner told census taker Lorenzo Labadie, a former Indian agent and Juan Patrón's brother-in-law, that he was born in Missouri, that both of his parents were born in Missouri, and that he was twenty-five years old at the time. Except for those who are enamored of his legend, there does not seem to have been any credible reason for him to have lied about either his place of birth or his age. The problem that has existed stems primarily from those who created the legend insisting he was born elsewhere and that he was younger than he said he was. It is documented that his given name was Henry McCarty and that in 1866 he was living in Marion County, Indiana with his mother Catherine McCarty and his elder brother Joseph McCarty. It was at this time that Catherine McCarty became acquainted with the man she would eventually marry, William H. Antrim of the town of Huntsville, located between Indianapolis and Anderson. Antrim had been honorably discharged as a private from Company "I" of the 54th Regiment of the Indiana Volunteer Infantry on 26 September 1862. On an application for the U.S. Bureau of Pensions executed on 2 April 1915 at El Paso, Texas, then his home, William H. Antrim claimed that it was his understanding that the natural father of Henry and Joseph had died in New York. This definitely need not have meant that Henry's father was a native of that state, merely that that is where he was living when he died.

Catherine McCarty suffered from tuberculosis. In 1869 she, her two sons, and Antrim left Indianapolis for Wichita, Kansas. On 14 September 1869 Mrs. McCarty purchased a town lot in her own name in Wichita and the following March she filed on a quarter-section of public land near the town upon which she settled on 10

August 1870. While Mrs. McCarty operated a hand laundry in Wichita, Antrim worked at farming and augmented his income by working as a carpenter and a part-time bartender. Henry Cook, to whom in August, 1871, the widow sold her town property, in a deposition recorded in the Deed Records of Sedgwick County, Kansas on 18 July 1892 asserted that it was his understanding that six months later the lady was in New Orleans. He may have misinterpreted what she said since New Mexico was a more appropriate place for her to go given her respiratory condition. Antrim is on record as saying that he left the Wichita area in October, 1872, while Joseph, known as "Josie" when a child, recalled in an interview with the *Denver Post* on 1 April 1928 that in 1871 he had gone to Denver with his "father."

As were many men during the post–Civil War period, Antrim was a part-time prospector and he prospected, without success, during his stay in the Denver area. On 1 March 1873, the couple identified as "Mr. William H. Antrim and Mrs. Catherine McCarty, both of Santa Fe, New Mexico," on the marriage certificate, were married by the Reverend D. F. McFarland of the First Presbyterian Church of Santa Fe.[1] Henry and Josie McCarty were recorded as among the witnesses. Almost immediately, perhaps because of the reports of rich silver strikes in the area, Antrim and his family departed for Silver City, New Mexico; but also, as in the previous moves to Colorado and to Santa Fe, Antrim may well have been searching for a climate that would prove beneficial for Catherine's tuberculosis. Until he settled in El Paso in October, 1912, Antrim never ceased making prospecting trips between periods of paid employment.

Those who knew Mrs. Antrim in Silver City later recalled that, despite her illness, she showed fortitude and good cheer. A young neighbor at Silver City, Lewis Abraham, remembered that "Mrs. Bill Antrim was a jolly Irish lady, full of life and mischief."[2] In order to assist in the support of the family, Mrs. Antrim took in boarders at the 30×25 wooden frame house which Antrim built on Lot 4 bounded by Main, Broadway, Hudson, and Yankee Streets, even when her health worsened and until four months prior to her death.[3]

Subsequent storytellers, for various reasons, fabricated incidents which supposedly occurred in the Kid's early years while in Silver City. The fact is that Henry McCarty's boyhood was an average one for a youth growing up in a frontier mining camp. Henry was, again according to schoolmate Lewis Abraham, "full of fun and mischief."[4] Harry Whitehill, son of the Silver City sheriff, said later that "my sister and I went to school with Billy the Kid. He wasn't a bad fellow."[5] Chauncey O. Truesdell, another schoolmate of the McCarty brothers, said that Henry was sometimes called by the name of his stepfather, Billy Antrim, and that, while neither boy was big for his age, Josie was the larger and sat toward the rear of the schoolroom with the more advanced students, whereas Henry "sat near the front with us younger ones."[6] Henry's teacher, Miss Mary Richards, recalled that "Billy (they called him Henry then) was no more of a problem in school than any other boy" and that he was "always quite willing to help with the chores around the schoolhouse."[7] Henry liked to sing and dance and he performed once as "end man" in the school minstrel show and in amateur theatricals at Morrill's Opera House. It would appear, based on the written documents he left behind, that this brief period in Silver City constituted the only formal schooling he was ever to have and that his literacy skills were marginal at best by the time he became too old to remain in school.

During the final months of her life, Mrs. Antrim developed acute tuberculous caseous pneumonia, what is commonly referred to as "galloping consumption." It is a condition characterized by lesions ulcerating through the walls of the bronchi in many places and infection being spread throughout the lungs through inhalation. A person is racked by coughing, with bloody effusions, stabbing pain from either coughing or deep breathing. One gasps for breath, so that all of one's conscious faculties are concentrated on the mere process of breathing, the face muscles usually constricted from involuntary anxiety. It was a painful death. Henry was approximately eighteen years old when his mother succumbed on 16 September 1874.

The weekly *Silver City Mining Life* reported on 19 September 1874 that "the funeral occurred from the family residence on Main Street at 2 o'clock on Thursday." After the wake, Henry went to live with Mr. and Mrs. Del Truesdell, parents of his schoolmate, Chauncey. Mr. Truesdell operated the Star Hotel and Henry earned his room and board by waiting on tables and washing dishes. "Henry was the only kid who ever worked there who never stole anything," Truesdell later recalled. "Other fellows used to steal the silverware—that kind of stuff was scarce in the camp."[8]

When Mr. Antrim secured employment at Richard Knight's butcher shop, he had his stepsons board with him at the Knight home in Silver City and Henry helped him around the shop. Occasionally Henry would venture out to the Knight ranch to visit with his boyhood friend, Anthony B. Connor, younger brother of Sarah Ann (Mrs. Richard S.) Knight at whose home he was boarding. Although still in his teens, Anthony regularly transported mail over the dangerous forty-mile stretch between Silver City and Ralston. His father was U.S. Mail contractor and his son continued to work for him until the elder Connor was ambushed and killed by Indians in 1878, some five miles from the Knight ranch. "Billy was about 12 and I was 13," Connor remembered concerning their first meeting. "I know he was a better boy than I was. . . . I never remember Billy doing anything out of the way any more than the rest of us. We had our chores to do, like washing dishes and other duties around the house."[9] When Mr. Antrim quit his job at the butcher shop to go to work in the mines at Chloride Flats, Henry chose to stay in Silver City and took a room in Mrs. Brown's house. By this time, he no longer seems to have been working at anything nor to have been very close to his brother. He seems to have had little use for his stepfather, even when his mother was alive, but he talked often in later years to friends about the affection he retained for his mother's memory.

It was shortly after this that Henry got into trouble for the first time through stealing a keg of butter from an unattended buckboard and selling it to a Silver City merchant. Sheriff Harvey W. Whitehill, a six-foot-two, two-hundred-and-forty pound ex-miner who had been recently elected to that office, confronted Henry with his action, appropriated the money he had made on the sale, and paddled his backside. Ash Upson would later say that the Kid's basic problem was that he wouldn't stay whipped. He certainly didn't in this case. A few months later the *Grant County Herald* for Sunday 26 September 1875 carried the following item: "Henry McCarty, who was arrested on Thursday and committed to jail to await the action of the grand jury, upon the charge of stealing clothes from Charley Sun and Sam Chung, celestials sans cue [queue, i.e., pigtail], sans Joss sticks, escaped from prison yesterday through the chimney. It is believed that Henry was simply the tool of 'Sombrero Jack' who done the actual stealing whilst Henry done the hiding. Jack has skipped out."[10]

What happened, apparently, was that George Shaffer, who was known locally as "Sombrero Jack," absconded with a bundle of laundry and two pistols valued at between $150 and $200 belonging to the two Chinese who had become Westerners (hence the description that they abandoned the queue and Joss sticks invariably associated with most men from China on the American frontier) while Henry and perhaps another young man kept a lookout. It was purportedly a joke, but Sheriff Whitehill arrested Henry and, when Henry refused to name his accomplice(s), locked him up in the jail. It was perhaps Whitehill's intention to frighten the young man thoroughly while teaching him a lesson. Henry seems to have been scarcely cognizant of this and—based on remarks he made later in life—was by now intensely hostile toward his stepfather. He chose instead of a hearing to squeeze his way up through the chimney—something which he was physically slight and lithe enough to accomplish—and strike out on his own. Dan McMillan, one of Antrim's coworkers out on Chloride Flats, recalled how Antrim "was called out of the mines one day to talk to his son who had gotten himself in a great deal of trouble and he had given him all of the money he had on him at that time and told him to leave town."[11]

A. M. "Gus" Gildea, who knew Henry in the Camp Grant district in Arizona in 1876–1877, told Colonel Maurice Garland Fulton in an interview at the home of John M. Kelly of Douglas, Arizona in August, 1932, that the youth from Silver City was known in Arizona as Kid Antrim or merely as "the Kid." Gildea had gone to Arizona in November, 1876, with a John Chisum cattle drive and had remained behind to work as a civilian scout at Camp Grant and, later, as a cowhand for Bill Whalen at Colonel Hooker's Sierra Bonita ranch, the Crooked H. "When we weren't at work," he told Fulton, "we used to hang out at the Bonita store, about six miles from the Bonita ranch house. There was a good eating house there and a saloon that had a little dance hall. It was only about four miles from Camp Grant and of course the men from the post used to go there a lot, too. I read a story in a magazine where some fellow said that Billy killed a Chinaman in Globe, but if that had really happened I am sure I would have known about it. That is like what Pat Garrett said about Billy being in Mexico, and all those other yarns somebody dreamed up after Billy was dead."[12]

Lewis Abraham, Henry's friend living back in Silver City, heard that he was working as a cowboy in Arizona. Henry was employed for some time by W. J. "Sorghum" Smith who ran a hay camp in what was at the time part of Pima County,

Arizona. "He came to my camp at Fort Thomas," Smith recalled subsequently, "(which is on the Gila below Solomonville) and asked for work. He said he was seventeen, though he didn't look to be fourteen."[13] Later the Kid went to work as a teamster for Captain G. C. Smith, post quartermaster at Camp Grant, driving a log team from the timber camp on Mount Graham to the sawmill at the post. The Bonita settlement near Camp Grant had grown considerably by the summer of 1877 when the abolition of the Chiricahua Indian reservation and the easing of warfare with the Apaches now attracted numerous cattlemen into the area, including John Chisum. The former little town of Bonita even changed its name to Camp Grant— rather as Laramie grew up some distance from Fort Laramie in Wyoming. Miles L. Wood, the sixteenth Anglo-American to settle in Arizona Territory (and so something of an old-timer by local American standards), became both sheriff and justice of the peace at the civilian Camp Grant.

Henry, no doubt because of his youthful appearance, was now commonly referred to as "Kid" by locals. Gus Gildea in an interview with J. Fred Denton described the Kid as "dressed like a 'country jake,' with 'store pants' on and shoes instead of boots. He wore a six-gun stuffed in his trousers."[14] Between sporadic periods of legitimate employment, Kid Antrim was part of a gang stealing horses and sometimes cattle in the Camp Grant area and driving them out to the mining camps where they were bought with no questions asked. "The soldiers would ride down to Bonita [civilian Camp Grant]," Sheriff Wood recalled, "and tie their horses in front of the saloon known as the 'hog ranch' and go in for a drink, and while [they were] doing so [Henry] and his chum [Johnny Mackie] would steal the saddles from the horses and sometimes would take the horses and hide them until they got a chance to dispose of them."[15]

In the latter part of November, 1876, Henry stole a saddled horse belonging to a cavalry sergeant by the name of Louis Hartman. The horse had been hitched outside McDowell's store. The Kid headed out toward the Globe mining camp. Hartman led a detachment of four enlisted men in pursuit. They recovered the horse but had to let Henry go free because they lacked a warrant for his arrest. Hartman remedied that situation on 16 February 1877 when he swore out a warrant for the arrest of "Henry Antrim, alias Kid." Sheriff Wood had no intention of troubling himself hunting up the Kid. He bided his time and on 25 March he saw Henry Antrim and Johnny Mackie entering the dining room of the Bonita Hotel for breakfast. Presumably the Kid thought his contretemps with Hartman had blown over. Wood arrested the Kid in the dining room and then marched him out to the military post and requested of the commanding officer, Major Charles Compton, that he hold them for trial in the guardhouse. There was no jail in civilian Camp Grant in which to hold the Kid and he certainly was not charged and held as a military prisoner. Perhaps Wood was able to get cooperation from the post because the warrant had been sworn out by Sergeant Hartman. At any event, that evening, despite being shackled, the Kid threw salt in the eyes of the soldier guarding him and escaped custody, shackles and all. Again, the Kid bided his time, then returned to civilian Camp Grant. He was identified once more in a theft and another arrest warrant for larceny was issued against him. He was again taken into custody and again broke free. It would seem even this early in his career the Kid had a blind side. As Frederick Nolan pointed out, "with two arrests for thieving in one six-month period notched up against him, a more careful man might have distanced himself from an area where he was clearly well known, but it appears the Kid's method for handling problems was to pretend they didn't exist; he would make the same mistake just a few years later at Fort Sumner."[16]

The Kid was next involved in his first shooting outside Adkins' dance hall in civilian Camp Grant. Frank P. Cahill was a civilian blacksmith attached to the post who had earned the nickname "Windy" because of his overbearing manner. He apparently found delight in tormenting the Kid and on 17 August 1877, after a card game, he became involved in a fatal quarrel with the Kid in which he called the Kid "a pimp" and the Kid called him "a sonofabitch." Cahill wrestled the Kid down. The Kid pulled a gun and shot the older and much heavier man through the stomach. "He had no choice," Gildea told Colonel Fulton; "he had to use his 'equalizer.' "[17] Frank Cahill died the following day.

Again the Kid was arrested by Sheriff Wood and this time, as justice of the peace, Wood conducted a coroner's inquest at which the jury decided that the killing "was criminal and unjustifiable, and that Henry Antrim, alias Kid, is guilty thereof."[18] The Kid was once more incarcerated at the military post to await formal trial.

The 30 March 1933 issue of the *Tombstone Epitaph* ran a letter from Colonel C. C. Smith, retired, about his father, Captain G. C. Smith who in 1877 had been post quartermaster at Camp Grant and for whom the Kid had worked as a teamster. "One night while a social function was in progress at my father's quarters," Colonel Smith wrote, "two or three shots rang out. This did not cause much excitement but when the officer of the day (I believe it was Lieutenant Benny Cheever, 6th Cavalry), who had gone out to investigate, returned to the party he announced that the shots were fired by the sentry at the guardhouse at a man who had escaped. . . . It has always been believed that the Kid had some soldier help in making his escape." Colonel Smith's view of what happened is supported by a telegram sent at the time dated 23 August 1877 by Major C. E. Compton to U.S. Deputy Marshal W. J. Osborn in Tucson in which the major confirmed "Cahill was not killed on the military Reservation L. R. 704. His murderer, Antrim, alias 'Kid,' was allowed to escape and I believe is still at large."[19] It would seem evident that the military tended to be particularly lax about civilian matters and escape was as a result rather easy for the Kid.

The Kid seized the fastest horse he could find, "Cashaw," a racing pony belonging to John Murphey. About a week later the pony was returned by a mounted traveler who told Murphey that the Kid had asked him to return the animal to its rightful owner. The Kid had fled to the Knight ranch, some forty miles south of Silver City. Knowing that he could not stay there indefinitely without being found out, after two or three weeks the Kid left. Sarah Ann Knight told the Kid he might select any horse he wanted from the corral. The Kid picked the scrubbiest of the lot and headed toward Mesilla.

It would seem, based on a letter written to Robert N. Mullin by Gustave Dore Griggs dated at Mesilla, New Mexico 4 September 1922 that the Kid was still going by the name Antrim, albeit calling himself Billy Antrim, when he reached Doña Ana County. A Mesilla valley rancher at the time, Eugene Van Patten, later told Griggs that he was surprised to learn that the boy named Antrim who had come to his ranch seeking work in the early fall of 1877 turned out to be the notorious William Bonney.

The Kid stayed in Mesilla only briefly before joining up with a youth his own age, Tom O'Keefe, who was going to the Pecos valley in search of work. They rode together through the Organ mountains and across the Tularosa basin. However, instead of taking the longer but safer route through the Tularosa, Ruidoso, and Hondo valleys, the young men took a shortcut straight over the northern portion of the Guadalupe mountains. They discounted the fact that travelers in this section were frequently victims to roving bands of renegade Apaches. They were climbing an old Indian trail on the second day of their journey when they saw a pool of water at the bottom of the canyon below them. Taking their empty canteen with him, the Kid made his way down the cliff wall to the water. He was about to return when the sounds of gunfire reached him. Taking cover behind rocks and brush, the Kid made his way back up to where he had left O'Keefe and the horses. There was no sign of either; gone also, therefore, were the Kid's bedroll and his rations.

Keeping himself hidden until nightfall, the Kid resumed the journey on foot. After two days of remaining concealed and three nights of walking through the arid foothills, the water in the canteen gone, the Kid finally made his way through the mountains and down Rocky Arroyo until he came upon the Jones ranch. Heiskell Jones and his wife Barbara, known generally as Ma'am Jones, and their ten children lived there. Ma'am Jones heard the Kid outside, went out to investigate, saw him, and half carried him into the kitchen. Removing his boots, which struck her as remarkably small, she saw that he wore no socks and that his feet were raw and swollen. She proposed to wash his feet and suggested he take a bath. Then she asked him how long it had been since he had eaten, and he responded that it had been three days. According to Eve Ball's account in MA'AM JONES OF THE PECOS (University of Arizona Press, 1969), Ma'am heated some milk. The strange boy sat hunched in a blanket with his feet in hot water. Ma'am held the cup out to him.

" 'I don't like milk,' he told her.

'Drink it. Later you may have some food, but not now. It's bad for you to eat before you're rested a little.'

"There was no reply."

" 'Do you want me to hold your nose and pour it down you?'

"He took the cup. When he tasted the milk he made a wry face, but he drank. He drank greedily. Ma'am took the cup and told him to sip the milk. He obeyed.

" 'Now, I'm going to put you to bed. You're worn out and need sleep.'

" 'I can sleep right here.'

" 'You can sleep better in a bed.' "[20]

The next day the Kid introduced himself as Billy Bonney. This was the first time he is known to have used this alias, but it is understandable in view of his desire to conceal his identity. There is no reason to believe that the fictitious surname was any reference to an old family name. Billy told of his experiences with the Indians, whom he had not seen, and he engaged in some target practice with John, the Joneses' eldest son. John asked the Kid how he was with his left hand. " 'Not so good,' " the Kid is reputed to have said. " 'Sometimes I hit, but if I was in a jackpot I'd use my right.' "[21]

When the Kid was sufficiently recovered to ride, John lent him a horse and he was again on his way.

II

Lincoln County in New Mexico Territory was established by an act of the Territorial legislature on 16 January 1869. General William Tecumseh Sherman, on a tour for the War Department in 1874, perhaps typified the attitude of the federal government of the United States toward New Mexico Territory when he remarked that it was "not worth the cost of defense."[22] In 1878 the Territorial legislature enlarged Lincoln County so as to include approximately one-fourth of the entire Territory, measuring 170 miles from north to south, from east to west about 150 miles.

At the beginning of the Civil War, New Mexico Territory, which had first come into the possession of the United States as a result of the Treaty of Guadalupe Hidalgo with the Republic of Mexico on 2 February 1848, was seized by Confederate troops, but they were summarily routed by General James Henry Carleton whose California Column entered the Territory flying the Stars and Stripes in mid-1862. On 27 September 1862 Carleton issued the following order: "Fort Stanton, on the Bonito river, in the country of the Mescalero Apaches, will without delay be reoccupied by five companies of Colonel Christopher Carson's regiment of New Mexico volunteers."[23] Carleton's orders to Carson regarding the Mescaleros were as follows: "All Indian men of that tribe are to be killed whenever and wherever you can find them. The women and children will not be harmed, but you will take them prisoners, and feed them at Fort Stanton until you receive other instruction about them."[24] On 4 November 1862 Carleton established a new post called Fort Sumner, located near an Apache campsite known as Bosque Redondo on the Pecos River, and here he tried his ultimately futile effort to force four hundred Mescaleros to live on the same small reservation with over seven thousand Navajos whom Kit Carson had rounded up. "Farming was a perennial failure," C. L. Sonnichsen noted in THE MESCALERO APACHES (University of Oklahoma Press, 1972). "Every year something would happen—worms, borers, blight, hail, floods, drought! The Apaches made a crop in 1863. After the Navajos came, not one successful harvest was brought in."[25]

Reservation conditions became so wretched that the Mescaleros broke away, seeking freedom in the White mountains in 1866. Through Kit Carson's interces-

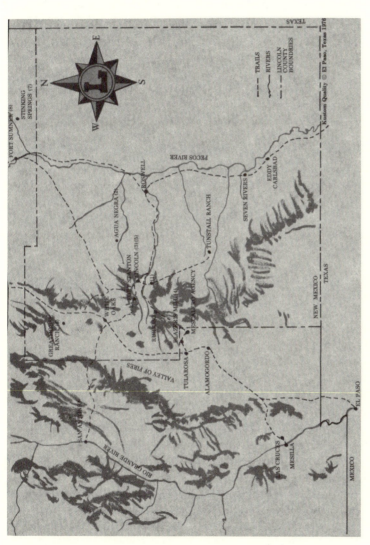

A map of Lincoln County during the Lincoln County War: (1) where John H. Tunstall was killed; (2) where Morton, Baker, and McCloskey were killed; (3) Lincoln, where Sheriff Brady and Deputy Sheriff Hindman were killed; (4) Blazer's Mill where Andrew L. "Buckshot" Roberts and Dick Brewer were killed; (5) Lincoln, again, the site of the siege at the McSween home during the five-day battle; (6) Greathouse ranch and trading post where James Carlyle was killed; (7) Stinking Springs where Billy the Kid, Dave Rudabaugh, and Tom Pickett were captured and Charles Bowdre was killed by Deputy Sheriff Pat Garrett and his posse; (8) Fort Sumner where on the night of 14 July 1881 Billy the Kid was killed by Pat Garrett. *Map courtesy of the Lincoln State Monument.*

sion the Navajos were restored to their traditional lands and Fort Sumner fell into disuse, the main buildings being purchased in 1868 by Lucien B. Maxwell, two years before he sold off the fabulous Maxwell Land Grant for $1,350,000. During the 1870s, Fort Stanton, in the western portion of Lincoln County, came again into prominence when the American military once more forced the Mescaleros to try reservation life and a garrison of soldiers was deployed to oversee their conduct and the safety of life and property among the Anglo-Americans. The Mexican-Americans in the Territory were generally expected to look out for themselves.

In 1867 John S. Chisum established himself at Bosque Grande, in the eastern portion of Lincoln County. As did many Texans at the time, he brought a herd of cattle with him from Texas, except in his case he claimed two hundred miles up and down the Pecos valley, calling it his by right of discovery. The land had not yet been opened to settlers and so Chisum squatted on it and made good his claim by his own means. La Placita del Rio Bonito was presently Americanized to Lincoln and was designated the county seat. Chisum himself, however many armed men might ride for him, never carried a gun, remarking that "a six-shooter will get you into more trouble than it will get you out of."[26] However, Chisum is said to have carried a pistol in a holster attached to his saddlehorn. Before long, he was considered the most powerful cattle baron in Lincoln County.

A year prior to his arrival in New Mexico Chisum had become inadvertently involved in an abortive packing house scheme at Fort Smith, Arkansas. Chisum was living in Texas when an Arkansas promoter by the name of Wilbur approached him and proposed that he join with him and an associate named Clark in opening a packing house. Chisum did not think much of the proposition or Wilbur's business acumen, but rather than say no he signed an agreement whereby he contracted to put up $33,333 worth of cattle at such a time as Wilbur and Clark would be able to invest $66,666 in cash. Using Chisum's name, Wilbur and Clark raised enough money actually to set up such a business, titling the firm, Wilbur, Chisum, and Clark. The firm continued to borrow heavily until it finally folded.

In 1875 Chisum, after thirty years in the cattle business in Texas and New Mexico, sold out his livestock holdings to Hunter & Evans of St. Louis, Missouri for $319,000. For the next year or two, Chisum, joined by his two brothers, James and Pitzer, was engaged in gathering Chisum cattle for transfer to ranges in Kansas owned by Hunter & Evans or transporting them to Arizona to fulfill government contracts. William Rosenthal, an associate of Thomas B. Catron, U.S. District Attorney at Santa Fe and principal organizer of the economic and political group known as the Santa Fe "Ring," while raising no cattle himself was the largest beef contractor for the U.S. Army and Indian reservations in the Southwest. Chisum was Rosenthal's chief competitor for beef contracts in southwestern New Mexico and in an effort to cut Chisum out of that market Rosenthal bought up many of the open notes for the Wilbur, Chisum, and Clark company and tried to collect on them. He retained the law firm of Catron and Thornton in Santa Fe and they succeeded in obtaining a court judgment against Chisum in Santa Fe. Chisum's sale of his cattle to Hunter & Evans, in fact, may have been precipitated by Chisum's hope to escape by this means having to settle the suit. Chisum went so far as even to assign all the land and other holdings still in his name to his brothers, James and Pitzer, but these manipulations did not deflect Rosenthal, or Catron and Thornton, and they continued to press for satisfaction, Catron and Thornton buying up as many more of the outstanding Wilbur, Chisum, and Clark notes as they could.

Chisum's difficulties were further compounded by the fact that he generally tried to avoid payment of his debts, including debts far more legitimate than those having to do with the packing house scheme. In an omnibus lawsuit filed in the district court of Lincoln County on 23 April 1884 Catron and Thornton added a number of other plaintiffs to their original suit and judgment and alleged in their accompanying complaint that Hunter & Evans, after the sale, retained possession of Chisum's property, in particular of his cattle herds, only as long as required to satisfy their claims, based on the sum they had paid to him, whereupon what remained was transferred to James and Pitzer. The suit was ultimately decided in favor of the multiple plaintiffs in the sum of $57,030.86, the decree coming down on 14 November 1884, a little more than a month before Chisum died of cancer. His brothers, joined by James' son-in-law, William Robert who married James' daughter Sallie, tried to continue the cattle operations they inherited, but they ultimately were to prove incompetent.

Emil Fritz and Lawrence G. Murphy in summer or fall of 1866 had set up L. G. Murphy & Company with a post store and brewery just beyond the eastern boundary of Fort Stanton. By 1868 they had a contract for supplying the Mescalero agency near Fort Stanton, including filling William Rosenthal's beef contracts. Murphy had joined the 1st New Mexico Volunteers in 1861 while Fritz had come to New Mexico with General Carleton's California Column. Major Murphy and Colonel Fritz were both mustered out of the service on 16 September 1866 and thereupon set up their partnership. Over the years Fritz became increasingly interested in his Spring ranch, located a few miles below Lincoln, and felt he had best take it easy since his tuberculosis bothered him more and more and he also suffered from kidney and heart disease. In the summer of 1873, Fritz left Lincoln to go to Germany to visit his childhood home and his relatives, intending to return in December. His health worsened, keeping him in Stuttgart through the winter, and he died there in the spring of 1874.

While Fritz was becoming less and less active, Murphy promoted a young Irishman he had hired first as a clerk in 1869, James J. Dolan. Dolan proved himself to be an extremely artful negotiator and it was probably Dolan who masterminded the arrangement whereby Jesse Evans and his gang would rustle beef from Chisum's herds, turning the cattle over to L. G. Murphy & Co. to fulfill Rosenthal's government contracts. Lily Klasner in her memoirs recalled that Dolan was expert in "crooked and underhanded deals, usually getting someone else to do the dirty work and take the consequences."[27] The situation got so bad that Captain James F. Randlett succeeded in evicting the Murphy store from Fort Stanton during the summer of 1873 and he even had Dolan arrested for a brief time for having threatened his life. "This firm I know to have been defrauding the government since my arrival at the post," Captain Randlett explained in a letter to the War Department. "Their contract as Indian agents have [*sic*] been fraudulent to my certain knowledge. So powerful is the ring to which they belong that I am able to prove that this firm has even attempted to force upon an officer of this post contract goods inferior to sample which they were bought at. I consider that L. G. Murphy & Co.'s store is nothing more or less than a den of infamy, and recommend the removal of this firm from this reservation."[28]

The Murphy company store was relocated to Lincoln where the firm already had a small operation known as the Placita store and an appropriately imposing structure was erected. However, for all of his monopoly in the district, Murphy was usually cash poor since he customarily advanced credit at his store to farmers in exchange for their produce. In the year 1874 and for the years following, his balance at the First National Bank of Santa Fe was usually between only $5,000 and $8,000, whereas prior to his eviction from the post he had a balance two or three times that much. In March, 1877, Dolan bought out Murphy's interest and renamed the firm J. J. Dolan & Co. This was more than agreeable with Murphy who had been diagnosed with inoperable cancer. Always a heavy drinker, after Fritz' death he was almost constantly drunk and spent more and more of his time at his Fairview ranch at Carrizo Spring. This change in ownership notwithstanding, for years afterwards the men working for Dolan were still termed "Murphy men."

John H. Riley had come to Lincoln County in the early 1870s to raise cattle. Once the Murphy store had become beef subcontractors for William Rosenthal, Dolan readily enlisted Riley's services to oversee that aspect of the business and in late 1876 Riley became a copartner in the operation and Dolan's partner in the new organization. The firm also became a subcontractor to Zadoe Staab & Brothers in supplying flour to the Indians, both of these contracts continuing in spite of Captain Randlett's previous complaints. When Dolan bought out Murphy and with Riley now openly a member of the firm, it was felt Riley should be replaced, especially in his dealings with Jesse Evans and other "suppliers." His job was taken over by Jacob B. "Billy" Mathews who had the status of a silent partner in the reorganized company. (Mathews had to buy his way in, however, which is how he came to sell John H. Tunstall the Peñasco ranch of which he was only coowner, a circumstance he failed to relay to Tunstall when making the sale).

S. B. Bushnell, a federal agent assigned to the Mescalero reservation, described the business tactics of the Murphy company in a report to the Bureau of Indian Affairs. "L. G. Murphy is the Indian trader; J. J. Dolan his confidential clerk," he wrote. "They control issues and the agents. 'It don't make any difference who the government sends here as agent. We control these Indians,' Major Murphy says. The Indians very likely would protect his life and property if occasion rose. The agent is dependent upon this firm for supplies; all they expect is that he will sign vouchers at the end of the month. L. G. Murphy claim that $60,000 is owing them. In 1871, the Indians numbered 400; in 1872, over 1,800; in 1873, over 2,200. Dolan's latest list calls for 2,679. Here is a rapidity of increase which leaves rabbits, rats, and mice in the shade. How this is done is very plain to one with his eyes open."[29] Officials in Washington, D.C., chose to take no action.

Dolan carried on Murphy's practices with the local farmers. Farmers were forced to buy merchandise on credit at exorbitant prices at the Dolan store and were compelled to turn over to the store their produce at prices determined by Dolan. The legal machinery in the county, including judge of the third district, Warren Bristol, District Attorney William L. Rynerson, and Lincoln County sheriff, William Brady, were all Murphy and then Dolan men. Should a farmer refuse to cooperate with the Dolan store, he would be subjected to immediate litigation and the legal process would accomplish what Dolan himself might not be able to do short of a show of force. In fact, Colonel Rynerson lent Dolan some of the cash he required to buy out Murphy's interest and it was to his advantage to see that Dolan's business interests were protected. Numerous lawsuits had been brought against Murphy during his tenure as head of the firm, every one of which without exception had been decided in his favor, and Dolan had no reason to think this would ever change.

A good case in point was that of Dick Brewer who had been born in St. Albans, Vermont on 19 February 1850 and whose family moved to Wisconsin in 1860. When Brewer first came to Lincoln County from Wisconsin, he had obtained his ranch from L. G. Murphy & Co. and had agreed to pay the asking price over a period of years. He was accommodated by the firm for all the supplies he required to start farming. As his produce never earned enough at the prices paid by the Murphy store to pay off what he owed, he found himself sinking year after year more deeply into debt without hope for improvement. Nearly in despair, Brewer took his case to a local attorney, Alexander A. McSween, and was astonished to learn that L. G. Murphy & Co. not only had not perfected ownership of his farm originally but that the firm had no title to it whatsoever. Of course this did not mean very much, since Colonel Rynerson and Judge Bristol would back up in court whatever claims Dolan might make. Dolan as Murphy before him was allied with Thomas B. Catron at Santa Fe and by making a "loan" of $1,800 to Samuel B. Axtell, governor of New Mexico Territory, he was assured of the governor's support as well.

McSween had arrived in Lincoln from Kansas in the spring of 1875. Shortly after receiving his license to practice law, in August, 1873, McSween had married Susan Hummer at Atchison, Kansas and he had come to New Mexico, he claimed, because he suffered from chronic asthma. There may have been more than reasons of health behind his departure, however. One of McSween's clients, Samuel Webster, a Canadian as was McSween, hired McSween while living in Eureka. Webster entrusted McSween with cash for investment and also turned over to him notes due for collection between October, 1873, and April, 1875, all of which were paid before term. The total sum involved was $746 of which McSween had only paid back $100 as of May, 1874, leaving $646 owing, a sum that was still outstanding three years after the McSweens had departed from Kansas for good. Webster later testified that he believed "the said monies and the proceeds of said promissory notes and mortgage were appropriated by the said Alexander A.

McSween to his own use and for his sole benefit."[30] Notwithstanding, McSween had a local reputation as a man of high—even, given his base of operations one might say, naïvely high—professional ideals and it is true that he frequently declined cases which he felt were without merit. It has been stated that McSween had once studied for the Presbyterian ministry, but that cannot be documented any more than the rumor that Major Murphy once studied for the Roman Catholic priesthood. In Murphy's case, however, there may have been something to it since he did upon occasion use Church Latin.

One day, shortly after McSween's arrival and once he had begun to understand how affairs were conducted in Lincoln County, when some freight wagons were stopped in the road outside his house, McSween went over and took some samples of the flour intended for delivery to the Indian reservation. It was nearly worthless. He placed some of the flour in an envelope. "Take good care of this," he said, handing the envelope to his wife. "Someday there will be an investigation to how the big store is handling its flour contract with the government, and then this sample will come in handy."[31]

In early November, 1876, John H. Tunstall came to settle in Lincoln County. He was the only son of John Partridge Tunstall of J. P. Tunstall & Co., merchants at Cheapside, London. John H. had first left Great Britain to work at the firm of Turner, Beeton, & Tunstall in Victoria, British Columbia in which his father had an interest, and had come to Lincoln in search of opportunities for long-range investments. McSween had encountered Tunstall in Santa Fe and had persuaded him there was indeed money to be made in Lincoln County. Tunstall was twenty-three years old; McSween at the time was thirty-two. Because he was a British subject, Tunstall filed on public land through a number of surrogates who were American citizens and who would surrender the land to him after the claims under the Desert Land Act had been perfected. Tunstall, as has been mentioned, bought Mathews' ranch on the Peñasco and then acquired through the surrogates and McSween's legal assistance land on the Rio Feliz. He built a small house on the latter site and purchased at auction a small herd of cattle which had been confiscated from the late Robert Casey. Casey had had a falling out with Murphy and it was rumored, but not proven, that Murphy had instigated his murder. Tunstall, due to his mercantile background, was more excited about the prospects of opening a store with which to compete with J. J. Dolan and, along with it, a bank to finance local farmers. He arranged for McSween to act as legal counsel and even drew up a partnership agreement whereby McSween, while investing no money, would be allowed a one percent share of the profits after an an eight percent deduction for Tunstall's capital investment in exchange for his legal assistance. When the partnership would be formalized in May, 1878, McSween would receive an eight percent portion of what was then on the books. Susan McSween later said that she had been opposed to the venture because Tunstall wanted to enter the store business. She added that her husband "went in against my will. Tunstall was the cause of his getting into it."[32] If Tunstall had been privy to Murphy's precarious financial state before selling out and more importantly had his father—who was financing him—been aware of it, it is almost certain he would not have attempted to open a store. As it was, there was barely enough business to support just the big store and in its case most of the profits came at the expense of the federal government.

Even as it was, the elder Tunstall had misgivings and warned his son of many potential dangers. "As regards the banking and store keeping and the intricate way of making money of course it is quite impossible for me to see that as you see it," he wrote in a letter, "my not being on the spot; but I have no doubt you may be right, and were we to meet you would make me see it the same as yourself. But in a poverty-stricken, cut-throat country like New Mexico, you would always be liable to be broken into and liable to be shot by some of your drunken customers; and that occupation would not be so good for your health. And now the importation of meat has so set in from the States to this country, I should think that the raising of cattle would be wonderful, providing you have the means of sending your cattle to market."[33]

Much has been made of Tunstall's schemes to get rich in Lincoln County, particularly by detractors such as Robert M. Utley. The only real source for what Tunstall was thinking at the time is found in his letters home to his father trying to persuade him to finance the various schemes he was propounding—so feverishly he once confessed that he had trouble sleeping. One of the most outspoken of Tunstall's letters dates from 27 May 1877 in which he outlined a plan for an operation of his own identical to that of J. J. Dolan & Co. Tunstall was convinced that the post trader would resign his position in the next twelve months and "if I get the chance of playing the right cards, I may very likely get the position. From what I can see, I think that about £2000 would run the business, the profits would not be less than £1000 & *be absolutely safe*! And if I could but get that position I could make *a great deal* of money every year, as I should so entirely control the county that I could make the prices of everything *just* to suit myself."[34] While it is possible to see another young Major Murphy in embryonic form here, to do so demands quite a stretch of the imagination —almost as great a stretch as it required Tunstall to think that as a British subject with no political connections in the Territory or in Washington, D.C., he could ever be considered even remotely for the position of post trader at Fort Stanton. The evident bravura in this letter, and others of a similar ilk, shows a man barely past his majority anxiously trying to wheedle money from a conservative and cautious parent by means of sure-fire arguments that there is no gamble, no possibility for failure, no potential for loss. Anyone in a similar position, either wheedling or being wheedled, well knows the amount of energy, enthusiasm, and excessive need for reassurances required by the former or, from the viewpoint of the latter, how much persuading and cajoling and special pleading will be necessary before, as John Partridge Tunstall, the parting with money in small, careful increments begins at all. Be that as it may, there was one person besides Tunstall's father who was taking in every hyperbolic word Tunstall was writing home, namely the Lincoln Post Master, Mr. James Joseph Dolan. His activity may have been technically illegal—and eventually Tunstall found him out—but more to the point the thought that an upstart Englishman and a conniving Canadian were going to set up their own ring and take away his business got up Dolan's fighting Irish. Cattle raising was one thing but a store, hopes to be post trader, the thought of unlimited capital from England when he had had to take in Rynerson as a partner to meet Murphy's asking price of $10,000 in promissory guarantees were more than Dolan was willing to countenance from an American, much less a foreigner.

There was no bank in southern New Mexico. The First National Bank of Santa Fe, founded by Lucien B. Maxwell, was now in the hands of the Santa Fe Ring, most notably Thomas B. Catron. Given John S. Chisum's attitude toward Catron and the Ring, Tunstall was able to persuade him to lend at least his name to the Lincoln County Bank, and Chisum was listed as president, Alexander A. McSween as vice president, and John H. Tunstall, whose father's money was financing the project, was the cashier. "His sense of honesty and fair play was ingrained and inflexible, best described as characteristically English or even sturdily mid-Victorian," Maurice Garland Fulton wrote of Tunstall in his HISTORY OF THE LINCOLN COUNTY WAR. "He had inherited business ideals in the best tradition which he did not intend to desert even in New Mexico, where business seemed to have lost all ethics in the mad scramble after wealth and power and where opportunities were so limited that men adopted the most cut-throat methods."[35] Most probably Fulton was correct. However, given his competition and the sources of its power, Tunstall should have acted more in the spirit of the way he wrote home it was his intention to behave instead, as was the case, to think fair business practices would inevitably win out against practices that were inherently dishonest and tyrannical.

If all that was not a sufficient drawback, Tunstall also had a tendency to take certain individuals under his wing and even to make injudicious loans on the basis of his reading of a man's character. The first of his adopted allies was Robert A. Widenmann who had drifted to New Mexico from Ann Arbor, Michigan and who impressed McSween as a hanger-on. Widenmann would prove to be a man who was essentially a parasite and who ingratiated himself with others through flattery, who talked much and did almost nothing. Another would be William H. Bonney.

III

The Kid's first stop after leaving the Jones family was John Chisum's South Spring River ranch where, as most visitors, he was made welcome. He remained there for a time, but he was not hired by Chisum. It may also be that during this period the Kid made the acquaintance of Jesse Evans and his rustlers, but he never joined in their activities. Evans, born in Missouri in 1853, was of slight build, five feet five and three-quarters inches in height and weighing 150 pounds. He had come to New Mexico in 1872 and had worked briefly for Chisum and others before he was enlisted by Dolan. The Kid rode on and soon made the acquaintance of George Coe and his cousin, Frank, and the Kid stayed with George at his ranch for several months, hunting with the Coes. According to George Coe they had first encountered the Kid at Dick Brewer's ranch on the Ruidoso where the Kid had stopped after leaving Chisum's. Dick Brewer by this time had been hired by Tunstall to act as his foreman while the Englishman was engaged running his store and bank in Lincoln and it was probably through Brewer that Tunstall ultimately met the Kid. In late January, 1878 Tunstall hired the Kid to work for him at his Rio Feliz ranch.

Tunstall "saw the boy was quick to learn and not afraid of anything," Frank Coe later recalled for an El Paso newspaper, "so when he hired him he made Billy a present of a good horse and a nice saddle and a new gun. My, but the boy was proud—said it was the first time in his life he had ever had anything given to him."[36] As soon as he could, Billy returned the horse John Jones had loaned him.

"He was universally liked," Mrs. Susan McSween told former New Mexico governor, Miguel Antonio Otero; "the native citizens, in particular, loved him because he was always kind and considerate to them and took much pleasure in helping them and providing for their wants. He thought nothing of mounting his horse and riding all night for a doctor or for medicine to relieve the suffering of some sick person. Billy was a graceful and beautiful dancer, and when in the company of a woman he was at all times extremely polite and respectful. Also while in the presence of women, he was neat and careful about his personal appearance. He was always a great favorite with women, and at a dance he was in constant demand; yet with it all, he was entirely free from conceit or vanity. It was just natural for him to be a perfect gentleman."[37] With regard to the Kid's relationship with Tunstall, Mrs. McSween observed that the Kid "often said that he loved Mr. Tunstall better than any man he ever knew. Just a few days before Mr. Tunstall was murdered, he told Sheriff Brady that he did not want any of his boys hurt either on his account or Mr. McSween's. I have always believed that if Mr. Tunstall had lived, the Kid, under his guidance, would have become a valuable citizen, for he was a remarkable boy, far above the average young men of those times and he undoubtedly had the making of a fine man in him."[38]

At the organization of Lincoln County in 1869, Major Murphy and Colonel Fritz were in a position to select the new county's sheriff and Major William Brady, who had served in the Army with them, had been their choice. When Brady took office for the second time in 1876, he pledged his loyalty to J. J. Dolan. No less devoted to Dolan's cause was Judge Bristol who had come to New Mexico in 1872, having been appointed judge of the third district by President Grant. William A. Keleher recorded a typical example of Judge Bristol's court procedure in his book THE FABULOUS FRONTIER: TWELVE NEW MEXICO ITEMS (University of New Mexico Press, 1962).

On 1 June 1881 "L. S. ('Bladder') Allen interfered in a quarrel between C. H. Keys and George Ulrich in the Pioneer saloon at White Oaks," Keleher wrote. "Before many seconds elapsed, 'Bladder' Allen whipped out a knife, stuck the blade into Keys' backbone, twisted it around and carefully put the knife back in his pocket. Allen then called a few bystanders to help him throw Keys bodily out of the saloon into the street. Under Allen's direction, four men did the job, one man to each arm, one man to each leg. Left to suffer out in the road for hours, Keys finally received medical aid. Suffering great pain, he died seventeen days later. A post-mortem examination of the body disclosed that an inch of Allen's knife blade still remained in the spinal column. For that incident, 'Bladder' Allen received from Judge Warren Bristol on 22 May 1884 a sentence of one year in jail. Before the year was up, 'Bladder' Allen got out of jail, went into the Will Ellis billiard hall in Lincoln on 5 May 1885, and 'accidentally' shot and killed Sam Anderson, the bartender. For that crime Judge Bristol sentenced him to serve five years in prison."[39]

Frontier justice even via due process was arbitrary, if not altogether capricious, in the Territories and even some of the States. The Kid knew from the hearing he had received by a jury made up of Frank Cahill's cronies in Camp Grant that due process could be partisan and so perhaps it did not surprise him to learn from John H. Tunstall that Colonel Rynerson and Judge Bristol were Dolan supporters, especially in view of the fact that Rynerson's money was behind Dolan. One of the first moves that Dolan made against the Tunstall/McSween combination was to loose Jesse Evans' gang to prey on Tunstall's livestock. He also took advantage of a situation that stemmed from some years before, when L. G. Murphy had hired McSween to represent the Fritz estate following Fritz' death in Germany.

Prior to his departure, Fritz had taken out a life insurance policy for $10,000 in favor of the beneficiaries of his estate. When, a year after Fritz' death, the insurance company still had not paid, Murphy had brought the matter to McSween for collection. Having received instructions from Mrs. Emilie Fritz Scholand and Charles Fritz, administrators of the estate, at his own expense McSween went to St. Louis and then on to New York in October, 1876. Although the insurance company had gone into receivership, McSween retained the New York financial firm of Donnell, Lawson & Co. to help him effect collection and they proved successful. On 1 August 1877 Donnell, Lawson & Co. informed McSween that his account had been credited with $7,148.49, the net proceeds of the policy less their fee. As soon as J. J. Dolan heard that McSween was in possession of this sum—he was a close friend of Charles Fritz' daughter Caroline and would soon marry her—he claimed the whole amount as due and owing him as successor to L. G. Murphy & Co., insisting the sum would contribute to what Fritz died owing to the firm.

On 21 December 1877 Dolan took an affidavit to District Attorney Rynerson to effect McSween's arrest on a charge of embezzlement. Mrs. Scholand, who could scarcely read or write, signed the complaint against McSween in Judge Bristol's court. Bristol, in turn, authorized that a warrant be issued. Rynerson also consulted with Thomas B. Catron about the matter and the plot deepened. Catron was by then in possession of the judgment against Chisum concerning the notes from the defunct Wilbur, Chisum, and Clark packing house venture. It was well known in the Territory that McSween and Mrs. McSween were planning a trip to St. Louis and that they were to be accompanied by John Chisum. Catron and Thornton, representing now both J. J. Dolan and William Rosenthal, wired the sheriff of San Miguel County to detain both A. A. McSween and Chisum when they should arrive there on their way East.

There was a statute that required a person under judgment to furnish a list of his assets. This Chisum had done, but having transferred all of his property to either his brothers or Hunter & Evans, what he owned did not amount to much. The statute permitted Catron and Thornton to resort to imprisonment if and until Chisum would furnish a more credible list of assets. Chisum was disgusted by their chicanery—after all, his name had been used on notes by Wilbur and Clark without his knowledge, much less consent—and chose confinement of eight weeks in Las Vegas in San Miguel County rather than comply. It was while in jail that Chisum wrote a narrative of recent events, including his arrest and that of McSween. "In December, 1877, I started for St. Louis, Mo.," he wrote, "on some business and got to Las Vegas on the night of Dec. 24. Upon arriving there I found that T. B. Catron had telegraphed to Las Vegas to know if Chisum and McSween had passed Las Vegas yet. The sheriff commanded us not to leave the city. I was traveling in company with McSween and his wife, all going to St. Louis on business, and of course in a hurry, as all travelers are. So the McSweens and I waited for forty-eight hours and no warrant came for the arrest of either one of us. The sheriff held us as long as he could without papers. So we hitched up our horses to an ambulance and started to St. Louis two days after Christmas. After going some half mile, we were overtaken by the sheriff and stopped on the public highway. The sheriff had thirty or forty men with him, some armed with pistols, some with rocks, some with clubs, but all making a desperate charge upon us and surrounding the ambulance we were traveling in. I was jerked out head foremost and fell upon my face on the hard road. I was then seized by the throat by one of the sheriff's men until I said to the sheriff, 'Will you please be so kind as to loosen the grip of this man?' The sheriff spoke and the man loosened his hold. So I breathed once more of the fresh air of New Mexico that they brag so much about. McSween was also jerked out of the ambulance and dragged by a lot of the gang. Mrs. McSween was left sitting all alone crying in the ambulance without a driver or even protection. The sheriff and his party were somewhat excited; McSween was somewhat confused; I was laughing and cool. I looked the gang over and noticed one young man that had on a clean shirt, who had just arrived at the scene of the excitement. I asked him if he would be kind enough to drive Mrs. McSween to the hotel, and the young fellow consented to do so and drove her there."[40]

On 4 January 1878 McSween left Las Vegas accompanied by two San Miguel deputy sheriffs, A. P. Barrier and Antonio Campos. He was to be kept in their charge until delivered at Mesilla, Doña Ana County, where Judge Bristol was to be holding court and where the warrant summoned him. Upon arriving in Lincoln, on their way to Mesilla, the party learned that Judge Bristol was not at Mesilla and would not be there for two or three weeks. Barrier, remaining with McSween, agreed to hold him in custody in Lincoln until they could start for Mesilla. This was the situation which existed at the time the Kid went to work for Tunstall.

When Judge Bristol returned to Mesilla, McSween, still in the charge of Deputy Sheriff Barrier, and accompanied by Tunstall, eager to help his friend and business associate, David P. Shield, McSween's brother-in-law (he had married Susan's older sister Elizabeth in Columbus, Ohio on 11 November 1859) and also an attorney who with his family shared half of the McSween home in Lincoln, Squire Wilson, and others, started for Mesilla. The party arrived in Mesilla on 28 January whereupon Judge Bristol postponed his examination of McSween until 2 February, but the actual hearing, with a Sunday intervening, ran over into 4 February. McSween and Shield asked for a continuance until a grand jury could be called in Lincoln in early April as some important witnesses were unavailable. Bristol acquiesced to this request, set bail at $8,000, but in a master stroke left the approval of bail up to District Attorney Rynerson. Deputy Sheriff Barrier was ordered by the bench to transport McSween back to Lincoln and turn him over to Sheriff Brady in whose custody he was to remain until satisfactory bond was made.

Dolan, who had been present during the hearing, did not leave Mesilla immediately, although McSween did, his party riding out on 5 February. When they put up at Shedd's ranch at sundown that day, they were met by Jesse Evans, Frank Baker, and John Long. Evans had been charged with horse theft by McSween and Tunstall, had been arrested by Sheriff Brady, but had escaped, and so was technically "at large." He made no secret of his enmity toward McSween and Tunstall, but claimed that he was only stopping at the ranch because he was looking for Dolan and heard he might be passing this way. During the brief period while McSween had been in Lincoln in Barrier's custody John H. Tunstall had committed an act, in good conscience, which now it would seem had sealed his fate. He had sent the following letter to the *Mesilla Independent* and it had been published only a short time before McSween's hearing. McSween had paid his Territorial taxes in a check made out to "Wm. Brady, sheriff and ex-officio collector" in the sum of $1,543.03, and the check had come back to McSween, cashed and endorsed by "Jno H. Riley." Tunstall had felt this evidence too damning to be let pass unnoticed.

OFFICE OF JOHN H. TUNSTALL

Lincoln, Lincoln County, N.M. 18 January 1878

"The present sheriff of Lincoln County has paid nothing during his present term of office."—Governor's Message for 1878.

Editor of the *Independent*:

The above extract is a sad and unanswerable comment on the efficiency of Sheriff Brady and cannot be charged upon "croakers." Major Brady, as the records of this county show, collected over Twenty-five Hundred Dollars, Territorial funds. Of this sum Alexander A. McSween, Esq. of this place paid him over Fifteen Hundred Dollars by cheque on the First National Bank of Santa Fe, 23 August 1877. Said cheque was presented for payment by John H. Riley, Esq. of the firm of J. J. Dolan & Co. This last amount was paid by the last named gentleman to Underwood & Nash for cattle. Thus passed away over Fifteen Hundred Dollars belonging to the Territory of New Mexico. With the exception of Thirty-nine Dollars, all the taxes of Lincoln County were promptly paid when due.

Let not Lincoln County suffer the delinquency of one, two or three men.

By the exercise of proper vigilance, the taxpayer can readily ascertain what has become of what he has paid for the implied protection of the commonwealth. It is not only his privilege but his duty. A delinquent taxpayer is bad: a delinquent tax collector is worse.

J.H.T.[41]

While in Mesilla, Dolan himself had answered these charges, albeit ineffectually, in a letter dated 29 January 1878 at Las Cruces. Obviously Rynerson and Bristol had made it quite plain to him that Tunstall had to be silenced. In the meantime, Catron himself paid up the delinquent taxes to stop the embarrassment there.

Dolan arrived very early the next morning, an hour or two after midnight, but stayed in camp with Jesse Evans and the others until nine o'clock. Then Dolan and Evans approached Tunstall at the corral, Dolan throwing down his Winchester on Tunstall and demanding they fight it out.

"Do you want me to fight a duel?" Tunstall asked him.

"You damn coward," Dolan replied, "I want you to fight and settle our difficulties." Dolan moved the rifle as if to take aim.

Deputy Sheriff Barrier then stepped between them.

"You won't fight this morning, you damn coward," Dolan told Tunstall, turning away, "but I'll get you soon." He walked some twenty yards or so and then paused, again facing Tunstall. "When you write to the *Independent* again," he jeered, "say I'm with 'the boys!' "[42]

With that, Dolan hurried on his way to Lincoln. Rynerson, for his part, sent the writ of attachment by courier so it, too, would arrive in Lincoln before McSween and his party. John H. Riley swept out the jail for Sheriff Brady, laughing that he had cleaned up the cell in which McSween would be staying. Brady immediately levied his attachment on McSween's home and its furnishings and then, accompanied by John Long, James Longwell, both Evans gang members whom he had deputized, and his regular deputies, George W. "Dad" Peppin and F. G. Christie, he placed a levy on the Tunstall bank and store, an action protested by Widenmann whom Tunstall had left in charge during his absence.

"I guess we all know that McSween's got a part interest in the store," Brady told Widenmann and, when Widenmann refused to surrender the keys, Brady had him searched and the keys were taken. The writ had required the sheriff to attach property in the sum of $8,000; Brady had attached property easily worth four or five times as much.[43]

Tunstall parted from the McSween party outside of Lincoln and headed for Dick Brewer's ranch. Widenmann met him there and told him about the attachment. On 11 February, Tunstall, sided by Widenmann, Fred Waite (a half-breed in Tunstall's employ), and Billy Bonney rode toward Lincoln. Arriving at the store, Tunstall and Widenmann went inside, leaving Waite and the Kid outside, holding rifles in addition to their sidearms. Both Tunstall and Widenmann wore sidearms. Tunstall found F. G. Christie making an inventory while the others loafed. He spoke his mind at once, objecting to the attachment of his property "for a debt of McSween" and calling it a "damned high-handed business."[44] Longwell suggested to Tunstall that he take up the matter with the court.

"Do you think," Tunstall demanded, having seen Judge Bristol and Colonel Rynerson in action, "that I can get any justice in the district court? Haven't I just seen how prejudiced are both Judge Bristol and Colonel Rynerson?"

"Well," responded Longwell, "if you can't get justice in the district court, you can carry your case before the United States court."

"God, man," Tunstall exclaimed, knowing full well that T. B. Catron was U.S. District Attorney, "you can't get justice there either. It's the worst outfit of all and is completely in the hands of that damn Santa Fe Ring."[45]

Tunstall next went to see Brady and scored a minor victory. Brady was willing to release the six horses and two mules in the corral adjacent to Tunstall's store since they were indisputably Tunstall's private property. Tunstall dispatched these animals to his Rio Feliz ranch in the charge of John Middleton, a cowboy who rode for him, Godfrey Gauss, his ranch cook, and William McCloskey, a roustabout who had worked at various jobs for a number of people and who may well have volunteered for the job at the instigation of J. J. Dolan to keep an eye on things for him. Widenmann asked permission to go along and Tunstall granted it. He sent Waite and the Kid with Widenmann while he himself intended to stay in town and help McSween raise his bond so that the attachment could be lifted.

Upon arrival in Lincoln Deputy Sheriff Barrier had refused to surrender McSween to Brady and instead kept him in his custody while McSween worked on his bond. Brady in the meantime had already got up a posse and sent it out to Tunstall's ranch to attach Tunstall's cattle. Billy Mathews, Dolan's silent partner, had been deputized and led the force which included Jesse Evans, Frank Baker, Tom Hill, George Hindman, Johnny Hurley, Andrew L. "Buckshot" Roberts, Manuel "The Indian" Segovia, and they were joined *en route* at the Rio Peñasco by more Dolan men led by William "Buck" Morton.

The posse, with all its riders, moved slowly, more slowly than the Tunstall group with the horses and mules, and so they were already at the ranch when the posse showed up. Shortly after Jesse Evans, Tom Hill, and Frank Baker had escaped Sheriff Brady's jail for stealing horses from Tunstall and McSween, Widenmann had had himself appointed a deputy U.S. marshal so as to pursue them with federal warrants concerning horse theft from the Mescalero reservation with which they had also been charged. Widenmann was visibly shaken to see those three now in the posse, but Dick Brewer took matters in hand at once. He rode out alone and had Mathews halt the posse about fifty yards from the house and himself to come forward similarly alone so the two could parley. When Mathews told Brewer that he had come to attach the cattle in the McSween case, Brewer countered him by saying that he would only be allowed to round up the cattle to see if any belonged to McSween and, even at that, the cattle could not be taken from the ranch but must be left there until the matter could be settled in court.

Mathews could see nothing wrong with this reasonable proposal when Widenmann, having got up his nerve, came up to them and demanded that he be permitted to arrest Evans, Hill, and Baker on the federal warrants he held for them. This request Mathews denied but he did agree to Brewer's terms, whereupon the posse was invited inside the house to eat.

"Do you want to arrest me?" Jesse Evans demanded insolently of Widenmann once they were all inside.

"You will find it out quickly enough when I want to arrest you," Widenmann responded.

"Have you got a warrant for me?"

"It's none of your business."

"If ever you come after me," Evans warned, "you are the first man I am going to shoot at."

"All right," Widenmann told him, "I can play a hand at that game as well as you." Then he turned to Mathews. "Billy, why did you allow those fellows to come along with you?" he asked.

"I did not summon them," Mathews replied. "They came along of their own accord. Jesse told me he wanted to find out if you had a warrant for him."

At this point Frank Baker turned to Buckshot Roberts and muttered, "What the hell's use of talking? Let's pitch in a fight, and kill all the damn sons of bitches."[46]

Mathews was not sure how Dolan and Brady would want him to proceed, so he proposed going back to Lincoln for further instructions.

"Billy," Brewer addressed him, "you see we want to do the right thing. What's the use of bringing so many along when you come back? Just yourself and another man will be enough, don't you think?"[47]

Mathews agreed and left, taking the posse with him. As soon as he was gone, Widenmann proposed to Brewer that he should go to town and inform Tunstall. Brewer concurred but insisted that he should take Bonney and Waite with him and go by way of the Pajarito mountain shortcut. Since the first part of the route was the same as that taken by the posse, Widenmann, Waite, and the Kid caught up with Billy Mathews and rode the distance with him and the posse. Before they separated, Mathews asked Widenmann what he thought would happen if the posse seized the cattle.

"We will not forcibly resist your doing so," Widenmann told him, "provided you leave the cattle on the ranch. But if you drive them away to the Indian agency or any other place, as we heard you intend doing, then you may be sure we will put up a fight."[48]

In Lincoln, McSween was able to submit a bond to Rynerson which represented a number of pledged sureties which in the aggregate came to $35,000. Rynerson rejected the bond on the grounds that he did not believe the sureties were properly represented. This was 12 February. On the evening of the next day, 13 February, Widenmann, Waite, and the Kid reached Lincoln and told Tunstall about the proposed attachment. Tunstall's first response was that he would not resort to any means other than due process to fight the attachment, but then he heard from George Washington, a black ex-cavalryman who worked occasionally for McSween, that the Dolan men were boasting that Dolan was presently getting together a posse of forty-three men in order to "settle the difficulties with Tunstall and McSween once and forever."[49] They also were boasting that they had the district attorney behind them, the district judge, and the Santa Fe Ring. Under the circumstances, Tunstall decided to ride out to Chisum's ranch to consult him and perhaps gain his support. However, upon his arrival at the ranch, he learned that Chisum was still in jail at

Las Vegas and his brothers were unwilling to allow their cowboys to become involved in the dispute without John's permission.

Before leaving Lincoln, Tunstall had confided to McSween, "I will not sacrifice the life of a single man for all the cattle. I am going to the ranch to do all I can to prevent trouble. If needful, I will have all my men leave and come to Lincoln. Mathews and his crowd can take my property, and I will seek remedy in the courts."[50] The side trip to Chisum's was evidently an effort to make perhaps a sufficient show of force to dissuade Dolan and the others from resorting to violence.

The distance from Chisum's ranch to Tunstall's Rio Feliz ranch was some sixty miles and Tunstall and his party did not arrive until the night of 17 February at ten o'clock. He learned at once that the Mathews posse was organizing about eight miles distant and was intent on driving the cattle with them and destroying all resistance. Tunstall found all of his men willing to fight, but he vetoed this idea. Instead he instructed McCloskey, who was known to be friendly with a number of the men in the Mathews posse, to start at about three in the morning, ride to where Mathews was with the posse, and inform them that they could have the cattle under the terms proposed by Brewer, that he would leave a repre-sentative in charge of the herd and Mathews should do likewise. McCloskey was then to ride to "Dutch" Martin Martz's ranch, a nonpartisan, and ask him to ride over and watch over the proceedings. Tunstall was going to leave Godfrey Gauss, the cook, behind as his representative, while he and the rest of his men headed in to Lincoln. The question came up about the horses that had been taken to the ranch from Lincoln and Tunstall decided that they would take them to Lincoln with them. "That will be proper enough," he observed, "since Brady himself released them."[51]

The next morning, 18 February, at half past eight Tunstall started out toward Lincoln, accompanied by Dick Brewer, Fred Waite, Robert A. Widenmann, John Middleton, Henry Brown, and Billy Bonney. Their progress was slow because of the herd. When Dolan and Mathews and their large posse arrived at Tunstall's ranch, they found that McCloskey had told them the truth. Tunstall and the others had left. Dolan then decided to get up a sub-posse to give pursuit to Tunstall. Pantaleon Gallegos was in charge of writing down the names of the posse for the official record and, when Jesse Evans and his group came forward to be included in the sub-posse, Gallegos was told not to write down their names. Evans was quick to comment that not writing down his name did not mean he was not coming.

"You bet your damn life we are going," he said, "for we want our horses we loaned to Billy the Kid. They tell me they have been taken away with the other horses."[52]

Fred Waite was driving a wagon and he and Henry Brown split off from the main group now so as to take a shortcut. Continuing on with the horses, near five o'clock in the afternoon, with Tunstall, Brewer, and Widenmann riding point ahead of the horses which followed in single file, Middleton and the Kid some five hundred yards in the rear, their passage stirred up a flock of wild turkeys. Brewer and

Widenmann immediately wanted to bag some of them. Widenmann offered his gun to Tunstall, but Tunstall declined.

"I'll stay with the horses," he said. "You and Dick go after the fowls."[53]

Brewer and Widenmann, chasing the turkeys, were out of sight of Tunstall when Widenmann heard the sounds of hoofs. An advance guard of the sub-posse led by Morton, Evans, and Hill, rode out in front of Tunstall, seeking to cut him off. Other members of the posse rode toward Middleton and the Kid and, seeing themselves outnumbered, they called to Tunstall to seek shelter and cut away themselves. Tunstall, rather than follow them, rode toward Morton, Evans, and Hill. When he was well within range, Morton raised his rifle and fired, the bullet hitting Tunstall in the chest, his body falling from his horse. Jesse Evans then rode up, dismounted, and snatching Tunstall's revolver fired a shot into the back of Tunstall's head and then sent another bullet into the head of Tunstall's horse. By the time the remainder of the sub-posse arrived, Evans showed them Tunstall's gun, recently fired with the empty chambers, and said they had had to shoot him while resisting arrest. By this means he transformed a *tiro de gracia* into an instance of the infamous *ley de fuga*.

In his report to Colonel Rynerson, dated 5 March, Sheriff Brady gave this as the official version, writing that "J. H. Tunstall fired on the posse and in the return fire he was shot and killed." Brady also concealed the presence of the Evans group with the sub-posse. "It has been falsely averred that attached to the deputy's posse were men against whom U.S. warrants had been issued. To disprove this, I present you a letter which reached him before he attached and in addition to my minute verbal instructions."[54] Here is the letter he supposedly sent:

Lincoln, N. M., 15 Feb. 1878

J. B. Mathews

Dept. Sheriff,

Dear Sir:

You must not by any means call on or allow to travel with your posse any person or persons who are known to be outlaws. Let your Mexicans round up the cattle and protect them with the balance. Be *firm* and do your duty according to *law* and I will be responsible for your acts.

I am, Sir,
Respectfully yours,
Wm. Brady, Sheriff
Lincoln County[55]

William Morton also beat the head of Tunstall's corpse with his rifle butt, shattering bone. To disguise this would require more than a letter *ex post facto*. Brady certainly must have known who had been in that sub-posse to make his denial of their presence so emphatic before a question had even been raised.

IV

It was ten or eleven at night before the men who had been with Tunstall, including Billy the Kid, reached Lincoln. Widenmann apparently went to inform McSween, everyone figuring he would be the next victim. Fully aware that Brady would be of no help to them in bringing Tunstall's murderers to justice, Widenmann next set out alone for Fort Stanton to seek the assistance of the Army, but found the officers there either sympathetic to Dolan's side or indifferent. In Lincoln, near midnight, a group of sixty men congregated outside McSween's house, both to learn details of the killing and to pledge their support in bringing in the men responsible. This show of public support alarmed those Dolan forces who were in town—Dolan, himself, of course, was still with the posse—and John Riley, quite drunk, came over to see McSween. To prove that his intentions were not hostile, he took off his revolver and laid it on the table and then proceeded to turn his pockets inside out. In the process he let drop a memorandum book. Once he left, the memorandum book was discovered. In it, among other items of interest, was a record of the occasions on which stolen cattle had been purchased from the Evans gang.

McSween arranged for the body of Tunstall to be located and brought into Lincoln. The next day he sent Dick Brewer and Billy Bonney to Squire Wilson, the justice of the peace, and had them make affidavits against the men they had recognized in the posse that had charged at Tunstall. Squire Wilson then issued warrants for their arrest and gave the warrants to Atanacio Martínez, the local constable. That same day, 19 February, Dr. Taylor F. Ealy, a physician and minister, arrived in Lincoln with his wife, their two children, and Miss Susan Gates, a teacher, with the intention of establishing a church and school in Lincoln. Dr. Ealy had heard the previous night at Fort Stanton of the murder of Tunstall and he sought out McSween.

"You are likely, Doctor, to find this what the Bible calls stony ground," McSween told Ealy, after welcoming him and his party. "What we are drifting into is really a struggle of the people to throw off a galling yoke of corruption, robbery, and persecution. We have locally the Dolan store, which holds several government contracts; it accumulates money by purchasing cattle from irresponsible parties for a small part of their actual value and by getting part of its stock of goods from government supplies, through collusion with government agents. They have been carrying on their business in this way, arrogantly and oppressively because they render themselves useful to the closed corporation dominating New Mexico, the Santa Fe Ring. They that sow the wind, shall reap the whirlwind."[56]

A speech as this was no doubt impressive to Dr. Ealy, but it also reveals McSween's naïve interpretation of what indeed was going on around him. If it had been sheer, stubborn distrust of Dolan's claim against the Fritz insurance money which had prompted him to hold off paying it out until he could satisfy himself that all potential legatees had been located, in New Mexico and in Germany, and if he recognized Dolan's financial predicament, he did not assess it properly by placing it into a moralistic and Biblical context. Dolan had gone on the line to buy a business that depended on monopoly to make money, and enough money had to be made to support the business, himself, and pay off Rynerson and Major Murphy. Perhaps somewhere deeply inside McSween knew that with Dolan, it was not a matter of right and wrong; it was a matter of economic survival. If he did, he certainly was not prepared for the prospect of total war and that is about the only option Dolan perceived.

Darkness was approaching when Tunstall's body was brought in and Squire Wilson impaneled a coroner's jury which took testimony and found Tunstall to have been killed by Jesse Evans, Frank Baker, Thomas Hill, George Hindman, James J. Dolan, William Morton, and others as yet unidentified.

The next day, 20 February, McSween sent for Dr. D. M. Appel, the post surgeon at Fort Stanton, to perform the postmortem. Appel, in his official report, noted that "there were two wounds on the body, one in the shoulder passing through and fracturing the right clavicle near its centre, coming out immediately over the superior border of the right scapula passing through in its course the right sub clavicle artery. This wound would have caused death within a few minutes and would have been likely to have thrown him from his horse. It would not have produced immediate insensibility. The other wound entered the head about one inch to the right of the median line almost on a line with the occipital protruberance of the left orbit. There was a fracture of the skull extending around the whole circumference from the entrance to the exit of the ball, and a transverse fracture across the middle portion of the base of the skull extending from the line of fracture on one side to that of the other. In my opinion the skull both on account of its being very thin and from evidence of venereal disease was likely to be extensively fractured from such a wound and this fracture in this case resulted entirely from said wound. A wound of this kind would cause instantaneous death passing as it did through the most vital portion of the brain. There were no marks of violence and bruises on the body except the above two wounds nor was the body or skull mutilated."[57] This is Dr. Appel's official report. In a curious private report that he supplied to Widenmann—for which Widenmann offered to pay him $100 only later to renege on the promise—so that Widenmann could send it on to Tunstall's family, he contradicted what he had stated in his official report. "Wounded in the head, entered 3 in. behind and in a line with the superior border of the right ear, made its exit $1\frac{1}{2}$ in. above the left orbit and $\frac{1}{4}$ in. left of the middle line of the forehead. The wound in the chest entered 2 in. to the right of the medium line, breaking the Clavicle, and made its exit $3\frac{1}{2}$ in. from the external border of the Acromian [acromial] process and scraping the upper border of the Scapula. The fracture of the bones of the skull extended completely around its circumference, passing through the two wounds and extending downward through the horizontal plate of the frontal bone, the greater [illegible] of the ephinoid [sphenoid] bone and cribuform [cribriform] plate of the ethmoid bone."[58] Dr. Ealy, who apparently also had assisted in the postmortem and did the embalming, could not help but notice as well as Dr. Appel that Tunstall's skull had been badly mutilated in ways not related to the bullet wound to the head or the progress of disease. Ruth R. Ealy recorded her father's opinion that "Tunstall's body was in bad shape as he had been shot and then beaten until his forehead was battered very badly."[59] This observation, however, did not find its way into the official report, and the official report was all that concerned the House. It is also worth a comment here that based on the symptoms of illness Tunstall described in his correspondence home it is indeed quite probable that he was suffering from Spirochaeta pallida which either had gone undiagnosed or which he had chosen to ignore. Indeed, when Tunstall believed he had been felled by smallpox, he may have misdiagnosed the spots which might have been syphilitic maculae that have the same appearance as the red spots in the roseolae stage of variola. There would also be an accompanying rise in temperature. For the texture and density of the skull to be affected as it was in his case, meningovascular degeneration typical of the secondary stage of the disease would have had to be somewhat advanced.

Atanacio Martínez that same day, accompanied by Fred Waite and Billy Bonney, went to the Dolan store to serve the warrants he had, Dolan and the other posse members having since returned to Lincoln. Sheriff Brady was at the store also and he refused to permit Martínez to serve the warrants. Instead, he arrested Martínez and Waite and the Kid with him. Brady let Martínez go by dark, but he kept Waite and the Kid in custody. In the interim Dolan had been able to secure a detachment of soldiers from Fort Stanton to protect his store and his men, a move he felt necessitated by the popular sentiment. The War Department frowned upon the use of soldiers in civil disturbances, so Captain G. A. Purington, who was partial to Dolan's interests, issued orders to Lieutenant Cyrus M. DeLany, the officer in charge of the black detachment, that "until instructions are received from Judge Bristol, judge of the United States court, no interference will be made with the civil authorities in the execution of their duties than the protection of life and property."[60] Nonetheless, the soldiers were there, and Brady instructed them to feed their horses from hay belonging to the Tunstall store.

The Kid was still in jail on 22 February, a Friday, when Tunstall was buried a short distance from his store and behind it. After the burial, a mass meeting was held at McSween's house and the townspeople sent a delegation to see Sheriff Brady. He was asked why he had arrested Martínez, Waite, and Bonney, and why he was still holding the last two? Brady's answer was to the point: "Because I had the power." He was next asked what he intended to do about McSween's bond in the Fritz case? His answer was equally succinct: "I will not take a bond from McSween of any kind or amount."[61]

Dolan, as soon as he heard about this visit to Brady, started for Mesilla to get Judge Bristol to issue an alias warrant for McSween which would compel Deputy Sheriff Barrier to surrender his prisoner to Brady. Dolan also hoped to hire John Kinney, a brutal outlaw, and his gang in Doña Ana County to join with his forces in Lincoln now that the soldiers had vacated and were to return to Fort Stanton.

Robert Widenmann, once Dolan was gone, did not waste any time. He went to Fort Stanton himself and asked for soldiers to assist him in serving the federal warrants he had for Jesse Evans and his associates. His request was honored and Lieutenant M. F. Goodwin was dispatched with a detachment of soldiers to accompany Widenmann on his return to Lincoln. Bonney and Waite were then released from custody by Brady and so they were able to join Widenmann when he arrived, along with Martínez, in making a search of the Dolan store. Evans and the others were nowhere to be found. However, afterward members of the Dolan faction insisted that it was during the search of the Dolan store that Widenmann came upon a letter dated 14 February 1878 from District Attorney Rynerson addressed to Riley and Dolan which read in part: "I believe Tunstall is in with the swindlers—with the rogue McSween. They have the money belonging to the Fritz estate and they know it. It must be made hot for them, all the hotter the better. . . . It may be that the villain 'Green Baptista' Wilson will play into their hands as alcalde. If so, he should be moved around a little. Shake that McSween outfit up until it shells out or squares up, and then shake it out of Lincoln. I will aid to punish the scoundrels all I can. Get the people with control—Juan Patrón if possible. You know how to do it, and be assured, I shall help you all I can, for I believe there was never found a more scoundrelly set than that outfit."

Next Widenmann went to the Tunstall store where there were five Dolan men on guard, George Peppin, Jim Longwell, John Long, Charley Martin, and a black ex-trooper named Clark. Widenmann disarmed them and, with the soldiers to back his play, marched them over to Brady's jail where they were kept overnight. The next day they had a hearing before Squire Wilson and were released, but by that time the store was again in the possession of the McSween faction and no further attempt was made by the Dolan forces to reoccupy it.

McSween could see that he was a marked man. The Rynerson letter was enough to indicate that due process could avail him nothing. On 25 February he made out his will, leaving his entire estate to his wife. He appointed John Chisum to become executor without bond; if he did not serve for any reason, then Mrs. McSween was to become executrix. Deputy Sheriff Barrier agreed with McSween that were he to surrender him to Brady, he would probably be killed. Either knowing or suspecting what Dolan and Bristol were up to, on 27 February Barrier and McSween left Lincoln and made camp about thirty or forty miles outside town.

While McSween was thus engaged, a number of men including former Tunstall employees such as Bonney, Waite, and Middleton, along with a stock detective for Hunter & Evans, Frank MacNab, and others such as "Doc" Scurlock, Charlie Bowdre, Henry Brown, Sam Smith, and Jim French, allied themselves under the leadership of Dick Brewer and declared themselves to be "Regulators." In effect, they composed a vigilante organization determined to serve the warrants against Tunstall's killers which Brady refused to honor. They swore an oath to remain loyal to each other no matter what happened and announced that their purpose was to arrest, not to execute, the wrongdoers and to bring them to Lincoln where they would be held for trial. They also dissociated themselves from the contretemps over the Fritz insurance money, claiming this was McSween's private affair and no business of theirs.

The Regulators reached the Pecos around 4 March and two days later, after a running fight, succeeded in capturing Morton and Baker. The Kid argued for immediate justice.

"Dick," he said, "we've got two of them and they are the worst of the lot. Let's avenge John Tunstall by killing them right now."[62]

Brewer rejected the Kid's proposal and instead started back to Lincoln with the prisoners. They stayed at Chisum's South Spring River ranch the night of 8 March and the next day resumed their journey. It was, however, at Chisum's ranch that the Regulators received the news that Dolan had returned from Mesilla and was in the process of organizing a large posse to overtake them. This made a number of the men apprehensive as to whether or not Morton and Baker could indeed be kept in custody long enough to be brought to trial. William McCloskey was with the Regulators. While he had occasionally been employed by Tunstall, in fact had been sent by Tunstall on an errand the day before he was killed, it was also known that McCloskey had not followed instructions; he had remained with the Mathews posse when they rode in to the Tunstall ranch and found Tunstall had already departed. He had first joined the Regulators after Morton and Baker had been captured and he was increasingly regarded as a possible spy, especially because of his sympathetic attitude toward the prisoners and his concern over their welfare. While staying at the Chisum ranch, Morton wrote a letter to a kinsman in Virginia in which he listed the names of the Regulators, professed his innocence, and remarked that "there was one man in the party who wanted to kill me after I had surrendered, and was restrained with the greatest difficulty by others of the party. The constable himself [Brewer?] said he was sorry we gave up as he had not wished to take us alive."[63]

On their way the Regulators also stopped at Roswell where Marion Turner and John Jones, the latter the same John Jones whom the Kid had met when he first entered Lincoln County, owned a general store. Marshall Ashmun Upson, known more familiarly there as Ash, was the local postmaster. Since Tunstall had first come to suspect Dolan of tampering with his mail, Upson by special arrangement with McSween had seen that McSween's mail was delivered in a private mail sack directly to him. Morton gave Upson his letter to post. Occasionally Upson, who was an aspiring journalist, would write up local happenings for newspapers, and he subsequently published a story concerning the arrest of Morton and Baker in the *Las Vegas Gazette* dated at Roswell, 9 March 1878.

What exactly happened late in the afternoon on 9 March on the winding road through Blackwater Canyon, in a place five miles below Agua Negra, is not known. Given McCloskey's sentiments and his connection with certain of the Dolan forces, it is unlikely in the extreme that the story the Regulators told—that Morton grabbed his gun, shot him, and then tried to make a getaway with Baker—was the truth. More probably the Regulators were jittery about the posse Dolan had raised overtaking them and despaired that justice would ever be done in Lincoln or anywhere else in the Territory. It is also probable that someone among the Regulators shot McCloskey and it was this action which may have prompted Morton and

Baker to make a break for their lives. There may also have been some kind of impromptu trial held. At any rate, Morton and Baker were killed according to the *ley de fuga* and there were at least nine bullets in Morton's body, all of them in the back—which makes a break for freedom more probable than an organized execution. The Kid's desire for vengeance was the order of the day, but the Kid himself alone did not kill either man, as he was later reputed to have boasted. Thenceforth the site of the shooting became known as Dead Man's Draw. Brewer by himself headed toward Lincoln, arriving late Sunday evening, 10 March. The others rode toward San Patricio.

As it turned out, the Regulators need not have been concerned about Dolan or his supposed posse, although they were correct in their surmise that Morton and Baker would never have been held as prisoners for trial. On 8 March Governor Axtell paid a brief visit to Lincoln and the three hours he stayed he spent in Dolan's company. After listening to Dolan's statement of the case, he issued a proclamation, on 9 March, which declared that "John B. Wilson's appointment by the county commissioners as a justice of the peace was illegal and void, and all processes issued by him were void, and said Wilson has no authority whatever to act as justice of the peace." Axtell also revoked Robert Widenmann's appointment as a federal marshal. Lastly, he called on the post commander at Fort Stanton "to assist Territorial civil officers in maintaining order and enforcing legal process" and avowed "that there is no legal process in this case to be enforced, except the writs and processes issued out of the third judicial district court by Judge Bristol, and there are no Territorial civil officers here to enforce these except Sheriff Brady and his deputies."[64]

When Brewer reached Lincoln, he found McSween in town. He had come back during the governor's visit, believing he would be safe. He advised Brewer to tell the others to give Lincoln a wide berth until court convened. Wishing to avoid a reprisal for the killings which Brewer reported to him, McSween, still in Barrier's custody, decided to leave Lincoln a second time, riding down the Pecos to seek refuge at Chisum's ranch. Brewer rode out to his farm on the Ruidoso and then got word to the others near San Patricio that they were all virtually outlaws. Chisum had finally been released from jail in Las Vegas and he therefore was present to provide the fugitive McSween sanctuary.

While McSween and the Regulators were lying low, Jesse Evans and Tom Hill made a raid on the camp of John Wagner, on 14 March, and Hill was killed and Evans wounded by Wagner. A few days later, seeking medical aid for his wound, Evans turned himself in at Fort Stanton. Should anyone ask him, Evans was more than willing to swear that Tom Hill had murdered Tunstall. No one asked.

McSween decided to return to Lincoln to be present when district court would begin its open session. As a result, MacNab, French, Waite, Middleton, Brown, and Bonney rode into Lincoln on the night of 31 March and stayed at the Tunstall store. The more they talked about it among themselves, the more convinced they became that Sheriff Brady was as much responsible for Tunstall's murder and the disorder in the district as anyone. When it came to shielding Tunstall's murderers, no one, it seemed to them, was more in the forefront. A decision was reached to ambush Brady. McSween was known to be on his way into Lincoln and there is no doubt that Sheriff Brady was aware of it. In fact, it was Sheriff Brady's intention to arrest him. After analyzing all the evidence and the contradictory testimony, Frederick Nolan arrived at "the inescapable conclusion that Brady was on his way to arrest McSween as the lawyer rode unprotected into Brady's eminent domain. There was absolutely no need for Brady to kill him on the street. Once in Brady's power, McSween's life would not be worth a plugged nickel."[65]

At nine o'clock the morning of 1 April Brady, Hindman, Mathews, Long, and Peppin began walking west up Lincoln's main street past the Tunstall store toward the far edge of town where McSween was supposed to arrive. They had no doubt heard a rumor that some of the Regulators were in town and thus the show of force. Brady, in addition to his sidearm, contemptuously held in his hands the rifle he had taken from Billy Bonney when he had arrested him. There is even a tradition in the Brady family that on that morning Francisco Anaya had sent his twelve-year-old son Timoteo to warn the sheriff that an ambush was rumored to have been set for him. Brady obviously was not intimidated by the warning, if he received it. Two-thirds of the distance between the rear and front of the Tunstall store there was a wooden gate. It was behind this gate that the six Regulators hid. When rifle shots rang out, Brady fell in his tracks. Afterwards it was determined that there were eight bullets in his body. Hindman was wounded by a single bullet and managed to stagger a few feet before he, too, fell. Jack Long was also hit. Squire Wilson, who was unaware of what was going on and had been in fact hoeing in his onion patch at the time, received flesh wounds in both legs between the hips and knees. The Kid concentrated his fire on Billy Mathews, but missed him. Mathews fled into the Cisneros' house. The Kid then ran out into the street to retrieve his rifle from near Brady's body and Mathews fired a shot at him which hit the Kid on the inside of the left thigh. Later José Chávez y Chávez claimed that he, too, was among the assassins and that it was he who killed Brady. It is possible he was there, but he didn't fire all the shots that downed the sheriff. Robert A. Widenmann was also later placed in the corral behind the Tunstall store and a case was alleged against him that he had participated in Sheriff Brady's murder.

Ruth R. Ealy's memoir of this time contains Dr. Ealy's account of the shootings. "Father stated that someone ran out to pick up either Brady's or Hindman's gun," Ruth R. Ealy wrote, "and was shot as he stooped over, not through the bowels as reported, but through the left thigh. Father said that the man came walking through the door and he treated him by drawing a silk handkerchief through the wound and binding it up. Soon the Murphy/Dolan crowd, who had tracked the man by his blood, came to search the house. It seems that Sam [Corbet] had taken the wounded man in charge and they disappeared. Afterwards, Father learned that Sam [Corbet] had sawed a hole under a bed and laid the man there with a gun in his hand."[66] Corbet was the clerk in the Tunstall store where Dr. Ealy had set up his temporary quarters. It was also probably in the store that Corbet hid the Regulator. According to Frederick Nolan, the man who was wounded in the thigh by the same bullet fired by Mathews that supposedly only clipped the Kid was Jim French. According to Colonel Fulton, the wounded man was the Kid. Since Fulton interviewed those who had seen or knew about the shooting at the site over a period of years, the preponderance of evidence is in his favor and it is further supported by Norman J. Bender's comment on Dr. Ealy's memoir of the incident. "Taylor Ealy did not name the wounded man who 'came walking into our back door.' However, the only one wounded at that time among those who ambushed Brady and Hindman was Henry McCarty."[67] The other Regulators involved in the shooting left town hurriedly.

Ruth R. Ealy also recorded that her mother thought Billy "a charming looking chap with splendid manners. He loved to sing in a beautiful tenor voice when he came to Sunday School, as he did when he happened to be in Lincoln." Ruth remarked in her own right that Billy had many attributes which were admired by those who knew him, including "his intelligence, his courtesy, his love for beauty, his capacity for leadership, his acceptance without fear and without complaint of the rough as well as the smooth in life, and his capacity for making friends." She went on to say that Tunstall won the Kid's "unending friendship by presenting him with a horse and a lovely saddle. So when Tunstall was killed, Billy vowed vengeance upon the enemies of Tunstall."[68] It is generally thought that MacNab masterminded the assassination plot. The Kid can certainly be accused of having been an accomplice in it. Beyond this, it was a particularly stupid crime to have committed on the part of the Regulators. It lost them sympathy and was readily construed for what it was—outright murder. Even though partisan to the Dolan faction since he owed money to the House, Brady was also at best an accomplice himself, following orders from Dolan, Rynerson, and Bristol, and beyond them the Santa Fe Ring. Tunstall had once declared him to be a tool. This he may have been and, if not quite the hero Donald R. Lavash portrayed him as having been in his biography SHERIFF WILLIAM BRADY: TRAGIC HERO OF THE LINCOLN COUNTY WAR (Sunstone Press, 1986), his death was most certainly a tragedy. Moreover, there is some question just how much of a willing tool he had been. There is no evidence that he condoned the murder of Tunstall, although he may have passively allowed it to occur. Partisan he was, but perhaps not quite the besotted derelict he was painted to be by the other side. It would seem more likely he was a man concerned with preserving the *status quo* and looked with suspicion on Tunstall and McSween as ambitious upstarts. The talon law of an eye for an eye might have been justified had Dolan been murdered in retaliation for his orchestrated murder of John H. Tunstall. By contrast, Brady's death was senseless and unjustified.

McSween arrived in Lincoln about noon, accompanied by John Chisum, Calvin Simpson, Albert Howe, and Dr. Montague R. Leverson. Dr. Leverson had come to the Pecos valley from Colorado seeking a fitting place to set up a colony of settlers and had significant influence with the Hayes administration. Deputy Sheriff Barrier had decided at the Chisum ranch to head back to Las Vegas without ever turning his prisoner over to Sheriff Brady. Dolan, as soon as he learned of this, rode again to Mesilla and had Judge Bristol issue a warrant for Barrier's arrest, but before it could be served McSween's hearing was held and McSween exonerated.

George Peppin, right after the shooting, had ridden to Fort Stanton and returned to Lincoln just about the time McSween did, leading Captain Purington and twenty-five troopers. Peppin, although his authority had vanished when Brady died, considered himself acting sheriff and he set about arresting McSween partisans with the help of the troopers. Widenmann was arrested at the Tunstall store. Peppin, taking Lieutenant C. W. Smith and two troopers with him, went down to the Ellis home to arrest McSween, having heard that McSween was staying there. Peppin told Issac Ellis that he was there to arrest McSween, but McSween, from within, refused to recognize Peppin's authority. McSween, however, was willing to place himself under military protection and Lieutenant Smith accepted this condition. As they were coming away from the Ellis home, they encountered Captain Purington and he rejected the offer Lieutenant Smith had made to protect McSween unless Peppin approved of his doing so. McSween put up an argument. Peppin countered by saying that it was also his intention to search McSween's house for Brady's murderers. McSween objected even more vociferously to this, insisting that Peppin had no authority to make such a search.

Dr. Leverson, who was a bystander at this altercation, interposed now, reminding Captain Purington that the Constitution protects individuals and property from search or seizure without proper warrant.

"Damn the Constitution and you for a fool," Purington told him.

Leverson then turned to the enlisted men present and advised them to disobey their officer in a violation of Constitutional rights such as this.

"Shut up!" Purington told him. "You are making a damn fool of yourself!"

"God knows," Leverson replied, irate, "I would not live in a country where such outrages as these I have witnessed this afternoon are countenanced."

"Sir," Purington said, "you have my permission to suit yourself."

"If your soldiers were not here," McSween interjected, "Peppin would never dare to enter and search my house."[69]

Purington's response to this was an order to his men to prepare to make the return journey to the fort. McSween felt it necessary to remain under the protection of the military so he climbed into the wagon which had been brought to transport him to Fort Stanton. He was joined by his wife, who wished to remain close to him, David P. Shield, his brother-in-law, Widenmann, and two black retainers, George Washington and George Robinson.

Dr. Leverson immediately began his own investigation of what had happened and, in consequence, wrote two letters to Washington, one to Carl Schurz, Secretary of the Interior, and one to President Hayes. The letter to President Hayes does shed some light on just where Brady and his group were actually going when they were ambushed. Apparently Brady had learned that McSween was on his way into Lincoln because McSween had applied to Fort Stanton for protection prior to his entering Lincoln and this information had been communicated to the Dolan forces. "Brady had started out with Hindman, his deputy Peppin, and two other men to go down the creek and meet McSween (really there can be no doubt to murder him) and who . . . was on his way to the road to the fort, but had to pass through Lincoln to reach it. Brady and his party were met by seven citizens, some of them, I am assured on excellent authority, being among the best citizens of the county; how the firing commenced I have been unable as yet to learn, but Brady and Hindman were killed and two of the citizens were wounded."[70] Actually only the Kid had been wounded, and there were only six men lying in ambush. It is possible that the Regulators involved in the assassination did not know what Sheriff Brady's intentions were regarding McSween. In any event, it is a bit hyperbolic to describe this group as "among the best citizens of the county," since even to partisans they were scarcely that.

As soon as he could do so, the Kid slipped out of Lincoln undetected and headed for San Patricio. It was there that Billy met Tom O'Folliard and the two became instant friends. O'Folliard was a young man of about Billy's age who had drifted in to New Mexico from Uvalde, Texas. The Kid persuaded him to take a hand in the war against the Dolan forces and to become a Regulator.

Dick Brewer, while he disapproved of the killing of Brady and Hindman, objected even more strenuously to Dolan's countermove, which was to place a bounty of $200 on any Regulator. Riding through the Ruidoso valley, Brewer enlisted the aid of Frank and George Coe who shared his alarm at the turn which events were taking. Brewer had heard that Tunstall's cattle had been removed from the Rio Feliz ranch and had been driven to the corrals at the Shedd ranch where Dolan had once confronted Tunstall after McSween's first hearing before Judge Bristol. The Coes agreed to assist in returning the cattle. John Middleton and Charlie Bowdre were with Brewer and on the way the group encountered the Kid and Tom O'Folliard. On 4 April they put in at Blazer's Mill, a building owned by Dr. Joseph Blazer which he leased to the Mescalero Indian agency. The agent's wife, Mrs. Frederick Godfroy, was known to serve dinner to passers-by and the Regulators entered that part of the complex reserved for an eating place and gave her their orders.

Andrew L. Roberts, who had been with the sub-posse when Tunstall was killed, was prowling around the countryside now, hoping to earn the bounty money that Dolan had offered. "We had no idea," George Coe recalled in his autobiography, "that 'Buckshot' Roberts was on our trail, waiting for an opportunity to catch us off guard and kill as many of us as he could on the first round."[71] If Roberts had indeed been trailing the Regulators, he must have had no idea whatsoever as to their strength. When he rode up to the compound, he dismounted and proceeded toward the room in the northwest corner of the building which Dr. Blazer had reserved for his office to carry on his work as postmaster and oversee the operation of the sawmill.

"Here's Buckshot Roberts!" shouted out someone among the Regulators.

It would have been possible for one of them to have taken a shot at Roberts, but Brewer restrained them. He had a warrant for Roberts' arrest and he wanted to try negotiation first. He sent Frank Coe, who knew Roberts well, to talk over the matter with him. Coe approached Roberts who, by this time, was holding his rifle and Roberts suggested to Coe that they adjourn to Dr. Blazer's office. Coe declined. He informed Roberts that Brewer had a warrant for Roberts' arrest and assured him that he would be protected while in custody.

"Give me your rifle," Coe said, "and we will walk around to the crowd. I will stand by you whatever happens."

"Surrender?" Roberts scoffed. "Never, while I'm alive. Kid Antrim is with you and he would kill me on sight. Don't I know what happened to Morton and Baker?"

Apparently it had already become second nature among the Dolan forces to characterize the Kid as homicidal. No doubt the search for him after the deaths of Brady and Hindman had contributed significantly to this prevailing sentiment. Coe continued to argue with Roberts, but Brewer could see from his position that more persuasion of the hopelessness of his situation had to be impressed on Roberts and so he sent George Coe, John Middleton, and Charlie Bowdre over to join Frank.

Roberts was a man of small stature whose right arm had been crippled so that he could not raise a rifle to his shoulder.

"Roberts," Bowdre called out, as the trio approached the two men, "throw up your hands." He already had his six-gun in his hand.

"Not much, Mary Ann," Roberts said.

"With his refusal to throw up his hands," George Coe recalled, "they fired simultaneously. Bowdre's bullet struck Roberts right through the middle, and Roberts' ball glanced off Bowdre's cartridge belt, and with my usual luck, I got there just in time to stop the bullet with my right hand. It knocked the gun out of my hand, took off my trigger finger, and shattered my hand which still bears record of the fight. The wound did not seem to affect me, but I was stunned, not knowing just what to do. Instead of offering my back as a target for his bullets, I ran forward right in front of Roberts. He shot once at John Middleton, and the bullet entered his breast. He fired three times at me, but missed. Dick Brewer was enraged and swore vengeance against Roberts, declaring: 'I'll get him now at any cost.' "[72]

The bullet which had hit Middleton seriously injured his lung. The Kid, who ran out toward a wagon near the building, had his arm grazed by another bullet. Roberts quickly retreated into Dr. Blazer's office, tore the mattress off a bed in the room, and propped it in the doorway as a makeshift breastwork. Also in the room was Dr. Blazer's Springfield rifle and a thousand rounds of ammunition.

Brewer directed the others to remain out of the line of fire while he himself sought protection behind some logs piled near the sawmill. He raised his head so as to see what Roberts was doing some 140 yards away. Roberts snapped off a lucky shot at the thin strip of forehead. The bullet hit Brewer, taking off part of his skull. This placed the other Regulators in a quandary and, presently, they departed *en masse*, heading for George Coe's ranch on the Ruidoso.

The shooting had lasted only a few minutes.

Major Godfroy, the Indian agent, and Dr. Blazer were swiftly on the scene and sent to Fort Stanton for Dr. Appel, the post surgeon, but it was too late. The next day Roberts died and was buried in a grave near to that of Dick Brewer.

"He never drank and he never quarrelled except upon extreme provocation," Maurice Garland Fulton wrote of Brewer in the HISTORY OF THE LINCOLN COUNTY WAR; "he was esteemed by everyone as an honest, hard-working farmer. In buying from Murphy the farm which the latter did not own, he had gotten into debt to 'The House,' and when through the advice of McSween he had escaped the trap they had set for him and his property, their hostility had descended upon him. As Tunstall's foreman, he had been loyal to the interests of his employer, ready instantly to do anything. If Tunstall's horses were stolen, it was Brewer who went after them when Brady would make no move. If Tunstall's cattle were to undergo attachment, it was Brewer who withstood the posse that Brady dispatched. If Tunstall's murderers were to be brought to justice, it was again Brewer who shouldered the responsibility of leadership."[73]

Dolan wrote his own account of recent events for the *Santa Fe New Mexican* dated 16 May 1878, a newspaper dominated by the Ring. "They say 'outraged prominent citizens,' 'regulators,' " he started off, naming his enemies. "Who are these prominent citizens and regulators? I will here state William H. Antrim, alias 'the Kid,' a renegade from Arizona, where he killed a man in cold blood." Dolan may not have realized it, but by calling attention to the Kid in this fashion he was laying the foundation for the Kid's legend as a bad man and ruthless murderer. What he doubtless did intend was to make the Kid, along with others such as Fred Waite and Alexander A. McSween, a convenient scapegoat on which could be blamed all the troubles in the district. In this, he was ultimately to prove successful.

V

The McSween faction was momentarily helped, albeit inadvertently, by Judge Bristol. Bristol wanted McSween, Widenmann, Shield, George Washington, and George Robinson, who were still at Fort Stanton under military protection, to be arrested and arraigned in his court. He appointed John S. Copeland to serve the warrants which Brady had had in his possession at the time of his death but had been unable to serve and which included a warrant for McSween. He had not suspected that the county commissioners of Lincoln County would approve of this action and at a special meeting on 27 April actually appoint Copeland officially to the office of sheriff. When this indeed did happen, Dolan had to go at once to Santa Fe and see Governor Axtell personally to rectify Bristol's error and Axtell, accordingly, removed Copeland from office as of 28 May 1878 and appointed George W. Peppin in his place. The *faux pas* gave the McSween faction almost two months of freedom from local persecution by the sheriff's office.

Bristol's second error in judgment was even more a disaster. He was mistakenly convinced that he could control anyone impaneled in a grand jury within his courtroom. By 13 April, with McSween and the others now under arrest and in Copeland's custody, he impaneled a grand jury with Dr. Joseph H. Blazer as foreman and consisting of several prominent citizens of Lincoln, Juan B. Patrón and Vicente Romero among them. Bristol commenced by lecturing the grand jury that the McSween "embezzlement" was "the immediate starting point and occupied a conspicuous place in all the violence and bloodshed" and that "the circumstances of the case point to but one conclusion as to the motive, and that was to induce desperate men to come to the aid of McSween, armed with deadly weapons, for the purpose, among other things, of offering open and violent intimidation or resistance to this court. They have so far succeeded as to resist successfully by force the processes of the court under circumstances which I shall hereafter relate to you."[74] He then proceeded to tell his version of McSween's villainy in a long, and at times bitter, diatribe.

Bristol was probably shocked when on 18 April the grand jury reported to him its findings concerning the matters related to the recent violence in Lincoln County and concluded: "We fully exonerate him [McSween] of the charge and regret that a spirit of persecution has been shown in this matter." The grand jury further declared that "had his excellency, S. B. Axtell, when here, ascertained from the people the cause of our troubles, as he was requested, valuable lives would have been spared our community; especially do we condemn that portion of his proclamation relating to J. B. Wilson as J. P. Mr. Wilson acted in good faith as such J. P. for over a year. Mr. Brewer, deceased, arrested, as we are informed, some of the alleged murderers of Mr. Tunstall by virtue of warrants issued by Mr. Wilson. The part of the proclamation referred to virtually outlawed Mr. Brewer and posse. In fact, they were hunted to the mountains by our late sheriff with U.S. soldiers. We believe that had the governor done his duty whilst here, these unfortunate occurrences would have been spared us."[75]

Indictments were brought against Jesse Evans, George Davis, Miguel Segovia, and John Long (under his alias of Frank Rivers) as principals in the murder of John H. Tunstall and against James J. Dolan and J. B. Mathews as accessories. Of the principals, only Jesse Evans was available, still at Fort Stanton recovering from his bullet wound, and he was arrested and placed under a bond of $5,000. Dolan and Mathews were arrested and placed under a $2,000 bond each. Indictments were brought against William H. Bonney, John Middleton, Fred Waite, and Henry Brown for the murders of Brady and Hindman. Charlie Bowdre was indicted for the death of Andrew L. Roberts. As none of these was available, warrants for their arrest were turned over to Sheriff Copeland. Robert Widenmann, David P. Shield, George Washington, and George Robinson were released on their own recognizance as there were no charges against them. Lastly, indictments were found against Dolan and Riley who were charged with cattle stealing.

No such travesty would ever occur again as far as Judge Bristol was concerned. Henceforth all juries in his court would be handpicked to bring in the desired verdict. When Jesse Evans was put on trial on 2 July 1878, charged with Tunstall's murder according to the grand jury's indictment, S. B. Newcomb, a close associate of Colonel Rynerson's who would eventually replace Rynerson as district attorney, represented Evans. Rynerson represented the Territory. The defense and prosecuting attorneys and Judge Bristol were extremely careful in their selection of a jury. Evans testified that he was in the company of James J. Dolan twenty-five miles from the scene when Tunstall was murdered. Dolan corroborated Evans' testimony. The chief witness for the prosecution was Robert Widenmann. Judge Bristol himself questioned Widenmann to impress the jury with Evans' innocence. "Mr. Widenmann: You say you were running horseback, dust flying, balls whistling around, yet you could casually look back, see a large party of 15 or 20 coming at full speed behind," he scoffed; "that you recognized Mr. Dolan in the party, when everybody knows that a number of reliable witnesses swear positively that Mr. Dolan was 25 miles from there at the time. Mr. Widenmann, your testimony in this matter will be taken with a good deal of allowance."[76] The charges against Evans and, therefore, against Dolan were thus demonstrated to be without substance and in due course both men were acquitted.

What neither Bristol nor Rynerson could salvage was Dolan's hold on his business. Major Murphy, whose health was rapidly deteriorating from his terminal condition, left Lincoln County and moved to Santa Fe where he died on 19 October 1878. Frank Coe later recalled that "the Sisters of Charity would not let him have whiskey, and that cut his living off."[77] If true (and it probably is just hearsay), Murphy's suffering must have been intensified. Dolan accompanied Murphy on this trip and met with T. B. Catron in Santa Fe where it was decided that Dolan and Riley must assign their shares and interest in J. J. Dolan & Co. to Catron. Catron, in turn, appointed his brother-in-law, Edgar Walz, to go to Lincoln and manage the Dolan store and oversee its activities. Riley emigrated to Las Cruces for a time, but eventually returned to Lincoln to help Dolan assist Walz in winding up their affairs.

When the indictments of the grand jury were originally brought against Dolan and the others, Constable Atanacio Martínez overheard a conversation between Dolan and Colonel Rynerson.

"Don't give up," Rynerson had told Dolan. "Stick to that McSween crowd. I will aid you all I can, and will send you twenty men. Stick to the fight, and give it to those rascals. That is the only way to win."[78]

Dolan's assignment of his interest in J. J Dolan & Co. was at first to be taken no more seriously than John Chisum's assignment of all his property to his brothers. It was an artful legal manipulation which would leave Dolan free to pursue the war against McSween and his followers while Walz would protect the investment both Catron and Rynerson had in the company and its operations. Shortly thereafter John Kinney and his hardcases from Doña Ana did arrive in Lincoln, backed by Dolan locally and Rynerson on the part of the Territory.

Colonel Hatch, the military commander for the District of New Mexico in Santa Fe, removed Captain Purington as the commanding officer at Fort Stanton on 2 April, the day after the shooting of Brady and Hindman. His successor was Colonel Dudley, an inveterate believer in coercion and force as the best means by which to maintain control over a civilian population. A year before this appointment, while he was at Fort Union, Dudley had tried to force a marriage between a young man residing in the vicinity of the fort and a young woman who was a relative of the post chaplain. He was also known as a very heavy drinker. This fact was brought out during his court-martial hearing in November, 1877, regarding the attempt to force the marriage. Dudley had been defended by the firm of Catron and Thornton and, presumably, his new appointment to Fort Stanton met with Catron's endorsement.

Ash Upson, the postmaster at the Turner & Jones store in Roswell, was himself an ardent Dolan supporter. He would later write THE AUTHENTIC LIFE OF BILLY THE KID, although under the byline of Pat F. Garrett, sharing equally with Garrett in the royalties. He gave his verbal approval and helped draft a letter dated 28 April 1878 signed by Marion Turner detailing the righteousness of the Dolan cause. Presently Turner and John Jones organized a posse—ten of whose members had been in the posse the day that Tunstall was killed, including Billy Mathews and George W. Peppin—and they set out for Lincoln to offer their services to Sheriff Copeland in maintaining the peace. Also in this posse were two sets of brothers who would play important roles in the future course of events, Bob and John Beckwith and Wallace and Bob Olinger. They became known as the Seven Rivers gang, to distinguish them from John Kinney's Doña Ana bunch. Both groups saw J. J. Dolan as the certain victor and so backed him. Nor would they be proved wrong by history. Even in terms of patriotism, Dolan clearly had the backing of officialdom in the Territory, from Governor Axtell and U.S. District Attorney Catron to Judge Bristol and Colonel Rynerson. Moreover, John Chisum was perceived as McSween's ally, and many of the Seven Rivers gang resented Chisum's flagrant land claims as much as farmers resented laboring beneath the Dolan yoke. In terms of power and economics, it was a question of who was to control the Territory. Ash Upson in the open letter signed by Marion Turner which was printed in the *Las Vegas Gazette* called it "but a contest for 'the best of the fight,' which any good man will try to get."[79] A later, more romantic generation would call it fulfilling the American dream. One figure still loomed in their way and he would have to be removed, he and all his followers, Alexander A. McSween.

As the Seven Rivers gang was making its way to Lincoln, they encountered Frank Coe and Ab Saunders who were riding from Lincoln back to Coe's farm on the Hondo in the company of Frank MacNab, the cattle detective for Hunter & Evans. The presence of this last was indeed unfortunate since most of the Seven Rivers gang had been making their living stealing cattle from Chisum and, more recently, from Hunter & Evans and MacNab had been a virtual scourge to their activities. The gang opened fire and MacNab fell at the first volley, his body riddled with bullets. Saunders fell also, severely wounded. Coe dropped off his horse and hid himself, keeping up a steady fire as long as his ammunition lasted. By the time he was down to his last bullet, the gang had discovered that MacNab was dead and their ardor subsided enough for Coe, who was friendly with Wallace Olinger, to surrender with a guarantee as to his personal safety. Saunders was classed as a noncombatant, was cared for on the spot, and then was transported to nearby Fort Stanton for treatment at the post hospital.

The gang then proceeded cautiously on its way to Lincoln, ten or twelve of them slipping in to the Dolan store under the cover of darkness—the town was thought to be infested by McSween sympathizers who constituted, in fact, most of Lincoln's residents—and another contingent went to the house of Captain Baca, located east of the Tunstall store.

By the morning of the next day, 1 May, the gang realized that the members of the McSween faction who were in town and were ready and willing to fight were fortressed in the Ellis place. It would be too risky to attempt an attack, so the gang sent word to Copeland that they were on hand and prepared to assist in making arrests for the Brady and Hindman killings. Copeland rejected their offer but immediately dispatched a messenger to Fort Stanton to Colonel Dudley requesting troops to preserve order.

Close to noon, George Coe, who with Henry Brown was positioned on the roof of the Ellis place, espied a man sitting on a cow's skull in a distant field.

"See that fellow way off yonder?" he asked Brown. "I am going to take a shot at him."[80]

Coe aimed and fired, hitting the man who fell to the ground. He was Charlie Kruling, or "Dutch Charlie," who had just ridden in the previous night with the gang. The incident touched off firing by both sides. When Lieutenant C. W. Smith and fourteen troopers arrived, the hostilities were called off and the gang surrendered to the soldiers to be taken to the fort. Copeland at this time had his own group of prisoners, including Dolan, and he turned them over to Lieutenant Smith as well.

Word finally reached Lincoln about the attack on MacNab and McSween went to J. G. Trujillo, justice of the peace for the second district (since Squire Wilson was deposed by Governor Axtell no replacement had as yet been appointed for the first district), to make affidavits against Bob Beckwith and others of the Seven Rivers gang for the murder of MacNab and the attempted murder of Saunders. Copeland was supplied with warrants and rode out to the fort and served them on those who had been charged. McSween also wrote to Colonel Rynerson asking why none of the indicted parties in the Tunstall murder had been served with warrants, why, in fact, warrants for them had yet to be issued? Rynerson wrote back contemptuously that he intended to issue no warrants regarding the Tunstall murder until something was done about serving warrants on those indicted for the murders of Brady, Hindman, and Roberts.

Dolan's presence at the fort gave him an opportunity to visit at length with Colonel Dudley and he was readily able to make Dudley a partisan. Dudley now threw the Army behind Copeland, after lecturing him about doing his duty, and insisted that McSween and several others of his faction be arrested at once in connection with the murders of Roberts, Brady, and Hindman. McSween, Doc Scurlock who lived in Lincoln, Widenmann, George Washington, Issac Ellis and his son, Will, Sam Corbet, and others were arrested and brought to Fort Stanton to be held for a preliminary hearing along with the Seven Rivers gang members before Squire Trujillo on 6 May. The hearing never took place. Copeland could not control such a mob, so he counseled each to go home and everyone was released on his own recognizance.

Doc Scurlock, Charlie Bowdre, George Coe, Billy Bonney, and others quickly resumed their activities as Regulators to offset the threats of the combined gangs from Doña Ana and Seven Rivers which were now roaming about, looking for them. Manuel Segovia, known as "The Indian," had been with the first Mathews posse sent to attach the Tunstall herd and it was learned that he was now at the Dolan and Riley cow camp where all of the horses on Tunstall's ranch, those on Brewer's farm, and those ridden by MacNab, Saunders, and Coe had been taken. The Regulators decided to retrieve this herd and attacked the cow camp, wounding two of the herders and killing "The Indian." Frank Coe later claimed to former Governor Miguel Otero that it was he who killed Segovia.

This depredation outraged T. B. Catron who claimed the horse herd as part of his assignment from Dolan and he wrote an angry letter to Governor Axtell demanding action, in particular military action. "I also learn that all the stock men on the lower Pecos" [by which he meant the Seven Rivers gang] "have been compelled to abandon their stock and go to the mountains where they are now awaiting an attack."[81] Axtell responded promptly by removing John H. Copeland from his office as sheriff of Lincoln County—Dolan's visit to Axtell neatly coincided with Catron's letter—and appointed, at Dolan's recommendation, George W. Peppin in his place.

Peppin's first official act was to appoint a number of men from the Dolan forces as his deputies, Marion Turner and John Long, the latter still under indictment by the grand jury for the murder of Tunstall, among them. Further, although the claim was false, Peppin insisted he be appointed a deputy U.S. marshal and that federal warrants be issued for all the Regulators involved in the killing of Buckshot Roberts because the incident supposedly had occurred on federal land. Armed with these federal warrants, he could now call upon Colonel Dudley's soldiers to join in a posse composed of John Kinney and his Doña Ana bunch to search for the Regulators. Dolan offered Kinney $500 personally if he were to kill McSween. Kinney made so little of a secret about this private commission that Lieutenant Goodwin, in command of the detail assigned to Peppin's posse and himself a staunch Dolan supporter, found his presence in their group an embarrassment and he insisted Kinney and his gang leave the posse.

McSween at once felt compelled to take flight from Lincoln, traveling to San Patricio in the company of the most dedicated of the Regulators who now were to serve as his bodyguard. Prior to leaving, McSween mortgaged the Beatty piano which had arrived during Susan's absence and been used for Dr. Ealy's Sunday service to Issac Ellis for $500. It had been acquired from the Fritz estate. He hoped with this money to pay each man in his bodyguard $3 a day.

Peppin, however, vacillated. He seemed satisfied just to occupy Lincoln and made no effort to pursue McSween and the others at San Patricio. Colonel Dudley became so disgusted with what he regarded as a lack of grit on Peppin's part he recalled his troops to the fort. This spurred Peppin to action, it would seem. He organized a posse under John Long and sent it to San Patricio to arrest McSween and the others.

Once at San Patricio, a short skirmish took place wherein Long's horse was shot from under him. There were no casualties, since the McSween faction quickly fled toward the nearby mountains. Long, however, swore out affidavits against both McSween and Bonney for assault with a deadly weapon. Colonel Dudley, hearing news that Peppin had actually sent a posse after McSween, dispatched thirty-five men to San Patricio under the command of Captain Carroll, charged with maintaining the peace. Carroll, however, was abruptly recalled by Dudley before he reached his destination. On 18 June an amendment had been attached to an Army appropriations bill prohibiting the use of any part of the U.S. Army as a posse comitatus, or otherwise, in civil disturbances except where violations of the Constitution or acts of Congress were involved.

The situation was becoming ever more desperate for the Dolan forces and a decisive battle had to be fought. As a result of Dr. Leverson's letter to President Hayes, and numerous other complaints, the president had sent Judge Frank Warner Angel to Lincoln County as a special agent for the Department of Justice. Judge Angel talked to numerous participants in the struggle, including such minor players—at least so far—as Billy Bonney. In his report to the U.S. attorney general Judge Angel would find, among other things, that "John H. Tunstall was murdered in cold blood and was not shot attempting to resist an officer of the law." He would also discover many of the irregularities of Dolan's and Riley's dealings with the Indian agency and take testimony from Captain Henry Carroll—the same officer Dudley had dispatched to San Patricio and then recalled—that when rations were issued in October, 1877, there were about 250 Indians present but ration tickets were collected and paid on 901 Indians. Judge Angel also had "no doubt that Wm. Morton, Jesse Evans, and Tom Hill were the only persons present and saw the shooting, and that two of these persons murdered him [Tunstall]."[82]

However, this was still some months in the future. As it stood in June, Morton and Hill were dead. Evans was about to be acquitted. The time for Dolan was now, "to give it to those rascals," as Colonel Rynerson had counseled, to win "the contest for 'the best of the fight,' " as Ash Upson had rallied. The McSween faction, too, it would appear was ready for such an engagement. A sheriff's posse under the leadership of Marion Turner and Buck Powell trailed the McSween faction after their exodus from San Patricio to their refuge at Chisum's ranch. McSween, to keep his bodyguard alive, had had to draw on money from the Tunstall estate and it was just prior to this time that John Chisum more or less implied that he could be counted on for financial backing, in deferred wages perhaps, but for right now the store he maintained at the ranch for supplies and ammunition was open and available to them. Early in July several of the Seven Rivers gang, a portion of the trailing posse, discovered the twelve or fourteen men in the McSween faction at Chisum's ranch and laid siege. After a day and a night of desultory fighting, Powell decided his force insufficient to storm the stronghold and on 4 July he withdrew to get reinforcements in the Seven Rivers area. The McSween faction withdrew at once for San Patricio and when Powell returned, with Turner and his men backing him, he found them gone. However, before reaching San Patricio, McSween decided that he had reached the Rubicon. He would now cross over. He changed direction and headed with his men for Lincoln.

The pursuing posse, in the meantime, convinced that McSween was indeed heading for San Patricio got in touch with Sheriff Peppin and presently Peppin, Dolan, and an additional posse joined up with them. When they found that the McSween faction was not at San Patricio, Dolan ordered the town ransacked. The incident was probably reported by McSween in the *Cimarron News and Press* on 25 July, although the dateline was 11 July 1878. "Headed by Axtell's sheriff and J. J. Dolan," the article read, "the Rio Grande posse killed and stole horses in San Patricio last week; at the same time and place, they broke windows and doors, smashed boxes and robbed them of their contents; from an old woman who was living alone they stole $438. They tore the roof off of Dow Bros. store; they threw goods out on the street and took what they wanted. Towards women they used the vilest language. Citizens working in the fields were fired upon but made good their escape up the river. Dolan and Panteleon Gallegos, late clerk to the 'House,' killed a horse lariated near the town because the owner was supposed to sympathize with the Regulators. Dolan informed the people that there was no law in the county that he could recognize and that when certain Regulators and sympathizers were killed, he would leave the d--d country. Kinney, who was present, remarked those were his sentiments. Kinney said in town that he was employed by the governor and that he and his men would have to be paid $3.50 a day by the county, and that the sooner the people helped him arrest the Regulators, the sooner their county would be relieved of this expense; Dolan endorsed this speech. Peppin stated that he would turn those who sympathized with the Regulators out of their houses, that he would take all of their property, that he had power to do as he pleased. Dolan and Kinney enthusiastically endorsed this sentiment."

Shortly after the siege at the Chisum ranch and shortly before the sacking of San Patricio by the Dolan forces, Bob Beckwith wrote a letter to his sister.

My dear sister:

Today we will start to look after them. We do not know where about in the country they are but suppose they are at Ruidoso or the Feliz. Our party or sheriff's posse number about 35 men. The Mob are too cowardly to come to us and fight—we will have to look for them like Indians. The Mob was routed on the 3rd and the sheriff pursued them down to the Pecos. We would have captured them but they returned to the plaza and 12 of us only had to contend against them at South Spring River. We held them there the 4th all day and they did not dare to come out and fight us —they shot a few shots at us from the house and did not touch any of us. Had the men from here come to our assistance we would probably have got some of them but they did not come until we sent for them, and when they came McSween's mob had escaped.

Now, Dear Sister, do not fret yourself about us, it does no good—and tell Mother and Camilia and Ellen not to either. God will be with us, and these murderers will not touch a hair on our heads. Dear Sister we are having a rough time of it but ere long we will be about ready to go home again.[83]

The women of San Patricio complained so vehemently to Colonel Dudley that to satisfy them he sent Captain Blair to report on conditions there. Captain Blair's report merely confirmed the newspaper account. One of the McSween faction (the handwriting was identified as belonging to Charlie Bowdre), disgusted with what had happened at San Patricio, wrote a letter to Edgar Walz, warning him "that if any property belonging to the residents of this county is stolen or destroyed, Mr. Catron's property will be dealt with as nearly as can be in the way in which the party he sustains [Dolan] deals with the property stolen or destroyed by them." The letter was dated 13 July 1878, "In Camp."[84] By the night of Sunday, 14 July, the McSween faction, now numbering fifty or sixty riders, entered Lincoln and deployed themselves among three strongholds.

VI

Shortly after they had first met, when Billy and Tom O'Folliard were on their way to join the Regulators to retrieve stolen Tunstall stock, the two stopped at Martín Chávez' small ranch. He had been stripped of every animal he owned by the rustlers, save for the one horse with which he was trying to plow. Billy and Tom had a pack horse with them. They switched their gear from this animal to the horses they were riding. Chávez did not want to accept the gift, but the Kid and O'Folliard rode off before he could do anything about it. "Billy was one of the kindest and best boys I ever knew," Chávez later told former Governor Otero when he was preparing his account of the Kid. "He was not bloodthirsty, he was forced into killing in defense of his own life. In all his career he never killed a native citizen of New Mexico, which was one of the reasons we were all so fond of him."[85] Now that matters with the Dolan forces had come to a showdown, Martín and between twenty and twenty-five Mexican adherents under his command rode in with the McSween faction and occupied the Montaño place. Another group established themselves at the Ellis place so as to control the eastern access to Lincoln. McSween and the men acting as his bodyguard—Jim French, Billy Bonney, Tom Cullins, Tom O'Folliard, Joseph J. Smith, José Chávez y Chávez, Francisco Zamora, Yginio Salazar (who was fifteen), Vicente Romero, Ignacio Gonzales, and Harvey Morris (who was a young law clerk in McSween's office who had come West because of a lung ailment and who was not technically a combatant)—occupied the McSween house itself.

This action took Sheriff Peppin completely by surprise. Most of his posse was still in the San Patricio area. In town with him were only Billy Mathews, a man called "Dummy" because he was supposed to be deaf and dumb, and three other deputies whom Peppin deployed in an old *torreón*, a stone structure known as the "Indian tower" which stood in a clearing near the house Captain Saturnino Baca was renting from McSween. Peppin dispatched a messenger at once to summon the San Patricio posse. Meanwhile the McSween faction dug in, barricading windows and piling sandbags in doorways. They were ready for a protracted siege.

On the morning of 15 July, Monday, the first day of what would prove a five-day battle, McSween tried to clear the Indian tower of men by serving written notice on Baca that he must surrender his house. "You have consented to so improper use of the property by murderers for the purpose of taking my life, and I can no longer consent to your occupancy thereof," McSween wrote.[86] Baca responded by at once appealing to Colonel Dudley at the fort for protection, recalling his own service in the New Mexico Volunteers from 1863 to 1868. Dudley, upon receipt of Baca's appeal, felt impotent to take a hand, but he did tell Dr. Appel to ride to Lincoln and investigate matters.

Dr. Appel interpreted his role as that of a mediator. Upon arriving in Lincoln, he called on McSween and found him insistent that only if Captain Baca would clear the *torreón* of Peppin forces he would be allowed to stay on the property. The Peppin forces, on the other hand, refused to leave the *torreón* unless soldiers from the fort were to come and occupy it, thus making it neutral ground. Dr. Appel, frustrated at McSween's obduracy, returned to Fort Stanton and declared matters at an *impasse*.

By afternoon, the Dolan forces were brought to full strength with the arrival of Dolan, John Kinney and the Doña Ana bunch and Marion Turner and the Seven Rivers gang. In addition to Robert and Wallace Olinger, John and Robert Beckwith, Andrew Boyle, Jesse Evans, Joseph Nash and approximately three dozen others, John Jones, Marion Turner's business partner, brought along his younger brothers, James and William. William was only thirteen years old and he was to be employed chiefly loading guns and molding bullets for the older combatants.

Peppin's first ploy was to send John Long to the McSween house with warrants for McSween, Doc Scurlock, Charlie Bowdre, Henry Brown, Billy Bonney, Frank Coe, George Coe, and several others and to demand they put themselves in custody. He was fired at several times as he approached the house and his demand for surrender was rejected. Long went to the Wortley Hotel, which was being used as the headquarters of the Dolan forces, to report his failure. Peppin, in the interim, because his background was that of a stonemason and not that of military strategist, permitted Dolan and others to instruct him as to how he should best deploy his men, which was done, with the Dolan forces spreading themselves out so as to surround the McSween fortifications. By late afternoon an outburst of heavy shooting occurred when some of Martín Chávez' *caballeros* foolishly tried to cross from the Montaño place to the McSween house and were met with gunfire from the sharpshooters located in the Indian tower. The shooting lasted for about half an hour.

The McSween house was a double dwelling, the west wing of which was occupied by the McSweens, the east wing by David Shield, who was presently safely out of town, his wife and their five small children. Elizabeth Shield and the children were barricaded in their part of the house. Susan McSween stayed by her husband's side, even though she knew that he was the most vulnerable, since it was his life Dolan wanted and the presence of the principal Regulators in his house did not make McSween less of a target. Dr. and Mrs. Ealy, their two children, and Miss Gates, the schoolteacher, were barricaded in the Tunstall store, to the east of the McSween house, and were quite definitely noncombatants. The few residents of the town who were not involved in the standoff and who remained in town kept off the streets. The only casualties after the first day's fighting were a horse and a mule.

On 16 July, Tuesday, the second day of battle, the Dolan sharpshooters in the Indian tower were reinforced and threw a sporadic fire at the McSween strongholds. In a counter-move, Martín Chávez located several excellent marksmen on the roof of the Montaño place to return the fire at the Indian tower and to attack other Dolan positions. To counteract this, five of the best shots among the Dolan forces were dispatched to the rocky hillsides south of town to pin down the men atop the Montaño roof with a steady fire. It required much shooting, but the Dolan sharp-shooters were finally successful. Sheriff Peppin, while this was going on, sent a note to Colonel Dudley, declaring the McSween faction to be a lawless mob and requesting the loan of a cannon to restore order. Dudley wanted to assist Peppin, but he could not accede to his request. He did not hesitate to affirm, however, in his return note that "in my opinion you are acting strictly within the provisions incumbent upon you as deputy U.S. marshal and sheriff, and were I not so circumscribed by law and orders, I would most gladly give you every man and all the material at my post to sustain you in your present position, believing it to be strictly legal." Dudley sent this missive by way of a black soldier named Berry Robinson.

When Robinson reached town and was riding up to the Wortley Hotel, a shot was fired in his direction. It is doubtful that it was fired by one of the McSween faction since they were all well aware of the sympathy the commanding officer at Fort Stanton had toward the Dolan forces and were not about to precipitate an incident. However, Peppin took advantage of the episode by claiming in a note back to Dudley that the McSween faction had fired on the soldier and that "my men on seeing him tried their best to cover him, but of no use." Berry returned to the fort.

On the third day, 17 July, Wednesday, the Dolan sharpshooters deployed along the hillsides grew impatient with their positions and decided to go back to the Wortley Hotel. In evacuating their positions they afforded the men on the Montaño roof with splendid targets. Fernando Herrera, one of the sharpshooters with Martín Chávez and Charlie Bowdre's father-in-law, brought down Charlie "Lallacooler" Crawford from among the Dolan forces, wounding him so badly that after falling to the ground he was unable to crawl to shelter behind a rock. None of the other Dolan men was willing to take the risk of going to his aid, so Crawford remained where he was throughout the hot morning.

At the fort, Dudley dispatched a board of inquiry to determine what had happened while Private Robinson was in Lincoln and, predictably, the finding was that he had been shot at several times by "parties concealed within Mr. McSween's house."[87] This "hearing" was held at the Wortley Hotel after Captain Blair, Dr. Appel, and a detachment of the 9th Cavalry arrived at midday. Besides taking testimony from the Dolan forces, Blair tried to pry some admission of guilt out of McSween, even visiting his house, but was only met with an emphatic denial. Since this denial contradicted every other statement the board had heard at the hotel, the board felt fully justified in the conclusion it reached. While in town, Captain Blair, together with Dr. Appel and two other soldiers, was also able to rescue the wounded Crawford. After bringing him down from the hillside, Dr. Appel ministered to him, and then sent to the fort for an ambulance to convey Crawford thither to the post hospital. Crawford's injury was a serious one—a bullet wound in the left side, not fatal in itself, but compounded by the effects of exposure—and, although he survived for a time, he died on 24 August.

On the fourth day, 18 July, Thursday, there was very little firing of any kind from either side. Colonel Dudley was beside himself with frustration, unable to decide what to do. The board of inquiry had recommended immediate action, but to interfere would be to go against a Congressional directive. What settled the matter for him was a visit he received that afternoon from James J. Dolan (who subsequently denied he ever made such a visit). Dolan, apparently, reminded Dudley of what his patriotic duty must be, and he must have been rather convincing since that same afternoon Dudley dictated a memo which was signed by all of his officers, Dr. Appel included, in which they endorsed Colonel Dudley's decision to place "soldiers in the town of Lincoln for the preservation of the lives of the women and children, and in response to the numerous petitions received from persons in that town."[88] He also ordered that all pieces of artillery be put into condition for immediate use. On this fourth day Dr. Ealy braved the Lincoln street, vacating his quarters in the Tunstall store, to minister to Ben Ellis, one of Issac Ellis's sons, a man in his early twenties who had been hit by a stray bullet. Mrs. Ealy and her two children accompanied the doctor, in defiance of the Dolan forces who were positioned all around them as they walked up the street past the Indian tower toward the far eastern edge of town where the Ellis place was located.

On the fifth day, 19 July, Friday, Dolan was confident of Dudley's intercession on his behalf and so began making preparations to storm the McSween house. Firing was exchanged between the two sides as early as seven in the morning, the men in the McSween house concentrating on the Dolan men in the Wortley Hotel. Dolan's strategy, despite the McSween gunfire, was to deploy his men around the McSween house and John Long, who was still under an indictment for Tunstall's murder, was placed in charge of distributing the men. The McSween faction was convinced that even if the Dolan forces charged the house, they could defend it. Their sanguine mood was somewhat dissipated when, at 10:30 in the morning, Colonel Dudley rode into Lincoln with all of his officers, thirty-five enlisted men, a Gatling gun, this with 2,000 rounds of ammunition, and with a mountain howitzer. The men had a three days' supply of rations, if that much time was needed. Dolan was certain it would not be.

Arriving at the Wortley Hotel, Dudley summoned Sheriff Peppin to see him. Dudley stressed to Peppin that he was there solely to protect the lives of women and children. He next directed his troops to march down the street and station themselves directly across from the Montaño place on the south side of the street and between the McSween house to the west and the Ellis place to the east. The Wortley Hotel was to the west of the McSween house and, therefore, due to Dudley's position, was now cut off from the other McSween fortifications.

Dudley's next move was to send Dr. Appel to the Ellis place and Dr. Appel decided on the way to bring Issac Ellis back with him so he could hear from the colonel what the military intended. Charlie Bowdre, Doc Scurlock, and John Middleton were at the Ellis place, but they were not invited to accompany Ellis to Dudley's headquarters. Dudley informed Ellis, and Peppin also, who now joined them, that he was there to protect noncombatants and that his men would only fire should they be fired upon. Dr. Appel then went back to the Ellis place with Issac Ellis where he attended to his son's wound and changed the dressing. Dudley summoned the doctor back to his headquarters because he wanted his signature on the affidavit that would back up the warrant he had almost had to slap literally out of Squire Wilson and which, Dudley had stipulated, must be sworn out against McSween personally. Even before he had deployed in town, Colonel Dudley had halted at Squire Wilson's house and made his forceful demand for a warrant for Alexander A. McSween's arrest, based on the findings of Dudley's board of inquiry. Both Dolan and Judge Bristol had obviously convinced the pugnacious Dudley that McSween was at the root of all the trouble.

Martín Chávez and his riders at this point pulled out of the Montaño place, realizing that with the soldiers in such close proximity they could not possibly lend any kind of support to the men in the McSween house. They were also Mexicans and, even if the 9th Cavalry *was* one of the two black cavalry regiments in the U.S. Army, they were officered by white Anglo-Americans who considered most Mexican-Americans as a cut below the Mescaleros. The men at the Ellis place, seeing Chávez' withdrawal, also mounted up to evacuate, being in a still more impotent position to lend support to the men in the McSween house. Since Bowdre, Scurlock, and Middleton were in this group and Peppin had warrants for them, he took a few men and rushed up to the Ellis place, demanding that they surrender. It was too late. The men were out of range before he arrived.

Squire Wilson, now at Colonel Dudley's headquarters, needed someone to execute the warrant he had signed for McSween. Marion Turner and four or five men from his Seven Rivers gang volunteered to undertake service. Turner went up to the McSween house and yelled out that he had a warrant for McSween as well as warrants for several of the others.

"Yes," someone inside called out in response, "and we hold warrants for some of your men."

"Where are they?" Turner yelled.

"In our guns, you cock-sucking bastard!" a shout came from within the house.

Turner shrugged and with his men returned to the Wortley Hotel.

Thereupon McSween drafted a note on his law office stationery and sent it to Colonel Dudley via his niece Minnie, one of the Shield children. "Would you have the kindness to let me know," McSween wrote, "why soldiers surround my house. Before blowing up my property, I would like to know the reason. The constable is here and has warrants for the arrest of Sheriff Peppin and posse for murder and larceny." McSween's alarm about his house being blown up had obviously been occasioned by Dudley's having placed his cannon directly facing the McSween house. However, Dudley chose to ignore this circumstance in his reply, which he sent back with Minnie. "I am directed by the commanding officer," he wrote, as if it were his adjutant speaking and not himself, "to inform you that no soldiers have surrounded your house and that he desires to hold no correspondence with you; if you desire to blow up your house, the commanding officer does not object, provided it does not injure any United States soldiers."[89]

While this letter-exchange was going on, Dolan men attached themselves to various soldiers and improved their positions around the McSween house, confident that no one inside would dare shoot in the proximity of anyone in uniform. Dolan men also broke into the house opposite the McSween home and hung out a black flag. Everyone knew its meaning. At the battle of the Alamo, Santa Anna's soldiers had raised a black flag to let the Texans known that no one would be spared. The Dolan forces were now notifying McSween and his partisans of the same thing. McSween, irked at how adroitly Dudley had misconstrued his language, wrote to him a second time, offering to surrender to the military, but not to Dolan's gunmen. Dudley responded succinctly that he had nothing to do with the situation, except to protect women and children.

John Long together with Dummy procured a can of coal oil from the Ellis place and they approached the McSween house from the east. They soaked the unguarded kitchen floor with the kerosene and set it afire. There was a strong easterly breeze blowing and it fanned the flames. This was the Shield portion of the house. Little Minnie Shield, entering the kitchen, saw the fire and reported it to Mrs. Shield who put it out with their meagre supply of water.

On Thursday, George Coe had changed his position from the Montaño place to the rooftop of the warehouse behind the Tunstall store, east of the McSween house. With holes drilled in the adobe for gun ports, he, Henry Brown, and Joseph Smith were able to see Long and Dummy attempt to escape through the back yard of the McSween house and they opened fire. Long and Dummy, joined by Buck Powell who had been approaching the back yard rather than trying to exit from it, all sought cover together, racing into the McSween privy the vault of which was at the edge of the Rio Bonito embankment at the extreme rear boundary of the city lot. The men managed to duck the fire from the Coe group by "forting up" in the vault, where they remained for the rest of the day until they could slip away under the protection of darkness.

Andrew Boyle tried to fire the McSween house half an hour later, this time with success. He was supported by intensive fire from the Dolan forces and confined his attempt to the west side, or McSween portion, of the house. Every effort on the part of those inside to extinguish the flames was frustrated by this withering fire, but the house, being made of adobe, burned very slowly, the wood confined to the flooring, rafters, door and window casings. Some of Dudley's soldiers may also have poured their rifle fire into the house.

Mrs. McSween, joining Mrs. Shield and her children, discussed the perilousness of their situation, but Mrs. Shield was no more willing to flee at this time than was Mrs. McSween. Leaving the house from the Shield side, Mrs. McSween made her way to Dudley's headquarters and asked him for his protection of clothing and domestic items, so these might be saved. Dudley refused her request. "So I returned again with a heavy heart to tell Mr. McSween," Mrs. McSween later wrote in a letter to John Tunstall's father in England, "and remained with him until the last room was on fire."[90] She did, however, try once again to see Dudley and walked directly down the middle of the street. Passing the Indian tower on her way, she saw Sheriff Peppin.

"Peppin!" she cried out to him. "Peppin! What does this mean? Why have you set our house on fire? Why are you letting it and all we have in it be burned up?"

Peppin's response was to tell her that he was going to serve the warrants he had against McSween and the others inside even if it cost the lives of everyone involved.

Arriving at Dudley's headquarters, she went directly to see Dudley.

"Colonel Dudley," she asked, more angry than during her previous visit, and perhaps a trifle hysterical, "what do you mean by having my husband's house surrounded by your soldiers?"

"I have come," Dudley told her, in his most officious tone, "I have come to Lincoln with my small command solely for the purpose of giving protection to women and children and such others as may care to avail themselves of it. I do not intend to take sides in the fight, nor shall I permit any of my men to do so."

"Why, then, Colonel Dudley, do you have that cannon pointed toward our house, if you do not intend to take sides in the fight?"

"Madam," Dudley said, more amused than irritated, "if you will take a careful look, you will find that gun is not pointed towards your house at all, but in exactly the opposite direction. I intended using it, if needful, on the men I found this morning in Montaño's house. I expected trouble, but they took the hint and vamoosed."

"Colonel Dudley," Mrs. McSween asked then, nearly in tears, "why have you allowed Peppin's posse to try to burn our house?"

"I am not aware, madam, that your house has been set on fire by Peppin's men. A few hours ago I received from your husband a note saying that he was going to destroy his house. How am I to know that he has not carried out that intention and that is the reason the building is on fire?"

"I don't believe you have any such statement from McSween," she protested vehemently.

"Indeed, I have," Dudley insisted, "and to prove it to you I will produce it." He pulled out McSween's first note from his pocket.

"Give me that letter, sir," Mrs. McSween demanded, reaching for it.

"Hold, madam, hold," Dudley warned her. "If you try to snatch that letter, I will call the guard, and have you escorted from the camp."

"You are a cruel and hard-hearted man, Colonel Dudley," Mrs. McSween said in despair, "to sit here in your camp and allow Peppin and his men to do what they are doing. Some day these deeds will recoil on your head! If I live, I will do all in my power to bring that about."[91]

In her bitter disappointment, Mrs. McSween made her way back to the burning house.

McSween was made only more apathetic when his wife reported to him the conversation she had had with Dudley. He seemed almost in a state of emotional collapse. The Kid felt compelled to take charge.

"We can stick it out," he told the others, "if the fire does not burn any faster than it is now. Some of us are certain to get hit, but most of us can make it across the river. It's only a few hundred yards, and, if we run fast and shoot fast, we can hold off Peppin's crowd so they can't do us much damage."[92] He then turned to Mrs. McSween and regarded her with sympathy. "I expect, Ma'am, you had better leave before. A dress ain't very good to make a run in."

Mrs. McSween agreed grudgingly to leave early enough so that she would not impede the others when the time to make their break came. It was agreed that the Kid with two or three volunteers would run out first, drawing the fire of the Dolan forces and the soldiers and thus making it possible for McSween and those remaining to slip out undetected and get to safety. All exhibited courage, including Yginio Salazar, the youngest of the group, save for Ignacio Gonzales who had taken to whimpering since he had been wounded in the arm.

"Brace up and behave like a man," the Kid told Gonzales.

Gunfire increased from the Dolan forces around four o'clock when Martín Chávez tried to return with his men, leading them as far as the far bank of the Rio Bonito. No one was hit on either side—the distance was 800 yards—but in time Chávez was forced to admit the hopelessness of his position and, again, gave the signal to retreat.

Miss Gates, the schoolteacher in the Ealy household, went to Colonel Dudley with a note requesting help from the soldiers in removing the Ealy family and their belongings from the Tunstall store. Dudley dispatched Captain Blair, Lieutenant Goodwin, and three enlisted men—Miss Gates was reputedly very attractive—to give the good doctor a hand. He also sent a wagon to assist in transporting their household goods. Dudley regretted his action when he heard that Ealy had spoken without the proper humility to an enlisted man, but Ealy hastened to apologize to Colonel Dudley and Dudley permitted the removal work to continue. Before the soldiers were finished, Mrs. McSween came over and asked Captain Blair if she, Mrs. Shield, and the Shield children could join the Ealy group. Blair told her he could only protect her if she and the others were away from the McSween house. She went back and got the Shields. The expanded party was escorted to the house of Juan Patrón, outside the firing zone.

Dusk came at eight o'clock. By nine, those still in the McSween house were huddled together in the kitchen in the McSween portion of the house. Then the Kid made his move, taking Tom O'Folliard, Jim French, José Chávez y Chávez, and Harvey Morris with him. Morris was killed as he crossed the back yard. The others were able to make it through the rear gate, past the rear of the Tunstall warehouse, where Coe and his group had been earlier, and down the embankment to the security of the Rio Bonito. The firing was continuous but the figures were difficult to make out in the darkness. Both the Kid and Chávez y Chávez later said that they were fired upon by three soldiers as they ran. McSween, who was to use this fusillade at the Kid and his group to cover his own exodus with Francisco Zamora, Vicente Romero, and Yginio Salazar, waited too long. He seemed to be petrified by apprehension and merely cowered with these others near the woodpile outside the kitchen door. Tom Cullins and the others who had so far remained inside the house now ran past them and hid in the chicken coop.

John Jones, upon seeing the Kid heading for cover, yelled after him that they were there to kill McSween, not him. He did not know whether or not the Kid heard him. Ignacio Gonzales was the last one out of the house and, seeing McSween and the others hovering by the woodpile, he called out.

"We want to surrender. Is there anybody who will receive our surrender and protect our lives?"

"Yes," replied Bob Beckwith who, with John Jones, Joe Nash, and Dummy, who had escaped from the privy a half hour before, now entered the back yard, "I can receive your surrender."

As soon as John Jones caught sight of McSween, he raised his rifle to shoot him. Beckwith, who obviously from his letter to his sister regarded the whole affair somewhat differently than most of the Seven Rivers gang, tried to grab Jones's rifle out of his hands or at least to deflect his aim. The consequence was that Jones's bullet went through one of Beckwith's wrists and then into his brain. Beckwith was shot again in the head, probably also by Jones. These shots instigated a new round of firing and presently the shooting was concentrated on the group near the woodpile.

"I surrender, oh, my God, save me," McSween said, when first he was hit, falling to his knees. "Oh, Lord, Lord, save me."[93] His body was torn by four more slugs. Romero and Zamora were also killed, Romero with three bullets in his body and leg. Salazar fell to the ground, unconscious but not dead from his wounds.

When on 25 May 1879 the Kid was called upon to give evidence at Fort Stanton at the court of inquiry which had been appointed to investigate Colonel Dudley's possible complicity in the death of McSween, his testimony offered several sidelights to the events on the night of 19 July 1878.[94]

The Recorder [Captain Humphries] began the questioning.

Q.—What is your name and place of residence?

A.—William Bonney—my name is William Bonney; I reside in Lincoln.

Q.—Are you known or called Billy Kid? Also Antrim?

A.—Yes, sir.

Q.—Where were you on the 19th of July last, and what, if anything, did you see of the movements and actions of the troops that day? State fully.

A.—I was in Mr. McSween's house in Lincoln, and I seen the soldiers come down from the fort with the sheriff's party—that is, the sheriff's posse joined them a short distance above there—that is McSween's house. [The] soldiers passed on by [but] the men dropped right off and surrounded the house—that is, the sheriff's party. Shortly after, three soldiers came back with Peppin, passed the house twice afterwards. Three soldiers came down and stood in front of the house in front of the windows. Mr.

McSween wrote a note to the officer in charge asking him what the soldiers were placed there for. He replied saying that they had business there; that if a shot was fired over his camp or at Sheriff Peppin or any of his men he would blow the house up; that he had no objection to [Mr. McSween] blowing up his own house if he wanted to do so. I read the note; Mr. McSween handed it to me to read. I read the note myself. I seen nothing further of the soldiers until night. I was in the back part of the house when I escaped from it. Three soldiers fired at me from the Tunstall store—from the outside corner of the store. That is all I know in regard to it.

Q.—Did the soldiers that stood near the house in front of the windows have guns with them there?

A.—Yes, sir.

Q.—Who escaped from the house with you, and who was killed at that time, if you know, while attempting to make their escape?

A.—José Chávez escaped with me; also Vicente Romero, Francisco [Zamora], and Mr. McSween.

Q.—How many persons were killed in the fight that day, if you know, and who killed them, if you know?

A.—I seen five killed. I could not swear as to who it was killed them. I seen some of them that fired.

Q.—Who did you see that fired?

A.—Robert Beckwith, John [Kinney], John Jones, and those three soldiers —I don't know their names.

Q.—What were the names of the persons who were killed?

A.—Robert Beckwith, Francisco [Zamora], Vicente Romero, Harvey Morris, and A. A. McSween.

Q.—Did you see any persons setting fire to the McSween house that day? If so, state who it was, if you know?

A.—I did, Jack Long, and there was another man I did not recognize.

The Recorder stated at this point that he had finished with the witness and Colonel Dudley exercised his right to cross-examine him.

Q.—What were you, and the others there with you doing in McSween's house that day?

A.—We came there with Mr. McSween.

Q.—Did you know, or had you not heard, that the sheriff was endeavoring to arrest yourself and others there with you at the time?

A.—Yes, sir. I heard so; I did not know it.

Q.—Had you not been there for two or three days previous?

A.—Yes, sir. I never went out of the house.

Q.—Then you were not engaged in resisting the sheriff at the time you were in the house?

[The Recorder interrupted, "I object," and Colonel Pennypacker, the president of the court of inquiry, responded, "Objection sustained." Colonel Dudley asked a new question.]

Q.—Were you in the habit of visiting and stopping at the house of McSween before that time?

A.—Yes, sir.

Q.—In addition to the names which you have given, are you now known or styled in Lincoln County as "the Kid"?

A.—I have already answered that question. Yes, sir, I am; but not "Billy the Kid" that I know of.

Q.—Were you not, and were not the parties with you in the McSween house on the 19th day of July last and the days immediately preceding, engaged in firing at the sheriff's posse?

[The president objected here to his line of questioning and Colonel Waldo, Colonel Dudley's defense counsel, argued in favor of it. There was a pause until the president announced his decision on the point at issue.]

Q.—How many did you see them fire?

A.—I could not swear to that; on account of the firing on both sides, I could not hear. I seen them fire one volley.

Q.—What did they fire at?

A.—Myself and José Chávez.

Q.—Did you not just now state, in answer to the question who killed [Zamora], Romero, Morris, and McSween, that you did not know who killed them, but you saw Beckwith, Kinney, John Jones, and the three soldiers fire at them?

A.—Yes, sir, I did.

Q.—Were these men, the McSween men, there with you when the volley was fired at you and Chávez by the soldiers?

A.—Just a short way behind us.

Q.—Were you looking back at them?

A.—No, sir.

Q.—How then do you know they were just behind you then, or that they were within range of the volley?

A.—Because there was a high fence behind and a good many guns to keep them there. I could hear them speak.

Q.—How far were you from the soldiers when you saw them?

A.—I could not swear exactly—between 30 and 40 yards.

Q.—Did you know either of the soldiers that were in front of the windows of McSween's house that day?

A.—No, sir, I am not acquainted with them.

Colonel Dudley stated at this point that he had completed his cross-examination of the witness. The Recorder had additional questions on redirect examination.

Q.—Explain whether all the men that were in the McSween house came out at the same time when McSween did, and the others who were killed by the firing from the soldiers and others?

A.—Yes, sir, all came out at the same time. The firing was not done by the soldiers until some had escaped.

The Recorder then stated that he was finished with the witness and Colonel Dudley began redirect cross-examination.

Q.—How do you know, if you were making your escape at the time, and the men [Zamora], Romero, Morris, and McSween were behind you, that they were killed at that time? Is it not true that you did not know of their deaths until afterwards?

A.—I knew of the death of some of them. I did not know of the death of one of them. I seen him lying there.

Q.—What time of day was it when you escaped from that house?

A.—About dusk in the evening—a little after dark.

Q.—Whose name was signed to the note received by McSween in reply to the one previously sent by him to Colonel Dudley?

A.—[It was] signed "N.A.M. Dudley"; did not say what rank. McSween received two notes; one had no name signed to it.

Q.—Are you as certain of everything else you have sworn to as you are to what you have sworn to in answer to the last preceding question?

A.—Yes, sir.

Q.—From which direction did Peppin come the first time the soldiers passed with him?

A.—He passed up from the direction where the soldiers camped, the first time I seen him.

Q.—From what direction did he come the second time?

A.—From the direction of the hotel from McSween's house.

Q.—In what direction did you go upon your escape from the McSween house?

A.—I ran towards Tunstall's store; was fired at, and then turned towards the river.

Q.—From what part of the McSween house did you make your escape?

A.—The northeast corner of the house.

Q.—How many soldiers fired at you?

A.—Three.

Q.—How many soldiers were with Peppin when he passed the McSween house each time that day, as you say?

A.—Three.

Q.—The soldiers appeared to go in companies of three's that day, did they not?

A.—All that I ever seen appeared to be three in a crowd at a time, after they passed the first time.

Q.—Who was killed first that day, Bob Beckwith or the McSween men?

A.—Harvey Morris, McSween man, was killed first.

Q.—How far is the Tunstall building from the McSween house?

A.—I could not say how far; I never measured the distance. I should judge it to be 40 yards, between 30 and 40 yards.

Q.—How many shots did those soldiers fire, [those] that you say fired from the Tunstall building?

A.—I don't know.

Q.—Did you see either of the men last mentioned killed; if so, which of them?

A.—Yes, sir, I did. I seen Harvey Morris killed first. He was out in front of me.

Q.—Did you not then a moment ago swear that he was among those who were behind you and José Chávez, when you saw the soldiers deliver the volley?

A.—No, sir; I don't think I did. I misunderstood the question if I did. I said that he was among them that was killed, but not behind me.

Yginio Salazar continued to lie with the McSween dead even after he regained consciousness, too injured to move. He pretended unconsciousness when on two different occasions men from the Dolan forces looked over the bodies. Burning boards were torn up and thrown on the corpse of McSween, and he was left to burn. One of the Dolan forces advised a man looking at Salazar not to waste another bullet on the "greaser." Eventually Salazar pulled himself away to safety and the next day he was attended by Dr. Appel. Salazar had been born on 14 February 1863 and, when he died, he was buried in the Lincoln cemetery, the date given 7 January 1936. The inscription on his tombstone reads, "Yginio Salazar, Pal of Billy the Kid."

Who all shot McSween, or whose bullet definitely terminated his life, will never be known.

"I am tired of being a refugee," he had told Mrs. McSween when he returned to Lincoln for the last time. "I want to die in my own home."[95]

Judge Frank W. Angel's verdict in his report to the Department of Justice summed up the case: "Both have done many things contrary to law; both violated the law. McSween, I firmly believe, acted conscientiously; Murphy & Co. for private gain and revenge."[96] This was written in a private government report. The versions that were printed in the local newspapers, and reprinted in other newspapers farther East, especially the versions in those newspapers directly controlled by the Ring, the *Mesilla News* and the *Santa Fe New Mexican*, had only praise for Sheriff Peppin and his forces and Colonel Dudley's timely intervention which, once again, permitted the forces of truth and justice to triumph over criminality and brigandage and murder.

Following the burning of McSween's body, the Peppin deputies and Dolan forces in general commenced a celebration in which they stormed the Tunstall store and raided its shelves. The more calculating entered the room used for a bank and carried off all available cash.

Robert Beckwith's body was recovered but the others were let lie until the next day. A coroner's jury, appointed by Sheriff Peppin, found that A. A. McSween, Harvey Morris, Francisco Zamora, and Vicente Romero died "while they were resisting the sheriff's posse . . . with force and arms" and that Robert Beckwith died as a consequence of "trying to arrest the parties for whom he had warrants to arrest."[97] With Peppin's deputies and Dolan's other forces ravaging the town, Mrs. McSween was terrified for her life and so did not attend the funeral for her husband who was buried by George Washington and George Robinson in a grave near that of Tunstall.

After making good his escape, Billy Bonney became the leader of what was left of the Regulators. Despite his testimony at the Dudley hearing, he was openly called "Beely" and "the Keed" and occasionally "Beely the Keed" as well as *el chivato* by Mexican-Americans in the area. On the morning of 5 August the Kid said to George Coe whose right hand was still bandaged:

"George, we must go over and see what they did with poor old Dick. You need a change from your hand-nursing, so we'll just make you captain of the guard."[98]

On the way to Blazer's Mill, Billy, George Coe, and Henry Brown met up with a posse of Mexican-Americans under the leadership of Constable Atanacio Martínez. Mrs. McSween, administratrix now of the Tunstall estate, had heard that half of Tunstall's cattle were in the possession of Frank Wheeler and his San Nicholas Spring rustlers and had sent Martínez to repossess them. Martínez convinced the Kid not to venture to Blazer's Mill because of all the trouble that had occurred recently at Lincoln. Instead, he would ride over with his men, check on Brewer's grave, and see if he could get a line on the route the rustlers took with the cattle.

As Martínez and his men were approaching the agency, a party of Mescaleros, perhaps suspecting they were rustlers intent on running off a nearby herd of Indian ponies, opened fire. Morris J. Bernstein, Agent Godfroy's clerk, and Godfroy were issuing supplies at the agency when they heard the gunfire and Bernstein set out to investigate.

The *Cimarron News and Press* for 19 September 1878 carried an account of what happened next. "It is positively asserted," the account stated, "that Bernstein was killed by a Mexican who was with a party going from San Patricio to Tularosa to assist in recovering a lot of stolen stock in the possession of Frank Wheeler and others. When the Mexicans reached the water alongside of the road above the agency, they stopped to water their horses. Bernstein saw them and probably supposing them to be a party of the 'Regulators' attacked them with a party of Indians; he rode up on one Mexican and fired two shots at him; the man took shelter behind a tree. Bernstein still advancing rode close to the tree and fired again at the man, who returned the fire and killed Bernstein. The Mexican says he acted strictly in self-defense and will at any time deliver himself up for trial. His name is Atanacio Martínez."

When Bernstein's body was discovered, he was lying face downwards with four bullets in him. His guns and ammunition were gone and his pockets were left turned inside out—it could not be determined by whom. But this condition of the body suggested more theft and pillage than merely justifiable homicide. Since the Kid was known to be the leader of what was left of the Regulators, the Ring-dominated newspapers and the Dolan forces blamed him for the killing. Colonel Dudley accepted Dolan's identification of the Kid personally as the culprit and, since the depredation had occurred on federal land, this permitted him to dispatch soldiers to search for the Kid and any and all of the McSween faction which remained at large. Lieutenant Goodwin and a detachment were sent in pursuit while Lieutenant Smith and ten troopers were ordered to guard the agency.

"One night a party of soldiers from Fort Stanton, working in the interest of the Murphy gang, was on the trail of Billy for some offense committed on the Mescalero reservation," Mrs. McSween told former Governor Otero. "A party of Mexicans from San Patricio was responsible for the trouble, but as usual it was charged to Billy, and the soldiers seemed determined to get him dead or alive. The trail followed by the soldiers led to a small adobe house occupied by a poor Mexican and his wife. As the adobe had but one room, the man and his wife were sleeping on a mattress in one corner of the room, while Billy was sleeping on another mattress in another corner. The soldiers first surrounded the house and then pounded on the door for admission. Billy instantly crept to the bed in which his friends slept and whispered to the woman and her husband, both of whom immediately got up. Billy quickly lay down on their bed, and the man and woman covered him with his own mattress and bedding. They then lay down on top of the newly made bed.

"When the pounding at the door was renewed, the woman got up and unlocked the door, asking: 'Who is there?' But before the soldiers could enter she got back into bed. When the soldiers piled into the room demanding to know if Billy was there both the man and the woman gruffly answered, 'No!' The soldiers looked around the room with the aid of lighted matches, and failing to discover signs of any person other than the man and woman, they finally gave up; and mounting their horses rode away. When they had gone, Billy reappeared from his place of concealment, though he was almost smothered to death between the two mattresses and the bedding. This was just one of his many wonderful escapes. His plans were always formed and executed as swift as lightning, no matter what the emergency. He never seemed to hesitate or to be at a loss—at least, on only one occasion—and that was the time he and Pat Garrett met in the room at Pete Maxwell's."[99]

One thing was certain to the Kid at this point: he had been hopelessly outlawed by the Dolan forces. This meant that he had no employer nor was there anyone in Lincoln County who would dare employ him. He had only three options: to leave the Territory, to be killed, or to try to survive by his wits and by theft, although this option, too, might well lead to his being killed. There was one other potential alternative. John Chisum might make the difference. That, however, was not to be.

VII

Hugh M. Beckwith's brother-in-law, W. H. Johnson, had been one of the ringleaders of the Seven Rivers gang's cattle rustling from the Chisum herds. He had taken Hugh's two sons with him, John and Bob, when the Seven Rivers gang set out for Lincoln and, of course, the boys had been involved in his various rustling activities. Hugh was not the least concerned with who actually shot Bob during the five-day fight. He blamed his brother-in-law since, had it not been for Johnson, Bob would not have been in the fight in the first place. About four weeks after the conclusion of the five-day fight, Hugh went over to Johnson's house carrying a shotgun, called Johnson to the door, and in front of his wife and their infant son, whom Mrs. Johnson was holding, he shot down Johnson.

The Kinney Doña Ana bunch ran rampant throughout the county, fearing no restraint, raping women, shooting down native New Mexicans. Recent immigrants into the area began to pull up stakes and leave the county. Many ranchers and farmers refused to join the various Dolan posses roaming the countryside searching for Regulators, preferring to leave rather than to become involved in the fighting.

John Chisum had gone to St. Louis in June to seek medical attention for an old leg injury. He had not been in the county when the five-day fight occurred. His brothers made themselves scarce, departing from the South Spring River ranch after the Seven Rivers gang laid siege to it, and moved, Pitzer and James and James' daughter Sallie, to Chisum's ranch on the Bosque Grande where, according to Sallie Chisum's diary, they arrived on 31 July. On 13 August, after having eluded Lieutenant Goodwin's search detail, the Kid, having joined up again with some of the Regulators, showed up at the Bosque Grande ranch, looking for Chisum. "Regulators came to Bosque Grande," Sallie's diary reads for that date. "Indian tobacco sack presented to me on the 13th of August by William Bonny [Bonney]." Rather than become further associated with the Regulators, the Chisum brothers moved again on 14 August, heading for Fort Sumner. The Kid apparently followed them to Fort Sumner since on 22 August Sallie noted in her diary: "Two candi hearts given me by Willie Bonney on the 22nd of August."[100]

Chisum had kept a small but very select herd of cattle separate from the herds he had turned over to Hunter & Evans and on his return from St. Louis he intended with his brothers to close up the South Spring River ranch and to begin a trail drive to a new range on the Canadian River in the Texas Panhandle.

Even before John arrived at Fort Sumner to join his brothers and begin the drive, the Kid perhaps knew what he intended to do. When the Kid did meet him, he reminded Chisum of the backing he had promised McSween and before him Tunstall. He had left for St. Louis before the Seven Rivers gang laid siege to the South Spring River ranch. His brothers had refused to come to McSween's aid when the five-day battle was going on, just as they had refused to help Tunstall when he had gone to them shortly before he himself was killed. Now Chisum was preparing to leave the Territory. The Kid felt that Chisum owed the Regulators at least $500, if for nothing else, than interfering with Jesse Evans's rustling activities, whereupon the Kid drew his pistol.

"Let me get a smoke, Billy, for then I can talk better," Chisum said, ignoring the gun pointing at him. After he had filled his pipe and lit it, he resumed. "Now, Billy, listen. If you talked about that money until your hair was as white as mine, you could not convince me that I owed it to you. Billy, you couldn't shoot an honest man, could you, while he was looking you square in the eye? You have killed several men, I know, but they needed killing."

Chisum could see that what he was saying was impressing the Kid, so he pressed his advantage, reminding the Kid that he had let the McSween faction hide out at the South Spring River ranch and have free use of his store, even in his absence. The Kid lowered and then holstered his pistol.

"All right, Mr. Chisum," he said, "but only for the present. If you won't pay me that $500 in money I'll steal from your cattle until I get it."[101]

Doc Scurlock and Charlie Bowdre, among the Regulators then at Fort Sumner with the Kid, when they heard that Chisum did not intend to back them financially, went to Pete Maxwell, who managed his family's ranching interests outside of Fort Sumner, and secured employment working for him. George and Frank Coe, also at Fort Sumner, were contacted by Lou Coe, Frank's brother, who offered them a job on the Sugareet helping him move his cattle to the San Juan country in New Mexico. A shooting contest occurred with some buffalo hunters who had just arrived and the Kid backed Coe.

"I'm putting my last dollar on George to beat the crowd," Billy said. "Am I covered?"

The shooting contest was held and the Kid won eight dollars. The Coes then told him and the others they intended to pull out.

"Well, boys," the Kid said, "you may all do exactly as you please. As for me, I propose to stay right here in this country, steal myself a living, and plant everyone of the mob who murdered Tunstall if they don't get the drop on me first. I'm off now, with any of my *compadres* who will follow me, after a bunch of horses at the Charlie Fritz ranch. He has more horses than he can manage, and I need *dinero*. I'm broke, fellows, and I've got to make a killing."[102]

Half a century later, Frank Coe recalled the Kid for an El Paso newspaper. "Billy the Kid," Coe said, "took sides with the people of the country, to fight for our property and our lives. He stood with us to the end, brave and reliable. He never pushed in his advice or opinions, but he had a wonderful presence of mind; the tighter the place the more he showed his cool nerve and quick brain. He was a fine horseman, quick and always in the lead, at the same time he was kind to his horses and could save them and have them ready and fresh when he needed to make a dash. I hope I have made it clear that at the beginning he was not the blood-thirsty, hard desperado that history has made him out to be. That he ever killed as many men as he is given credit for, or ever killed for money, is absurd. He never seemed to care for money, except to buy cartridges with; then he would much prefer to gamble for them straight. Cartridges were scarce, and he always used about ten times as anyone else. He would practice shooting at everything he saw and from every conceivable angle, on and off his horse. He never drank. He would go to the bar with anyone, but I never saw him drink a drop, and he never used tobacco in any form. Always in a good humor and ready to do a kind act to some one. Billy never talked much of the past; he was always looking into the future. He often spoke of his mother."[103]

John Middleton, Henry Brown, and Fred Waite also wanted to pull out, now that Chisum refused them backing. Unlike the Coes, none of them had traveling money, so they agreed to join Tom O'Folliard and the Kid in staging the projected raid on Dolan stock at the Fritz ranch. The Kid took time to assist Doc Scurlock to move his belongings on 1 September from Lincoln to Fort Sumner and then the gang set out. Jim French also joined them. The Fritz ranch was known as a stronghold of the Dolan forces and the raid netted the gang fifteen horses and 150 cattle. French and O'Folliard were the only ones recognized, apparently, since they were the only ones charged.

Jim French left when they sold the cattle but the horses were driven to Tascosa, in the Texas Panhandle. Cattlemen in the area knew the Kid by reputation—the Lincoln County War was national news—and they met with him to advise him that, while he had not been indicted by them, they did not want him to think he could misbehave in their district. The Kid countered that all his friends and he wanted was to be left alone and, should one or another of them be interested in some fine horse flesh, he was willing to sell one from the *remuda* they had brought with them.

While in Tascosa, the Kid made the acquaintance of Henry F. Hoyt who left behind a memoir of their meeting in his autobiography, A FRONTIER DOCTOR. "For some time Bonney's party mingled freely with all, sold and traded horses with anyone so inclined, varying their business dealings with drinking, gambling, horse-racing, and target shooting. Billy was an expert at most Western sports and dissipations with the exception of drinking. Much has been published of his exploits during drinking bouts, but it is my opinion they are mostly fiction. I never knew of his taking a drink of liquor all the time he was in the Panhandle. . . . Billy's men, however, made up for his abstinence. John Middleton was drinking heavily one day at Howard & McMasters' store and began to get ugly, evidently looking for trouble. . . . He had his hand on his gun and during his boasts glared fiercely around hoping some one would give him the slightest excuse to begin hostilities. Just at this juncture in walked Billy the Kid.

"In a mild voice that contained, however, a curious note of challenge as well as command, he said, 'John Middleton, you damned idiot, light out for camp and stay there till I come.'

"Wheeling toward him, Middleton, his eyes flashing, replied, 'Billy, you'd never talk that way to me if we were alone. You think you're showing off.'

" 'If that's the way you think just come with me out behind the store and we *will* be alone,' was Billy's quick reply, as he backed toward the door, hand on his gun.

"Middleton's face turned an ashen color, his lower lip dropped, and with a sticky grin he stuttered out, 'Aw, Billy, come off, can't you take a joke?'

" 'You bet I can,' said Billy, 'but this is no joke. You heard me. Git for camp and git quick.' And old John shuffled out the door like a whipped dog."

The Kid also broke up another near gunfight between Tom O'Folliard and a Mexican who had been playing monte. "In spite of his discipline," Dr. Hoyt concluded, "his men fairly worshiped him and would have backed him with their lives any time it might become necessary."[104] Just how true this was became apparent a few nights later when the Kid and his gang attended a *baile* put on by the Romero family. The Kid and Dr. Hoyt took time out from the dancing to stroll across the plaza. On the way back Hoyt challenged Billy to a footrace. Hoyt kept the lead until they neared the entrance to the dance hall. The Kid overtook him but tripped on the foot-high threshold of the doorway, falling in a sprawl in the center of the ballroom. His four pals, pulling out their guns, soon stood back to back around the Kid on the floor, thinking that his stumble meant trouble. Of course it did not, but the men were supposed to be unarmed and, as a result, they were barred from all future *bailes* put on by the Romeros.

Dr. Hoyt presented the Kid with a watch and chain as a gift, which greatly pleased him. Before leaving, the Kid sold Dr. Hoyt a fine horse of Arabian stock, writing out a bill of sale for the animal and signing it W. H. Bonney. The horse, called Dandy Dick, had presumably once belonged to Major Murphy and then Sheriff Brady and had been kept at the Fritz ranch by Dolan after Brady's death. In departing, the gang split up. John Middleton and Henry Brown decided to head for Kansas. Fred Waite set his course for the Nations, from which region he had originally come. Only Tom O'Folliard and the Kid returned to Fort Sumner.

VIII

President Hayes was under some degree of pressure to find a place for General Lew Wallace in his administration. The intensification of hostilities in Lincoln County provided him with an opportunity. Dr. Leverson's letter confirmed by Judge Angel's report helped him to decide to remove Governor Axtell and on 4 September 1878 he offered the post to General Wallace. It was scarcely the sinecure Wallace hoped to receive, but he was in need of money and a position which would grant him time to pursue a literary career and so he accepted.

Thomas B. Catron could perceive the course events were taking. Although the Territorial delegate in Congress, Stephen B. Elkins, Catron's former law partner and good friend, tried to stem the tide, he failed, and early in October Catron resigned as U.S. district attorney, effective 10 November, although he would continue to function in this capacity until his replacement arrived, S. M. Barnes. Behind the scenes, as one of the most powerful men in the Republican machine in New Mexico, Catron encouraged the Republican effort in the Senate to prevent Wallace's confirmation in the post of governor, a situation which required Wallace to proceed very inoffensively when he appeared in Santa Fe to assume his new duties.

Wallace was charged by the Hayes administration with establishing peace in the Territory and his first step to do so was to issue, on 13 November 1878, a proclamation of amnesty, providing "a general pardon for misdemeanors and offenses committed in the said County of Lincoln against the said laws of the said Territory in connection with the aforesaid disorders, between the first day of February, 1878, and the date of this proclamation."[105] Because of the charges being laid against Colonel Dudley and others in the military in the Territory, Wallace also extended the pardon to include officers in the U.S. Army "stationed in the said County during the said disorders." This action on the new governor's part did anything but placate Dudley whose position was that he had acted in a wholly honorable way throughout the difficulties.

Fearful for her life after the five-day battle, Mrs. McSween moved to Las Vegas where she hired Huston I. Chapman, a lawyer who had recently entered the Territory from Portland, Oregon to represent her in prosecuting Dudley, Peppin, and Kinney in connection with her late husband's murder. As administratrix of the McSween estate—John Chisum being unwilling to serve—she was in a financial position to continue the fight in the legal arena. Chapman was a particularly aggressive and outspoken man and undertook the case in such a way as to make it a crusade. After his murder, Chapman's father wrote to Judge Ira E. Leonard that he felt his son's aggressive temperament was an outgrowth of a physical disability. "On account of an accident in his early youth our son lost one arm and he was always an object of our most anxious solicitation," the elder Chapman wrote in his letter of 20 March 1879. "We preferred that he should remain nearer home but his energy and enterprise knew no bounds. He spurned the idea that he could not accomplish with one hand anything that others could do with two."[106]

It was Chapman's feeling that Mrs. McSween must accompany him back to Lincoln in order to collect evidence. He wrote to Colonel Dudley requesting a safeguard for Mrs. McSween. However, Dudley had not forgotten the threats Mrs. McSween had made to him the final day of the fight and denied the request. Chapman then wrote to Governor Wallace, asking for the safeguard and complaining that Dudley was involved in the killing of McSween. Wallace's response was to request of Colonel Hatch that he direct Dudley to provide Mrs. McSween with military protection and included with his request Chapman's letter to him. Hatch forwarded both the Chapman letter and the governor's to Dudley who threw a fit, answering what he felt was a personal attack with affidavits from various members of the Dolan forces unfavorable to both McSween and his wife. Most of this testimony had to do with Susan McSween's flagrant promiscuity and indicated that McSween had been impotent. Whether or not there was any truth in these charges of sexual indiscretion was irrelevant since they scarcely addressed the issue which remained: Colonel Dudley's culpability in the occasion of McSween's murder.

Wallace, having included the military amnesty to placate Dudley in his proclamation, also wrote a conciliatory letter to Dudley on 16 November insisting that Mrs. McSween was to be accorded protection no matter what her character. Dudley's reaction was to publish a blunt attack against the Hayes administration in general and Governor Wallace in particular in the Ring-controlled *Santa Fe New Mexican* which appeared on 30 November. At the same time, aware of the Republican efforts to cast aspersions on him, Governor Wallace opened his files to the

Rocky Mountain Sentinel, a rival Santa Fe newspaper, and, unfortunately for Colonel Dudley, the *Cimarron News and Press* on 5 December exposed Dudley's effort to cover up Catron's use of stolen beef to fill his beef contract with William Rosenthal for the Mescalero reservation (Catron having merely continued Dolan's practices when he assumed the management of Dolan's business).

It was at this moment—now that Mrs. McSween had returned to Lincoln —that Billy the Kid chose to ride into Lincoln with those of his followers who had remained with him. Sheriff Peppin had recently resigned due to lack of pay. This action may have given the Kid a sense of false security. Alarmed at the Kid's arrival, Dolan, Billy Mathews, and John Long went at once to Fort Stanton. Edgar Walz, for his part, had no trouble at all convincing Colonel Dudley to dispatch a detachment of troops to guard the Dolan store. George Kimbrell, appointed to replace Peppin for the duration of his term as sheriff, arrested the Kid and put him in the Lincoln jail on 22 December 1878. This action apparently was sufficient to convince the Kid that his presence in Lincoln was not desirable and, upon his release, the Kid left town, heading for Las Vegas. There, at a hot springs, about six miles outside Las Vegas, the Kid met Dr. Hoyt again, shortly after Christmas, and also made the acquaintance of Jesse James, who was traveling in the Southwest under the alias Thomas Howard from Tennessee.

By the end of January, Chapman in Lincoln had carried his campaign against Dudley to Colonel Hatch himself and was contemplating a trip to Washington, D.C. Mrs. McSween had located the other half of Tunstall's cattle, the half that had not been disposed of by Frank Wheeler, through the agency of a private detective named Charles Scase whom she had hired. They were in the possession of Robert Speakes of the Seven Rivers district and she requested from Colonel Dudley his assistance in securing their return. Dudley responded that if Mrs. McSween were to make out the necessary legal papers and if she could get Sheriff Kimbrell to request his intervention, he would cooperate. This move seemed to frustrate any immediate action.

Perhaps the Kid had discussed with Jesse James the motion in the Missouri legislature to grant the James gang a general amnesty and how the motion had failed finally to win endorsement. One thing is certain. The Kid now wanted to take advantage of Governor Wallace's proclamation and, in February, he returned to Lincoln intent on working out a peace accord with the Dolan forces. Sheriff Kimbrell, upon the Kid's reappearance, requested troops from Colonel Dudley, since there was but one man in all of Lincoln willing to assist him in arresting the Kid, and the Kid warned Kimbrell that if an arrest warrant for murder were served on him he would not be taken alive. Jesse Evans was also in Lincoln. He had been acquitted on the murder charge but was under a warrant for stock theft. U.S. District Attorney Barnes was intent on having this warrant served and both Evans and the Kid felt it prudent, if they were to stand trial, to insure that members of neither side would be permitted to testify variously against one or the other of them. On 18 February, the Kid, Tom O'Folliard, Jesse Evans, and James J. Dolan held a peace parley and actually worked out a six point agreement among themselves. Having done so, Dolan insisted they all celebrate the action with several rounds of drinks, from which, of course, the Kid himself abstained.

Chapman picked this inauspicious moment to come to Lincoln from Las Vegas. He went first to consult with Mrs. McSween. Leaving her, he headed for his sleeping room at the now defunct Tunstall store. On the way he ran into Dolan, Evans, and Bill Campbell from the Dolan forces and the Kid, O'Folliard, and José Salazar from what was left of the McSween faction. Also following this entourage were others of the Dolan forces, including Billy Mathews, Edgar Walz, and Deputy Sheriff Redman (the "one man" who had been willing to aid Kimbrell in arresting the Kid). Campbell called out to Chapman, asking who he was.

"My name is Chapman" the lawyer returned curtly.

"You are the contemptible cur that has come in here and stirred up trouble," Campbell told him, drawing his pistol and punching it into Chapman's breast. "But we've settled it all now, and we are going to be friends. Now, just to show you are peaceable too, you've got to dance."

"Am I talking to Mr. Dolan?" Chapman demanded.

"No," said Jesse Evans, "but you are talking to damn good friends of his."

The exchange grew more heated until Dolan, drawing his gun, fired into Chapman. Campbell fired a second shot a moment later.

"My God, I am killed," Chapman exclaimed and collapsed.

Dolan then poured whiskey on the prostrate body and it was set on fire.

O'Folliard and the Kid had tried to draw themselves away from the scene as soon as the interchange began, but Evans had moved behind them and compelled them to remain. It was not until some time later that the two were able to escape from the Dolan forces. Chapman's body remained where he fell until soldiers from the fort arrived about 11:30 that night.

"I promised my God and Colonel Dudley that I would kill Chapman, and I have done it," Campbell is reported to have said as he walked away from the scene.[107]

The next day, naturally concerned about appearances, Dolan with Evans and Campbell went to Fort Stanton and consulted with Colonel Dudley. The citizens of Lincoln, as intent perhaps as the Kid to secure peace, invited Colonel Dudley to come as a guest of the town. The burial of Chapman was the occasion for this goodwill gesture. Dudley, taking advantage of the situation, dispatched a detail under Captain Carroll to Seven Rivers to get the Tunstall cattle Mrs. McSween wanted from Speakes, hoping thereby to assuage any hard feelings she might have. The cattle were ultimately sold for $1,000, but the sum was only sufficient to pay for the trouble of locating them in the first place and holding them until a sale could be effected. On 5 March a ball was held in Lincoln with Dudley and all the other officers invited from the fort by formal resolution.

It was on this date that, after delaying for months, Governor Wallace finally paid his long-awaited visit to Lincoln. He was shocked to learn that Jesse Evans, Billy Mathews, and Bill Campbell, implicated in the Chapman killing, were staying at the old Murphy ranch and that no effort had been made to arrest them, nor were witnesses such as Billy the Kid anywhere to be found. The townspeople, given their new attitude toward Dudley, which they felt was merely being realistic, if not patriotic, were unwilling to testify against Dudley or any of the Dolan forces.

Unlike Governor Axtell's visit to Lincoln the previous year, Governor Wallace attended a mass meeting at the courthouse and expressed his desire to hear anyone who had any information to contribute. He also made a public announcement that he had requested the removal of Colonel Dudley as commanding officer at Fort Stanton, an action which, somewhat ironically, was greeted with repeated applause. Giving Captain Carroll temporary command of the garrison at the fort, the governor then issued a list of thirty-six names of men who were to be arrested and impounded at the fort. Jesse Evans, Billy Mathews, and Bill Campbell were the first to be arrested. Wallace ordered that they be kept in close confinement at the fort, and he demanded the same treatment be accorded Dolan who, until this time, had his freedom, even though technically under arrest, to leave the fort for Lincoln any time he pleased. Wallace also offered a thousand dollar reward for the apprehension of the Kid. An undated, semiliterate letter, written on either 12 or 13 March, was sent by the Kid to Governor Wallace.

Dear Sir:
I have heard that you will give one thousand $dollars for my body which as I can understand it means alive as a Witness. I know it is as a witness against those that Murdered Mr. Chapman. if it was so as that I could appear at Court I could give the desired information, but I have indictments against me for things that happened in the late Lincoln County War and am afraid to give up because my enemies would kill me. the day Mr. Chapman was murdered I was in Lincoln at the request of good Citizens to meet Mr. J. J. Dolan to meet as Friends. so as to be able to lay aside our arms and go to Work. I was present When Mr. Chapman was Murdered and know who did it and if it were not for those indictments I would have made it clear before now. if it is in your power to Anully those indictments I hope you will do so as to give me a chance to explain. please send me an answer telling me what you can do You can send answer by bearer I have no Wish to fight any more indeed I have not raised an arm since Your proclamation. as to my Character I refer to any of the Citizens. for the majority of them are my Friends and have been helping me all they could. I am called Kid Antrim but Antrim is my stepfathers name,

Waiting an answer I remain

Your Obedeint [sic] Servant

W. H. Bonney[108]

Wallace replied at once in a note dated 15 March 1879.

W. H. Bonney,
Come to the house of old Squire Wilson (not the lawyer) at nine (9) o'clock next Monday night alone. I don't mean his office, but his residence. Following along the foot of the mountains south of the town, come in on that side, and knock at the east door. I have authority to exempt you from prosecution if you will testify to what you say you know.

The object of the meeting at Squire Wilson's is to arrange the matter in a way to make your life safe. To do that the utmost secrecy is to be used. So come alone. Don't tell anybody—not a living soul—where you are coming or the object. If you could trust Jesse Evans, you can trust me.

Lew Wallace[109]

The Kid kept the appointment the following Monday night and what the governor saw was a young man about five feet eight inches in height with light brown hair and steel-gray eyes. Wallace himself gave an account of it for the *Indianapolis World* on 8 June 1902. "Billy the Kid kept the appointment punctually," Wallace related. "At the time designated, I heard a knock at the door, and I called out, 'Come in.' The door opened somewhat slowly and carefully, and there stood the young fellow generally known as the Kid, his Winchester in his right hand, his revolver in his left.

" 'I was sent for to meet the governor here at 9 o'clock,' said the Kid. 'Is he here?' I rose to my feet, saying, 'I am Governor Wallace,' and held out my hand. When we had shaken hands, I invited the young fellow to be seated so that we might talk together. 'Your note gave promise of absolute protection,' said the young outlaw warily. 'Yes,' I replied, 'and I have been true to my promise,' and then pointing to Squire Wilson, who was the only person in the room with me, I added, 'This man, whom of course you know, and I are the only persons in the house.'

"This seemed to satisfy the Kid, for he lowered his rifle and returned his revolver to its holster. When he had taken his seat, I proceeded to unfold the plan I had in mind to enable him to testify to what he knew about the killing of Chapman at the forthcoming session of court two or three weeks later without endangering his life. I closed with the promise, 'In return for your doing this, I will let you go scot free with a pardon in your pocket for all your misdeeds.'

"When I finished, the Kid talked over the details of this plan for his fake arrest with a good deal of zest. He even ventured the suggestion that he should be kept hand-cuffed during his confinement in order to give a bona-fide coloring to the whole proceeding. He did not commit himself definitely to the proposal, but promised to write me in a few days what his decision was."

On 19 March Jesse Evans and Bill Campbell escaped their confinement at Fort Stanton. One day after the escape, on 20 March, the Kid wrote to Squire Wilson.

Please tell you know who that I do not know what to do, now as those prisoners have escaped, to send word by bearer, a note through you may be that he had made different arrangements if not and he still wants it the same to send: William Hudgens as Deputy to the Junction tomorrow at three o'clock with some men you know to be all right. Send a note telling me what to do.

W. H. Bonney

P.S. Do not send soldiers.[110]

Governor Wallace, to whom Squire Wilson forwarded the Kid's note, wrote back to the Kid that, for appearance's sake, it would look better if Sheriff Kimbrell were to make the arrest and that Kimbrell would be instructed "to see that no violence is used." The Kid replied to the governor in a matter of hours.

Sir:

I will keep the appointment I made but be sure and have men come that you can depend on. I am not afraid to die like a man fighting but I would not like to be killed like a dog unarmed. tell Kimbal [Kimbrell] to let his men be placed around the house and for him to come in alone; and he can arrest us. all I am afraid of is that in the Fort we might be poininered [poisoned] or killed through a window at night. But you can arrange that all right. Tell the commanding officer to watch Lt. Goodwin he would not hesitate to do anything There will be danger on the road of somebody waylaying us to kill us on the road to the Fort. You will never catch those fellows on the road. Watch Fritzes, Captain Bacas ranch and the Brewery. They will either go to Seven Rivers or to Jicarilla mountains. They will stay close until the scouting parties come in give a spy a pair of glasses and let him get on the mountain back of Fritzes and watch and if they are there will be provision carried to them. It is not my place to advise you, but I am anxious to have them caught, and perhaps know how men hide from soldiers better than you. Please excuse me for having so much to say and I still remain

Yours truly

W. H. Bonney

P.S. I have changed my mind. Send Kimbal [Kimbrell] to Gutierrz [sic] just below San Patricio one mile, because Sanger and Ballard are or were great friends of Conuls' [Campbell's]. Ballard told me yesterday to leave for you were doing everything to catch me. It was a blind to get me to leave. Tell Kimbrell not to come before 3 oclock for I may not be there before.[111]

On 21 March the Kid and Tom O'Folliard were arrested by Sheriff Kimbrell at the place the Kid had designated and Governor Wallace sent a note to Colonel G. A. Purington, again commanding the garrison at Fort Stanton, to the effect that the two would be kept in Lincoln for a few days before being transferred to the fort. The Kid was convinced that he was trading his testimony against Evans, Campbell, and Dolan in exchange for a pardon from the governor. Additionally, the Kid agreed to testify in the case pending against Colonel Dudley. What Wallace did not know, and evidently the Kid was as yet too naïve to suspect, was that the Santa Fe Ring, Judge Bristol, and District Attorney Rynerson were not about to convict Jesse Evans, J. J. Dolan, or anybody else associated with the Dolan cause. Now, though, all of these men knew that the Kid was willing to turn state's evidence, was willing to testify against them, and that could mean only one thing: the Kid himself had to be removed.

At first, the Kid and Tom O'Folliard were put in the Lincoln jail and the Kid wrote on the wall:

William Bonney was incarcerated here first time, December 22nd, 1878; second time, March 21st, 1879, and hope I never will be again.

W. H. Bonney

The jail was actually a cellar, the only access being by means of a small door through which a ladder could be lowered. The Kid apparently complained about his accommodations and Wallace, not yet wanting him and O'Folliard to be taken to the fort, had the prisoners transferred to Juan Patrón's house. The Kid had begun to smoke cigars, and these were readily available. He was also well fed and whiled away his time playing cards or talking with those who came to visit him. Among his visitors was Governor Wallace himself who recalled his impressions in the same newspaper interview previously cited concerning his first meeting with the Kid. "I did not require that the Kid and his companion be kept under strict confinement," Wallace said, "and was entirely willing for him to have a good many privileges. I went down one day to see him, and having some curiosity to know whether the stories I had heard about his marksmanship were true, I asked him to give me some exhibition of his skill. After he had shown me what he could do—and it was remarkably good shooting with both the rifle and the revolver—I complimented him and coupled with my praise the questions, 'Billy, isn't there some trick in your shooting? How do you do it?'

"'Well, General,' he replied, 'there is a trick to it. When I was a boy, I noticed that a man in pointing to anything he wished to observe, used his index finger. With long use the man unconsciously learned to point with exact aim. I decided to follow suit with my shooting. When I lift my revolver, I ask myself, "Point with your finger" and unconsciously, it makes the aim certain. There is no failure. I pull the trigger and the bullet goes true to its mark. That's the trick, I suppose, to my shooting.' "

When the Kid's guards had asked Governor Wallace how he dared be around the Kid when the Kid was armed, Wallace related in the interview, "I knew that I was the last man in New Mexico Billy wanted to kill, for I was the only man who could give him a pardon." This was true enough, but Governor Wallace was also a political appointee whose residence was temporary at best and who would, given the prospect of a more salubrious or prestigious post, resign in an instant. His status reports to Secretary of the Interior Schurz and others in Washington indicate that he was committed to bringing peace to the area and honestly felt he was making progress, even if his methods might appear extreme. At the same time, in his private correspondence he was constantly angling for a different appointment. "A precious specimen named 'The Kid,' whom the sheriff is holding here in the Plaza, as it is called, is an object of tender regard," Wallace wrote to Schurz on 31 March. "I heard singing and music the other night; going to the door, I found the minstrels of the village actually serenading the fellow in his prison."[112] The Kid regarded the governor as his means to a pardon. The governor regarded the Kid as his means to getting convictions and ridding the Territory of much of its so-called "criminal" element. The Kid can perhaps be excused for believing that the governor's power was greater than that of the Territorial bureaucracy. Nor did he appreciate fully Wallace's position and his intentions. Frederick Nolan concluded that to Wallace the Kid "was just a means to an end. Wallace never had any real intention of fulfilling any of the promises he made. That he was a sophisticated, intelligent man dealing with an unlettered thief who, no matter what his origins and crimes, deserved better than the cynical exploitation of his naïve desire to clear himself, redounds less than favorably upon Wallace. No doubt he justified his later actions by telling himself that deals struck with the likes of William H. Bonney were as worthless as the 'precious specimens' who struck them."[113] Even if Wallace is given the benefit of the doubt about his good intentions toward the Kid initially, both of them were about to receive a lesson in *Realpolitik*.

IX

On 14 April, after repeated objections from Judge Bristol to Governor Wallace's insistence on a grand jury being convened (after all, Bristol had learned his lesson about grand juries the previous year), Bristol finally complied with Wallace's request. However, he had studied the law carefully and both he and Rynerson were confident they could meet any and all contingencies through the adept use of the right to change of venue. Issac Ellis, a McSween supporter, was foreman of the grand jury, and Martín Chávez was a member, as were several from the Dolan forces. The Kid had agreed to testify, but he was not represented by counsel and therefore, in answering "not guilty" to the charge of killing Brady and Hindman, he could not prevent Rynerson from bringing a motion to change the venue of his trial to Doña Ana County. Judge Bristol, who would be presiding there as well, made his home at Mesilla and was certain he could have a jury selected that would convict the Kid and get him out of the way once and for all. John Middleton and Henry Brown were also indicted on the same charges but, as they had left the Territory, there was little chance they would be brought to trial. Further indictments were brought against Dolan and Campbell, with Jesse Evans as accessory, in the murder of Chapman. Campbell and Evans, of course, were absent, and Dolan secured a continuance and a change of venue to Socorro County where his case would be heard. He was assured that he would be cleared of this charge as he had been in the Tunstall case. Most of the men indicted for their involvement in the five-day war were represented by Catron and Thornton and were pardoned under Governor Wallace's amnesty proclamation. Marion Turner and John Jones appeared in the greatest danger, since they were indicted for the murder of McSween. Colonel Dudley, George Peppin, and John Kinney were indicted for having set the McSween house on fire. The colonel was released on bail of $2,000 until his case could be heard. Kinney was also arrested and placed under bond, pending his trial at the next session of court.

These indictments, such as they were, were obtained without the Kid's testimony. Rynerson, as the prosecuting attorney, felt it within his discretion whether or not to have the Kid testify, and he decided against it. Rynerson claimed to the press that, no matter what the governor had told the Kid, the Kid was a murderer and he would be tried as such at Mesilla.

Next the court of inquiry at Fort Stanton sat to hear charges brought against Colonel Dudley by Mrs. McSween, and others, concerning his role in the death of McSween. Judge Ira E. Leonard, a friend of the governor's, was Mrs. McSween's counsel, Colonel Henry L. Waldo, retired, a Ring man, defended Dudley. Governor Wallace himself gave testimony, but most of it was discounted as hearsay since he was not on the scene at the time the events occurred. The Kid also testified, as cited above, but the court found that "none of the allegations made against Lieutenant

Colonel Dudley by his Excellency the Governor of New Mexico, or by Ira E. Leonard, have been sustained and that proceedings before a court martial are therefore unnecessary." The governor did not stay for the entire hearing, but left after his own testimony. Susan Wallace recalled in a letter to her sister that upon their departure the Kid, in her words "a gentlemanly looking fellow," came to shake hands. " 'I hope,'" she quoted him as saying, " 'you have a sentinel in camp.'To which Lew answered, 'I always have, and was never surprised in my life.' "[114]

When the findings were published, Judge Leonard wrote to Governor Wallace. "It is a farce on judicial investigation and ought to be called and designated 'The Mutual Admiration Inquiry,'" he observed. "I hope the evidence may go to the War Department, so that they can see how things are managed. The evidence against Dudley would hang a man in any country where right and justice prevailed. . . . I sent you a petition signed by a large number of citizens asking the removal of Bristol."[115]

General John Pope at Fort Leavenworth reviewed the record of the case on its way east on 15 October 1879. "Having carefully considered the evidence in the foregoing case," he remarked, "the Department Commander disapproves the opinion expressed by the court of inquiry." D. G. Swaine of the judge advocate general's department in Washington, D.C., in reviewing the proceedings observed that "the conclusion is irresistible that Dudley both actively and passively aided and abetted the Sheriff's party in its doings." However, Swaine also recommended that "it would not be in the best interests of the public or military service to attempt to bring Colonel Dudley to trial by court-martial."[116] It might be thought that the disapproval of the Department Commander would have made a difference in Washington. It did not, as Swaine's recommendation makes clear. The decision of the War Department was to drop the matter, in the spirit that the less said about it the better.

On 6 December 1879 the civil charges against Colonel Dudley brought by Mrs. McSween were heard at Mesilla before Judge Bristol and the jury, selected with Rynerson's and Bristol's approval, deliberated all of two minutes before bringing in a verdict of "not guilty." All the suits, however, brought against McSween, including the embezzlement suit, were now transferred against Mrs. McSween as administratrix.

After Dudley's hearing before the court of inquiry, the Kid remained in custody in Lincoln for another six weeks, waiting to learn of the findings and interested to see what good, if any, the petition on the part of seventy percent of the people against Judge Bristol's appointment might do. Bristol's appointment prevailed. When Dudley was exonerated, word came that Judge Bristol was now ready to hear the Kid's case at Mesilla, where he would be taken by Dolan supporter, Deputy Sheriff James Redman. The Kid realized by now that Governor Wallace was not about to issue him a pardon. In one instance, that before the grand jury, his testimony had been rejected, and in the other, the court of inquiry, it had been less than useful, and the governor had no pressing motive to pardon him.

"Kid," Juan Patrón is reputed to have said to him, "I'll give you a horse and a Winchester. Then let's see if they can capture you."

The Kid thought about the offer for a day or two.

"Boys," he said finally, walking past his guards out of the house, "I'm tired of this. Tell the general I'm tired."[117]

Wallace, even if he had wanted to, no doubt knew by this time there was nothing he could do for the Kid or against the Dolan forces. Peace of a sort had been established. He busied himself, writing on his novel about Caesar and Christ, working days going through the motions of office, waiting for a transfer. In the meantime, the local press began to have a field day, criticizing Wallace for every possible failing, and not just the Ring newspapers. Other papers defended his actions, especially the extreme of having employed the military to make mass arrests. The attitude of the War Department with regard to Dudley became the governor's attitude toward his job: he intended to leave well enough alone.

On 9 July, Dolan had his preliminary hearing before Judge Bristol at Mesilla. Because Billy the Kid was loose, he was escorted there by Deputy Sheriff Redman and six troopers from the fort. On 13 July he was released on bail. He then married Caroline Fritz, Charles Fritz' daughter, and in August, at his hearing before Judge Bristol at Socorro, where he was represented by Catron and Thornton, all charges against him were summarily dismissed.

"Jimmie Dolan was acquitted of the two murders for which he was indicted by the grand jury," Godfrey Gauss, who had once been Tunstall's ranch cook, wrote to his deceased employer's father. "He married the daughter of the farmer Fritz and lives here in town. In this county he would have without doubt been convicted, but he took a change of venue to Socorro, and had not much trouble to find a jury to acquit him. This is law and justice in New Mexico."[118]

On 2 July 1879, without knowledge of it coming back to New Mexico, Jesse Evans was arrested by Texas Rangers near Alamito Creek in Texas on charges of murder and robbery. He was sentenced to twenty years in prison. After serving a year and a half of his term, he escaped, and vanished to history. His example, as concerns his disappearance, might have been a worthy one for the Kid to have followed. The Kid, however, would not have it that way. By remaining in the Territory, the Kid's options for making a living were circumscribed and limited to gambling and stealing. After Wallace's failure to help him, he certainly could look on no one in government as an ally.

Because of the indictments against them, Marion Turner and John Jones sold out their store at Roswell to Captain Joseph C. Lea, a land speculator and cattle rancher who had served on the side of the Confederacy in the 6th Missouri Regiment and was called later the "Father of Roswell." Captain Lea fully realized the business opportunities in New Mexico, maintained amicable relations with the Ring and the Dolan forces, and was also a close friend of John Chisum's who seemed increasingly to be contemplating a return to New Mexico now that the trouble appeared to be dying down.

Marion Turner had registered some cattle which belonged to John Jones in his name and, before leaving the Territory, sold them to John Beckwith. On 26 August, trying to reclaim the stock, Jones had a quarrel with Beckwith and shot him to death.

On 29 August, stopping at Milo Pierce's ranch, John Jones was lured into a trap by Pierce and shot twice in the back by Bob Olinger. Despite the fact that John Jones had been part of the Seven Rivers gang and on the other side in the five-day battle, the Kid regarded himself as a friend of the Jones family and swore to avenge the murder.

On 9 July 1879 *Thirty-Four*, a newspaper published at Las Cruces, complained that "Kid and Scurlock and others are still in the country. They are reported as getting a crowd together again. No effort is being made to arrest them." As far as the Kid was concerned, John Chisum was at the bottom of the reversal of fortune he had suffered, ever since Chisum had pulled out of the McSween cause at Fort Sumner and moved to Texas. In October, the Kid with Scurlock, O'Folliard, Bowdre, and two Mexican-Americans crossed into the Texas Panhandle and rustled a hundred head of cattle from Chisum. They turned around and sold them to beef-buyers from Colorado for $800. Doc Scurlock, reputedly dissatisfied with his share but also probably able to see the future course of events, pulled out of the gang and moved his family to Texas. Chisum, discovering the theft, sent his brother James and some picked men after them.

The cattle were herded back to the Panhandle through the Fort Sumner area and the Kid, together with Barney Mason, Pat Garrett's brother-in-law, and another hand working for the Maxwell ranch, had the effrontery to ride out to the Chisum camp and claim the right to look through the retrieved herd for Maxwell strays. To show that there were no hard feelings, he invited James Chisum and his crew to come to Fort Sumner that night to Bob Hargrove's saloon and have a drink on him. At the saloon the Kid encountered a man named Joe Grant, a hardcase who was extremely drunk. First Grant threatened James Chisum, believing him to be his brother, John, and then he threatened the Kid. Then Grant took to showing his ability with a gun by firing at the bottles on the backbar.

"Let me help break up housekeeping, pard," the Kid said to Grant, proposing to join him.

Grant, perhaps anticipating trouble or merely irked at the Kid's manner, threw his gun down on the Kid and pulled the trigger. The gun failed to fire. The Kid drew his own gun and shot Grant in the head.[119]

When James Chisum got back to the new home ranch and reported this incident as well as the Kid's effrontery about the herd of cattle he had stolen in the first place, John Chisum's patience was exhausted.

As early as 15 April 1879 Chisum had written to Governor Wallace that a body of twenty men stationed at Pope's Crossing might effectively put a stop to all the rustling going on in the district since most of the rustlers were concentrated in this area. Pat Garrett had made every effort to become friends with Chisum when he had first met him at Fort Sumner despite his own petty dealings as a cattle rustler (most Anglo-Americans and many Mexican-Americans had engaged in such an enterprise at one time or another, including John Chisum himself). He convinced Chisum that he wanted most of all to work as some kind of stock detective on behalf of the major cattle owners. Chisum, writing his letter to Wallace from Fort Sumner, mentioned Garrett by name as a good choice to head up a similar posse around the Fort Sumner area.

"I hope Gov you will not think I show any disposition to meddle or dictate," Chisum concluded the letter. "I know the County well, and I am satisfied you are more than anxious to give the Citizens protection and I am equally anxious to see the Robers [sic] kept out hence I make these suggestions. Robers cannot very well reach the Pecos by any other route on account of the water."[120]

After the raid on his Panhandle herd and the subsequent events at Fort Sumner, it became evident to Chisum, as it was already to James J. Dolan, Judge Bristol, Captain Lea, and a number of others that there was only one solution to the problem posed by Billy the Kid. The Kid had to be killed and a man to kill him had to be found.

X

Patrick Floyd Garrett was born on 5 June 1850 in Chambers County, Alabama, the son of John and Elizabeth Garrett. In 1852, a few months after Pat Garrett's maternal grandfather died, he moved with his family to Louisiana and in 1853 his father purchased a plantation in Claiborne Parish of that state. In 1867 Pat's mother died, at thirty-eight years of age, and his father died the next year. With the death of John Garrett, the Garrett plantation began to disintegrate. A squabble developed over who would manage the estate and oversee its liquidation—John Garrett had been in debt—and in early 1869, somewhat bitter, Pat Garrett left home and his elder sister, his three younger sisters, and his three younger brothers.

Pat tried dirt farming in Dallas County, Texas in 1870, but stayed at it only a year. In 1871 a Dallas County rancher offered Pat a job and he pursued a career as a ranch worker for three years, probably marrying and living with his wife near Sweetwater, Texas. Early in 1875, Garrett seems to have wanted to visit his family in Louisiana. In later years, after he had relocated to New Mexico, he would regularly visit his home state of Louisiana and family members who continued to live there. It would appear that he killed a black man in Bowie County, on the Texas/Louisiana border. He did not return to Sweetwater, but instead, deserting his wife and perhaps a child, he headed toward the Llano Estacado and the buffalo country. In Fort Worth he made the acquaintance of a youngster by the name of Joe Briscoe. In October, 1875, Garrett joined with Skelton Glenn and Luther Duke in pooling resources in a partnership to go buffalo hunting in the Fort Griffin area. Against the objections of the other two men, who would have preferred a more experienced hunter, Pat prevailed in his insistence that Briscoe accompany them. At Fort Griffin, the group hired Nick Buck, an experienced skinner, and Grundy Burns, a camp cook.

Young Joe Briscoe was a devout Roman Catholic who kept a small crucifix around his neck. When they had been out hunting for several months, Joe tried to wash a few pieces of clothing in some rain runoff that was nearly frozen. Coming up to the camp fire to warm his hands, Garrett growled at Briscoe that only a damned

Irishman would be stupid enough to wash anything in such muddy water. Briscoe took umbrage and began to fight, with Pat Garrett at six feet five inches towering over him. Garrett beat Briscoe down several times until Joe, feeling he needed an equalizer, grabbed an ax and rushed at Pat. He chased Pat around the cook wagon for several turns before Garrett paused long enough to pick up his Winchester. Garrett shot Briscoe, the latter collapsing in the camp fire. Briscoe clung to life for another thirty minutes.

"I'm dying, Pat," he is reputed to have said. "Won't you come over here and forgive me?"[121]

Garrett went out alone, riding, for the rest of the day and all night. When he returned to camp the next day, Glenn suggested he go to Fort Griffin and report himself to the authorities. Garrett left the camp. When he came back a few days later, he said that the officials at Fort Griffin had refused to prosecute him.

Comanche raids against the buffalo hunters were continuous—the buffalo were their main food supply and the white men were intent on wiping them out. In 1877, cashing in what they could at Fort Griffin, Garrett and Glenn set out for St. Louis by train where Garrett gambled away what little money he had made. When, in November, 1877, Garrett and Glenn returned to Texas, Garrett, instead of being a partner, went to work for Glenn as a hunter at a wage of sixty dollars a month. This arrangement lasted until January, 1878, when Glenn, Garrett, and Nick Buck, discouraged by the scarcity of buffalo, set out to seek their fortune farther west. In February, 1878, they arrived at Fort Sumner, New Mexico.

Lucien B. Maxwell had died in 1875, leaving his wife, Maria de la Luz Beaubien Maxwell, a son, Pedro, and daughters Odila, Amilia, Virginia, Sophia, and Paulita. Señora Maxwell remodeled the thirteen-room adobe officers' quarters adjacent to the parade ground of the old fort into a suitable home. Several Mexican-American families settled here and with the establishment of a post office and the building of a Roman Catholic church, by 1876 the pueblo of Fort Sumner came into existence.

Upon his arrival, Garrett sought out Pedro Maxwell, known as "Pete" to the Anglo-Americans, and was hired for range work. His two companions continued on their travels. Garrett married for the second time to Juanita Gutiérrez. She died soon after, presumably from a miscarriage, but Garrett, in later years, claimed it was due to heartbreak at not having been married in the Church. Garrett himself was an agnostic and he could only have regarded such a ceremony as superstition. Pat also became friends with Barney Mason, a local hardcase who perhaps was the first one to convince him that cattle stealing, on a small scale, could be profitable. It may have been this circumstance which caused Pete Maxwell to fire Garrett in July, 1878. Garrett then tried operating an eating place and, when that did not work out, he was hired by Beaver Smith as a bartender. On 14 January 1880 Garrett married Apolinaria Gutiérrez, his sister-in-law, at a double wedding at which Barney Mason was also married into the large Gutiérrez family, a marriage in the eyes of the Church at which Pat was Barney's best man, and Mason was Garrett's best man. This third marriage lasted for the rest of Garrett's life. Although he philandered occasionally, Apolinaria stayed with him, presenting Garrett with several children. Judging by their correspondence, Garrett was rather formal, addressing Apolinaria as "Dear Wife" and closing with "Pat F. Garrett."

In late 1879, Garrett had gone into a hog-raising venture with Thomas L. "Kip" McKinney, a local cowboy who, as Barney Mason, would eventually join Garrett in the hunt for Billy the Kid. Apparently, Garrett had been trampled one day by a hog and it was while recovering, being nursed by Apolinaria, that the two were drawn to each other.

"There seems to be no doubt that he [Garrett] knew Billy the Kid," Leon C. Metz wrote. "It has been claimed that Pat Garrett often rode with the Kid and sometimes helped him rustle cattle, but no documentary evidence exists to support such claims."[122] What Garrett did was to nurture, as *"un laquais à louange,"* acquaintances with leading cattlemen in the district, especially John Chisum and Captain Joseph C. Lea. When George Kimbrell was up for reelection as sheriff of Lincoln County, Garrett assured both Chisum and Lea that he would be willing to hunt down and kill Billy the Kid and all other cattle rustlers. Lea persuaded Garrett to move to Roswell so as to qualify for the Democratic nomination. Kimbrell was a Republican and Lincoln was almost completely Democratic. Before Garrett came on the scene, Kimbrell had been confident that he could win the endorsement of both parties and run unopposed. But neither the Dolan forces nor the cattlemen were inclined to believe that he would kill the Kid and, for Dolan since the Dudley hearing and for Chisum since the stock theft, killing Billy must be the primary objective of the sheriff of Lincoln County. Dolan had taken over the Tunstall store in Lincoln and had also gained possession of the Tunstall ranch on the Rio Feliz. T. B. Catron had sold the old Murphy/Dolan store in Lincoln to the township to be used as a courthouse. At the local Democratic convention, both Will Dowlin, formerly a post trader at Fort Stanton for Major Murphy and then Dolan's store manager in Lincoln, and James J. Dolan gave stirring speeches in support of Garrett's candidacy. The motion was carried.

Having, therefore, been nominated by the Anglo-American minority, Kimbrell and Garrett had to go out and woo the Mexican-American vote. Both men had Mexican-American wives, and so this factor was not decisive. The ideology of one-settlement culture had begun to take hold and probably it was this, more than any other factor, which worked in Garrett's favor. Dolan and Chisum were backing the same man and Garrett's election might well heal all the wounds of the Lincoln County War which still festered. What the community most needed was law and order. Outlaws had to be dealt with summarily. Once peace was established, everyone, Anglo-Americans and Mexican-Americans, could march forward proudly and participate in the great civilization the future was somehow going to see. Lea, Chisum, and the other *ricos* backed Garrett because he swore to kill outlaws and so did Dolan. It seemed for a brief, fluttering moment as if Lincoln County was at last on the verge of a majestic consensus of the people—those with money and influence, anyhow.

Shortly before he was murdered, many years hence, Pat Garrett would write to then governor of the Territory of New Mexico, George Curry: "Dear Curry: I am in a hell of a fix. I have been trying to sell my ranch but no luck. For God's sake, send me fifty dollars."[123] Garrett had Curry's check for $50 on his person the day he died. During the campaign for the office of sheriff in 1880, George Curry was living in Lincoln County, managing the Block Ranch, in which Will Dowlin was a partner. A young man rode into the ranch complex, on his way to a *baile* a few miles away. According to William L. Keleher, the young man, after caring for his horse, was invited to supper by Curry. He told Curry where he was going and asked him along, but Curry could not accompany him because his employers had told him he must go out and garner votes for Pat Garrett.

"Do you know Garrett?" the stranger asked Curry.

"No, I don't," Curry replied, "but from all I hear he is a splendid man."

"Do you think he will be elected?"

"I don't know, but I'm sure he will carry this precinct. I have a gallon of whiskey on hand, and I think that will help carry it."[124]

The stranger rode out to the dance, returning very late. He was up at dawn, however, and joined Curry for breakfast. As he was about to depart, the stranger thanked Curry for his hospitality.

"You are a good cook and a good fellow," he said; "but if you think Pat Garrett is going to carry this precinct for sheriff, you are a dam'd poor politician."

Sometime after he rode off, Curry learned that his guest had been Billy the Kid and that he had been campaigning the previous night against Garrett. Kimbrell carried the precinct in the election.

Captain Lea would soon be elected a commissioner of Lincoln County. He dominated the region around Roswell and could deliver its votes. He also had influence, as did Chisum, with all of the big ranchers. Dolan and T. B. Catron together were able to swing the votes of many indebted to them. Perhaps because Garrett was a Democratic candidate, perhaps because he was not really associated openly with the Ring or the previous factionalism, and perhaps because many Mexican-Americans did not vote, Pat Garrett won, 320 votes to Kimbrell's 179.

In October, 1880, while Garrett was still out campaigning, Azariah F. Wild, an agent for the Treasury Department, came to Lincoln County to investigate counterfeiting. Dolan and T. B. Catron, after the demise of the Jesse Evans gang, had been servicing their federal beef contracts with stolen cattle which they purchased from Pat Coghlan of Tularosa, New Mexico. Coghlan had set up a masterful rustling ring between the large cattle ranches in the Canadian River section of the Texas Panhandle and his ranch. The rustling on the Texas end, it would appear, was done by Tom Cooper and his gang. The cattle then would be driven across New Mexico to Coghlan and then sold to Dolan and Catron. On the way, Dan Dedrick's ranch near Bosque Grande was a frequent stopping-off place. Dan's brother, Sam Dedrick, was a partner with W. W. West in a livery stable at White Oaks. Separate from this group was a gang headed up by David Rudabaugh which had come into New Mexico in 1879 from Kansas. Rudabaugh had been arrested for train robbery in Kansas by Bat Masterson. John Joshua Webb, who had been in Masterson's posse, also came to New Mexico at this time and got himself appointed city marshal at

Las Vegas. Striking up an association with Rudabaugh, Webb offered Rudabaugh and his gang "protection" while they plundered stages and trains in the Las Vegas area. This association lasted until March, 1880, when Webb was arrested for murder. On 9 April Webb was sentenced to hang. On 30 April Rudabaugh managed to break Webb out of jail, but he also killed a jail guard in the process. Henceforth, Rudabaugh was wanted for murder. Also there was "Whiskey Jim" Greathouse who operated a trading post and bar on the White Oaks/Las Vegas road and who had a station and depot in Anton Chico. Greathouse often acted as a "fence" for stolen horses.

Shortly before Wild showed up, Tom Cooper had a falling out with Pat Coghlan. He had also got his hands on some $30,000 in counterfeit money. With Billie Wilson, who had joined his rustling gang, Sam Dedrick, and W. W. West, Cooper planned to purchase a large herd in old Mexico with the money. James J. Dolan had one of the counterfeit hundred dollar bills in his possession and he showed it to Wild, claiming that it had been passed by Billie Wilson. There appears to have been a falling out between Cooper and Wilson and perhaps Wilson had taken some of the counterfeit money with him. Wilson, on the dodge, became friends with Billy the Kid.

When Doc Scurlock pulled out of Fort Sumner, Charlie Bowdre went to work for T. G. Yerby, managing his ranch. Bowdre took his young Mexican-American wife with him and was often joined by Tom O'Folliard. Tom Pickett, who had come to Las Vegas with David Rudabaugh and had ridden in his gang, after Webb's arrest went out to the Yerby ranch and Bowdre hired him.

Communications on the New Mexico frontier were anything but good and rumors were rampant. Billy the Kid, because of his past activities and the constant complaining about him in Ring newspapers, was only the most visible, if at the same time perhaps one of the more negligible, among all of these desperadoes. Nonetheless, it was his name which was usually linked with any depredation which might occur. That the Kid ever headed up a complex and sophisticated cattle rustling ring, employing some or all of these men, can no more be documented than that he and Garrett were for a time engaged in this enterprise as full partners.

What the Kid had become, besides a drifter and gambler, was a petty horse thief. Alexandre Grzelachowski, who had been with the New Mexico Volunteers during the Civil War, operated a general merchandise store and saloon at Puerto de Luna and also raised cattle, sheep, and horses on three different ranches. He gave the Kid unlimited credit at his store. He also looked the other way when the Kid occasionally stole some horses from him to raise enough money to keep in provisions. Jesus Silva, who worked for Pete Maxwell, once told former Governor Otero of how one day John Singer, the Las Vegas butcher to whom Garrett and Barney Mason disposed of their rustled beef while they were engaged in penny-ante rustling, "came to Fort Sumner to buy some stolen cattle from Pat Garrett. Singer was riding a pinto pony to which the Kid took a fancy. While Singer was in one of the stores, Billy went to the hitching post, untied the rope with which the horse was hitched, remarking: 'I'm not stealing this horse; I'm just taking him.' John Singer hunted for the horse until he realized the futility of his search and had to buy another one. The Kid felt that since John Singer had stolen the horse from someone in Las Vegas, it might just as well be his as anybody's."[125] Much of the Kid's illegal activity had about it the quality of what some might regard as "adolescent" defiance, ridiculing the hypocrisy of the ruling classes and exposing their vulnerable dishonesty. It is entirely within the realm of possibility that the Kid put Wilson up to passing the hundred-dollar bill on Dolan as a kind of ironic joke. If so, the attempt failed, since Wild became increasingly convinced that all of the robbery, murder, and passing of counterfeit money was being directed by the Kid.

Pat Garrett felt he understood the power structure in New Mexico. The future, if there was to be one, rested with Captain Lea, John Chisum, T. B. Catron, J. J. Dolan, Judge Bristol, Colonel Rynerson, and the other men whose wealth and influence manipulated that power. Together they had frustrated Governor Wallace's efforts at reform and the governor was now mostly a figurehead. After Garrett was elected, Captain Lea and the others did not want him to wait two months, until January, 1881, to take office. They wanted the manhunt and killing of outlaws to begin at once and so pressured Sheriff Kimbrell to appoint Garrett a deputy sheriff in the interim. Garrett saw to it that Bob Olinger and "Kip" McKinney were appointed his deputies as well as Ash Upson, at Roswell, who became a "clerical" deputy to handle Garrett's paperwork. It is untrue that Garrett could neither read nor write, but he preferred to do as little of either as possible.

According to Wild's official reports back to Washington, all of the bad element in Lincoln County was not only in collusion with Billy the Kid, but the situation was so grave that no one dared ride anywhere without an armed escort. At least, Wild himself did not, except when he was working undercover. Wild wrote to Captain Lea at Roswell, saying that he needed a discreet and reliable person to infiltrate Fort Sumner and get the goods on the counterfeiters. The U.S. government would pay this man two dollars a day plus expenses. A meeting was set up at which Captain Lea and Deputy Sheriff Garrett introduced Wild to Barney Mason and swore to his "honesty and fidelity."[126] Wild hired Mason. Between themselves, Garrett and Mason must have had a good laugh at Wild's gullibility. He was to them an auspicious "pigeon." Garrett and Mason soon got Wild to sign their vouchers for hotel, stable, feed bills, and meals. Mason began to scout around the countryside, looking for clues, while actually hoping to get a line on the Kid for Garrett, since the men who had put Garrett in office wanted the Kid removed first. It is improbable that Mason and Garrett agreed with Wild's contention that the Kid was somehow involved in the counterfeiting. But they were willing to use his money and influence to finance their operations and Wild got Bob Olinger appointed a deputy U.S. marshal. He got Garrett and even Captain Lea similarly appointed around 2 January 1881.

After John Jones was murdered by Bob Olinger, his body was transported back to the Jones ranch for interment. Shortly after Garrett's election and the manhunt for him had begun, the Kid stopped to express his condolences to Ma'am and the

Jones family. After going out to John's grave with Ma'am, where the two of them knelt for a time, they walked back together to the Jones homestead.

"I don't know, Ma'am, whether you can talk about it or not," the Kid told her. "I've already asked Pa Jones not to take up the fight and not to let the boys take it up. He's promised and so has Jim. Pa Jones said he'd given his word to you many years ago that he'd never fight a duel. I've told Jim that I have personal reasons, and I think he'll respect them, because he's given his word. But I haven't seen Bill. Your boys are not mixed up in anything, and I don't want them to be. I know how it feels. Besides, I want to take care of Olinger myself."

"Billy, don't do it," Ma'am told him then. "It won't bring John back and you'll be next on the list."

"I'm already on the list."

"There's been far too much killing already. I don't want any other mother to suffer as I have."

"You're the only mother I have, Ma'am."

"And I don't want you to live the life of the hunted. I've seen men who hide. When they come for supplies they always face the door. I'm thankful John was spared that. And I don't want you to endure it."

"I know that, Mother. And I'll give you my word that I won't seek a meeting with Olinger. But if it comes to a showdown. . . ."

"No, Billy. You're a good boy. You've been driven to things you wouldn't otherwise have done. Drop this. Go away before it's too late. . . . There's time to go elsewhere and make a new start."

"It's too late."[127]

It was characteristic of the Kid, after having worked for Tunstall and then fought for McSween, to appoint himself a guardian over those he felt unable to defend themselves. It was also a foolish and, under the circumstances, hopelessly unrealistic posture.

Billy remained for several days, helping Ma'am prepare meals, washing dishes, selling merchandise, and assisting her in feeding pilgrims. When Heiskell Jones hitched up his wagon and started for Fort Sumner, Billy tied his horse to the end gate and rode beside him, young Sammie Jones standing behind the seat, listening to their conversation.

"There's nobody like her," Billy remarked of Ma'am. "I've seen many mighty brave men, and John was the bravest of all; but Ma'am has more courage than anyone I've ever known."

"Know the new sheriff at Lincoln?"

"Pat Garrett? Everybody knows him. Chisum put him in to get me."

"He's sheriff, Billy, regardless. Whatever he does will have the protection of the law. You haven't a chance."

"I'm outlawed," Billy conceded. "And it hasn't been long since I was a law and old Pat an outlaw. Funny thing, the law."

"Why does Chisum want to own the sheriff?" Pa Jones asked.

"Several things. It's commonly thought that the Murphy/Dolan bunch paid no taxes when they owned the sheriff. Maybe old John thinks it's his turn now."

"Nobody's ever asked us for taxes."

"They will. All this takes money. Bob Olinger's been deputized by Garrett. That means he's scared. Safest place in the world for a murderer is to get a job as deputy."

"We've always thought well of Wallace Olinger. Ma'am likes him, and where there's a man or a horse involved nobody fools her."

"She's had plenty of chances to study them."

"I'd like to know what she'd think of Garrett," Pa Jones mused.

"Ol' Pat can act all right when he wants to."

"Billy, I still wish you'd go somewhere and make a fresh start."

"It's too late, Pa Jones."[128]

Notwithstanding, the urgings of the Jones family apparently did influence the Kid. After leaving Pa Jones at Fort Sumner, the Kid struck out on the road to White Oaks where Judge Ira E. Leonard lived. He had come to know the judge during the Dudley hearing and knew that he was now representing Mrs. McSween. He had been told by the judge that he might be willing to take on his case and perhaps it was worth one more try. The Kid had behaved this way in the past, when he had decided to make peace with the Dolan forces before Chapman was killed and again when he had met with Governor Wallace. Why not try once more?

At Anton Chico, on the way to White Oaks, the Kid ran into Dave Rudabaugh, who had been introduced to him by Whiskey Jim Greathouse, and Billie Wilson. The three set out together for the Greathouse trading post, which was some miles outside White Oaks and to the north. Knowing that he would have to pay the judge something and being low on funds, the Kid rustled six horses on the way, planning on selling them to Whiskey Jim. Greathouse bought four of the horses and the remaining two were turned loose. The Kid learned that Judge Leonard was not at White Oaks at the moment, having left on a trip to Lincoln. The Kid was at the Greathouse trading post on 28 November because he was seen there and his presence was reported by Lieutenant Clark who passed through with his twelve-man detail guarding the paymaster on the way to Fort Stanton.

In the meantime, on 29 November, Barney Mason reported to Wild at Roswell that he had just left the Kid and the counterfeiter gang at White Oaks and they had wanted Mason to join them in a scheme whereby they would take the counterfeit money to El Paso and purchase a herd of cattle. The money was being brought by an Easterner named Duncan who would deliver it to the Kid and his gang at the Dedrick ranch near the Bosque Grande. A posse consisting of Deputy Sheriff Garrett, Deputy U.S. Marshal Olinger, Barney Mason, and Wild, as well as others, set out to make the capture. Wild agreed to finance the posse's expenses.

Garrett probably would have looked for a reason to ditch Wild if one had not presented itself, so that he could proceed with a freer hand. A short distance outside Roswell, the posse encountered Joseph Cook, a Texas outlaw, who had two stolen horses with him. Convincing Wild that Cook no doubt could provide information about the whereabouts of the counterfeiters, Garrett had him chained and dispatched back to Roswell with Wild and two deputies. Wild was to question the prisoner and then get in touch with any information he received. Garrett and the rest of the posse would continue on their way.

The citizens of White Oaks, hearing that the Kid was in the vicinity, helped organize a posse of eight men to be led by Deputy Sheriff Will Hudgens. It was suspected that Mose Dedrick, Sam and Daniel's brother, had been sent to town to buy supplies for the Kid and his gang. Deputy Hudgens and the posse trailed Mose out of town and so were on hand when he was met by the Kid, Billie Wilson, and Dave Rudabaugh. The Kid had evidently decided to follow Judge Leonard to Lincoln and had ordered the supplies to take on the journey. The outlaws and posse exchanged shots and both the Kid's horse and Billie Wilson's were hit. They were able, despite this, however, to elude the posse.

The next night, 30 November, Deputy Sheriff James Redman, the deputy who was supposed to have accompanied the Kid on the trip from Lincoln to Mesilla for his trial, claimed the Kid had ridden into town and tried to assassinate him. Simultaneously, Wild, back at Roswell with Cook, saw the town gripped by a similar paranoia. The citizens heard that the Kid and his gang were in the vicinity and were intent on rescuing Cook. The talk grew more and more strident until the townspeople gathered at the post office, still run by Ash Upson at Captain Lea's store, and prepared for a last stand, fighting off the Kid and his myrmidons. When, after hours of waiting, nothing at all happened, the men sheepishly dispersed. Also on 30 November Garrett and his posse stormed the Dedrick ranch at Bosque Grande, expecting to fight it out with the Kid. Instead, they captured John Joshua Webb, whom Rudabaugh had broken out of the Las Vegas jail the previous April, and George Davis, a horse thief. These captives were placed in irons and the posse set out for Fort Sumner.

On 1 December, outraged at the Kid's brazen lawlessness, the citizens at White Oaks formed another posse under the leadership of James Carlyle, a local black-smith and deputy sheriff. They rode out of town and trailed the Kid from where the shooting had occurred two days before to Greathouse's trading post. They quickly surrounded the trading post and prepared for a siege. The weather was extremely cold and, intermittently, it snowed. Greathouse himself was not in favor of the idea of a siege and he came out to speak with Carlyle, offering himself as a hostage while Carlyle was to go inside the house and negotiate a surrender from the Kid, Billie Wilson, and Dave Rudabaugh. Although it was a stupid play at best, this Carlyle agreed to do. However, once inside, confronted by desperate men who refused to surrender, Carlyle could do nothing but send back word to the posse that there was no chance for a peaceful solution. It grew colder and colder as it grew dark outside and the Kid was unwilling to let Carlyle go, knowing that as soon as he did those outside the building and surrounding it would commence firing.

Around midnight a note was passed in to the Kid from the posse declaring that if Carlyle were not released in five minutes, Greathouse would be shot. The Kid remained adamant in his refusal. When a shot was fired by one of the posse outside, Carlyle must have thought it was Greathouse who had been killed. He lunged through a window, sprawling on the snow-covered ground. In the very poor light, the posse could not make out who it was and, believing that it was probably the Kid trying to make a getaway, cold and jittery as the posse men had become, they opened fire. Carlyle, who had risen to his feet, was hit, fell again on the ground, struggled to his feet, and was again cut down by gunfire. The posse men raced forward to see whom they had dropped and were aghast when they discovered it was Carlyle. They immediately called off the siege and, rounding up every horse they could find, set off back to White Oaks, leaving Carlyle dead in the snow. The story, as they told it later, was that Carlyle had been shot down by the Kid. The Kid, Wilson, and Rudabaugh made their escape on foot. The *Las Vegas Gazette* on 3 December 1880 ran a scathing editorial in which it claimed that a gang of forty to fifty men, all hardcases and murderers, was "under the leadership of 'Billy the Kid,' a desperate cuss, who is eligible for the post of captain of any crowd, no matter how mean and lawless. . . . Are the people of San Miguel County to stand this any longer? Shall we suffer this horde of outcasts and the scum of society, who are outlawed by a multitude of crimes, to continue their way on the very border of our country?" Leader of the gang or not, the Kid was convicted according to an old adage, *noscitur a socio*. This editorial marked the first time Henry McCarty was ever referred to as Billy the Kid in print.

On 5 December Garrett telegraphed Wild from Fort Sumner that some of his horses had distemper and that Wild should send him more horses and more men since he did not have force enough to guard his prisoners and stock and make the arrests he had in view, as Wild explained in his subsequent report to Washington. However, Wild did not comply with Garrett's request. Frustrated when he heard nothing from Wild, Garrett dismissed his posse, sent Bob Olinger on to Las Vegas with Kip McKinney to try and get a new line on the Kid, rented a wagon, and with Barney Mason set out to transport the prisoners to Puerto de Luna after wiring Sheriff Don Desiderio Romero of San Miguel where he was going and that the sheriff should meet him there with a posse to take the prisoners off their hands.

On the way from the Bosque Grande to Fort Sumner, Garrett and the posse had raided the Yerby ranch, on the off-chance that the Kid might be there. All they found were Charlie Bowdre's wife and another woman and two mules. They impounded the two mules but let the women go. About twelve miles east of Fort Sumner, Garrett and the posse had put in at the Wilcox ranch for supper and word had been brought to Garrett that Bowdre wanted to parley. Garrett met with Bowdre about two miles out of town and informed him that Captain Lea had promised leniency to any one of the Kid's gang who would defect. Lea had put this message in writing and Garrett showed it to Bowdre.

Bowdre was at Fort Sumner when Garrett and Mason pulled out with their prisoners. A few days later, the Kid, Wilson, and Dave Rudabaugh, footsore and weary, walked in. Bowdre told the Kid about Lea's offer. In the meantime, Wild in Roswell heard a rumor and reported to Washington that the Kid and his gang had been in Lincoln, romping in a brothel.

At Puerto de Luna, Garrett and Mason turned their prisoners over to Deputy Sheriff Francisco Romero (no relation to Sheriff Romero who did not come himself) and retired to Alexandre Grzelachowski's store and saloon to get drunk. In a surly mood, Garrett got into a shooting scrape with Marino Leyba, a local roughneck. Deputy Sheriff Romero, having signed for the prisoners and taken them to a room especially prepared for their safekeeping, heard the shots and went to investigate. "While going towards Mr. Grzelachowski's place," he later swore in an affidavit, "I met Marino on horseback cursing and very furious, without a coat and his shirt unbuttoned. . . . With his right hand he opened his shirt and found a wound in his left shoulder, and kept going on his horse, galloping."[129] Romero went into Grzelachowski's store where he disarmed both Garrett and Mason and insisted they remain on the premises until the next day when they would have a preliminary hearing before the justice of the peace. At the hearing the charges were dismissed. Garrett and Mason set off in the direction of Las Vegas.

On 12 December, feeling boxed in, the Kid decided as a final resort to write a letter to Governor Wallace.

Gov Lew Wallace
Dear Sir

I noticed in the *Las Vegas Gazette* a piece which stated that Billy "the Kid," the name by which I am known in the country was the captain of a band of outlaws who hold Forth at the Portales. There is no such organization in existence. So the gentleman must have drawn very heavily on the imagination. My business at the White Oaks at the time I was waylaid and my horse killed was to see Judge Leonard who had my case in hand. he had written to me to come up, that he thought he could get everything straightened up I did not find him at the Oaks & should have gone to Lincoln if I had met with no accident. After mine and Billie Wilsons horses were killed we both made our way to a station, forty miles from the Oaks kept by Mr. Greathouse. When I got up next morning the house was surrounded by an outfit led by one Carlyle, who came into the house and demanded a surrender. I asked for their papers and they had none. So I concluded it amounted to nothing more than a mob and told Carlyle that he would have to stay in the house and lead the way out that night. Soon after a note was brought in stating that if Carlyle did not come out inside of five minutes they would kill the station keeper (Greathouse) who had left the house and was with them. in a short time a shot was fired on the outside and Carlyle thinking Greathouse was killed jumped through the window breaking the sash as he went and was killed by his own Party they think it was me trying to make my escape. the Party then withdrew.

They returned the next day and burned an old man Spencer's house and Greathouses also. I made my way to this place afoot and During my absence Deputy Sheriff Garrett acting under Chisums orders went to Portales and found nothing. on his way back he went to Mr. Yerberys ranch and took a pair of mules of mine which I had left with Mr. Bowdre who is in charge of Mr. Yerbys cattle he (Garrett) claimed that they were stolen and even if they were not he had a right to confiscate any outlaws property.

I have been at Sumner since I left Lincoln making my living gambling. The mules were bought by me the truth of which I can prove by the best citizens around Sumner. J. S. Chisum is the man who got me into trouble and was benefited Thousands by it and is now doing all he can against me There is no Doubt but what there is a great deal of stealing going on in the Territory and a great deal of property is taken across the Plains as it is a good outlet but so far as my being at the head of a band there is nothing of it in several instances I have recovered stolen property when there was no chance to get an officer to do it.

One instance for Hugh Zuber post office Puerto de Luna another for Pablo Analla same place

if some impartial party were to investigate this matter they would find it far different from the impression put out by Chisum and his tools

Yours Respect.
W. H. Bonney[130]

Charlie Bowdre also wrote the governor, declaring that he had thought about Garrett's amnesty offer and would be willing to surrender if the indictment against him for the murder of Buckshot Roberts was dropped.

On 15 December, as a consequence of pressure from T. B. Catron and other parties as well as the editorial in the *Las Vegas Gazette*, Governor Wallace ran the following notice:

$500 REWARD

NOTICE IS HEREBY GIVEN THAT FIVE HUNDRED DOLLARS REWARD WILL BE PAID FOR THE DELIVERY OF BONNEY ALIAS "THE KID" TO THE SHERIFF OF LINCOLN COUNTY.

LEW WALLACE
GOVERNOR OF NEW MEXICO [131]

The notice was careful not to make the usual demand of "dead or alive," but indeed stressed delivery. When Governor Wallace received the Kid's letter, he was powerless to stop the forces congealed against him, but he could and did cause it to be published in New Mexican newspapers so that the Kid would have a hearing before the public. The *Las Vegas Gazette* in an editorial commented that "the Kid's band showed very good taste in reading the GAZETTE religiously."

Dating his letter 15 December 1880 at Fort Sumner, Charlie Bowdre also wrote to Captain Lea:

Capt. Lea,

I have broke up housekeeping and am camping around, first one place & then another on the range, so that no one can say that Yerbys ranch is the stopping place for any one. So no party will have any excuse for going there unless they are after me. I thought this a duty due Mr. Yerby, for if there is nothing to eat at the ranch no one will go there & there will be no chance for a fight coming off there & Mr. Yerby's property injured. If I don't get clear I intend to leave some time this winter, for I don't intend to take any hand fighting the territory, for it is different thing from what the Lincoln Co war was. The only difference in my case & some of the officers in Lincoln Co. is that I had the misfortune to be indicted before the fight was over & did not come under the Gov's pardon. It seems to me that this would come to their minds once & a while, when they are running around after me, but I suppose it is human nature to give a man a kick when you have the upper hand.

I saw the two Billies the other day & they say they are going to leave this county. That was my advice to them for I believe it is the best thing they can do. Don't you think if you can get the Gov interested in my case, that it could be thrown out by the Dist Att'y without my appearing at court. I don't doubt your good intentions, but during the present state of the country I think there is some danger of mobing. For my name has been used in connection with a good many things that I have had nothing to do with, which outside parties can't know. I have taken your advice in regard to writing to Mr. Yerby & have no doubt but what he will do all he can for me. I know of nothing to urge in my favor, now than that others were pardoned for like offences. Experience is a good but slow teacher & I think if I keep my mind, I will let every man do his own fighting so far as I am concerned & I will do my own.

Respt
Chas. Bowdre.[132]

Tom Pickett had come to Fort Sumner with Bowdre. The Kid probably argued that there would be strength in numbers while waiting to see what official reaction would be to these various missives. O'Folliard and Bowdre, two of the original Regulators, the Kid, Tom Pickett, Dave Rudabaugh, and Billie Wilson congregated under Billy's leadership and rode twelve miles out of town, to hole up at the Wilcox ranch.

Garrett and Mason, arriving in Las Vegas on 15 December, were apprised of the reward for the Kid being offered by the governor. Garrett also heard that Frank Stewart, a representative of the Canadian River cattle owners, had been in the area five days previously searching for rustled stock and sent Barney Mason in pursuit of him. James East, who was in the posse of Texans under Stewart's leadership, wrote a letter on 19 August 1927 to Western author Eugene Manlove Rhodes in which he described the composition of the Texas group. "Some writers," he wrote to Rhodes, "have had a good deal to say about us Texans 'bringing the law to the Pecos.' After these long years I don't believe Garrett's posse from Tascosa thought much about establishing the law. We were just a bunch of ordinary cowpunchers— not professional 'gunmen'—working for $30 per mo. and told to go down to the Pecos and try to recover cattle strayed or stolen and incidentally to get any rustlers that came in the way. Didn't get many cattle but some of the rustlers."[133]

Stewart had with him Lon Chambers, Lee Hall, James East, Tom Emory, Louis Bozeman, Bob Williams, Charles Siringo, and Big-Foot Wallace (Frank Clifford), as well as several others of lesser distinction. Stewart did not bring his posse back with him to Las Vegas, but instead sent them on to wait at White Oaks. Garrett convinced Stewart to halt his search for strays and assist him in tracking down the Kid. They rode to White Oaks where Garrett explained to Stewart's men that they would be pursuing the Kid because he had in his possession a stolen herd of panhandle cattle.

"How can that be?" one of the Texans asked, having heard about the shoot-out at Greathouse's trading post and that the Kid had been left afoot.

" 'Don't know,' " Charles Siringo quoted Stewart as responding in his book, A TEXAS COWBOY. " 'If you doubt my word about it, just ask Mr. Garrett, there.' "

Siringo concluded: "Of course we all did doubt his word, and were well satisfied that it was a put up job, to gain the reward."[134]

After more argument, Garrett chose only some members of Stewart's posse to accompany him: Stewart himself, Lon Chambers, Lee Hall, James East, Tom Emory, Louis Bozeman, and Bob Williams. Charles Siringo, Big-Foot Wallace, and the others were to remain at White Oaks cooling their heels.

Garrett set his course for Puerto de Luna, a hundred miles northeast, the men riding single file through the bitter cold. Putting up at Grzelachowski's store, Garrett sent on a local man to scout around Fort Sumner while he and the posse spent a few days sampling the various wares. At a little past midnight on 18 December Garrett and the posse were on the outskirts of Fort Sumner. He stationed the posse around the town while he and Barney Mason entered. Finding a Mexican-American, Juan Gallegos, who was known to be friendly with the Kid, Garrett arrested him and worked on him until the man confessed that the Kid was at the Wilcox ranch, but that he would be returning soon. Garrett summoned the rest of the posse into town and took over the old adobe hospital where Charlie Bowdre's wife was staying. They set up an ambush. Around eight o'clock, the Kid and the five men with him returned to Fort Sumner, hunched over against the cold, strung out. When the men had ridden into the trap, Garrett, who had his rifle aimed as had the others in the posse, opened fire. James East, in a letter he wrote to Charles A. Siringo, described what happened. "Lon Chambers was on guard," East stated. "Our horses were in Pete Maxwell's stables. Sheriff Pat Garrett, Tom Emory, Bob Williams, and Barney Mason were playing poker on a blanket on the floor. . . . Tom O'Folliard was shot through the body, near the heart, and lost control of his horse. O'Folliard's horse came up near us, and Tom said, 'Don't shoot any more, I am dying.' We helped him off his horse and took him in and laid him down on my blanket. Pat and the other boys went back to playing poker. I got Tom some water. He then cussed Garrett and died, about thirty minutes after being shot."[135] After this incident, East no longer completely trusted Garrett. "I camped with him and slept with him alone and always watched him," East wrote years later in an inscription in Harrison Leussler's copy of THE SAGA OF BILLY THE KID (Doubleday, 1926) by Walter Noble Burns. "A cold and dangerous man."[136]

The Kid, with Rudabaugh straddling behind Wilson on the latter's horse because his own had been shot, Pickett, and Bowdre returned that night to the Wilcox ranch. There was snow on the ground which would make tracking relatively easy. Garrett remained in Fort Sumner until the morning of 21 December. At midnight on the previous night Emanuel Brazil, a partner of Wilcox', had come to Fort Sumner to inform Garrett that the Kid and the others had pulled out. The posse tracked the outlaws to an abandoned rock house at Stinking Springs. The posse was split in half, one half under Stewart covering the rear of the house, the other under Garrett covering the front. Three horses were tied outside which meant that there were at least two being kept inside. The posse spread out and took up positions.

"I had told all the posse that, should the Kid make his appearance, it was my intention to kill him, and the rest would surrender," Ash Upson wrote as Garrett in THE AUTHENTIC LIFE OF BILLY THE KID. "The Kid had sworn that he would never yield himself a prisoner, but would die fighting, with a revolver at each ear, and I knew he would keep his word. I was in a position to command a view of the doorway, and told my men that when I brought up my gun, to all raise and fire."[137]

It was the morning of 23 December.

Charlie Bowdre was the first one out the door. Garrett and other posse members raised their rifles and shot him. Staggering in pain, Bowdre tottered toward Garrett and the posse, then collapsed. The gunfire was then concentrated on the house. Garrett shot down one of the three horses tied outside, dropping it in the doorway, effectively cutting off any attempt from those inside to ride out and escape. As the day wore on, the firing became more sporadic. East, in a letter, described how some of the posse managed to creep close enough to the rock house to have a conversation with the Kid. "He said they had no show to get away," East wrote, "and wanted to surrender, if we would give our word not to fire into them when they came out." It was extremely fortunate for the Kid that Garrett had persuaded the Texans to come with him. "We gave the promise and they came out with their hands up, but that traitor, Barney Mason, raised his gun to shoot the Kid, when Lee Hall and I covered Barney and told him to drop his gun, which he did."[138]

Garrett had sent back to the Wilcox ranch for food and he fed the prisoners, the Kid, Rudabaugh, Wilson, and Pickett, before having them mount up to ride back to Fort Sumner. At a blacksmith shop in town, the prisoners' ropes were removed and replaced with irons. Garrett gave the Kid's horse to Frank Stewart in gratitude for all the help he and his men had been—a point of contention later. That afternoon Maria de la Luz Beaubien Maxwell sent Deluvina "Maxwell," an old Indian retainer who had assumed the family name, to ask Garrett if Señora Maxwell and her daughter, Paulita [Pablita in Spanish], could be allowed to say good-bye to Billito. Out of deference to the family, Garrett agreed. The Kid, shackled to Rudabaugh, and guarded by James East and Lee Hall, was marched lockstep to the Maxwell home. Señora Maxwell pleaded with the guards to unlock the Kid's irons so he could enter a private room for an affectionate farewell to Paulita. This East refused to do, feeling that to release the Kid for any reason would be unwise. "The lovers embraced, and she gave Billy one of those soul kisses the novelists tell us about, till . . . we had to pull them apart, much against our wishes, for you know all the world loves a lover."[139]

Still later that afternoon, Garrett with a posse now consisting of Barney Mason, Frank Stewart, Lee Hall, and Tom Emory set out with the prisoners to Las Vegas. On Christmas day they made Puerto de Luna where, again, they pulled in to Grzelachowski's store and celebrated after their own fashion. The captives were transported in irons in a mule-drawn wagon the entire distance from Fort Sumner to the jail at Las Vegas.

XI

J. H. Koogler, editor of the *Las Vegas Gazette*, obtained an interview with Garrett on 27 December about the capture of the Kid and an Extra was put out to tell of it.

A day later, in the regular edition, Koogler ran his interview of the Kid while in jail. "Through the kindness of Sheriff Romero," Koogler recounted, "a representative of the *Gazette* was admitted to the jail yesterday morning. Mike Cosgrove, the obliging mail contractor, who often met the boys while on business down the Pecos, had just gone in with five large bundles. The doors at the entrance stood open and a large crowd strained their necks to get a glimpse of the prisoners, who stood in the passageway like children waiting for a Christmas tree distribution. One by one the bundles were unpacked, disclosing a good suit for each man. Mr. Cosgrove remarked that he wanted 'to see the boys go away in style.'

"Billy 'the Kid' and Billie Wilson, who were shackled together, stood patiently while a blacksmith took off their shackles and bracelets to allow them an opportunity to make a change of clothing. Both prisoners watched the operation which was to set them free for a short while, but Wilson scarcely raised his eyes and spoke but once or twice to his compadres. Bonney, on the other hand, was light and chipper and was very communicative, laughing, joking and chatting with the by-standers.

" 'You appear to take it easy,' the reporter said.

" 'Yes! What's the use of looking on the gloomy side of everything? The laugh's on me this time,' he said. Then, looking around the *placita*, he asked, 'Is the jail in Santa Fe any better than this?'

"This seemed to trouble him considerably, for, as he explained, 'this is a terrible place to put a fellow in.' He put the same question to every one who came near him and when he learned that there was nothing better in store for him, he shrugged his shoulders and said something about putting up with what he had to.

"He was the attraction of the show, and as he stood there, lightly kicking the toes of his boots on the stone pavement to keep his feet warm, one would scarcely mistrust that he was the hero of the 'Forty Thieves' romance which this paper has been running in serial form for six weeks or more.

" 'There was a big crowd gazing at me, wasn't there,' he exclaimed, and then smilingly continued, 'well, perhaps some of them will think me half a man now; everyone seems to think I was some kind of animal.'

"He did look human, indeed, but there was nothing very mannish about his appearance, for he looked and acted a mere boy. He is about five feet, eight or nine inches tall, slightly built and lithe, weighing about 140; a frank and open countenance, looking like a school boy, with the traditional silky fuzz on his upper lip; clear blue eyes, with a roguish snap about them; light hair and complexion. He is, in all, quite a handsome looking fellow, the imperfection being two prominent front teeth, slightly protruding like squirrels' teeth, and he has agreeable and winning ways.

"A cloud came over his face when he made some allusion to his being made the hero of fabulous yarns, and something like indignation was expressed when he said that our Extra misrepresented him in saying that he called his associates cowards. 'I never said any such thing,' he pouted, 'I know they ain't cowards.'

"Billie Wilson was glum and sober, but from underneath his broad-brimmed hat, we saw a face that had a by no means bad look. He is light complexioned, light hair, bluish grey eyes, is a little stouter than Bonney, and far quieter. He appears ashamed and is not in very good spirits.

"A final stroke of the hammer cut the last rivet in the bracelets, and they clanked on the pavement as they fell.

"Bonney straightened up and then rubbing his wrists, where the sharp edged irons had chaffed him, said: 'I don't suppose you fellows would believe it, but this is the first time I ever had bracelets on. But many another fellow had them on, too.'

"With Wilson he walked toward the little hole in the wall to the place which is no 'sell' on a place of confinement. Just before entering he turned and looked back and explained: 'They say, a fool for luck and a poor man for children—Garrett takes them all in.'

"We saw them again at the depot when the crowd presented a really war-like appearance. Standing by the car, out of one of the windows on which he was leaning, he talked freely with us of the whole affair.

" 'I don't blame you for writing of me as you have. You had to believe others' stories, but then I don't know as anyone would believe anything good of me, anyway,' he said. 'I wasn't the leader of any gang. I was for Billy all the time. About that Portales business, I owned the ranch with Charlie Bowdre. I took it up and was holding it because I knew that sometime a stage line would run by there, and I wanted to keep it for a station.' " [It was rumored that the ranch at Los Portales which the Kid had homesteaded with Bowdre was a rendezvous for stolen stock, but none was ever found there.] " 'But I found there were certain men who wouldn't let me live in the country so I was going to leave.

" 'We had all our grub in the house when they took us in, and we were going to a place about six miles away in the morning to cook it and then light out. I haven't stolen any stock. I made my living gambling but that was the only way I could live. They wouldn't let me settle down; if they had I wouldn't be here today,' he held up his right arm on which was the bracelet. 'Chisum got me into all this trouble and wouldn't help me out. I went to Lincoln to stand my trial on the warrant that was out for me, but the Territory took a change of venue to Doña Ana, and I knew that I had no show, and so I skinned out. When I was up to White Oaks the last time, I went there to consult with a lawyer, who had sent for me to come up. But I knew I couldn't stay there either.'

"The conversation then drifted to the question of the final round-up of the party. Billy's story is the same as that given in our Extra, issued at midnight on Sunday.

" 'If it hadn't been for the dead horse in the doorway I wouldn't be here. I would have ridden out on my bay mare and taken my chances at escaping,' said he. 'But I couldn't jump over that, for she would have jumped back, and I would have got it in the head. We could have stayed in the house but there wouldn't have been anything gained by that for they would have starved us out. I thought it was better to come out and get a square meal—don't you?'

"The prospects of a fight (at the train) exhilarated him, and he bitterly bemoaned being chained. 'If I only had my Winchester, I'd lick the whole crowd,' was his confident comment on the strength of the attack party. He sighed and sighed again for a chance to take a hand in the fight, and the burden of his desire was to be set free to fight on the side of his captors as soon as he should smell powder.

"As the train rolled out, he lifted his hat and invited us to call and see him in Santa Fe, calling out '*Adios!*' "

In Las Vegas, Garrett had dismissed the posse, retaining only Frank Stewart and Barney Mason, and adding Bob Olinger who met him there and Mike Cosgrove. Stewart's men had been sent to New Mexico to find loose stock, not hunt the Kid, and it was best they get back to it. Garrett had no warrant for Tom Pickett, so he relinquished custody of him to Sheriff Romero. The Kid, Billie Wilson, and Dave Rudabaugh were to be transported to Santa Fe and there turned over to U.S. Marshal John Sherman. The excitement at the depot was caused by resentment among certain citizens of Las Vegas who did not want Dave Rudabaugh taken from the vicinity, but instead tried and hanged on the spot. It had nothing whatsoever to do with the Kid. Rudabaugh was so apprehensive for his life that he extracted a special promise from Garrett regarding his safety. A noisy mob, gathered at the depot, on 27 December, the day after Garrett had brought in the prisoners, intended to seize Rudabaugh by force if necessary rather than let him leave town. Garrett and his men were heavily armed and he threatened to arm the Kid as well, but this had no effect. It was then that Miguel I. Otero, father of the later governor and a Territorial legislator, made a mollifying speech to the mob. While he was talking, someone climbed into the engineer's cabin and started the train. Otero and his two sons stayed on the train and Miguel A. Otero later recalled that "on the way we talked with Billy the Kid and Dave Rudabaugh. We knew Rudabaugh well; he had been on the police force in East Las Vegas [during John Joshua Webb's term as city marshal]. Though we had never seen the Kid before, we were familiar with his part in the Lincoln County War and in the reign of terror he had created. In Santa Fe we were allowed to visit the Kid in jail, taking him cigarette papers, tobacco, chewing gum, candy, pies, and nuts. He was very fond of sweets and asked us to bring him all we could. The Kid's general appearance was the same as most boys of his age. I liked the Kid very much, and long before we even reached Santa Fe, nothing would have pleased me more than to have witnessed his escape."[140]

The train to Santa Fe stopped at the station at Bernalillo. Dr. Hoyt, who was standing on the platform waiting for a southbound train, happened to see the Kid through a Pullman window. Hoyt hastily climbed aboard and walked down the aisle toward the Kid. The Kid recognized him at once. After identifying himself to the Kid's armed escort, he asked the Kid if there was anything he could do for his comfort.

"Sure, Doc," the Kid said in high spirits, "just grab and hand me Bob's gun for a moment."

"My boy," Olinger cut in on him, "you had better tell your friend good-bye. Your days are short."

"Oh, I don't know," the Kid quipped, "there's many a slip 'twixt the cup and the lip."[141]

Later that day, Garrett turned the prisoners over to Charles Conklin, deputy U.S. marshal at Santa Fe.

W. G. Ritch, a staunch Axtell supporter, had fought against Governor Wallace's appointment in the U.S. Senate. As part of his effort to make peace with everybody who mattered in New Mexican politics, Wallace appointed Ritch to serve as acting governor whenever he was away from Santa Fe. Ritch was serving in that capacity the day the Kid and the others were brought in and he released Charles Bowdre's letter to the press. On 29 December the Ring newspaper, the *New Mexican*, commented on the letter in an editorial that "Charlie is now where no indictments will reach him."

The Kid was unaware that Wallace was in the East, among other things being fêted for the appearance of his novel, BEN-HUR: A TALE OF THE CHRIST, and trying to politic himself a new position in the recently elected Garfield administration. On 1 January 1881 from jail the Kid wrote Wallace.

Gov Lew Wallace
Dear Sir

I would like to see you for a few moments if you can spare time.

Yours Respect.
W. H. Bonney[142]

Discouraged by the governor's lack of response, the Kid joined with Rudabaugh and other prisoners, using spoons, forks, boards, and bedsprings, to dig his way out of jail. On 1 March the cell was searched and a tunnel was discovered, hidden under a mattress. Rudabaugh was the most in despair. In January he had been sentenced to ninety-nine years for federal mail robbery and next he was to face charges for the murder he had committed in Las Vegas. For the latter crime he was sentenced to hang. He did not, however. In fact, before the end of the year both Webb and Rudabaugh successfully broke out of prison. On 2 March, the Kid again wrote to Wallace.

Gov Lew Wallace
Dear Sir:

I wish you would come down to the jail to see me. It will be to your interest to come and see me. I have some letters which date back two years and there are Parties who are very anxious to get them but I shall not dispose of them until I see you. that is if you will come immediately.

Yours Respect—
Wm H. Bonney[143]

The Kid was in solitary confinement as a result of the abortive attempt to escape. He did not hear from Wallace, but knew that he was in town. He wrote again on 4 March.

Gov Lew Wallace
Dear Sir

I wrote you a little note the day before yesterday but have received no answer I expect you have forgotten what you promised me this month two years ago, but I have not; and I think you had ought to have come and see me as I have requested you to. I have done everything that I promised you I would and you have done nothing that you promised me I think when you think the matter over you will come down and see me, as I can explain everything to you.

Judge Leonard passed through here on his way east in January and promised to come and see me on his way back but he did not fulfill his promise. it looks to me like I am getting left in the cold. I am not treated right by Sherman. he lets every stranger that comes to see me through curiousity in to see me, but will not let a single one of my friends in, not even an attorney. I guess they mean to send me up without giving me any show but they will have a nice time doing it. I am not entirely without friends. I shall expect to see you some time today

Patiently waiting
I am very truly yours Respect.
Wm H. Bonney[144]

On 18 March 1881 the Kid learned that the San Miguel grand jury had indicted him on a charge of cattle stealing. On 28 March he was to be transferred to Mesilla for his hearing before Judge Bristol. On 27 March, he wrote again to the governor.

Gov Lew. Wallace
Dear Sir

For the last time I ask. Will you keep your promise. I start below tomorrow. send answer by bearer.

Yours Resp.
W. Bonney[145]

On 4 March 1881 President Garfield had been inaugurated. Governor Wallace saw to it that he received a specially bound and autographed copy of BEN-HUR. Dr. Hoyt was also a guest at the governor's Palace and heard Wallace telling a group, sitting around him, spellbound, how the fight during the five-day battle had occurred, reputedly just as the Kid had first told it to him. Hoyt asked the governor if there was any hope for the Kid. "The General," as Hoyt referred to Wallace, "was thoughtful for a moment. Then he shook his head and replied, 'Too late.' "[146]

On his way to Mesilla, the Kid and Billie Wilson, who was also to be tried, were guarded by Chief of Police Frank Chávez and Deputy Sheriff and Deputy U.S. Marshal Tony Neis. "When at last they did reach Rincon," the *Santa Fe New Mexican* reported, "there were some six or seven roughs on hand, who showed a very bristling front. Deputy Marshal Tony Neis hurried the prisoners from the train [which they had taken from Santa Fe to Rincon; the rest of the journey would be by coach] "into a saloon in order to get them out of the way as soon as possible and having done so hired a back room for them. One of the men said so that the officers could hear the remark, 'Let's take them fellows anyhow' whereupon Neis replied, 'You don't get them without somebody being killed,' and then the party entered the house. The men on the outside then endeavored to organize, while the officers and prisoners awaited anxiously in the room. Neis had a double-barreled gun and a six-shooter, and Chávez a rifle. The Kid and Wilson were evidently uneasy, and Neis not being acquainted with the intentions of the mob and suspecting that their object was to release the prisoners, told them that if it came to the scratch he would turn his guns loose on both of them before they should be taken. . . . Some disinterested men finally succeeded in dispersing the mob, whom they assured that if any attempt was made to rescue the men they would have a hard fight for it, and the project was abandoned. The officers with their charges took the coach at Rincon for Mesilla, to which place they proceeded unmolested."

The trial of Billy the Kid, which commenced 6 April 1881, was perhaps the most brilliantly staged judicial drama which Judge Bristol ever engineered in his courtroom. Colonel Rynerson, who had retired from the office of district attorney to devote himself full-time to the cattle business he was engaged in with J. J. Dolan, had been replaced by his very close friend, S. B. Newcomb. On 2 November 1877 in Judge Bristol's court, with Rynerson prosecuting and Newcomb defending, John Kinney had been acquitted of a murder charge. Kinney was now a special deputy assigned to guarding the Kid. Newcomb had also successfully defended Jesse Evans when Evans had been charged with John H. Tunstall's murder.

Two federal indictments were open against the Kid, one for the killing of Buckshot Roberts, the other for the murder of Morris J. Bernstein. Newcomb admitted that the prosecution's case was weak on both counts and Judge Ira E. Leonard, who was on hand to defend the Kid, had no trouble in getting them dismissed. Newcomb then switched gears and declared that the Kid would be tried in Territorial court (same judge, same building, same prosecutor) for the murder of Sheriff Brady. Judge Bristol dismissed Judge Leonard as defense counsel and in his place appointed Colonel Albert Jennings Fountain to be assisted by John D. Bail. Judge Bristol had been a close friend of Sheriff Brady's and Fountain, having been long sympathetic to the Dolan and Catron interests, was scarcely impartial. Fountain belonged to the same Masonic lodge as did S. B. Newcomb, James J. Dolan, Thomas B. Catron, Henry L. Waldo, and W. G. Ritch. Together with Bristol presiding, Newcomb and Colonel Fountain handpicked the jury.

On 8 April Colonel Fountain announced that the defendant was ready for trial. By 10 April, with J. J. Dolan and Billy Mathews as key prosecution witnesses, it was all over but for the hanging. Judge Bristol confined the jury to only two verdicts: murder in the first degree or acquittal. Before the jury retired, Judge Bristol sternly instructed them to remember that "there is no evidence before you showing that the killing of Brady is murder in any other degree than the first." Further, Bristol reminded them that the prosecution did not need to prove that the Kid fired the shot that killed Brady. If it was demonstrated that he was on the scene, that would be sufficient evidence to warrant conviction. When the jury quickly returned a verdict of guilty, Judge Bristol asked the Kid if he had any remark to make before sentence was passed. The record shows that the Kid said nothing.[147] Even so partisan a source as Robert M. Utley found it necessary to remark on the curiosity that the Kid's "defense attorneys seem to have directed most of their efforts toward influencing Judge Bristol's charge to the jury, although it is difficult to understand how their view of the case favored their client."[148] This and the astonishing fact, in Utley's words, "that a trial of such public interest then and since should have left so little record is baffling and disappointing," are readily comprehensible once it is realized that Fountain and Bail were appointed to represent the Kid precisely because they would make no case for him and the records were obscure because it was known beforehand that there would be no appeal then, or one even possible posthumously.[149]

On 13 April President Garfield began reading BEN-HUR. On 15 April Judge Bristol ordered that the Kid be remanded to the custody of Sheriff Pat Garrett and there on Friday, 13 May 1881, William Bonney, alias the Kid, alias William Antrim, "be hanged by the neck until his body be dead." From the moment Garrett had turned over the Kid to the Santa Fe authorities, he had been trying to secure payment from Governor Wallace of the $500 reward. Acting Governor Ritch had declared the claim without merit since the reward as posted had called for "capture and delivery of the Kid to the sheriff of Lincoln County" and Garrett, still a deputy, had not surrendered his prisoner to Sheriff Kimbrell. W. T. Thornton of the law firm Catron and Thornton personally paid Garrett $500 in exchange for an assignment of the claim. James J. Dolan, from various sources, was able to raise another eight hundred dollars for Garrett. This money, combined with Garrett's *per diem* expenses for months of manhunting at four dollars a day and six and one-half cents a mile, netted Garrett a sum sufficient to buy a small ranch near Bear Canyon and a hotel in town. Billie Wilson's case was continued by Judge Bristol on 30 March 1881. It was finally heard in Santa Fe, but Wilson escaped from jail. His attorney in Santa Fe was W. T. Thornton. Wilson went to Texas where he changed his name to D. L. Anderson. He soon married and became a respectable citizen. When Thornton became governor of the Territory of New Mexico, he submitted a petition to the Attorney General, including testimonial letters from James J. Dolan and Pat F. Garrett, and Wilson received a presidential pardon dated 24 July 1896. On 19 April 1881, having finished BEN-HUR, President Garfield made the decision to appoint Lew Wallace to the American ambassadorship at Constantinople.

"Well, I had intended at one time not to say a word in my own behalf, because persons would say, 'Oh, he lied,' " the Kid said in an interview with the *Mesilla News* shortly after sentence was passed. " 'Newman, editor of *Semi-Weekly*, gave me a rough deal; has created prejudice against me, and is trying to incite a mob to lynch me. He sent me a paper which shows it; I think it is a dirty mean advantage to take of me, considering my situation and knowing I could not defend myself by word or act. But I suppose he thought he would give me a kick down hill. Newman came to see me the other day. I refused to talk to him or tell him anything. But I believe the *News* is always willing to give its readers both sides of a question.

" 'If mob law is going to rule, better dismiss judge, sheriff, etc., and let all take chances alike. I expect to be lynched in going to Lincoln. Advise persons never to engage in killing."

Editor—Think you will be taken through safe? Do you expect a pardon from the governor?

" 'Considering the active part Governor Wallace took on our side and the friendly relations that existed between him and me, and the promise he made me, I think he ought to pardon me. Don't know that he will do it. When I was arrested for that murder, he let me go and gave me my freedom of the town, and let me go about with my arms. When I got ready to go, I left. Think it hard I should be the only one to suffer the extreme penalties of the law.' "

"Here the sheriff led us away," the reporter later stated, "and said we had talked long enough."

The Kid had first met Edgar Caypless, a Santa Fe attorney, when the latter had come to visit Dave Rudabaugh. He had heard that the mare he had been riding at the time of his capture which Garrett had given to Frank Stewart had been traded by Stewart to W. Scott Moore of Las Vegas for a revolver valued at $60. On 15 April the Kid wrote from Mesilla to Caypless in Santa Fe.

Dear Sir:

I would have written before this but could get no paper. My United States case was thrown out of court and I was rushed to trial on my territorial charge. Was convicted of murder in the first degree and am to be hanged on the 13th of May. Mr. A. J. Fountain was appointed to defend me and had done the best he could for me. He is willing to carry the case further if I can raise the money to bear his expense. The mare is about all I can depend on at present, so I hope you will settle the case right away and give him the money. Please do as he wished about the matter. I know you will do the best you can for me in this. I shall be taken to Lincoln tomorrow. Please write and direct care of Garrett, sheriff. Excuse bad writing. I have handcuffs on.

I remain as ever
Yours respectfully,
William Bonney.[150]

XII

The Kid has been praised by those who knew him for resourcefulness and for courage. Based on his letters to Governor Wallace and to Edgar Caypless, he was hopelessly naïve and totally incapable of assessing his situation, what it was about him that had so uniformly congealed to destroy him. In his letters he was urgent, insistent, but never desperate. If ever he did know fear, it must have been on the trip from Mesilla to Lincoln with the hated Billy Mathews, John Kinney, and Bob Olinger leering and stroking his shotgun among his guards. Yet Newman reported in his *Semi-Weekly* that the Kid "appeared quite cheerful and remarked that he wanted to stay with the boys until the whiskey gave out anyway. Said he was sure his guard would not hurt him unless a rescue should be attempted, and he was certain that would not be done, 'unless perhaps those fellows over at White Oaks come to take me,' meaning to kill him. It was, he said, about a stand-off whether he was hanged or killed in the wagon. The Mesilla jail was the worst he had ever struck. The sheriff wanted him to say something good about it when he left, but he had not done so. He wanted to say something about John Chisum, and it would be some satisfaction to him to know that some men would be punished after he had been hung. He was handcuffed and shackled and chained to the back seat of the ambulance. Kinney sat beside him. Olinger on the seat facing him. Mathews facing Kinney, [W. A.] Lockhart driving, and [D. M.] Reade, [Deputy Sheriff Dave] Woods, and [Tom] Williams riding along on horseback on each side and behind. The whole party were armed to the teeth, and any one who knows the men of whom it was composed will admit that a rescue would be a hazardous undertaking."

The party set out on 16 April. They arrived, without incident, in Lincoln on 22 April. The Kid's prison cell was Murphy's former bedroom in the Dolan store. One window looked out into the main street, another out into the yard. The Kid's chains were fastened to the floor. On the other side of the stairs was the armory, in the room Dolan and Riley had shared. Dolan had built himself a home across from the old Tunstall store, which he was operating with success, and it was here that he stayed when he was in town. It was an indication of how in the revolutions of *rota Fortunae* there were those who had been favored, and those who had not been. Once the Kid was chained to the floor, Garrett dismissed the possemen except, of course, for Bob Olinger who as a deputy sheriff was appointed along with J. W. Bell to guard the Kid, a job Olinger relished.

On 28 April Sam Corbet, who had been a clerk in Tunstall's store, came to visit the Kid. He passed him a note on which was written one word, "privy." That day José M. Aguayo, a devoted admirer of the Kid although related to the Baca family which was on the side of the Dolan forces, went to the privy behind the courthouse with a revolver wrapped in a newspaper under his arm. When he left the privy, he no longer had either. Other prisoners were being held in the west wing on the second floor of the courthouse and Olinger and Bell customarily alternated between themselves escorting them across the main street at mealtime to eat at Wortley's Hotel. Pat Garrett was not in town. In March, 1881, John Poe had arrived at White Oaks, Frank Stewart's replacement as special agent for the Canadian River cattlemen's association. Garrett had met him at White Oaks and had made him a deputy. Poe had been at work tracing stolen stock and Garrett had gone to meet with him to receive his report. It was Olinger's day to take the prisoners across to the hotel. Olinger placed his shotgun in the armory and led the prisoners out and down the stairs. While they were at the hotel, the Kid asked Bell to be permitted to go to the outhouse. Finding the revolver in the privy, the Kid hid it in his clothes until he and Bell were on the steps leading to the second floor. When he produced the revolver, Bell did a very foolish thing. Instead of throwing up his hands, as the Kid demanded he do, Bell turned and ran. The Kid shot him.

Still shackled, the Kid hopped the distance to the armory and got hold of Olinger's shotgun. He hopped to the window overlooking the path Olinger would take, coming from Wortley's Hotel. Olinger, hearing the gunfire, ran toward the courthouse to investigate. The Kid called to him from the open window, pointing the shotgun. Olinger was looking up when the blast from his own shotgun hit him.

Godfrey Gauss, who had once been Tunstall's cook, was now the courthouse janitor. Having made his way to a hall window at the rear of the building, the Kid called out to Gauss, who was in the yard below, and asked for a tool with which to remove the shackles. Gauss' account of what happened appeared in the *Lincoln County Leader* on 15 January 1890. "When I arrived at the garden gate leading to the street, in front of the courthouse," Gauss recalled, "I saw the other deputy sheriff, Olinger, coming out of the hotel opposite, with the other four or five county prisoners where they had taken their dinner. I called to him to come quick. He did so, leaving his prisoners in front of the hotel. When he had come close up to me, and while standing not more than a yard apart, I told him that I was just after laying Bell dead on the ground in the yard behind. Before he could reply, he was struck by a well directed shot fired from a window above us, and fell dead at my feet. I ran for my life to reach my room and safety, when Billy the Kid called to me: 'Don't run, I wouldn't hurt you—I am alone, and master not only of the courthouse, but also of the town, for I will allow nobody to come near us.' 'You go,' he said, 'and saddle one of Judge Leonard's horses, and I will clear out as soon as I can have the shackles loosened from my legs.' With a little prospecting pick I had thrown to him through the window he was working for at least an hour, and could not accomplish more than to free one leg. He came to the conclusion to await a better chance, tie one shackle to his waistbelt, and start out. Meanwhile I had saddled a small skittish pony belonging to Billy Burt, as there was no other horse available, and had also, by Billy's command, tied a pair of red blankets behind the saddle. I came near forgetting to say, that whilst I was busy saddling, and Mr. Billy Kid was trying hard to get his shackles off, my partner, Sam Wortley, appeared in the door leading from the garden where he had been at work, into my yard, and that when he saw the two sheriffs lying dead he did not know whether to go in or retreat, but on the assurance of Billy the Kid that he would not hurt him he went in and made himself generally useful. When Billy went down stairs at last, on passing the body of Bell, he said, 'I'm sorry I had to kill him but couldn't help it.' On passing the body of Olinger he gave him a tip of his boot, saying, 'You are not going to round me up again.' We went out together where I had tied up the pony, and he told me to tell the owner of same, Billy Burt, that he would send it back next day. I, for my part, didn't much believe his promise, but, sure enough, next morning, the pony arrived safe and sound, trailing a long lariat, at the courthouse in Lincoln. And so Billy the Kid started out that evening, after he had shaken hands with everybody around and after having had a little difficulty mounting on account of the shackle on his leg, he went on his way rejoicing. . . . In regard to the guilt or innocence of Billy the Kid I will here state, that Billy himself, in many conversations I had with him during the two or three years I was acquainted with him prior to his death, never denied that he was in the habit of stealing cattle from John Chisum, of Roswell, against whom he professed to have a claim, for wages I believe, which Chisum refused to pay, and hence he was determined to secure himself."

The Kid rode the short distance to the foothills of the Capitan mountains and spent the night at the goat ranch of his friend, José Cordova, a schoolmaster. He released Billy Burt's pony, knowing that the pony would find his way back, and worked to rid himself of the remaining leg iron. He borrowed a horse and saddle from Cordova, with Cordova's consent, and rode toward Fort Sumner. Pat Garrett was sitting in a saloon in White Oaks with John Poe when he heard the news of the Kid's escape.

"Now I'll have to do it all over again," he is reputed to have said.[151]

Bob Olinger's mother, in a conversation with Mrs. McSween, said that her son was a murderer from the cradle until the moment he died and confessed that he got his just deserts when Billy shot him.

When Garrett got back to Lincoln, he found an execution order for Billy from Governor Wallace and returned it, commenting that he could not execute the Kid because he had escaped. Garrett led several search posses after the Kid, but with no results. On 12 May the *Las Vegas Gazette* reported that "William Bonney, alias Kid, has been seen near Fort Sumner, riding a horse stolen from [Montgomery] Bell's ranch. It is believed Billy is on the lookout for Barney Mason, who was then in Fort Sumner. The Kid never had any great love for Barney, and especially since he assisted in the capture of Billy and party at Stinking Springs. If Bonney remains much longer in Lincoln County, hovering about to pay off old scores, he is likely to be shot when he is not prepared to do his best shooting."

On Pioneer Day, 26 February 1931, at the Old-Timers meeting in Roswell, John Meadows recalled his meeting with the Kid after his escape. "The Kid come to my place three or four days after he made his escape from jail," Meadows said, "and Tom [Norris] and me was in the cabin cooking some supper and the Kid come around the corner of the house and saw nobody there but us, and stepped in and said, Well, I got you, haven't I. And I said, Well, you have, so what are you going to do with us. He says, I'm going to eat supper with you. I says, That's all right as long as you can stand them beans. . . .

"We talked until eleven that night. He said, if I was laying out there in the arroyo and Pat Garrett rode by and didn't see me, he would be the last man I would kill. I wouldn't hurt a hair on his head; he worked pretty rough to capture us, but he treated me good after he got me; he treated us humane and friendly and was good to us after he did get us captured, I have ever such a good feeling for Pat Garrett.

"I said, What kind of a feeling do you have for Bob Olinger. He says, I expressed that a day or so ago. That was the first time I heard of it.

"I said, When I was sick and down and out, you befriended me, and there is two things I have never done, I have never kissed the hand that slapped me nor went back on a friend. Anyway, I'm going to befriend you now. I have got fourteen head of old Indian ponies, some of them ain't very much, but you go out and look 'em over, and if one of them does you any good, take it and you are welcome to them all. But don't go back to Fort Sumner for if you do, Garrett will get you sure as you do, or else you will have to kill him.

"He said, I haven't any money, what would I do in Mexico with no money? I'll have to go back and get a little before I go. Sure as you do, I said, Garrett will get you. He said, I have got too many friends up there and I don't believe he will get me, and I can stay there a while and get money enough and then go to Mexico. I said, You'd better go while the going is good, you go back up there and you will get killed or Garrett. He went back to Sumner."[152]

Garrett made very little effort, after the initial forays at reconnaissance, to hunt for the Kid. There is some speculation as to why. The newspapers at the time complained about his inactivity and found its cause in unconcern. The *Cimarron News and Press* on 26 May 1881 quoted him as about to resign unless citizens indicated "more readiness to support him in the execution of his arduous duties." The least likely explanation is that Garrett was giving the Kid a chance to flee to old Mexico and he was not merely indifferent. He was probably humiliated by what had happened and, later in life, often expressed his culpability for not having had the Kid guarded more closely. Garrett was firmly allied with the power structure which ran the Territory, but the majority of the citizens were unwilling to help him kill Billy. Garrett had sent Poe to scout around, but Poe learned nothing. It was not Garrett's way—as demonstrated in his original manhunt for the Kid—to go looking for his quarry. He preferred to lie in ambush. Nor did he have the funds to support a posse in the field. Wild had returned to Washington and Poe was a one-man replacement for Stewart's posse.

On 30 April 1881, Wallace's notice of a $500 reward appeared again in New Mexican newspapers. This time the prospect was anything but inspiring, given the problem Garrett had had trying to collect the reward the first time. Governor Wallace's post paid $2,400 a year and the governor, if indeed he personally had had anything to do with the notice, had not intended to pay it personally. Presently he was off to his new post in Constantinople and Pat had had quite enough of bargaining with Acting Governor Ritch.

The day before the Kid had escaped, Governor Wallace gave an interview to the *Las Vegas Gazette*. "The conversation drifted into the sentence of 'The Kid,' " the interview recounted. " 'It looks as though he would hang, Governor.' 'Yes, the chances seem good that the 13th of May would finish him.' 'He appears to look to you to save his neck.' 'Yes,' said Governor Wallace smiling, 'but I can't see how a fellow like him should expect any clemency from me.' Although not committing himself, the general tenor of the governor's remarks indicated that he would resolutely refuse to grant 'The Kid' a pardon. It would seem as though 'The Kid' had undertaken to bulldoze the governor, which has not helped his chances in the slightest."

There is no telling what Garrett would or would not have done had Pete Maxwell not informed on the Kid. "Such an arrangement, with the Mexicans covering up for him, might have gone on indefinitely had not Billy paid too much attention to pretty Paulita Maxwell," Leon C. Metz wrote. "The love affair so disturbed her brother Pete that he finally notified the authorities. A trusted vaquero slipped into White Oaks and gave the news to John Poe, who in turn relayed the message to Pat Garrett.

The sheriff thought the entire yarn unbelievable, and only after the strongest urgings by Poe did he agree to check it out. Then, because of the possibility of retaliation falling upon Maxwell's head, both men concocted the story that Poe had learned of the Kid's whereabouts through a conversation he had overheard in White Oaks."[153] The latter story was the one Garrett had Ash Upson narrate in THE AUTHENTIC LIFE OF BILLY THE KID and which Poe told in his account, later published as THE DEATH OF BILLY THE KID. There was one other fact which both men agreed to lie about: that the Kid was armed with a revolver at the time he was killed, near midnight on 14 July 1881.

It may well have been Paulita Maxwell who constituted the biggest inducement for the Kid to stay near Fort Sumner. It was she with whom the Kid was in love, and not Garrett's sister-in-law, Celsa Gutiérrez, as Walter Noble Burns would later claim. In January, 1882, Paulita married José Jaramillo. As Macrobius reported Julia's response to a lover on why her children looked so like Agrippa when they, in all probability, were not his, Paulita might well have explained the resemblance of her firstborn to the Kid in a similar fashion: *"Nunquam, enim nisi plena navi, tollo vectorem"* [I never take on a passenger unless the vessel is full].[154] What is certain is that Pete could see no future in the relationship and wanted it brought to an end.

"Billy the Kid had been stopping with me for several weeks," Francisco Lobato recalled. "He came to me after he had escaped from jail at Lincoln, thinking my camp was a safe place. He was with me nearly all the time Pat Garrett was seeking him. We were good friends; Billy would do anything for me and I would do anything for him. He often rode to Fort Sumner at night but always returned to the camp before daylight. On the night he was killed, he and I went to Fort Sumner together. We were hungry and stopped at Jesus Silva's to eat. Billy wanted some beefsteak and asked Silva if he had any fresh meat. Silva replied that he had none but had helped Pete Maxwell kill a yearling that morning. He told the Kid he could get all he wanted if he went over to Maxwell's for it."[155]

Because both Francisco Lobato and Jesus Silva were as intent in protecting Paulita as Garrett and Poe were in protecting Pete, it is impossible now to say whether the Kid stopped to see Paulita before going over to Pete Maxwell's. John Poe had not previously laid eyes on the Kid. He, Kip McKinney, and Garrett had arrived at Fort Sumner well after dark and it was near midnight when they crept across the peach orchard toward the Maxwell house. Pete was in bed, asleep, and Garrett went in to speak with him, regarding the message he had sent to Poe. He left Poe and McKinney outside, near the porch. "It was probably not more than thirty seconds after Garrett had entered Maxwell's room," Poe recalled, "when my attention was attracted, from where I sat in the little gateway, to a man approaching me on the inside of and along the fence, some forty or fifty steps away. I observed that he was only partially dressed and was both bareheaded and barefooted, or rather, had only socks on his feet, and it seemed to me that he was fastening his trousers as he came toward me at a very brisk walk."[156]

The Kid, carrying perhaps a butcher knife in his hand but otherwise unarmed, saw the two men congregated outside Pete Maxwell's bedroom and spoke to them in Spanish.

"*¿Quién es?*" he asked. "*¿Quién es?*"

Since neither was about to reveal their identities much less their reason for being there, Poe and McKinney remained silent. The Kid then stepped abruptly into Pete Maxwell's bedroom.

"Pete, who are those fellows on the outside?" he inquired.

Garrett was admittedly frightened at the prospect of the Kid's being in the vicinity and he probably had unsheathed his pistol as he entered the bedroom.

"That's him," Pete said in English.[157]

Garrett could see a silhouette and fired at it, twice. According to THE AMERI-CAN EPHEMERIS AND NAUTICAL ALMANAC for 1881 published by the Washington Bureau of Navigation by authority of the Secretary of the Navy, there was a full moon that night making it possible for Garrett to see such a silhouette by its illumination.

"Soon after Billy left we heard two shots from Maxwell's direction," Francisco Lobato recalled, "and Silva and I went over immediately. We found a great deal of excitement. Pat Garrett, and two other men whom I did not know, were standing outside the house, rifles in hand, and ready to shoot. Pete Maxwell and the household were standing at the door of Pete's bedroom. Someone had been shot in the bedroom and we were told it was the Kid. Jesus Silva and Deluvina Maxwell, the old Navajo woman, went in to see who it was. Deluvina came out sobbing, 'My little boy is dead!' "[158]

Poe, too, confirmed that there was initially some doubt about who had been shot. "I heard a groan and one or two gasps from where I stood in the doorway, as of someone dying in the room," Poe wrote. "An instant later, Garrett came out, brushing against me as he passed. He stood by me close to the wall at the side of the door and said to me, 'That was the Kid that came in there onto me, and I think I have got him.' I said, 'Pat, the Kid would not come to this place; you have shot the wrong man.' Upon my saying this, Garrett seemed to be in doubt himself as to whom he had shot. . . . A moment after Garrett came out the door, Pete Maxwell rushed squarely onto me in a frantic effort to get out of the room, and I certainly would have shot him but for Garrett's striking my gun down, saying, 'Don't shoot Maxwell.' "[159]

"The night Pat Garrett killed him," Jesus Silva said, "he and Francisco Lobato stopped at my house. Billy said he was tired, threw his hat on a chair and took off his coat and shoes. I got them something to eat and even went over to Beaver Smith's for more beer. But Billy said he wanted a beefsteak and hot coffee. I had no beef in the house, but told him I had helped Pete Maxwell kill and dress a yearling calf that morning. I suggested that he go over to ask Pete for some meat, I knowing he was welcome to anything of Pete's.

"We had heard strange voices coming from the peach orchard but had given no thought to who it might be. If we had, the Kid's life might have been saved. It was

Pat Garrett and his two deputies. Billy would not have walked into the trap laid for him. Someone in Fort Sumner must have given Billy away.

"Billy took the butcher knife and went over after the meat. He had been gone only a few minutes when Lobato and I were startled by two shots coming from the direction of Pete Maxwell's house. We ran over as quickly as we could, finding Pat Garrett and his two deputies by the open door of Pete Maxwell's bedroom.

"Deluvina, an old Navajo woman who had always been particularly devoted to the Kid, went into the room to find out whom Garrett had shot. I went in with her. There on the floor, we saw Billy—stretched out, face down. We turned him over, and when Deluvina realized fully it was the Kid, she began to cry bitterly, interspersing with her tears the vilest curses she could bestow on the head of Pat Garrett.

"We asked permission to remove the body, Pete Maxwell suggesting removal to the old carpenter shop. We laid the body on the carpenter's bench and placed lighted candles around the corpse. News of the killing spread quickly through the town and surrounding country, and consequently a large number of Billy's friends were gathered at the wake. Everyone's grief at the Kid's death was genuine and sincere. Pat Garrett and his two companions were badly frightened, and did not dare to sleep that night. They remained awake, arms in readiness for any emergency. The next morning, a coroner's inquest was held before Alcalde Segura and a jury, which declared that Sheriff Pat Garrett had killed William H. Bonney in the discharge of his official duty and that the homicide was justifiable.

"The morning after the killing, I measured Billy's body and made a rough box which we used as a coffin. That afternoon we dug his grave and buried him."[160]

After discovering the Kid's body, Deluvina Maxwell burst from Pete Maxwell's bedroom and pushed her way through the crowd that was congregating. "You piss-pot!" she screamed at Garrett. "You sonofabitch!"[161]

The mourners had to restrain her from attacking Garrett physically.

Many years later she told former Governor Miguel Otero that Garrett had been "afraid to go back to the room to make sure of whom he had shot! I went in and was the first to discover that they had killed my little boy. I hated those men and am glad that I have lived long enough to see them all dead and buried."[162]

In A FITTING DEATH FOR BILLY THE KID, Ramon F. Adams asked: "Did Garrett realize that he had killed an unarmed man? It has been suggested many times that he proposed writing [THE AUTHENTIC LIFE OF BILLY THE KID] to salve his conscience, to build up a super-gunman for his own purposes. He declared, 'It was either him or me,' but I think that deep down he was trying to convince the world his act was justified."[163] Former Governor Otero, who knew Garrett personally, recognized that "actually, Garrett was in no danger of being killed," but he hastened to add, with some justification, that for his own part Garrett "did not know that the Kid was unarmed, and he cannot be blamed for shooting when he did."[164] In any event, the Kid died exactly as he did not want to die, "killed like a dog unarmed."

On 20 July, Garrett petitioned Acting Governor Ritch for the reward money. A question was at once raised as to whether or not Garrett himself had actually killed the Kid. The coroner's report, it seems, had been misplaced. Charles Green, editor of the *Santa Fe New Mexican* and a solid member of the Santa Fe Ring, may have been the one to suggest to Garrett that, under the circumstances, he should have a new coroner's report drawn up. He certainly did agree, when asked by Garrett, to file a petition for the reward with Acting Governor Ritch. The document Garrett had drawn up by Manuel Abreu, Pete Maxwell's brother-in-law, had signatories who had not been present at the original hearing and it contains many obviously slanted statements which indicate for what use it was intended, most significantly the statement that "*dicho Garrett fué homicidio justificable y estamos unánimes en opinion que la gratitud de toda la comunidad es devida [debida] á dicho Garrett por su hecho y que es digno de ser recompensado.*" Pete Maxwell is also quoted as having said: "*A poco rato que Garrett se sentó entró William Bonney y se arrimó a mi cama con una pistola en la mano y me preguntó 'Who is it? Who is it?' y entónces Pat.*" It seems quite probable that the original document mentioned that the Kid was unarmed and was therefore suppressed. It is also extremely questionable that the coroner's jury, made up of men sympathetic to the Kid, would have concluded by saying that "Garrett deserves to be rewarded!"[165] Pete Maxwell, on the other hand, had a very good reason for going along with Garrett subsequently in claiming that the Kid was armed, namely Garrett's silence as to whom it was who had informed on the Kid.

While Acting Governor Ritch continued to balk over paying out the reward, James J. Dolan went out and raised a gratuity of $1,150. According to the *Las Vegas Optic*, John Chisum gave Garrett $1,000. It was apparently a time for giving, since Chisum also reportedly settled with Mrs. McSween, turning over to her two hundred head of cattle from which herd, in time, she built a considerable livestock ranch in the Tres Rios region of New Mexico. She also managed to salvage some money from her deceased husband's estate and realized a profit in selling Dick Brewer's ranch which she dishonestly and fraudulently persuaded Brewer's relatives in Wisconsin to deed to her in payment for monies Brewer according to her died owing Alexander McSween. John H. Tunstall's father in England never received a cent for his son's New Mexico holdings from Mrs. McSween who had acted as administratrix. What remained of the Fritz insurance money was never paid to the estate. Ironically, late in life the well furnished home Mrs. McSween owned in White Oaks also burned to the ground and she moved into an abandoned house in what was by then a ghost town.

In August, 1882, at the Armijo Hotel in Trinidad, Pat Garrett met with Joseph Antrim, the Kid's older brother, and, after conversing for several hours, the two parted, shaking hands. That same month, Charles Green of the *Santa Fe New Mexican* proposed to Garrett that he write an account of his killing of the Kid. Ash Upson agreed it would be a good money-making proposition and moved in with Garrett in order to write the book, at the ranch Garrett bought near Roswell with the windfall he had come into this second time around in pursuit of the Kid. Upson continued to live with Garrett wherever Garrett went until his death on 6 October 1894. Since Upson was indigent, Garrett paid for his funeral expenses.

On 18 February 1882, after spending almost $500 buying libations for the legislators, the Territorial legislature voted to award Garrett the reward money. Garrett felt that he might have a brilliant future in politics. However, he was told outright by Dolan and others that he would stand no chance to be reelected sheriff of Lincoln County in the 1882 elections. At first Dolan himself had intended to run, but changed his mind, and ran for county treasurer instead, which office he held until 1888 when he ran and was elected to the Territorial senate. John Poe ran for sheriff and was elected, to replace Garrett. Poe eventually became a successful banker at Roswell. T. B. Catron, so important a force in the Lincoln County War, albeit behind the scenes, served several terms in the Territorial legislature and when, in 1912, New Mexico became a state, he was elected to the office of U.S. Senator by the State legislature. He died perhaps the richest man in the state and specified in his will that he be buried according to the rites of the Masonic order.

John Chisum did not long outlive the Kid. He died of complications from cancer on 20 December 1884 at Eureka Springs, Arkansas, where he had gone for additional treatment after a tumor had been removed surgically from his neck. Before he died, Chisum turned over his holdings in the Panhandle and New Mexico to his brother, James, to manage for the family. The Jinglebob Land & Cattle Company was set up, named after the characteristic slit Chisum had customarily made in the ears of his cattle to mark his ownership, but by 1891 the company was defunct.

Catron and Dolan had fought the good fight and, if winning is measured by accumulation of wealth, social and moral and political standing within the community, then they were the winners of the war. Garrett had been little more to them than a convenient tool. They were willing to pay him for his services to the cause, but beyond that they had no interest in him. Nor was Garrett the businessman John Poe was. He liked to drink, and play poker, and spend time with prostitutes. In what was left to him of his life, he was occasionally hired to kill men, and, increasingly, this became the only attribute associated with his name.

In 1907, although still married to Apolinaria who resided at Las Cruces with the children, Garrett was living with a prostitute in El Paso. It was in El Paso, in January, 1908, that the indigent Garrett met "Deacon Jim" Miller who offered him three thousand dollars for Garrett's Bear ranch, which Garrett, because of where he got the money to acquire it, referred to as the Rock House and Stinking Springs ranch. Miller and Carl Adamson, related by marriage, supposedly had over a thousand head of cattle waiting in Mexico *en route* to a ranch in Oklahoma. Their scheme was to hold the herd for a time in New Mexico, to fatten them up, and, when negotiations with John W. Leatherman, who had a ranch near Bear Canyon, collapsed, Miller approached Garrett. Now that President Theodore Roosevelt had appointed George Curry governor of New Mexico, Garrett had hopes that Curry would appoint him superintendent of the Territorial prison at Santa Fe, to replace Holm O. Bursum. When, in 1921, Bursum was in the U.S. Senate he would introduce the Bursum Bill, designed to disenfranchise all of the Pueblo lands in New Mexico so they could be plundered for their rich mineral resources. If Garrett was willing, Miller also offered to pay him one dollar a head to drive the cattle from Mexico to his Bear Canyon ranch.

There was one problem in all this. On 11 March 1907 Garrett had leased the Bear ranch for a period of five years to Jesse Wayne Brazel who was presently raising goats there. To solve the problem, Garrett returned to New Mexico and offered to buy Brazel's goats from him, which Brazel numbered at 1,200. On 28 February 1908 Garrett was in a buggy with Carl Adamson. Brazel rode on horseback alongside. Garrett began arguing with Brazel, especially over the fact that it now appeared that Brazel had miscounted and there were actually 1,800 goats, more than Garrett could afford to purchase. Garrett, who was carrying a Burgess folding shotgun loaded with bird shot, asked Adamson to stop the buggy so he could get out and urinate. According to Adamson, Garrett's last words were: "Well, damn you. If I don't get you off one way, I will another."[166] His back to Brazel, holding the shotgun in his right hand and unbuttoning his trousers with his left, this was Garrett's position when the first slug from Brazel's gun slammed into him. Another slug went through his body as he fell.

Brazel turned himself in to the authorities, pleading self-defense. This was the plea entered by Brazel's attorneys at his trial and on this basis he was acquitted. Among those representing Brazel was Albert Bacon Fall. Along with T. B. Catron, he would be elected to the U.S. Senate when New Mexico achieved statehood. He bought part of Mrs. McSween's land holdings from her. She had since married and divorced Samuel Barber and was alone when she decided to retire from ranching and went to live in a small house in White Oaks. A. B. Fall became Secretary of the Interior in the Harding administration. In 1931, the year Fall finally went to prison as the architect of the Teapot Dome and Elk Hills scandals, Mrs. Barber died, at the age of eighty-six—itself a considerable achievement for a principal in the Lincoln County War. "It was said of Garrett," she told former Governor Otero shortly before her death, "that every man he ever killed was shot without warning, and I can well believe this was the case. Garrett finally got what he most richly deserved at the hands of a young man, Wayne Brazel. I will say this much for Pat Garrett; he did have some fine children."[167] Had she been willing—and she was **not**—Susan Hummer McSween Barber could have told a great deal more about the Lincoln County War than any of its other survivors with the possible exception of James J. Dolan who drank himself into an early grave on 26 February 1898. Pete Maxwell did the same and died the same year as Dolan. Frederick Nolan in THE LINCOLN COUNTY WAR: A DOCUMENTARY HISTORY in an antonomic paraphrase of the Latin translation of Diogenes Laertius's aphorism—*de mortuis nihil nisi bonum dicamus*—concluded that about the Kid it has been *de mortuis nil nisi malum*. The epitaph on his grave at Fort Sumner where he was buried next to Tom O'Folliard and Charlie Bowdre read simply: Pals. Better, I would suggest, in view of so much that has come to be said about the Kid's legend would be that Latin tombstone inscription so popular in antiquity despite the contrary teachings of the

Stoics, the Neo-Platonists, and the various Christian sects: *nil mali ubi nil est* [where there is nothing, there is nothing bad].

2

BILLY AND THE
HISTORIANS

It may have struck the reader of the foregoing historical construction of the life and death of Billy the Kid that the Kid's personality, to say nothing of his perception of himself and the character of his motivations, remains somewhat in shadow. Yet, this is the totality of what we know about him after more than a century of diligent historical research. Considerably less was known about his life and the particulars of even his participation in the Lincoln County War by virtually all of his contemporaries. In my anthology THE AMERICAN WEST IN FICTION (University of Nebraska Press, 1988), I included what Mark Twain wrote about another frontier desperado, Jack Slade, in his book ROUGHING IT (1872), being largely a collection of frontier exaggeration, hyperbole, tall tales, and baseless rumor, to demonstrate how a man could pay a terrible penalty on the frontier—death, in Slade's case as in the Kid's—not for what he was or what he had really done, but for what people thought about him.

Prior to the appearance of THE AUTHENTIC LIFE OF BILLY THE KID, eight sensational "cheap" novels, varying in price from five to twenty-five cents, appeared about the Kid, and mention of some of them is made in the next chapter. J. C. Dykes, who assembled BILLY THE KID: A BIBLIOGRAPHY OF A LEGEND, wrote the Introduction for the reissue edition of Garrett's book published by the University of Oklahoma Press in The Western Frontier Library—or, to give its full title: THE AUTHENTIC LIFE OF BILLY THE KID, THE NOTED DESPERADO OF THE SOUTHWEST, WHOSE DEEDS OF DARING AND BLOOD MADE HIS NAME A TERROR IN NEW MEXICO, ARIZONA, & NORTHERN MEXICO, A FAITHFUL AND INTERESTING NARRATIVE BY PAT F. GARRETT, SHERIFF OF LINCOLN CO., N.M., BY WHOM HE WAS FINALLY HUNTED DOWN & CAPTURED BY KILLING HIM. This reissue edition, first published in 1954, had been kept in print and subsequently had gone through ten printings as of 1976. Some of what Dykes wrote of a biographical nature about the Kid and Garrett in his Introduction would have to be modified in the light of later historical findings, but I agree with his observation that "while some of the strange tales about the Kid that were first published in dime novels do appear many years later in the 'factual' reminiscences of old-timers, it was the poorly circulated Garrett book that provided the foundation for the growth of the folk hero."[1]

I cannot, in the limited space I have, recount all of the errors of fact and omissions to be found in the Garrett/Upson book. However, what I can do is to provide at least a partial listing of the more significant fantasies about the Kid which the book did promulgate and which influenced numerous later writers, right down to the present day.

Garrett/Upson Fantasies

1. The Kid was born William H. Bonney at New York City on 23 November 1859. [23 November was Upson's birthday. There is no evidence it was the Kid's. The Kid himself told a Fort Sumner census taker in 1880 that he was twenty-five years of age and cited Missouri as his birthplace. This may have been no more the truth, but when he was in jail in Las Vegas a reporter from the *Las Vegas Optic* thought him about twenty-four years of age. Personally, I incline to the view that he was at least twenty-five when he died. His rightful name was Henry McCarty.]

2. Billy was the elder of the two brothers.

3. The Bonney family moved to Coffeyville, Kansas in 1862 where the Kid's father died. [Coffeyville had not yet been founded in 1862.]

4. Billy's mother married a man named Antrim in Colorado and in 1882 he was "the only survivor of the family of four."

5. The Antrim family moved to Santa Fe when Billy was "four or five years of age."[2]

6. In Santa Fe between the ages of five and eight the Kid "became adept at cards."[3]

7. Billy's mother's name was Kathleen. [Upson claimed to have lived in Mrs. Antrim's boardinghouse in Silver City and to have learned all of the facts of the Kid's early years from her. This is curious since he did not even know her name was actually Catherine.]

8. Billy was "a fair scholar" and "wrote a fair letter."[4]

9. Billy had a "fearful" temper and became "dangerous."[5]

10. Billy's "misfortune was, he could not and would not stay whipped."[6]

11. In Silver City Billy was the "constant companion of Jesse Evans."[7]

12. Billy killed his first man, stabbing him to death, because the man had insulted his mother.

13. Billy stole his first horse fleeing to Arizona.

14. Billy and a companion named Alias killed three Apaches near Fort Bowie in order to steal their horses and furs.

15. Billy and Alias successfully cheated Indians out of money at a horse race.

16. Billy killed a civilian blacksmith at Fort Bowie. [It was at Camp Grant, not—as it was then known—Camp Bowie.]

17. Billy fled to Sonora, Mexico and, while there, formed a coalition with Melquiades Segura.

18. In Sonora, the Kid shot Don José Martínez, a monte dealer who hated "gringos."

19. The Kid and Segura held up and killed a crooked monte dealer in Chihuahua and robbed three other monte dealers before fleeing.

20. In the year 1876 Billy again met up with Jesse Evans and together they committed "a hundred deeds of daring crime."[8]

21. The Kid's eyes were "deep blue, dotted with spots of hazel hue" and "one could scarcely believe that those blazing, baleful orbs and that laughing face could be controlled by the same spirit."[9]

22. Joined by Jesse Evans, the Kid, with a "pistol in one hand and a small Spanish dagger in the other," saved a wagon train of emigrants, killing eight Apaches. [Upson obviously used this image early in the Kid's career to foreshadow the image he would present of him the night he died.][10]

23. Instead of joining at once a gang with Jesse Evans which included William Morton and Frank Baker, the Kid wanted to wait to meet up with Segura. Jim McDaniels in this gang dubbed him "the Kid."

24. The Kid made a ride of eighty-one miles in "a little more than six hours" on the same gray horse in order to get Segura out of jail at San Elizario, Texas.[11]

25. The Kid drank whiskey, often to excess.

26. In another bit of foreshadowing, Segura's jailer, when the Kid knocked on the jail door, asked: "*¿Quién es?*"

27. Upson had probably heard of the incident with O'Keefe and the Mescalero raid from the Jones family with whom he was on close terms. In his version, the Kid, chased by twenty Indians, scaled a sheer cliff. Six braves climbed up after him. Billy paused midway to shoot one. He climbed further and killed another.

28. After scaling over the mountain top and escaping, the Kid went back to Las Cruces to retrieve his favorite gray horse and, while there, tried to talk O'Keefe, whom he met again, into joining him in the Lincoln County War about which he had just heard.

29. The Lincoln County War was fought between the small ranchers, united behind Murphy and Dolan, and John S. Chisum, "The Cattle King of New Mexico," and his allies, A. A. McSween and John H. Tunstall.

30. The small ranchers claimed "that at each round-up Chisum's vast herd carried with them hundreds of head of cattle belonging to others."[12]

31. The Kid, because of his "reckless daring, unerring markmanship [*sic*], and unrivalled horsemanship," was enlisted by Morton and Baker into the Murphy/Dolan cause.[13]

32. After thus spending the summer and a portion of the fall of 1877, the Kid became bored and switched sides, going to work for Tunstall.

33. The Kid, after telling the Murphy/Dolan side of his decision, rode off, "casting one long regretful glance at Jesse, with whom he was loth to part."[14]

34. William S. Morton "said to have had authority as deputy sheriff" set out with a posse "to attach some horses which Tunstall and McSween claimed." Tunstall's men all "ran away" and "Morton afterwards claimed that Tunstall fired on him and his posse." Tom Hill is said to have shot Tunstall in the back of the head with a rifle.[15]

35. The Kid first heard about Tunstall's murder from others and swore vengeance.

36. McNab killed McClosky [McCloskey].

37. The Kid alone shot the fleeing Morton and Baker, using only one bullet on each.

38. The Kid led Bruer's [Brewer's] posse to round up a man named Roberts and the Kid shot Roberts through the body. [In addition to Bowdre's letter to Captain Joseph C. Lea, Roberts on his deathbed told Dr. J. H. Blazer's son that it was Bowdre who shot him.]

39. Sheriff Brady was "an excellent citizen and a brave and honest man . . . a good officer, too, and endeavored to do his duty with impartiality." The Kid and the others ambushed Brady and Hindman by hiding behind an adobe wall. After the shooting, the Kid and his party "retired to the house of McSween." [It was a wooden gate, not an adobe wall. Note also the similarity between this fantasy and Trujillo Fantasy No. 3 below. This was obviously the source for the later fantasy.][16]

40. After Brady, Lincoln had no sheriff until Peppin was appointed.

41. The Kid agreed with Jesse Evans's claim that Evans had not been in the posse that killed Tunstall.

42. During the siege of McSween's house, the Kid refused to make terms. The fight lasted only three days. Marion Turner directed the sheriff's forces. The Kid shot Robert Beckwith.

43. The Kid killed Bernstein [the agency clerk] with a single bullet from his Winchester.

44. Dolan was innocent of killing Chapman and was "triumphantly acquitted."[17]

45. The Kid became the mastermind directing a far-flung, intricate cattle-rustling syndicate.

46. The Kid tampered with Joe Grant's revolver so it would not fire before he shot him.

47. The Kid, drinking heavily one time at Verando, fired at snowbirds until he killed several, claiming John Chisum was really his target.[18]

48. The Kid tried to assassinate Jim Redmond [Deputy Sheriff Jim Redman] on 23 November 1880 as part of a birthday celebration.

49. William Hudgens, not James Carlyle, led the posse that laid siege to the Greathouse trading post. The Kid shot Carlyle in the back. [It is interesting to note that Upson claimed that J. W. Bell was in this posse.]

50. Frank Stewart and his party were "on the trail of the Kid and his band; that he [Stewart] wanted to recover some stock stolen by them, but would much rather have the thieves."[19]

51. The Kid suspected the Garrett ambuscade at Fort Sumner and, accordingly, told Garrett subsequently with an eye that "twinkled mischievously" that he had contrived for O'Folliard to ride point so as to be the first to fall if the posse started shooting.

52. The Kid shoved the wounded Bowdre out of the rock house at Stinking Springs, telling him: "They have murdered you, Charley, but you can get revenge. Kill some of the sons-of--before you die."[20]

53. Bowdre had supposedly said after meeting Garrett outside Fort Sumner to discuss Captain Lea's offer that if he saw Garrett again he would just kill him and end all this trouble. Hearing this, Garrett felt better about killing Bowdre.

54. The Kid made Stewart a present of his mare while in irons at Fort Sumner.

55. Mention of Bob Olinger's name is omitted among the Kid's guards on the train to Santa Fe.

56. Garrett claimed, falsely, that he was a deputy U.S. marshal at this time. [Azariah F. Wild's report of 2 January 1881 at the National Archives in Washington, D.C., mentions that U.S. Marshal John Sherman, Jr., had mistakenly dispatched two deputy commissions for John Hurley and none for Garrett; Wild corrected the error by changing the name on one of Hurley's commissions to Garrett. By the time this report was filed, the Kid was already in jail at Santa Fe.]

57. Billie Wilson was in jeopardy for complicity in the murder of Carlyle. [Neither Wilson nor the Kid was ever indicted by the Lincoln County grand jury for this crime; the

only new indictment brought against the Kid came from San Miguel County for cattle stealing. The members of the White Oaks posse chose silence rather than to risk exposure.]

58. Again the names of guards are omitted on the Kid's trip from Mesilla to Lincoln, only Woods and Bob Olinger being mentioned.

59. The Kid, while in jail in Lincoln, did not deny killing Carlyle when charged with it by Garrett, but instead claimed there were extenuating circumstances.

60. "Bell was in no manner connected with the Lincoln County War, and had no animosity or grudge against the Kid. The natural abhorrence of an honest man towards a well-known violator of the law was intensified in Bell's case, by the murder of Carlyle, who was a friend of his; but never by word or action, did he betray his prejudice if it existed."[21] [It is my personal suspicion that Bell may have been one of those in the White Oaks posse who fired at Carlyle, mistaking him for the Kid, and, hence, Garrett's willingness to blame the Kid and protect Bell's memory.]

61. It is claimed that the Kid, after a trip outside, bounded up the stairs in his chains, broke into the armory, got a revolver, and fired at Bell, all this before Bell, who was following him, could draw and fire his own revolver.

62. Upon seeing Bob Olinger, the Kid said, " 'Hello, old boy.' " Olinger said, " 'Yes, and he's killed me, too.' "[22]

63. Old man Geiss [Gauss] brought the Kid a file to file through his leg irons.

64. The horse the Kid mounted broke away. The Kid sent another prisoner, named Andrew Nimley, after it. When Nimley brought back the horse, the Kid told him: " 'Old fellow, if you hadn't gone for this horse, I would have killed you.' "[23]

65. The town was not so much sympathetic with the Kid as terror-stricken.

66. Garrett did not learn of the escape until 29 April because he was out collecting taxes.

67. After his escape, the Kid stole a horse from Andy Richardson and another from Montgomery Bell.

68. The Kid had no "known ties to bind him to that dangerous locality" [Fort Sumner].[24]

69. Garrett, using intuition, asked Poe and McKinney to accompany him to Fort Sumner to engage in a stakeout.

70. Garrett, although he did not recognize him, saw the Kid at Pete Maxwell's before he entered Maxwell's bedroom.

71. "From his step I could perceive he was either barefooted or in his stocking-feet, and held a revolver in his right hand and a butcher knife in his left."[25]

72. "His right hand almost touching my knee, . . . the Kid must have seen, or felt, the presence of a third person. . . . He raised quickly his pistol, a self-cocker, within a foot of my breast."[26]

73. "I told them [Poe and McKinney] I had made no blunder, that I knew the Kid's voice too well to be mistaken." [Yet, in this account, it was Pete Maxwell who said to Garrett: " 'That's him!' " before Garrett fired.][27]

74. "I told them [Poe and McKinney] that he [the Kid] had fired one shot, between my two." [Garrett did conclude, however, that this might not have been true because no bullet could be found.][28]

75. "His exact age on the day of his death, was 21 years, 7 months, and 21 days."[29]

Garrett's book may not have sold well, but many of those who subsequently wrote accounts about the Kid followed it in most of its details. Foremost of these was Charlie Siringo who first told the Kid's story in his book A TEXAS COWBOY (1885) which, Siringo claimed, sold a million copies in his lifetime. "It was 'in print' for forty years," Dykes wrote in his Introduction to the reissue of the Garrett/Upson book, "and was reissued in 1950 with an excellent Introduction by J. Frank Dobie and with illustrations by Tom Lea [this very edition is still in print from the University of Nebraska Press]. Siringo's version of the Lincoln County War and the career of the Kid was Garrett's version, and Siringo's book achieved the wide distribution that Garrett's book deserved and probably would have had with a different publisher. Through Siringo the Garrett version became the best known and most quoted of all those published to date."[30]

Of the editions of the Garrett/Upson account which appeared prior to the current University of Oklahoma Press edition, perhaps the most notable is that edited by Maurice Garland Fulton and published by Macmillan in 1927. Fulton did include many helpful footnotes correcting a few of the errors in the book—he had only begun his own exhaustive research into the subject of the Lincoln County War—but he also tinkered here and there with the style and cut out certain passages. The Garrett/Upson account in his edition is not reliable history, nor is it the full account as Upson wrote it. What does make it of value are several rare photographs of the various physical *loca* where events occurred and the mention of certain odd bits of information which Fulton had gathered. For example, he was the first to note that "Roberts himself in a dying statement asserted that Bowdre had fired the shot that struck him."[31] He also corrected Upson's statement that the Kid was acquitted for the murder of Roberts. He was not. This case was set aside because of Judge Leonard's motion to do so, prompted by the fact that the shooting had not occurred on federal land and was therefore not a federal case. Most importantly, Fulton included photographs of the site of the rock house at Stinking Springs, both in a medium shot and in a long shot, a point to which I shall return below when I come to discuss Leon C. Metz's book on Garrett.

Had the Garrett/Upson book not been written, it is probable that the entire legend about Billy the Kid, if indeed one were even to have come into being, would have been different. For one thing, the Garrett/Upson book established the image of Garrett as a capable lawman discharging his duty and acting always from the best motives and in the best interests of the community. Garrett, in short, is the hero; and, if you have a hero, you must have a villain. But not just any villain would do. Consistently throughout Upson made elaborate claims for the Kid, did all he could, in fact, to make him a glamorous and romantic desperado. It was this image, when it began to appear and be perpetuated elsewhere, that became a part of American folklore. In a very real sense, Garrett's existence seemed to stop the moment he killed the Kid. He was remembered for nothing else.

Siringo not only repeated the Garrett/Upson version in A TEXAS COWBOY, albeit with a few of his own emendations, but he repeated it periodically in other books he wrote subsequently, such as A HISTORY OF "BILLY THE KID" (Santa Fe, 1920) and RIATA AND SPURS (Houghton Mifflin, 1927). THE TRUE LIFE OF BILLY THE KID (1881) by Don Jenardo [pseudonym for John Woodruff Lewis], #451 in the "Wide Awake Library," contains the first fanciful reference to Mrs. McSween's playing the piano while the McSween home burned during the five-day battle. "Mrs. McSwain [McSween]," Jenardo wrote, "opened the piano, and as coolly as though she was entertaining an evening party, seated herself before it. Her jeweled fingers ran over the keys and sent forth soul-stirring notes. High above the roar of battle, crash of bullets and cries of combatants, rose the sweet clear voice, in soul-stirring songs. The sound of that beautiful voice and sweet-toned piano, in such cheering strains seemed to make demons of the outlaws."[32] Such an image was too attractive for Siringo to ignore entirely. "There was a fine piano in the parlor," he wrote in A TEXAS COWBOY, "the property of Mrs. McSween, who was absent, and on this the 'Kid' played during the whole time, 'just to amuse the crowd outside,' he said."[33] This, too, Siringo repeated in his later accounts of the Kid. Siringo concluded his chapter on the Kid's life in A TEXAS COWBOY with a sentimental reference to the Kid's burial and to "a pretty young half-breed Mexican damsel, whose tears, no doubt, has [sic] dampened the lonely grave more than once."[34] He did not identify her by name. In A HISTORY OF "BILLY THE KID" he told of how "on one of his trips to Fort Sumner, Billy the Kid fell desperately in love with a pretty little seventeen-year-old half-breed girl, whom we will call Miss Dulcinea del Toboso. She was a daughter of a once famous man, and sister to a man who once owned sheep on a thousand hills."[35] By the time he wrote RIATA AND SPURS, he apparently felt no further need for subterfuge and called her by her name, Paulita Maxwell.

In A HISTORY OF "BILLY THE KID" Siringo introduced an anti-Semitic element into the killing of Bernstein which later writers, such as Walter Noble Burns, were quick to incorporate. "The Kid drew his rifle," Siringo wrote, "and shot the poor Jew dead. This was the Kid's most cowardly act. His excuse was that he 'didn't like a Jew, nohow.' "[36] In repeating the Kid's life in A LONE STAR COWBOY (Santa Fe, 1919), Siringo had the Kid alone when he shot Carlyle in the back, but in A HISTORY OF "BILLY THE KID" he reverted to the Garrett/Upson version. And in RIATA AND SPURS he had the Kid all alone when he shot Sheriff Brady and neglected any mention whatsoever of the killing of Deputy Sheriff Hindman. In all of his accounts he also differed with the Garrett/Upson account in describing the Kid's break from the Lincoln jail, claiming that the Kid hit Bell over the head with one of his handcuffs and, thereby, got hold of his gun with which he shot him. Robert M. Utley would later incorporate this fantasy into his BILLY THE KID: A SHORT AND VIOLENT LIFE (University of Nebraska Press, 1991). Fantasies seem to be always more attractive than an admission that in many cases there simply are not documents to explain what may have happened.

One characteristic that is especially noteworthy in both the Garrett/Upson account and in Siringo's many repetitions is the ambivalent image they present of the Kid, thus engendering at the very beginning a potential for two separate legends about Billy the Kid—a factor which will be probed at greater length in the chapter on the Kid's legend. The Garrett/Upson account stresses that the Kid was "the peer of any fabled brigand on record, unequalled in desperate courage, presence of mind in danger, devotion to his allies, generosity to his foes, gallantry, and all the elements which appeal to the holier emotions."[37] In A TEXAS COWBOY Siringo took pains to point out that "the 'Kid' was not the cruel hearted wretch that he was pictured out to be in the scores of yellow-back novels, written about him. He was an outlaw and maybe a very wicked youth, but then he had some good qualities which, now that he is no more, he should be credited with. It has been said and written that he would just as soon shoot an innocent child as a mule-eared rabbit. Now this is all wrong, for he was noted as being kind to the weak and helpless."[38] To illustrate what he was saying Siringo included an anecdote about how the Kid, "who had just come into town from one of his raids," found a sick man "who had been placed in an old outhouse on a pile of sheep skins. The 'Kid' hired a team and hauled him to Las Vegas, a distance of over a hundred miles, himself, where he could receive care and medical aid. He also paid the doctor and board bills for a month, besides putting a few dollars in money in the sick man's hand as he bid him good bye."[39] Inspired by this apocryphal tale, Eugene Manlove Rhodes subsequently fashioned his own fiction based on the Kid's life in which Pat Garrett by name was a character, PASÓ POR AQUÍ (Houghton Mifflin, 1927).

I think Siringo can be relied upon for one incident only in all of his books and that is the account he gave in A TEXAS COWBOY of how Garrett and Frank Stewart lied to the Texans in order to persuade them to join in the hunt for the Kid. James East's version I take to be closest the truth, i.e., that the Texans were in New Mexico to retrieve missing stock and not to hunt Billy the Kid. This view, in fact, is even supported indirectly by Siringo insofar as Garrett had to lie and say that the Kid was driving a herd of stolen Texas cattle to get Stewart's posse to participate in the manhunt. This is also the only incident with regard to the Kid of which Siringo had firsthand knowledge. Perhaps because Siringo did not believe Garrett, Garrett chose to leave him behind during the pursuit to Stinking Springs. It must have been a lifelong regret of Siringo's that he did not accompany the Garrett posse.

John W. Poe's account was first provided in written form to E. A. Brininstool to accompany an article Brininstool wrote for WIDE WORLD MAGAZINE, published in London, England, November and December, 1919. Brininstool later wrote a short preface to Poe's account and had it published privately in Los Angeles in 1922. It was finally issued posthumously in book form in 1933 by Houghton Mifflin with an Introduction by Maurice Garland Fulton, photo illustrations, and copies in both Spanish and English of the "new" death certificate which Garrett had drawn up to assist him in his claim to Governor Wallace's reward. Poe had not laid eyes on the Kid prior to the night the Kid died. His account of the pursuit to Fort Sumner and the Kid's death in Pete Maxwell's bedroom, as noted above in the chapter on the Kid's life, follows the Garrett/Upson version and, by design, excludes mention of Pete Maxwell as the source of information as to the Kid's whereabouts and Pete's motivation. What alone can perhaps be relied upon is the more significant confusion as to whom Garrett shot that night, and Garrett's own doubts. Even in the Garrett/Upson version, Pete Maxwell is quoted as having said "That's him!" before Garrett pulled the trigger. Such a statement is hardly consistent with Garrett's subsequent confidence: "I told them I had made no blunder, that I knew the Kid's voice too well to be mistaken." It is also to Poe that is owed the real explanation of why Garrett was not in Lincoln when the Kid escaped. He was not collecting taxes but meeting with Poe in White Oaks where Poe was to give his report on rustling activities.

BUCKBOARD DAYS (Caxton Printers, 1936) by Sophie A. Poe edited by Eugene Cunningham was reissued by the University of New Mexico Press in 1981 with a new Introduction by Sandra L. Myres. It is a vivid and interesting record of a woman's impressions of New Mexico during its later Territorial days, but the account of the Kid which she wrote basically follows that of her husband and the Garrett/Upson version. She is most to be trusted, in fact, only after her meeting for the first time with John William Poe and, of course, this was after the Kid was already dead.

Interest among the general public was running high with regard to the Kid after Walter Noble Burns's "saga" became a best-seller in 1926 and it is this which explains the reason that Garrett's "biography" was reissued as was Poe's account, Sophie Poe's memoirs of the Kid's death, and George W. Coe's autobiography which was published under the title FRONTIER FIGHTER (Houghton Mifflin, 1934) "as related to and with an Introduction by Nan Hillary Harrison." I recall when Hollywood stunt man Yakima Canutt was at work on his autobiography, published as STUNT MAN (Walker, 1979), I lived only a short distance away from his home. I dropped in on him one day and was surprised to see him reading a book on the making of GONE WITH THE WIND (M-G-M, 1939). He told me that the publisher wanted him to stress his work on this picture and, since he did not remember much of what had occurred, he was "reading up" on it so he could write about the picture. It must have been a similar situation for George Coe since he was most reliable when recounting incidents such as his trigger finger being shot off by the bullet fired by Buckshot Roberts which first grazed Charlie Bowdre's gunbelt, but when he sought to write about the events of the Kid's life he found himself having to rely on the Garrett/Upson account and Burns's "saga."

Frequently, in writing history, a historian is forced to depend on oral accounts since much of what occurred has not been otherwise recorded. For a long time it was thought that what a person might write down is somehow more trustworthy than what he or she might say. This attitude, fortunately, has begun to disappear and, accordingly, Eve Ball's historical construction, based upon firsthand testimony, in MA'AM JONES OF THE PECOS (University of Arizona Press, 1969) has acquired a reputation for accuracy which it justly deserves. Her book is dedicated to Maurice Garland Fulton and Robert N. Mullin and all that she was told was taken in balance against the documents and weighed against other accounts, including those of Fulton and Mullin. Of particular value are the portraits her book contains of the Kid and his relationship to the Jones family and, in view of the influence he exerted on the growth of the Billy the Kid legend, that of Ash Upson.

MY GIRLHOOD AMONG OUTLAWS (University of Arizona Press, 1972) by Lily Klasner, edited and with an Introduction by Eve Ball, is generally unreliable in the comments made with regard to the Kid—they were based primarily on rumor and hearsay—but her physical descriptions of him are noteworthy and the course of his life would have been entirely different, it may be presumed, had Lily's mother accepted the Kid's proposal that he accompany them on their journey from New Mexico to Texas. Even more important historically is her portrait of John Chisum, whom she did know well, and it is the best firsthand account we are likely to have of him.

LEW WALLACE: AN AUTOBIOGRAPHY (Harper's, 1906) was published in two volumes. There is one letter in which Wallace's wife makes a reference to the Kid, but other than that the former governor of New Mexico was conspicuously mute about the events of the Lincoln County War and the role he played. Probably he felt the less said the better, since, in a real sense, his role was a minor one. His brief mention is confined to an observation that "a rich stock raiser from Texas came up to New Mexico, and in a short time had three hundred thousand dollars worth of cattle. He settled on the Pecos River, and in a little while succeeded in driving away almost all the grazers. To retaliate, they began stealing from him. Now, they do not steal in that country as they do farther East, but drive off large herds of cattle, sometimes 500 at a time. To protect himself, the Texan went down into his native state and recruited about 70 men—murderers, thieves, and dangerous men of all classes, together with a number of sharp-shooters and buffalo-hunters."[40] Wallace had a good deal more to say in his various newspaper interviews and in his correspondence and it is on these that the historian must rely.

I believe that Henry F. Hoyt's testimony in his book A FRONTIER DOCTOR (Houghton Mifflin, 1929) is generally to be trusted, including the appearance of Jesse James in New Mexico since he himself demonstrated the authenticity of this last point in what I feel to be a convincing manner.[41] Where he cannot be followed—because of the weight of contrary evidence—is in his assertion that the Kid rejected Governor Wallace's pardon.

The typescript of the memoir WATER IN A THIRSTY LAND (1955) by Ruth R. Ealy is on deposit at the Wisconsin State Historical Society and is even more valuable since Dr. Ealy was on the scene during many of the most controversial events of the Lincoln County War, including the assassinations of Brady and Hindman and the five-day battle, and this record by his daughter sheds decisive light on the attempt of Dolan and Brady to cover up the mutilation of the body of John H. Tunstall. Ealy's own autobiographical writings have been combined to comprise MISSIONARIES, OUTLAWS, AND INDIANS: TAYLOR F. EALY AT LINCOLN AND ZUNI, 1878–1881 (University of New Mexico Press, 1984) edited and annotated by Norman J. Bender and is another valuable resource.

Emerson Hough was probably the most influential of the authors who sought to carry forth the legend of Billy the Kid into the early years of the 20th Century. On 21 July 1881 the *Santa Fe Weekly Democrat* noted that "Billy Bonny [Bonney], alias Antrim, alias Billy the Kid, the twenty-one year old desperado, who is known to have killed sixteen men, and who boasted that he killed a man for every year of his life, will no longer take deliberate aim at his fellow man and kill him, just to keep in practice." The Garrett/Upson account stuck with the figure of sixteen men, as did Siringo. By the time Hough came to write his first account of the Kid, in

THE STORY OF THE COWBOY (1897), the number had changed. "The whole region was full of horse thieves and outlaws," Hough wrote, "the worst of these being under the leadership of the notorious cut-throat, Billy the Kid, a name famous even yet along the border. Billy the Kid died at the ripe age of twenty-three, and at that time had killed twenty-three men, committing his first murder when he was but fourteen years of age. He and his men inaugurated a reign of terror, which made his name a dread one from one end of the country to the other."[42] In part Hough accounted for this expanded number of dead by telling of how the Kid once shot seven Mexicans at a water hole "just to see them kick."[43]

Hough had graduated from law school at the University of Iowa and set up practice in White Oaks in 1883 and perhaps he was recalling in this book some of the gossip he had overheard. There is no internal evidence that he was as yet familiar with the Garrett/Upson account. Chisum's name is spelled Chisholm. His version of the Kid's death is that the Kid was on his way to say goodbye to his girlfriend at Fort Sumner. Holding his boots in one hand, he entered a darkened bedroom in which Garrett was concealed behind a bed while holding down the rancher who was sleeping in the bed. Garrett shot the Kid.

Following up this account in "Billy the Kid, the True Story of a Western 'Bad Man,' " in EVERYBODY'S MAGAZINE in September, 1901, Hough told his readers that the Kid's grave was located at Las Cruces and that he had killed twenty-one men by the time he died in his twenty-first year. The Kid escaped from his Lincoln confinement by slipping off a handcuff while Bell was leaning out a window. He hit Bell over the head, shot him with his own gun which he snatched, and then finished off Orrendorf [Olinger] with a shotgun. Obviously, by this time Hough had read Siringo's account since that was the first time this fantasy appeared.

By the time Hough came to write THE STORY OF THE OUTLAW—A STUDY OF THE WESTERN DESPERADO (Outing, 1907), he had talked personally to Pat Garrett and had read the Garrett/Upson account. Therefore, his details about the Kid's life were changed to agree with Garrett/Upson. However, this did not prevent Hough from indulging in romantic flourishes. "On the trail from Roswell to Lincoln, at a point near Agua Negra," he wrote concerning the deaths of Morton and Baker, "both these men, while kneeling and pleading for their lives, were deliberately shot and killed by Billy the Kid."[44] He also claimed that Garrett went with him to Fort Sumner and there, in the former military cemetery, showed him where the Kid was buried. Picking up his canteen, Garrett offered a symbolic toast to O'Folliard, Bowdre, and the Kid. " 'Here's to the boys,' " Hough quoted Garrett. " 'If there is any other life, I hope they make better use of it than the one I put them out of.' "[45] Ramon F. Adams probably said it best. "After studying all his books on the West," he wrote in SIX-GUNS AND SADDLE LEATHER, "I have found Mr. Hough careless and unreliable as an historian."[46]

For the generation following the Kid's death, the Garrett/Upson account was more or less accepted as definitive. Walter Noble Burns's THE SAGA OF BILLY THE KID (Doubleday, 1926) did not substantially change many of the Garrett/Upson fantasies. What it did do was place them in a wider context, namely that of the

Lincoln County War, and hence the Kid was treated as a participant in events which came to overshadow and even consume him. And this book, unlike the Garrett/Upson account, became a best-seller.

This is not to say that Burns did not contribute his own fantasies to the growing legend, because he surely did. Indeed, his book is rightly classed as fiction by librarians and not as biography or history—although, when it appeared, it purported to be biography and, therefore, is best considered among biographies of the Kid. Burns made up some interesting variations on the Garrett/Upson fantasies. I would like to note a few of the more prominent of these since, henceforth, it is possible to determine whether an author was dependent on Garrett/Upson or Burns, based on which version is used.

Burns Fantasies

1. The Kid had "a baby brother named Edward" at Coffeyville, Kansas in 1862. [Joseph McCarty, after his meeting with Garrett in the lobby of the Armijo Hotel in Trinidad, spoke very rarely about his connection with the Kid and, indeed, would seem to have been ashamed of it. He died of apoplexy at the Murphy House, a gambling hall at 1617 Latimer Street in Denver, Colorado, on 25 November 1930. Because his antecedents were unknown, his body was turned over to the Colorado Medical School for dissection.]

2. William H. Bonney, Sr., died at Coffeyville.

3. The Kid moved to Silver City, New Mexico, in 1868. [Actually Silver City did not then exist, only a small grouping of adobe buildings known as Cienega de San Vicente. The city was founded after the turn of the decade when silver was discovered.]

4. Tunstall rode toward Lincoln accompanied by only Dick Brewer and the Kid.

5. Although six men were said to be hiding behind an adobe wall waiting to ambush Brady and Hindman, the Kid is the only one who shot at and killed Brady.

6. Hindman, before he died, was able to stumble and fall in front of the San Juan church.

7. Morton and Baker held out under siege for two days and the five-day battle, as in Garrett/Upson, lasted only three days.

8. While her house burned, Mrs. McSween played "The Star-Spangled Banner." "Facing death, the men felt the life and thrill of the old battle hymn. . . . The Kid whistled the tune. Tom O'Folliard beat time with his six-shooter."[47] [Burns also claimed that Mrs. McSween had the piano transported overland from St. Louis, whereas her husband bought it from Emil Fritz's estate.]

9. Andrew J. Roberts's name is given as "Buckshot Bill" Roberts and George Washington is viewed by Burns as a roving Negro minstrel, always singing and making music.

10. The Kid killed twenty-one men and would go to his grave peacefully and fulfilled if he could only yet kill Barney Mason and Pat Garrett. [On the basis of this fantasy, that "Pat Garrett must make twenty-two," a popular ballad was written and recorded, to help promote the book, particulars of which are discussed in Appendix A.]

11. The Celsa Gutiérrez/Billy the Kid romance emerges full-blown when for the first time Celsa Gutiérrez is identified as Billy the Kid's lover at Fort Sumner and, most interestingly of all, by none other than Paulita Maxwell Jaramillo: " 'Pat Garrett ought to have known who she was because he was connected with her, and not very distantly, by marriage.' "[48] [Henceforth, until Metz in his biography of Garrett would suggest the true situation, Celsa Gutiérrez, who was dead at the time Burns published his book and so could

not respond, was the name most often linked with the Kid's. Burns is not to be held totally responsible for this fabrication since in a letter to Judge William H. Burges of El Paso dated at Chicago on 3 June 1926 Burns noted that in the first version of his book he had identified Paulita Jaramillo as the Kid's *querida* at Fort Sumner but Doubleday's lawyers had insisted that he rewrite it because they feared a lawsuit for libel. It was as a consequence of this insistence by Doubleday that he substituted the deceased Celsa Gutiérrez' name for Paulita Jaramillo's. It is one of the curiosities with which Burns's fantasies continue to be held that Robert M. Utley, knowing full well the contents of this letter, should have identified *both* Paulita Jaramillo and Celsa Gutiérrez as among the Kid's *queridas*, ignoring entirely the stated reason that the one name was substituted for the other.]

12. Pat Garrett and Billy the Kid were the best of friends. Again, the words are attributed to Paulita Maxwell Jaramillo: " 'Pat Garrett was as close a friend as Billy the Kid had in Fort Sumner and was on friendly terms with every member of the Kid's gang. . . . Oh, yes, Garrett and the Kid were as thick as two peas in a pod.' "[49]

13. Garrett was out of town when the Kid escaped and was at White Oaks buying lumber for the Kid's gallows.

14. The Kid managed to draw Bell's revolver during a game of monte when Bell was distracted and used this pistol to kill Bell. Burns not only narrates the incident this way but offers as corroboration an unidentified Mexican who claimed: " '*Cogió la pistola de Bell mientras jugaban a monte y tiró una bala dejándole muerto.*' "[50] [Since John Poe does not record this statement as having been made during his meeting with Garrett in White Oaks, which is where Burns sets it, it is doubtless spurious.]

15. The Kid's last words were: "'*¿Quiénes son esos* [sic] *hombres afuera*, Pete?' "[51] [Had this been the case, using "*esos*" instead of "*estos*" would indicate that somehow Poe and McKinney were supposed to be standing nearer to Maxwell, who was in bed inside the room, than to the Kid who was standing in the doorway. Frazier Hunt in THE TRAGIC DAYS OF BILLY THE KID (Hastings House, 1956) rendered it thus: " '*¿Quien (sic) son estos hombres afuera, Pedro?*' "[52] Frederick Nolan in THE LINCOLN COUNTY WAR: A DOCUMENTARY HISTORY tried to clean up the Kid's ungrammatical Spanish and so had him asking " '*¿Pedro, quien (sic) sonos (sic) estos hombres afuera?*' "[53] These are almost as ridiculous. Based on the testimony of many Mexicans who knew and conversed with *el chivato*, as well as Anglo-Americans, the Kid spoke Spanish fluently and, I am sure, knew how to conjugate the verb *ser* as well as to have the relative pronoun agree in number with the plural direct object: "*¿Pedro, quiénes son estos hombres afuera?*" Poe, in his account, quotes the Kid as having said: " 'Pete, who are those fellows on the outside?' "[54] The Garrett/Upson account renders the Kid's almost last words: " 'Who are they, Pete?' "[55] Since no one has rendered the words in Spanish correctly from Burns through Nolan, I think it is safe to assume that what we have here is an attempt to seem authentic by a variety of authors who did not know even basic Spanish. Since Poe and Garrett have stated that the Kid spoke this sentence in English and no one ever stated he spoke it in Spanish prior to Burns, I think it safe to conclude, as I have in my construction of the Kid's last moments, the sentence was most probably rendered in English. It would also be logical, were it so, since the Kid had first addressed Poe and McKinney in Spanish (about which Poe and Garrett/Upson agree): "*¿Quién es?*" Receiving no answer, why wouldn't the Kid then try English, especially in addressing Maxwell?]

16. The Garrett/Upson account, and most after it, desisted from taking sides in the Lincoln County War. Burns did not. "Viewed impartially," he declared, "it is now clear that Murphy's cause was basically wrong and McSween's basically right; that Murphy was an

unscrupulous dictator, McSween the champion of a principle; that Murphy stood for lawlessness, McSween for law."[56] [By making Murphy the master villain, Burns was creating only one fiction among many. There is not a single episode from the Lincoln County War or from the Kid's life which he narrated accurately. What sympathy there may be for the Kid is derived from his being allied with the McSween cause. After McSween is killed, and Murphy dies, the Kid then takes over the role of the master villain and Pat Garrett is introduced as a hero. Thus what we have are two consecutive cycles of the forces of good battling against the forces of evil.]

17. As Burns conceived of the Kid, he was *primum mobile* of a cattle-rustling syndicate more ambitious than Ash Upson ever imagined and "his operations covered half of New Mexico."[57] The Kid, according to Burns, was "a Sir Henry Morgan of the purple sage, his flagship a bronco pony, the cattle ranges his Spanish Main."[58]

18. Burns expanded Siringo's charge about the Kid's anti-Semitism and, again, the Kid's only comment after he shoots down Bernstein is: " 'He was only a Jew anyway.' "[59]

19. Burns's Garrett says about the Kid that " 'he don't care no more about killin' a man than eatin' his breakfast. He's about as murderous a little hombre as ever stood in shoe leather.' "[60]

20. Garrett is quite definitely the hero of Burns's account. "New Mexico owes much to Garrett," Burns insisted. "He brought law and order west of the Pecos. He stabilized the land, made it safe to live in and build homes in, cleared the way for statehood. He was the last great sheriff of the old frontier, constructive through destruction, establishing peace on a foundation of graves, the leaping flame from the muzzle of his six-shooter the beacon of prosperity."[61]

21. In Burns's saga, Garrett himself goes to President Cleveland to get Billie Wilson's pardon. " 'I've done my part,' " Garrett tells Wilson, after giving him the pardon. " 'Now you do yours. Live straight. Make good. That'll be all the thanks I want.' "[62]

22. Burns claimed for Garrett that "he killed only three men in his life—Tom O'Folliard, Charlie Bowdre, and Billy the Kid—and in each instance the killing was justified by the circumstances."[63] [Given this posture, it is curious indeed that Eugene Manlove Rhodes in his essay "In Defense of Pat Garrett" in SUNSET MAGAZINE in July, 1927 should have attacked Burns's book for its damning portrait of Garrett, especially when Rhodes, in his defense, got the facts as confused as Burns had.]

23. Burns evoked the image of Fate as the ruling force in human lives, but it is more what the Greeks meant by Moira than the Romans did by Fortuna. "On this night of nights," Burns wrote of the Kid's walking to his death, "Fate, it might seem, was setting the stage."[64]

24. For Burns, in hiring Garrett to kill the Kid, "John Chisum had the future of New Mexico at heart."[65] Chisum was, according to Burns, "a labourer laying in the sweat of his brow the foundation stones on which arose civilization and law and order."[66]

Another of the curiosities about Burns's book is the firsthand conversations he supposedly had with some of the principals in his story. Most, if not all but two, of these were doubtlessly made up in his imagination. The whole last chapter is given over to a lengthy conversation with Pat Garrett which (given that Garrett was for everyone who knew him a man of few words and was dead by 1908) could scarcely have taken place. Others are made to say things about the Lincoln County War which it would have been out of character for them to have said, insofar as other interviews with them provide totally contradictory testimony and the only purpose served by what Burns quoted them as having said being to substantiate Burns's fantasies. For example, Burns quoted Sallie Chisum as remarking that " 'we never thought Billy stole any of our cattle, and it would be difficult to make me believe that he did. He had been a good friend of ours for several years, and, once a friend, it was hard to change him.' "[67]

The most intriguing of these quoted conversations—and, in retrospect, one of the two I suspect was genuine—was Burns's interview with Paulita Jaramillo. She denied that she was the one with whom the Kid was in love —for a number of obvious reasons, not the least being that the image of the Kid, even in Burns's account, was not such as to reflect well on her or her family. The truth she put in the subjunctive mood, remarking, " 'if I had loved the Kid and he had loved me, I will say that I would never have hesitated to marry him and follow him through danger, poverty, or hardship to the ends of the earth in spite of anything he had ever done or what the world might have been pleased to think of me.' "[68] I also do not believe she ever learned the role her brother played in the Kid's death.

The photograph which Billy posed for at Fort Sumner in 1879, she reputedly told Burns, was in possession of the Maxwell family for many years until it was given to John Legg, a Fort Sumner saloon keeper and friend of the family. " 'I never liked the picture,' " she is quoted. " 'I don't think it does Billy justice. It makes him look rough and uncouth. The expression of his face was really boyish and very pleasant. He may have worn such clothes as appear in the picture out on the range, but in Fort Sumner he was careful of his personal appearance and dressed neatly and in good taste.' "[69]

The same year Burns's book was published Harold Hersey included in his collection SINGIN' RAWHIDE (Doran, 1926) a ballad in which occur the lines:

> Thuh Kid was cold and arrogant
> He'd ride a good hawss lame,
> He played and sang, he shot tuh kill,
> He loved a poker game.
> But when Miz Maxwell smiled on him
> Thuh Kid grew limp and tame.[70]

Señora Jaramillo certainly stirred Burns's eloquence. "Time had dealt gently with Mrs. Jaramillo," he wrote. "No one would be so ungallant as to inquire how old she is, but it may be whispered that in 1881, when Billy the Kid met death in her home, she was a blooming girl of eighteen. Streaks of gray have only begun to show in her coal-black hair; when she smiled, the suspicion of a dimple still shows in the olive smoothness of her cheeks, and there is a sparkle in her black eyes that age has had no power to dim. It is easy to fancy her as the dashing beauty she is said to have been when she was the belle of Fort Sumner."[71] No other quoted conversation in Burns's book, save that with the aged Susan McSween Barber, has so many vivid details, physical descriptions of the speaker with each changing mood, so much attention to setting, and such a sense of background and presence. At any rate, Burns's quotation of Señora Jaramillo's denial coupled with her implication of

Señora Gutiérrez were not sufficient to dissuade Charles Siringo from naming Paulita Maxwell the next year in RIATA AND SPURS as the Kid's lover in Fort Sumner after having kept her name a secret for forty-two years in his many books.

The ultimate significance of Burns's book rests in its *Zweideutung*, its double meaning, its two cycles which provide the Kid with a Janus image, variously a hero and a villain. It made even more explicit the impression dormant but adumbrated previously in the Garrett/Upson and Siringo accounts.

The most significant body of new fantasies about the Kid to emerge since Burns's book, although admittedly based in part on some of the fantasies in the Garrett/Upson and Burns accounts, has been propounded in a total of three books by former Chief Historian and Assistant Director of the National Park Service Robert M. Utley. His early reputation as a historian of the 19th-Century West was based on several books he wrote about American military history during the Indian campaigns. If Garrett wanted his account to serve to bolster his image as a heroic lawman as well as to earn him some money, and if Burns was primarily interested in romanticizing historical figures among Western gunfighters and lawmen, Utley was more intent on condemning the Tunstall-McSween faction and exonerating Colonel Dudley's participation in the five-day battle. Above all, it seems to have been his objective to create the most negative image of the Kid as a ruthless killer since the turn of the century. His accounts employ the apparatus of the professional historian, with citations of documents and personal accounts as well as newspapers, but always in the service of his particular slant which also caused him to distort documents or draw conclusions scarcely warranted by the evidence.

Perhaps two illustrations of Utley's historical methodology will be instructive. On 7 October 1876 John H. Tunstall wrote a letter to his father in which, among other topics, he told of how on a recent trip surveying prospective sites in New Mexico offering investment opportunities, he had taken up cooking. "I don't know if you know it," Tunstall wrote, "but one of my determinations has always been that *I would not cook*; I have always felt that I would prefer going hungry or eating cold, dry biscuits to cooking but you have no idea how soon I altered my mind when the alternative arose as to whether I should cook? or our Mexican. . . . I would not have eaten what our Mexican touched, if you had paid me a dollar a mouthful. You would have laughed to have seen us, me with my coat & waistcoat off, & sleeves turned up above the elbows, shaking my frying pan, dusting its contents with flour, whilst squatting over the fire, then getting up, coughing the smoke out of my throat & rubbing my eyes, & standing with arms akimbo at a distance watching the progress of operations. We were not far from a small Mexican settlement & were honored by an invitation to a "bille" [*baile*] pronounced ('bylee') which is a dance which was to come off & at which we could have inspected the youth & beauty of the village."[72] Utley, intent on portraying Tunstall as a racist, wrote in HIGH NOON IN LINCOLN: VIOLENCE ON THE WESTERN FRONTIER (University of New Mexico Press, 1987) that Tunstall "continued to look with condescension on the territory's Hispanic population. Of the cook on the journey to the Pecos, he wrote: 'I would not have eaten what our Mexican had touched, if you had paid me a dollar a mouthful.' "[73] A less partisan reader would perceive that what Tunstall objected to was the man's cooking, not that he was a Mexican!

The Utley remark also introduces another difficulty about his three books. New Mexico, after 250 years of Spanish and then Mexican rule, was ceded to the United States by the Treaty of Guadalupe Hidalgo in 1848 although a formal territorial government was not organized there until 1851. In 1876 the majority of the population in Lincoln County consisted of native New Mexicans, politically Mexican-Americans but ethnically, culturally, and psychologically more Mexican than the Anglo-Americans who were coming in and who were regarded as Yankees, Texans, or simply gringos. When Pat Garrett ran against George Kimbrell for the office of sheriff of Lincoln County in 1880, he received 320 votes to Kimbrell's 179. It is obvious from these small numbers that most of these voters were not from the Mexican population and the few Mexicans who did vote followed the time-honored *patrón* system whereby employees voted the way the landowner for whom they worked voted or were expected to vote for Garrett because he had a Mexican wife. To apply late 20th-Century liberal notions derived from the ideology of one-settlement culture such as the term Hispanic is totally inappropriate. In the first place, the term carries a subtle brand of sophisticated racism unknown in 19th-Century New Mexico. Hispanic is a term which implies no national origin, no ethnic distinction, no cultural difference, and classifies a person strictly on the basis of language. The Mexican tradition was very strong in New Mexico at the time and to deny it to these people, justifiably proud of their ethnic heritage and splendid culture, is in its way no less derogatory than simply to call them "greasers." Similarly, it is inappropriate to group, as Utley does, Tunstall, McSween, Murphy, Dolan, Riley, Brady, Emil Fritz, and Dr. Ealy as "Anglos." It was a significant factor in the conflict that Tunstall was a British subject and could not own land, that McSween was a Canadian Scotsman, that Murphy, Dolan, Riley, and Brady were all Irishmen who had little use for a foreigner from England and another one from Canada, that Fritz was more German than an Anglo-American, and that Ealy was a Presbyterian white Anglo-Saxon who thought Roman Catholics inherently corrupted by their heresy. Only because Utley deliberately blurred ethnic distinctions with his one-settlement cultural terms was he able to conclude that "ethnic factors seem to have played only a minor part in the Lincoln County War."[74]

The second source of a number of the Utley Fantasies is his use of the reminiscences of Francisco Trujillo. "Although eighty-five at the time of the interview," Utley wrote of Trujillo, "his recollections of many of the incidents of the Lincoln County War contain too many verifiable specifics to be discounted."[75] The interview was collected by Edith L. Crawford in 1937 as part of the Federal Writers' Project. Trujillo's account which has been published in THEY "KNEW" BILLY THE KID: INTERVIEWS WITH OLD-TIME NEW MEXICANS (Ancient City Press, 1987) edited by Robert F. Kadlec and which is approximately nine pages long consists basically of eleven fantasies, all describing events concerning which there is absolutely no evidence that Trujillo was, or even could have been, present.

Since Trujillo's ramblings followed no chronology, I have followed none in listing his fantasies.

Trujillo Fantasies

1. Billy the Kid was with the gang that broke Jesse Evans and the other Boys out of jail on 16 November 1877. On their journey out of Lincoln, the Evans gang encountered Juan Trujillo on the road and stole a horse and his firearms. Francisco claimed he was present and was also robbed. [The only proof Utley advanced to substantiate Francisco Trujillo's veracity was the observation that Juan Trujillo's "loss of horse and arms"[76] is corroborated by an account of the robbery in the *Mesilla Valley Independent* (in HIGH NOON IN LINCOLN Utley dated the edition 13 December 1877 on p. 193 and in BILLY THE KID: A SHORT AND VIOLENT LIFE he dated the edition 15 December 1877 on p. 219). However, the one sentence that appeared in the article concerning this robbery states: "On their way to the Feliz, they met Juan Trujillo, and borrowed his saddle, gun, and pistol for Don Lucas Gallegos." This sentence does *not* place Francisco Trujillo at the scene, much less the Kid.]

2. No record exists from any source that Francisco Trujillo was with the Regulators when Morton, Baker, and McCloskey were killed. Trujillo claimed: "One of the gang named McLoska [McCloskey] said he preferred to be shot himself rather than to have one of those men killed. No sooner had he said this, when he found himself shot behind the ear. After they killed McLoska, Frank Baker and Billy Mote [Morton] were promptly executed."[77]

3. No record exists from any source that Francisco Trujillo was in Lincoln the day Sheriff Brady was killed. "Being in the [Dolan] store about eleven, the mail arrived and with it Macky Swin [McSween]. There also arrived Brady and a Texan named George Hamilton [Hindman]. At this juncture Brady also arrived where he found Billy the Kid, Jim French, Charley Barber [Bowdre], and John Melton [Middleton]. They were in the corral from whence two of the gang shot at one, and two others at the other, where they fell. Billy the Kid then jumped to snatch Brady's rifle and as he was leaning over someone shot at him from a house they used to call 'El Chorro.' Macky Swin [McSween] then reached the house where the nine Macky Swins were congregated—the four who were in the corral and five who had been at the river. There they remained all day until nightfall and then proceeded to San Patricio."[78] [This is an extremely well documented event and Trujillo didn't manage to get a single accurate fact into his account other than naming Brady, French, and the Kid along with a lot of other people who were not involved.]

4. There is no documentation that Francisco Trujillo was even in Lincoln, much less in the McSween house, on the last day of the five-day fight. This is what he recalled of that episode: "Chaves [José Chávez y Chávez] took Macky Swin [McSween] by the arm and told him to go out to which Macky Swin [McSween] answered by taking a chair and placing it in the corner stating that he would die right there. Billy and Jose Chaves [Chávez y Chávez] then jumped to the middle door, one on one side, and the other on the other. Then Robert Baker [Beckwith] and a Texan jumped and said, 'Here is Macky Swin' [McSween]. Drawing out his revolver he [Beckwith] shot him three times in the breast. When the last shot was fired Billy the Kid said, 'Here is Robert,' and thrust his revolver in his mouth while Jose Chaves [Chávez y Chávez] shot at the Texan and hit him in the eye."[79]

5. While, again, there is no evidence Francisco Trujillo was in Lincoln the day the Kid escaped, this is what he remembered: "Billy's next move was to rush to the hotel and to have

Ben Esle [Ellis] remove his shackles. He also provided for him a horse and saddled it for Billy upon the promise that he was to leave it at San Patricio."[80]

6. With obsessive regularity in Trujillo's reminiscences, the Kid is always headed for San Patricio. After he broke out of jail in Lincoln and arrived in San Patricio, "Billy now left San Patricio and headed for John Chisum's cattle ranch. Among the cowboys there, there was a friend of Billy Mote [Morton] who had sworn to kill the Kid wherever he found him in order to avenge his friend. But Billy did not give him time to carry out his plan, killing him on the spot."[81]

7. Near Puerto de Luna, where the Kid was hiding out with Tom O'Folliard, "there was to have been a dance and Billy sent his companion to make a report of what he saw and heard. While on his way there, and while he was passing in front of some abandoned shacks, Tome [Tom O'Folliard] was fired upon by one of Pat Garrett's men and killed. No sooner had Billy heard this distressing news than he set out for the house of his friend Pedro Macky [?] at Bosque Grande where he remained in hiding until a Texan named Charley Wilson, and who was supposed to be after Billy, arrived."[82]

8. Charley Wilson was the name by which Francisco Trujillo knew or remembered Joe Grant since Billy, according to Trujillo, went to meet Wilson in a saloon where Wilson started shooting at glasses at the bar until he came to the Kid's glass. "This he pretended to miss, aiming his shot at Billy instead. This gave Billy time to draw out his own revolver and before Charley could take aim again, Billy had shot the other in the breast twice. When he was breathing his last, Billy said, 'Do not whimper you were too eager to buy those drinks.' "[83]

9. We may not have "Kip" McKinney's reminiscences of what happened the night Garrett killed the Kid, but we do have Francisco Trujillo's: "Stepping to the door he partially opened it and thrusting his head in asked Pedro [Pete Maxwell] who was with him. Pedro replied that it was only his wife and asked him to come in. Seeing no harm in this Billy decided to accept the invitation only to be shot in the pit of the stomach as he stood in the door. Staggering back to his own room it was not definitely known that the shot had been fatal until a cleaning woman stumbled over the dead body upon entering the room the following morning."[84]

10. "When Marfe [Murphy] saw that he had lost out he ordered his men to get Macky Swin [McSween] or some of his companions. Macky Swin [McSween] hearing of the order that Marfe [Murphy] had given gathered up his people in order to protect himself. Among those he rounded up was Billy the Kid, Charley Barber [Bowdre?] and Macky Nane [MacNab?]. In addition to these three men, six more got together and Macky Swin [McSween] made them the same promise to the effect that a prize of $500 was to be awarded each person who killed one of the Marfes [Murphy men]."[85] [Not only was this wholly out of character for McSween to have done, but there is no corroboration for such a reward having been offered in any other document or in any of the testimony collected by Judge Angel including that taken from many members of the Dolan side who would have pounced on even the slightest hint of such a promise. Above all, it cannot be established that Francisco Trujillo was ever with the Regulators at any time.]

11. "We noticed that the Indian [Manuel Segovia] had gotten away from his captors and was riding away as fast as he could. Billy the Kid and Jose Chaves [Chávez y Chávez?] took out after him and began to shoot at him until they got him."[86] [There is no testimony or documentary evidence of any kind placing Francisco Trujillo with the Regulators when they raided the Dolan cow camp to retrieve stolen Tunstall horses and other stock belonging to various Regulators where Segovia was killed in the fray on 19 May 1878.]

These are the principal episodes—and fantasies—in the Trujillo account which Utley felt contained "too many verifiable specifics to be discounted." J. C. Dykes in his Afterword to Trujillo's and the other reminiscences in THEY "KNEW" BILLY THE KID more aptly concluded "these interviews . . . clearly indicate that legends do not die—they just grow."[87] It is for this reason that the word "KNEW" appears as it does in the title of this book. Yet it was from such whole cloth as the Tunstall letter—neatly highlighted out of context—and the Francisco Trujillo interview that Utley created his set of fantasies. Although he wrote three books on the same subject, they are essentially the same book, both HIGH NOON IN LINCOLN and BILLY THE KID: A SHORT AND VIOLENT LIFE being merely longer extensions of the vignettes first presented in FOUR FIGHTERS OF LINCOLN COUNTY (University of New Mexico Press, 1986). As a convenience to the reader, citations for the Utley Fantasies are provided for both of the later, expanded volumes since in most cases not even the prose is different, only the publisher.

Utley Fantasies

1. Outside of Tunstall's family back in England, "people existed simply to be manipulated and exploited for his own gain."[88] [This statement is set forth without any corroborating evidence. Yet, in his short life and relatively brief time in New Mexico, Tunstall manifested a generosity toward others that belies this charge, so much so that his largess to people such as Rob Widenmann was frowned upon by the more frugal A. A. McSween.]

2. Tunstall looked "with condescension" on the "Hispanics" in New Mexico.[89] [Utley's sole corroboration for this statement is the sentence quoted out of context in the letter cited above.]

3. Billy the Kid joins Jesse Evans's gang at Mesilla prior to Evans's arrest and imprisonment in Lincoln in late 1877.[90] [The sole source cited to substantiate this claim is the Francisco Trujillo interview when it cannot even be established that Francisco Trujillo was on the scene when his brother's horse was "borrowed" by the Boys.]

4. The Kid was with the gang that helped Evans and the others escape from the Lincoln jail and that Brewer acted as a "courier" with the rest of the gang.[91] [Again, Francisco Trujillo is the source for the Kid's participation. No citation is provided for the statement concerning Brewer's involvement and, since he went to great effort to capture the Boys, it would have been totally out of character for him then to have participated clandestinely in their escape.]

5. Tunstall was killed while resisting arrest.[92] [No supporting evidence is cited to support this contention other than the fact that Tunstall's revolver had two spent cartridges in its chambers.]

6. Tunstall was organizing a gang to strike back at the House.[93] [Instead of paying a visit to the Chisum ranch to consult John Chisum concerning what to do about Sheriff Brady's attachment of his property (which trip has been documented), Utley asserts Tunstall was instead out summoning the forces which arrived at McSween's house after Tunstall was murdered.]

7. The men who showed up at McSween's house following Tunstall's death had to have been summoned by him prior to his excursion back to Lincoln from his ranch because James

Longwell, a Dolan man, said this is what happened.[94] [Longwell's testimony is scarcely best evidence but it is the only evidence Utley adduced.]

8. McSween was nearly bankrupt when Tunstall was murdered.[95] [In a letter to me dated 6 February 1987 from Donald R. Lavash when Utley had stated this fantasy for the first time in FOUR FIGHTERS OF LINCOLN COUNTY, Lavash who had studied the records of the First National Bank of Santa Fe (one of the banks where McSween had an account) at the Special Collections of the University of New Mexico commented that "for anyone to say that McSween was insolvent in 1877–1878 . . . is ludicrous. His bank records . . . prove otherwise. . . . Utley is incorrect here. I do not understand why he said such a thing. I do recall we had discussed this and agreed that just before McSween's death in July, 1878, that he (McSween) was becoming short of funds. Perhaps this is what Utley meant to say." This was apparently not the case, however, since Utley repeated the fantasy in HIGH NOON IN LINCOLN after having been informed to the contrary by both Donald R. Lavash and myself and despite being presented with the hard evidence to the contrary.]

9. The letter revealing his bias to "Friends Dolan and Riley" from Colonel Rynerson was dropped by a drunken Riley in the McSween living room.[96] [The letter was more probably found when Widenmann searched the Dolan store accompanied by soldiers on the same day he took back possession of the Tunstall store. Unfortunately, in none of his three books does Utley supply a separate chronology which only adds to the confusion inherent in their texts where the chronology is generally inaccurate with events occurring on the wrong days. For example, Utley places the repossession of the Tunstall store by Widenmann on 20 February 1878 when it occurred on 22 February 1878 or he has Tunstall buried on 21 February 1878 when this also occurred on 22 February 1878.]

10. Atanacio Martínez was forced at gunpoint by the Kid and others to serve the warrants issued by Justice of the Peace Wilson.[97] [This fantasy is documented by a citation of Lieutenant Millard F. Goodwin's testimony to Judge Angel. Surely this is not best evidence. The Kid wrote to Governor Wallace that Lieutenant Goodwin "would not hesitate to do anything." Moreover, since Atanacio Martínez was also interviewed in private by Judge Angel, why, if true, would he not have said so in his deposition? It is one thing for a historian to cite partisan evidence for the record, another entirely to accept it as the truth when there is no corroboration.]

11. McSween offered the Regulators a reward if they killed Sheriff Brady.[98] [Trujillo Fantasy No. 10 is cited in support of this allegation. But then, Trujillo also had McSween present in Lincoln when Sheriff Brady was murdered and had him entertain the assassins for the rest of the day until nightfall when they rode to San Patricio.]

12. Susan McSween was even more bloodthirsty than her husband and "showed herself just as ready as the Regulators to fight back with violence and even homicide."[99] [Unfortunately for his case, Utley only cites the affidavits Colonel Dudley collected about Susan McSween. They do indicate that she was said to be promiscuous but scarcely violent, much less homicidal.]

13. Brady was on his way to the Lincoln County courthouse to post a notice that court day had been changed when he was ambushed.[100] [If this had been true, Brady's course would not have taken him past the Tunstall store and corral and into the ambush set there. As Frederick Nolan pointed out in THE LINCOLN COUNTY WAR: A DOCUMENTARY HISTORY, "there was no misunderstanding about the date court would open. . . . Which leaves us with the inescapable conclusion that Brady was on his way to arrest McSween as the lawyer rode unprotected into Brady's domain."[101]]

14. Jim French and the Kid rushing toward Brady's body were hit in the thigh by the same bullet and it was French who was treated by Dr. Ealy, hidden by Sam Corbet in the Tunstall store, and rescued that night by the Kid.[102] [As cited in the preceding biography chapter, Norman J. Bender who edited and annotated MISSIONARIES, OUTLAWS, AND INDIANS: TAYLOR F. EALY AT LINCOLN AND ZUNI, 1878–1881 noted in this connection that "Taylor Ealy did not name the wounded man who 'came walking into our back door.' However, the only one wounded at the time among those who ambushed Brady and Hindman was Henry McCarty . . . or, as he was already called, Billy the Kid."[103] Ruth R. Ealy in her unpublished memoir utilizing her father's memoirs does not mention the Kid by name as the person who was treated by her father. Mary R. Ealy, Dr. Ealy's wife, in a letter to Colonel Fulton on 16 January 1928 named Jim French as having been "pretty badly wounded and the Dr. dressed his wounds," but there is no mention of *when* this occurred. Fulton and Mullin in Fulton's HISTORY OF THE LINCOLN COUNTY WAR concluded that it was the Kid who was wounded and treated. The evidence is possibly equal on both sides that it was either the Kid or Jim French who was wounded by a bullet, probably fired by Billy Mathews. However, to say that it cannot be determined with exactitude and then to opt for one or the other is one thing. It is entirely another matter to try to blend the stories—supported by *none* of the testimony—and claim that *both* were wounded by the same bullet!]

15. With the death of MacNab, the Regulators "elected" Doc Scurlock as their "third captain."[104] [There is no documentation of any kind to support this assertion and Utley offers none. Sheriff Copeland had appointed Scurlock as his deputy but that was scarcely an election by the Regulators and Scurlock as a deputy was hardly a captain. In spelling Francis ("Frank") MacNab's name in this fashion, as opposed to McNab, I am following the way he himself signed his name.]

16. The Kid and Josefita Chávez executed Indian [Manuel Segovia]. [Utley's source for this is Trujillo Fantasy No.11. However, Trujillo identifies the other man with the Kid as Jose Chaves who at all other times is synonymous with José Chávez y Chávez in Trujillo's reminiscences. Obviously, Utley had to change this to Josefita Chávez who might have been there whereas José Chávez y Chávez definitely was not. This is shaping the evidence to fit the event rather than the evidence shaping the way the event is narrated.]

17. "The lawyer's [McSween's] talents did not run to field-soldiering. He may have departed from habit to shoulder a rifle, but he did not command."[105] [There is no testimony from any participant on either side or in any newspaper or other contemporary source that McSween ever shouldered a rifle or carried a gun. In fact, it was well known that he had no use for firearms. Utley did not (because he could not) substantiate this claim with a citation.]

18. During the five-day fight in Lincoln, the firing directed at Private Berry Robinson came from the McSween house.[106] [Utley cited as his source for this statement the board of inquiry Colonel Dudley sent the next day to Lincoln to investigate the matter. Colonel Fulton's view of the matter was more balanced: "Considering the officers' friendship with Dolan and his associates, and their open hostility to the McSween faction, their findings (that McSween men fired the shot) are not surprising."[107] Moreover, the preponderance of evidence is that it was a single wild shot that was fired, not the fusillade Utley describes. The board of inquiry interviewed Sheriff Peppin, Jesse Evans, J. J. Dolan and others at the Wortley Hotel before asking McSween what he knew about the incident. He denied it. The board chose to believe the Dolan side. Neither side adduced any hard evidence on which a conclusion reasonably could be based and the matter should have been adjudged that the shot had been fired by a person or persons unknown.]

19. McSween men fired at Dr. Appel and other military when they went to rescue Charlie Crawford who was wounded.[108] [Although Crawford would eventually die of his wounds, Dr. Appel in his report of the incident already referred to him as "the murdered man." Again, the only evidence supporting this claim came from the Dolan side and those in the military sympathetic with Dolan and hoping this would be the final straw necessary for Colonel Dudley to make his decision to intervene.]

20. Given Utley's military bias and his two previous fantasies, it ought to come as a surprise to no one that in Utley's view Colonel Dudley's intervention was for the sole purpose of protecting women and children, that he just simply "could no longer resist rushing to the aid of helpless citizens."[109] [If this had been the case, why did Dudley stop first to see Squire Wilson to have a warrant sworn out against McSween and, once he had the warrant, see that Sheriff Peppin's deputy Marion Turner try to serve it? Similarly, although there was much testimony to the contrary at Dudley's hearing, Utley stated unequivocally that "soldiers did not participate in the fighting."[110]]

21. Dolan fired into the street rather than into Huston I. Chapman's body.[111] [In FOUR FIGHTERS OF LINCOLN COUNTY, Utley had a variant of this fantasy, namely that Dolan "fired into the ground" rather than into Chapman.[112] This fantasy, of course, is closely related to Garrett/Upson Fantasy No. 44. Utley has no citation for this assertion. Dolan at the time was apparently too drunk even to remember afterwards whether or not he had been with the group, much less in what direction he may have fired the rifle he said he wasn't carrying. The *Mesilla Valley Independent* surveying Dolan's numerous contradictory versions concluded in its 5 July 1879 issue: "Fatal shot! Whether it was fired by collusion with Evans and Campbell, or whether he meant it as a signal or merely to attract attention, it caused the death of Chapman." The Kid, who was present, testified that Dolan's shot did not go into the ground or into the street but into its target. Frederick Nolan concluded, correctly I believe, that the truth lies "in two unargued facts: the first, that Campbell fired only once, and the second, that there were *two* bullets in Chapman's body."[113]]

22. The judge advocate general in Washington "pronounced the findings [of the Dudley court of inquiry] convincing and predicted that an expensive court-martial would reach the same conclusion."[114] [As quoted above in the biography chapter, D. G. Swaine of the judge advocate general's department stated that "the conclusion is irresistible that Dudley both actively and passively aided and abetted the Sheriff's party in its doings." He recommended no court-martial because such a public airing of the matter would not, in his opinion, "be in the best interests of the public or military service"—although, no doubt, less in the interests of the latter than the former!]

23. "Alcoholism killed him [Major Murphy]."[115] [According to medical records in the possession of the late Robert N. Mullin, L. G. Murphy was diagnosed with inoperable intestinal carcinoma. Because the prognosis was such that he would have at best eighteen months to live, he decided to sell L. G. Murphy & Co. to Dolan and Riley. Assistant Post Surgeon Daniel M. Appel prescribed morphine to Murphy when the pain became great and gave him permission to drink as much as he wanted to drink, since it could only ease the pain. Dolan accompanied Major Murphy to Santa Fe when he moved there on 10 May 1878 and there Murphy remained until his disease finally claimed him on 20 October 1878. He was buried in the Masonic and Odd Fellows Cemetery.]

24. There was "virtually no chance" that at least one of the bullets that hit Sheriff Brady was not fired by the Kid and "there can be no reasonable doubt of his guilt."[116] [There is no evidence that would substantiate such an absolute claim and even Judge Bristol, in league with the Kid's defense attorneys, was willing to settle on the Kid's mere presence with the

assassins as sufficient evidence for a conviction of first-degree murder on the basis of guilt by association.]

25. For "unknown reasons" Ira Leonard "bowed out of the defense of the Kid" on the Territorial charge of killing Sheriff Brady.[117] [He didn't bow out. He was dismissed by Judge Bristol who appointed Fountain and Bail in his place.[118] Bristol was taking no chances. Even the jury was made up exclusively of Mexicans who did not know the Kid personally and everything said had to be translated into Spanish for them and, if they had anything to say or ask, it had to be translated into English. Bristol was also certain Fountain and Bail would make no attempt at an appeal. "Unfortunately for Bonney and a number of his contemporaries, no appeal was taken in the Brady murder case to the Supreme Court of the Territory," wrote William A. Keleher, himself a lawyer. "It is idle to speculate on what the Supreme Court might have done with the case on appeal, but if an appeal had been taken, a transcript of the testimony would have been filed which would have been of considerable interest to posterity."[119]]

26. Omission of mention of J. J. Dolan as a prosecution witness against the Kid in his murder trial and omission of his name as among those who raised money to reward Garrett for capturing the Kid.[120]

27. Variation of Burns Fantasy No. 14 and verbatim the Siringo version wherein the Kid beats Bell down with his handcuffs and grabs his pistol.[121] [This fantasy does not tend to improve with age.]

28. "A sobbing Celsa Gutiérrez cursed Garrett and pounded his chest" after the Kid was killed.[122] [While testimony varies as to just when Deluvina Maxwell did this, it is gratuitous in the extreme to substitute Celsa Gutiérrez in the role.]

29. "For three months [after his escape from jail in Lincoln], Pat Garrett and his deputies pursued Billy tirelessly."[123] [Even the Garrett/Upson account details how Garrett was being criticized for his lack of activity in pursuing the Kid. "Pat defended himself by admitting that he spent a great deal of time on his ranch instead of seeking out the Kid's trail but claimed he was 'constantly but quietly at work, seeking sure information and maturing [his] plans for action,' " Leon C. Metz wrote. "The manhunter's confidence began to wane."[124]]

30. The coroner's jury was assembled the next morning after the Kid's death and convened in Maxwell's bedroom "where the body still lay on the floor."[125] [The reason for this patent absurdity is that Utley assumed Milnor Rudolph was the foreman of the coroner's jury. A. P. Anaya, a former member of the New Mexico legislature, reported to George Fitzpatrick, editor of NEW MEXICO MAGAZINE, and Fitzpatrick wrote to the late C. L. Sonnichsen on 19 January 1952, that Anaya and "a friend were called as members of the coroner's jury the night the Kid was killed and that this jury wrote out a verdict stating simply that the Kid had come to his death as a result of a wound from a gun in the hands of Pat Garrett, officer." Anaya clarified that "this verdict was lost and that Garrett had Manuel Abreu write a more flowery one for filing." New signatures of persons not originally members of the coroner's jury appear on this surviving document. "Milnor Rudolph, who signed as 'presidente' of the jury," Anaya concluded, "was not an original member of the jury who viewed the body."[126]]

To these thirty original fantasies or variations of the fantasies of others, Utley added a disproportionately generous share—larger than almost anyone else since 1932—of the Garrett/Upson Fantasies. In order of appearance in BILLY THE KID: A SHORT AND VIOLENT LIFE, they are: Nos. 1, 17, 9, 8, 37, 39, 46, 49, 52, 56, 55, 60, 66, 62, 64, 65, 67, 70, 71, and 73—nearly a fifth of them. Nor was Burns completely neglected. Utley also included Nos. 11 and 16 of the Burns Fantasies. Virtually all the photo illustrations in HIGH NOON IN LINCOLN are miscaptioned and, beyond all of these evident fantasies, the texts of all of Utley's books are riddled with inaccuracies on just about every page and in almost every paragraph. He is perhaps to be commended for having taken the time to examine most of the original documents in various archives, but the nagging question which remains is this: Why did he choose to write virtually the same book three times in succession without adding one single bit of new evidence? Anyone can take as an *Urtext* the Garrett/Upson account—as used to be so commonplace at one time—and add a few new "legendary" notions from highly questionable sources and thus come up with a new hodgepodge such as this. Certainly this was the case with Burns and Utley, too, in his own way very much in the Burns mode wrote fiction and presented it as history. However, it is doubtful that his work will have anywhere near the influence either the Garrett/Upson account or the Burns account had in their day. Other than Utley's own article "Billy the Kid Country" for AMERICAN HERITAGE (April, 1991), the Utley Fantasies have influenced only two articles: "Was Billy the Kid a superhero—or a superscoundrel?" by Jake Page in SMITHSONIAN (February, 1991) and "War Without Heroes" by Wilfred P. Deac in WILD WEST (April, 1991). Although Frederick Nolan incorporated two of the Utley Fantasies in THE LINCOLN COUNTY WAR: A DOCUMENTARY HISTORY—Nos. 14 and 23—and quoted documentary sources regarding Nos. 18 and 19 but without prejudice, there is no overt reference or citation of Utley anywhere in his text. This is perhaps as it should be. Indeed, anyone seeking to learn more about the Lincoln County War and the life and death of the Kid would be well advised to avoid reading the Garrett/Upson, Burns, and Utley accounts until the very last. The first two have prompted innumerable errors by other writers over the years and Utley's books have no information in them that cannot be found elsewhere with less quixotic and ludicrous interpretations which in his case also involve all too many errors of omission, commission, and distortion of documents.

Finally, to bring this "fantasy" section to a close there is another book which has appeared that also purports to be a biography of the Kid: ALIAS THE KID: THE MAN BEHIND THE LEGEND (Sunstone Press, 1986) by Donald Cline. Cline's book is shorter than either Utley's HIGH NOON IN LINCOLN or BILLY THE KID: A SHORT AND VIOLENT LIFE, but his historical methods are about as haphazard and partisan. On the other hand, unlike Utley, Cline appears to have been unfamiliar with most of what is documented about the Kid. His tone throughout is belligerent, his text without coherent organization, his prose frequently ungrammatical. "Readers who must have a sympathetic character to identify with may put this book down," Utley wrote in a preface titled "A War Without Heroes" in HIGH NOON IN LINCOLN.[127] This does hold true for all three of his books. With the exception of his forgiving posture toward Colonel Dudley and the military, Utley seems to have detested every person about whom he came to write. Cline, too, set out to prove something with his book, that the Kid was "a cowardly, petty outlaw" who has notwithstanding become a legend.[128] To do this, he often had to resort to his imagination. Most importantly, he failed to respect two cardinal rules for the historian: one voiced by Quintilian, that it is the historian's function to narrate but never to narrate just in order to give proof, and one by Fustel de Coulanges, that where there are no documents (or the documents are inadequate), there is no history. Following Garrett/Upson Fantasy No. 1, Cline would have his reader believe that Henry McCarty and his brother Joe were born in New York City. He claims to have found a birth certificate for a Michael McCarty born 20 November 1859, but he does not reproduce it, or provide the page and volume citation of where it is located in the Municipal Archives and Records Center. He cites three versions in newspapers concerning a murder committed by a Michael McCarty who had a brother named James and expects the reader simply to overlook the discrepancies in the names. Cline asserts that the Kid went back to New York just to commit this murder and that he later worked for Sheriff Brady, all without offering any proof. He departs from Utley when it comes to who offered payment to kill Brady, stating that "John Chisum offered to pay each participating man in the affair the sum total of $500 a piece [sic]."[129]

Cline tried to make a case that the Kid was arrested in Albuquerque with one John Wilson on a charge of horse-stealing, that he was convicted and sentenced to five years in the Bernalillo County Jail, and that he escaped. When I asked Katherine Dorman, archivist at the State Records Center and Archives in Santa Fe, if she could supply me with the Bernalillo County Court Docket Book for the May, 1880 term, she replied that the archives have a gap between 1878 and 1882 in the Bernalillo County Criminal Docket books. Cline was able to supply me with a photocopy, presumably made from the missing May, 1880 docket records, but the person tried and sentenced was identified only as "Kidd." Newspaper accounts of the trial in the *Albuquerque Advance* for 8 May and 22 May 1880 and in the *Albuquerque Review* for 20 May 1880, also supplied in photostats by Cline, do not identify this suspect by any other name than "Kid." Since by this time *the* Kid was well known throughout New Mexico, it seems unlikely the two were one and the same. Moreover, one of the articles mentions that "Kid" was formerly confined in jails at Trinidad, Las Vegas, and Santa Fe, and this was definitely never the case for Billy Bonney in Trinidad and only subsequently in the other two jails. In fact, the Kid complained about jail conditions without reference to any previous samplings of them.

The only thing Cline did get right is that the Kid had no gun when Garrett shot him, but he has the name of one of the two deputies with Garrett wrong and attributes to the other, John W. Poe, the statement that "he never saw the pistol until Garrett returned with it from Celsa Gutiérrez' room."[130] I do not know, since there isn't any citation, where Cline picked up this fantasy since Poe, in his published account in which he covered for Garrett, wrote that "we saw a man lying stretched upon his back dead, in the middle of the room, with a six-shooter lying at his right hand, a butcher knife at his left. Upon examining the body, we found it to be that of Billy the Kid."[131] I suspect Sabal Gutiérrez, Celsa's husband, would have been more than a little shocked since Burns's spurious linking of his wife with the Kid was still forty-five years in the future!

II

THE REAL BILLY THE KID WITH NEW LIGHT ON THE LINCOLN COUNTY WAR (Rufus Rockwell Wilson, 1936) by Miguel Antonio Otero marked the first true breakthrough in scholarship on the Kid's life and, in particular, on his death. As a former governor of New Mexico and a descendant of a family long associated with the New Mexican political scene, Miguel Otero was apparently able to win the confidence of bystanders at the Kid's death, such as Francisco Lobato, Jesus Silva, and Deluvina Maxwell. From them he learned that the Kid had not been armed with a revolver when Garrett shot him. In fact, Otero's firsthand account of his journey through Lincoln County and his record of the interviews which he conducted constitute extremely valuable historical documents. It is especially noteworthy that Otero was the first Mexican-American author to approach the subject of the Kid and the Lincoln County War. As such, he lacks the Anglo-American bias which has run through much of the fantasy fiction about the Kid from Garrett/Upson to Utley and his tendency to regard events and the Kid's life from the impact they had on native New Mexicans still seems to rancor some authors such as Utley. There is probably no book ever written about Billy the Kid that deserves to be reprinted in a modern edition more than this one, albeit with annotations and corrections of facts now much in evidence which had not yet been adduced when Otero conducted his research.

The weaknesses of his book are his reliance on the Garrett/Upson account for many of the details of the Kid's early life and his pursuit, adroitly blended with some of the images and sentiments of Burns's book. He also erroneously followed George Tower Buffam's account in his SMITH OF BEAR CITY (Grafton Press, 1906) for the apprehension of the Kid at Stinking Springs. It was not a mistake, however, as Ramon F. Adams claimed in BURS UNDER THE SADDLE, to refer to Squire Wilson as Green Wilson. In his letter of 14 February 1878 to John Riley and J. J. Dolan, Colonel Rynerson made reference to the justice of the peace at Lincoln as " 'Green Baptista' Wilson." Otero has also been unjustly criticized for talking primarily to those who were sympathetic with the Tunstall/McSween faction. Actually he did not have much choice in the matter, since the survivors who were in a position to have known the Kid and the events of the Lincoln County War came predominantly from this faction. Unfortunately, the influence of Otero's book has been confined almost exclusively to its use as a resource by historians while it has tended to be ignored by fabulists.

J. W. Hendron's THE STORY OF BILLY THE KID (Rydal Press, 1948), while hopelessly unreliable as history or biography, deserves recognition for incorporating the most amusing conjecture so far as to how the Kid managed his escape from the Lincoln jail. According to Hendron a small pocket knife and a small piece of *algerita*, or yellow wood, were smuggled to the Kid in a tortilla. The Kid hid the knife in his rectum and at every available opportunity whittled the *algerita* into a key that would fit the lock of his handcuffs!

Perhaps it was out of friendship for its author that Ramon F. Adams neglected to take to task Frazier Hunt's THE TRAGIC DAYS OF BILLY THE KID (Hastings House, 1956). The biography certainly is riddled with errors, occurring at the rate of at least one a page, and oftentimes more, errors which Adams corrected in numerous books by other authors and over which he, justifiably, berated them for their lack of disciplined scholarship. "Has much new material on Billy the Kid," Adams wrote of Hunt's book in SIX-GUNS AND SADDLE LEATHER (in its later, revised edition from 1969), the only annotation he provided for it. "It is perhaps the account nearest the truth to date. The author was fortunate in having the benefit of the studious research of such men as the late Maurice Fulton, Robert Mullin, and Phil Rasch. Altogether it is a reliable book, though there are a few minor errors, such as naming McNab [MacNab] Charlie instead of Frank in one place and getting Tunstall's name wrong."[132] In other annotations of other books on the Kid, Adams did not consider minor errors such statements as that there were no bruises on Tunstall's face and head or that the Kid had a revolver in his hand the night Garrett shot him. It could only have been a case of *amicitia ante veritatem*. Notwithstanding, there is value in the book, particularly in the source material supplied by Fulton, Mullin, and Rasch. What is possibly most frustrating about this information—including several documents not previously published in book form which do supplement our knowledge of events and the sequence of events—is that no citations are included.

Of interest primarily for its collection of photographs, some supposedly of the Kid quite spurious, is BILLY THE KID: A DATE WITH DESTINY (Hangman Press, 1970) by Marion Ballert with Carl W. Breihan. Most of the photos and other illustrations are interesting and valuable and some unique to this volume. With a subtitle such as "A DATE WITH DESTINY," obviously there is more than a little of the Burns "saga" about the text and for the most part it relies on Burns and Garrett/Upson for its contents. Ramon F. Adams reviewed it at length in MORE BURS UNDER THE SADDLE: BOOKS AND HISTORIES OF THE WEST. It is worth noting that Robert N. Mullin wrote the Introduction to this book (without having read the complete text) and a long letter is reproduced from Mullin tracing all of the research he and Colonel Fulton conducted in order to establish that the Kid was told by Sam Corbet that there would be a pistol hidden in the privy by José M. Aguayo. Both at the time were employed by Mrs. McSween.

Among articles of immense interest is "Billy the Kid: The Trail of a Kansas Legend" by W. A. Koop which appeared in THE TRAIL GUIDE (September, 1964) for its information about the Kid's early years, supplemented, of course, by Robert N. Mullin's THE BOYHOOD OF BILLY THE KID (Texas Western Press, 1967), published as a monograph, and Jerry Weddle's article "Apprenticeship of an Outlaw: Billy the Kid in Arizona" in JOURNAL OF ARIZONA HISTORY (Autumn, 1990). Beyond these are Mullin's A CHRONOLOGY OF THE LINCOLN COUNTY WAR (Press of the Territorian, 1966), provided it is amended by the chronology I have provided in Appendix B which is more up to date, and his monograph with W. H. Hutchinson, WHISKEY JIM AND A KID NAMED BILLIE (Clarendon Press, 1967), which is devoted to Greathouse and Billie Wilson. Of almost equal importance are Mullin's articles "Pat Garrett: Two Forgotten Killings" in PASSWORD (September, 1965) published by the El Paso County Historical Society, "The Key to the Mystery of Pat Garrett" in the LOS ANGELES WEST-ERNERS CORRAL (June, 1969), the monograph THE STRANGE STORY OF WAYNE BRAZEL (Palo Duro Press, 1969), as well as his articles coauthored with Philip J. Rasch "New Light on the Legend of Billy the Kid" in the NEW MEXICO FOLKLORE RECORD (1952–53) and "Dim Trails: The Pursuit of the McCarty Family" in the NEW MEXICO FOLKLORE RECORD (1954). Also well worth reading are Philip J. Rasch's solo articles, "The Twenty-One Men He Put Bullets Through" in the NEW MEXICO FOLKLORE RECORD (1954–55), "A Man Called Antrim" in the LOS ANGELES WESTERNERS BRAND BOOK (1956), "More on the McCartys" in the ENGLISH WESTERNERS BRAND BOOK (April, 1957), "John Kinney: King of the Rustlers" in ENGLISH WESTERNERS BRAND BOOK (October, 1961), "War in Lincoln County" in the ENGLISH WESTERNERS BRAND BOOK (July, 1964), "The Trials of Lieutenant Colonel Dudley" in the ENGLISH WESTERNERS BRAND BOOK (January, 1965), "The Hunting of Billy the Kid (Part One)" in the ENGLISH WESTERNERS BRAND BOOK (January, 1969), "The Hunting of Billy the Kid (Part Two)" in the ENGLISH WESTERNERS BRAND BOOK (April, 1969), "Prelude to War: The Murder of John Henry Tunstall" in the ENGLISH WESTERNERS BRAND BOOK (January, 1970), "They Fought for the House" in PORTRAITS IN GUNSMOKE (English Westerners Society, 1971) edited by Jeff Burton, "These Were the Regulators" in HO! FOR THE GREAT WEST (English Westerners Society, 1980) edited by Barry C. Johnson, "Gus Gildea—An Arizone [sic] Pioneer" in ENGLISH WESTERN-ERS BRAND BOOK (Summer, 1985), and "The Curious Case of Edward M. Kelly" in NOLA QUARTERLY (Fall, 1987). Rasch with Lee Myers also contrib-uted another important essay in "The Tragedy of the Beckwiths" in ENGLISH WESTERNERS BRAND BOOK (July, 1963).

Finally there is a very valuable, although hard to find, collection of essays published in the "Lincoln County Issue" of RIO GRANDE HISTORY No. 9 (1978) published by New Mexico State University available originally only to members of the Rio Grande Historical Collections and the University Library of New Mexico State University. Nora Henn, now Historian and Custodian of the Collection at the Lincoln County Historical Society, probably knows more about every person connected with the Lincoln County War than anyone else, including those of us who have written books about it and the Kid. She provided an excellent article "Lincoln County—An Historical Overview" for this special issue and Leon C. Metz provided a fine resumé of a number of the books which have been published on the subject of the Lincoln County War. It is worth quoting Metz' commentary on ALIAS BILLY THE KID (University of New Mexico Press, 1955) by C. L. Sonnichsen and William V. Morrison, since this issue—did the Kid escape Garrett's bullet?—

has persisted in the apocrypha from BILLY THE KID (M-G-M, 1930) to YOUNG GUNS II (20th-Fox, 1990) and more questions have been directed to me about it (including telephone calls from various countries around the world) than any other. "These two author-historians," Metz wrote, "presented evidence that the Kid did not die of Pat Garrett's bullet, but lived on under the alias of Brushy Bill Roberts. Although this version did not win much acceptance among historians, it was still a masterpiece of research. Information and documents turned up by Morrison and Sonnichsen dumbfounded many of the experts. Thus we have the interesting case of a book whose premise has been rejected and yet whose scholarly findings are a benchmark of what superb research is all about."[133]

A biography of Pat Garrett which enjoyed wide distribution but which is best ignored is PAT GARRETT: A BIOGRAPHY OF THE FAMOUS MARSHAL AND THE KILLER OF BILLY THE KID (Doubleday, 1960) by Richard O'Connor. There are sixty-four major errors in the text of those years pertaining to the Kid and the Lincoln County War (I regard the error in the title as a minor one) and most of them were addressed by Ramon F. Adams in his critical annotation for this book in BURS UNDER THE SADDLE. There is no documentary evidence—other than rumor—to attribute Garrett's murder to "Deacon" Jim Miller. O'Connor did so. To the extent that any kind of a case can be made for this proposition, the reader would be better advised to consult Glenn Shirley's SHOTGUN FOR HIRE: THE STORY OF "DEACON" JIM MILLER, KILLER OF PAT GARRETT (University of Oklahoma Press, 1970).

The best biography to appear to date on Garrett is Leon C. Metz's PAT GARRETT: THE STORY OF A WESTERN LAWMAN (University of Oklahoma Press, 1974). Ramon F. Adams in MORE BURS UNDER THE SADDLE corrected the most serious errors in this book, such as having the Kid armed when Garrett shot him, but I would criticize Metz more generally for having relied too heavily, and too naïvely, on the Garret/Upson account. In a letter to me dated 1 April 1981, Metz commented that he felt he was mistaken in having accepted the Garrett/Upson description of the landscape around the rock house at Stinking Springs. "Described was how the horses were hid behind a hill, etc. Well, a guy wrote me about a year ago saying he had visited the spot, and there are no hills. The land is flat. Garrett and the others crawling up and down banks is not correct, if my informant is correct. So if this guy knows what he is talking about, I goofed. I was enough of a professional to know that I should have gone and looked the area over myself—and drawn my own conclusions." It may well be, however, that a hundred years have produced some changes in the physical terrain of that area. The photographs Colonel Fulton supplied for his edition of the Garrett/Upson account do show something of a rise behind where the rock house stood and possibly the remains of a shallow arroyo nearby. Examining the area today would not necessarily settle the question as decisively as these photographs do. I think on this point—a shallow arroyo before the rock house along which the posse crept—Garrett and James East in his correspondence describing the episode may be trusted. Thanks to C. L. Sonnichsen's collection, Metz was able to see James East's letter of 20 May 1926 to Judge William H. Burges which describes the meeting between the Kid and Paulita Maxwell at Fort Sumner after the Kid's capture and confirms her relationship with him. This letter is to be supplemented with the letter to Charlie Siringo quoted by Miguel Otero in his THE REAL BILLY THE KID and East's letter to Eugene Manlove Rhodes quoted in W. H. Hutchinson's A BAR CROSS MAN: THE LIFE AND PERSONAL WRITINGS OF EUGENE MANLOVE RHODES (University of Oklahoma Press, 1956). Metz did make the mistake at one point of referring to Señora Maria de la Luz Beaubien Maxwell as "Mrs. Pete Maxwell," whereas Pete was her son; and, after uncovering the vital information—from an interview with Cliff McKinney, son of Kip McKinney—that it was Pete Maxwell who informed on the Kid to Poe and Garrett to get the Kid away from his sister, Paulita, Metz then tried to link the Kid romantically with Celsa Gutiérrez and, following Burns, had the Kid at Fort Sumner on the night of 14 July 1881 to see Celsa. Robert N. Mullin confirmed in an undated note to Colonel Fulton in the Fulton Papers at the University of Arizona that the Kid may have fathered two daughters by various women, but Eve Ball also had far more definite information about Billy the Kid's son who had died sometime before 22 June 1968 when Metz talked with her at Ruidoso, New Mexico, the family name of whom she refused to divulge in order to protect other family members. When and if this information is finally published, it will probably do little more than substantiate what is already known from other sources as to the identities of the father and mother. I think that for many, approaching the Lincoln County War and the Kid for the first time through the narratives of the Garrett/Upson and Burns accounts, it is very difficult subsequently to surrender all of these fantasies. There is some deep psychological, or perhaps archetypal, attraction which they exert which is the only way I can explain their persistence in the writings of contemporary historians. The wish to have them be true is stronger, in many cases, it would seem than any amount of professional and scholarly discipline. Moreover, some persist in defending them in the face of any contrary evidence, rather as doctrinaire theologians avoid even reading the research that has been done concerning the historical Jesus of Nazareth. If the very idea of such an analogy seems blasphemous, I apologize, but the compulsion to believe in connection with some of these matters seems to overwhelm reason itself, to say nothing of the documents in the case.

SHERIFF WILLIAM BRADY: TRAGIC HERO OF THE LINCOLN COUNTY WAR (Sunstone Press, 1986) by Donald R. Lavash is a problematic book. Frederick Nolan in THE LINCOLN COUNTY WAR: A DOCUMENTARY HISTORY termed it contentious and it definitely is that. The basic problem with the premise expressed in its title is that when you have a hero, you have to have a villain or villains. Since Brady was aligned with Dolan and Murphy, it has to be the other side. None of the questionable activities of the House is mentioned. Even Tunstall's death is glossed over by a superficial description: "It was nightfall making it difficult for the posse. Moments later shots were fired. Tunstall was dead."[134] Utley provided a Foreword to the book in which he commented: "Lavash sees Tunstall and McSween as unscrupulous adventurers intent on displacing

Murphy and Dolan as the overlords of Lincoln County. When the conflict intensi-
fied, Lavash charges, McSween put up the money to pay for Brady's assassination.
This is heady stuff—radical revisionism, no less."[135] The book, and most probably
Lavash himself, inspired Utley to come up with many of his own fantasies about
the Lincoln County War and the Kid. The basis for the charge against McSween is
Trujillo Fantasy No. 10. On the basis of his treatment of the Kid and the Lincoln
County War, Lavash's biography would more aptly belong in the section devoted
to fantasy books. However, what saves it from this fate are two important factors.
While it is not to be trusted in the least after McSween's arrival on the scene (and
the Kid's), the early background of William Brady's life and military career was
scrupulously researched and is invaluable in furthering our understanding of a
complex man. Moreover, because he had access to the Brady family records, Lavash
presents Sheriff Brady in a fuller light than merely as a Murphy-Dolan "tool," as
Tunstall put it. He was a farmer, a husband, a father, and a political leader in his
community. When Brady was assassinated, he left behind him his Mexican wife
and eight children, the oldest of whom was not quite fifteen. What did the Lincoln
County community do when Bonifacia Brady's husband was murdered? In a word:
nothing. Her husband, whatever his sympathies, was a law enforcement official
who had lost his life in service to his community and the response of the County
Commission should have been otherwise than this. Friends and neighbors came to
her assistance. This is something that happened so often on the frontier and which
is so frequently overlooked by historians, especially those concerned with conflicts
such as the Lincoln County War. It is also to the credit of J. J. Dolan that he
purchased the 320 acre Brady farm, paying off $1,600 in claims, debts, and liens
that had been filed against Bonifacia Brady. And he did more. He transferred to
Mrs. Brady 120 acres of cultivated land containing a ranch house and barn situated
on the Rio Ruidoso in the San Patricio district where Mrs. Brady moved with her
family. This aspect of Dolan's personality is as worthy of inclusion in the history
of the conflict as his violent response to economic and legal challenge. William
Brady's life, from his early years of poverty in Ireland to his military and civilian
career in the New World, is a part of his story worthy of inclusion in any balanced
account of the man rather than just his final years and his murder. Because it has
so long been the tendency of popular writers and fabulists to reduce the Lincoln
County War to the narrative structure of a formulary Western with clearly defined
heroes and villains, Lavash's attempt to portray Brady as a hero is scarcely unique.
However, the sum total of his portrait is to remind the reader that nothing about that
particular conflict was so simple as it has often been made to seem. In these terms,
Lavash, as ill-warranted as many of his assertions might appear, did add a vital
ingredient necessary for an adjustment in our perspective. Sheriff William Brady
emerges a far more complicated personality in this book than he does in any other
account and for this reason Lavash's biography, no less than Metz' equally flawed
biography of Garrett, deserves serious attention.

III

Colonel Maurice Garland Fulton's HISTORY OF THE LINCOLN COUNTY WAR (University of Arizona Press, 1968) edited by Robert N. Mullin is, notwithstanding the passage of the years, still required reading on the subject. Colonel Fulton worked on this book for most of his later life and even so it was in need of some editorial work upon his death. There are more than a few small errors in it and his chronology of events should be reconciled with the chronology in this book and with that in Nolan's book discussed below. The Kid's confrontation with John Chisum is definitely out of chronological sequence, among numerous other incidents. Green Wilson is not identified as Squire Wilson. The Kid is erroneously stated to have been visiting Bob Campbell at Fort Sumner the night he died rather than Jesus Silva. But these are perhaps minor oversights given the period during which the book was researched and some of them probably would not have been present had Colonel Fulton lived to complete his work.

This history is ably supplemented by William A. Keleher's VIOLENCE IN LINCOLN COUNTY: 1869–1881 (University of New Mexico Press, 1957) which has many rare documents and invaluable genealogies for a number of the participants. It is augmented, ideally, with Keleher's subsequent book THE FABULOUS FRONTIER: TWELVE NEW MEXICO ITEMS (University of New Mexico Press, 1945; revised edition, 1962). Keleher is almost always reliable, although, particularly in THE FABULOUS FRONTIER, he went out of his way, as did Fulton, to place as generous a construction as he could on everything—which may well be regarded as a virtue in a historical account of the Lincoln County War, given the passions of so many who have written about it or told only their side of the conflict. Yet, Keleher often carried this posture a bit too far. For example, standard operating procedure for Major Murphy in Lincoln County was to make loans and then hold mortgages. When a debtor would fall behind in payments—and this was usually the case—and was in danger of losing the mortgaged property, Murphy was then in a position to tell the debtor how to vote in a given election, e.g., that of sheriff. J. J. Dolan inherited this method and used it to good advantage in the election of Pat Garrett. At best, however, this was penny-ante compared to T. B. Catron's use of this same method. Catron "seldom filed a mortgage deed for record," Keleher wrote in THE FABULOUS FRONTIER; "none was ever foreclosed. Few notes were ever paid by borrowers. In making loans and accepting notes there was in Catron's mind a desire to help out friends and acquaintances, but at the same time he wished to control the borrower politically." Catron left, at his death, some $250,000 in such notes and mortgages. Surely, his motive was more the latter than the former!

There are some minor problems with Frederick Nolan's THE LINCOLN COUNTY WAR: A DOCUMENTARY HISTORY. While, according to his own testimony, Utley adopted generic racist terms such as Hispanic by his own volition, Nolan was required to do so by the editorial staff at the University of Oklahoma Press. I have already addressed this question with regard to Utley's books and would only add that it is to be hoped that in a future, revised edition of this fine and generally balanced account Nolan will be permitted to restore to native New Mexicans the rightful integrity of their culture and long history on this continent which pre-dated the advent of the United States that eventually annexed them. It is jarring to read constant references to the indigenous Mexican population in all the contemporary documents and then to have the author refer to these people as Hispanics, disenfranchising them more readily of their cultural heritage through nomenclature than the imposition at the time of Anglo-American mores and in many cases legal chicanery designed to rob them of their land and possessions. Should not historians at least permit them their cultural identity?

I have already noted that Nolan subscribed to Burns Fantasy No. 15 and he also fell victim to Burns Fantasy No. 11. It was his intention to conclude his history with the words of how the Kid rode into legend after his escape from the Lincoln jail. The same publisher that, according to Professor Gibson had earlier excised all references to the Kid in his book on Colonel Fountain, now insisted that Nolan include the pursuit and death of the Kid. By his own admission, Nolan had only a minimal interest in the Kid, his area of concentration being the subject of the Lincoln County War itself. As a consequence, this is an area he seems not to have researched as diligently as earlier events and for this reason probably found himself having to rely, as have so many others, on the Garrett/Upson account. He includes Garrett/Upson Fantasies Nos. 1, 62, 65, 67, 70, 71, 72, and 74. Since it should be obvious from his inclusion of Burns Fantasy No. 15 that Spanish is not a strong suit for Nolan, it is also not surprising to find in his text such linguistic absurdities as "the La Mesilla jail" or "jacals" for *jacales*. I think any reader conversant with Spanish or of Spanish-American origin will find these illiteracies as disturbing as the obsessive use of the term Hispanic. Nolan also flirts with the notion that the Kid may have once been a member of Jesse Evans's gang, but in this case he did not completely succumb to the blandishments of the Garrett/Upson account. Generally, his book is an example of splendid historiography, impartial and inclusive, and vital reading for anyone concerned in the least with the subject of the Lincoln County War. Nolan did conclude, perhaps correctly, that "the time has come now to render sterner judgment on Tunstall and especially on Alexander McSween." Unquestionably, it behooves everyone to desert finally and forever Burns Fantasy No. 16 that "Murphy's cause was basically wrong and McSween's basically right. . . . "[136] However, Nolan also added a caution that must also remain paramount in any consideration of the conflict when he wrote: "To state the case against the money-hungry McSweens, however, is not in any way to attempt to justify or condone the autocratic arrogance of Murphy or the murderous deviousness of his chief adjutant."[137]

The Kid plays only a limited role in the text of Frederick Nolan's earlier effort, THE LIFE AND DEATH OF JOHN HENRY TUNSTALL (University of New Mexico Press, 1965), but the book is vital for an understanding of Tunstall's character and just how his presence and ambitions acted as a catalyst for the Lincoln County War. The Kid does not figure at all in Arrell Morgan Gibson's THE LIFE AND DEATH OF COLONEL ALBERT JENNINGS FOUNTAIN (University of

Oklahoma Press, 1965). According to a letter Professor Gibson sent me as indicated above, all the material pertaining to the Kid's trial at Mesilla and Colonel Fountain's role in it had to be excised from his text at the request of the publisher—perhaps for reasons of space. However, Fountain's life and death are relevant to the Lincoln County War indirectly and were significant in Pat Garrett's later career as a lawman.

J. C. Dykes's BILLY THE KID: BIBLIOGRAPHY OF A LEGEND (University of New Mexico Press, 1952) is not complete, as I implied in my Preface to this book, but it is extremely valuable as far as it goes and in terms of the entries in it. Dykes annotated his bibliography with perspicacity so it is possible for a reader to gain an immediate impression as to what slant a particular entry takes with regard to the Kid and, above all, Dykes was thoroughly familiar with the material that he indexed and so can be trusted.

Ramon F. Adams's four books relevant to the Kid are indispensable: A FITTING DEATH FOR BILLY THE KID (University of Oklahoma Press, 1960), BURS UNDER THE SADDLE: A SECOND LOOK AT BOOKS AND HISTORIES OF THE WEST (University of Oklahoma Press, 1964), SIX-GUNS AND SADDLE LEATHER: A BIBLIOGRAPHY OF BOOKS AND PAMPHLETS ON WEST-ERN OUTLAWS AND GUNMEN (University of Oklahoma Press, 1954 and 1969), and MORE BURS UNDER THE SADDLE (University of Oklahoma Press, 1979). Fortunately, I can think of few others such as Frazier Hunt where Adams let down his critical guard. "Adams never took time to retire," Wayne Gard wrote in his Foreword to MORE BURS UNDER THE SADDLE. "Even in his last years, when he was in his eighties, he spent part of each day in research and writing, turning out new books and updating earlier ones. Yet he always had time to give a hand to another writer who might need help. Many will remember him as one who swept some of the cobwebs from the history of the American West and who set a fine example in telling the story of the frontier as it really happened." Frankly I do not know whom we will find to replace Adams. Indeed, anyone reading a book about the Kid or the Lincoln County War would be well advised to consult Adams's entry on it for a correction of errors in the text. His information on the Kid, of course, will date as more and more information comes to light, but what he had to say will always be applicable to the older efforts in the field.

The entries in Bill O'Neal's ENCYCLOPEDIA OF WESTERN GUNFIGHT-ERS (University of Oklahoma Press, 1979) pertaining to the Kid and other participants in the Lincoln County War are rarely reliable. For example, in describing the ambush of Frank Coe, James "Ab" Saunders, and Frank MacNab by the Seven Rivers gang on the night of 29 April 1878, O'Neal had Coe taken into custody by the ambushers "leaving behind both the wounded Saunders and McNab's [MacNab's] bullet-riddled body." Saunders was in fact not left behind but was instead cared for and ultimately taken to the Fort Stanton post hospital. A more serious, and less excusable, error occurred when O'Neal attributed Pat Garrett's assassination to Jim Miller rather than to Wayne Brazel who confessed to and was tried for the crime. O'Neal could have had no evidence—or, if he had, he did not show its source—to validate this statement, other than a citation of Glenn Shirley's

SHOTGUN FOR HIRE. It is one thing to suggest the guilt of Miller, another to state it unequivocally. In all justice to his sources and the documents in the case, O'Neal should not have been quite so positive about what remains a disputable attribution.

For a long time a definitive biography of Lew Wallace was needed and LEW WALLACE: MILITANT ROMANTIC (McGraw-Hill, 1980) by Robert E. and Katherine M. Morsberger goes a long way toward fulfilling this need. There are only eight major, and serious, errors in the section devoted to the Kid and the Lincoln County War—the reference to Walter Noble Burns's THE SAGA OF BILLY THE KID in the bibliography accounting for most of them—but it is my feeling that the authors did not stress sufficiently the ways in which Governor Wallace's good intentions were effectively frustrated by the Santa Fe Ring, nor does Wallace's personality emerge with the clarity I would have hoped. However, it does remain an impressive undertaking, on the whole, and is of more than passing interest to the student of the Lincoln County War.

Beyond these general histories and biographies, there are a handful of books which deserve some mention—not because they are accurate, but because they are not and because they have been widely distributed and continue to influence the growth of the legend of Billy the Kid. The many errors to be found in Carl W. Breihan's BADMEN OF THE FRONTIER DAYS (McBride, 1957) and GREAT GUNFIGHTERS OF THE WEST (John Long, 1961) and in TRAIL DRIVING DAYS (Scribner's, 1952) by Dee Brown and Martin F. Schmitt are addressed in Adams's BURS UNDER THE SADDLE. All three books base their accounts on a combination of Garrett/Upson and Burns.

Dane Coolidge's account of the Kid and the Lincoln County War in FIGHTING MEN OF THE WEST (Dutton, 1932) is generally garbled and actually of interest only for the light it throws on how Coolidge came up with his fictional narratives based on the Kid, discussed at length in the next chapter. However, Coolidge was the first to note that Poe built up his fictitious story about an informant in White Oaks to protect the real informant—albeit Coolidge implied that the person most in need of protection was Paulita rather than Pete Maxwell.

William MacLeod Raine in FAMOUS SHERIFFS AND WESTERN OUT- LAWS (Doubleday, 1929) tried to fit the Kid into his personal scheme of social Darwinism on the frontier, writing that Billy the Kid "by grace of natural fit- ness . . . was to become chief, because he was the worst bad man that ever strapped on a six-shooter in the West."[138]

The most unreliable chapter of all in Eugene Cunningham's TRIGGER- NOMETRY (Press of the Pioneers, 1934; Caxton Printers, 1941) is that devoted to the Kid and it is best skipped when reading this otherwise vivid and interesting series of vignettes. Cunningham depended almost totally on the Garrett/Upson and Burns fantasies in conceiving this narrative. One could wish, though, that Cunning- ham had documented one reference he made. "An old sheriff who knew the Kid (and knew Garrett) when neither was notorious," Cunningham wrote, "says: 'I remember one time he [the Kid] give Pat Garrett his horse and saddle and bedding and had to steal another outfit for himself. That was when Pat first come off the buffalo range and was going to be a cowboy for Maxwell.' "[139] Until some hard evidence can be cited, the conclusion reached by Leon C. Metz in his biography of Garrett is the one that has to stand, that while Garrett knew the Kid there is no basis on which to assume they often rode together or rustled cattle together.

Cunningham did later include an apologia of sorts for his chapter on the Kid which unfortunately appeared only in the British edition of TRIGGERNOMETRY (Transworld Publishers, 1957). "Over the years," Cunningham wrote, "a thousand [aficionadoes] have sifted the Billy the Kid midden, treasuring the tiniest shards of Fact and (I fear) getting better and brighter recollections from Oldtimer. But some skilled, hard-headed investigators have spent much time and money hunting evidence as distinguished from fifth-hand hearsay.

"W. H. Hutchinson, student of New Mexicana, while better known for his Eugene Manlove Rhodes biography A BAR CROSS MAN, has dredged up Kid data. J. C. Dykes has hunted down the slightest printed reference. Frederick Nolan of Liverpool has been 'muy perro' on the Tunstall trail in England, recovering from family and official records data we earlier writers knew nothing of save by implication.

"But Robert N. Mullin and Philip J. Rasch, logical, indefatigable, at horrific dollarage per gram, have built up facts on the Kid's mother and his small-boyhood. They have destroyed some of the myths which, as I wrote my preceding pages, were all that we had about the mother's journey to New Mexico, her marriage to Antrim, the Kid's youth. They show that between 1870 and 1873 a woman calling herself Catherine McCarty arrived in Santa Fe with two small boys—her sons, she said. She stated that her husband had died in New York. The boys were Joseph and Henry—who was to become 'Billy the Kid.' March 1, 1873 she married a man named Antrim. The four removed to Silver City, where she operated a boarding-house. September 16, 1874 she died of tuberculosis.

"Henry McCarty—'Kid' Antrim—'Billy the Kid'—killed nobody in Silver City! The tales of youthful homicides—and his stepfather's cruelty—were his own later inventions. He was arrested for theft in '76 or '77 and broke jail. Antrim gave him money for a run to Arizona. At Camp Grant, August 25, 1877 he killed F. P. Cahill—and ran. With Jesse Evans he was a member of a rustler gang. In the Fall of '77 Tunstall hired him—and after that his record is fairly clear to us. But from 1873 to 1877 little more is ours than hearsay and conjecture. Why he chose 'Bonney' for a go-by is still an unsolved puzzle."[140] Even if some of what he wrote hard on twenty-five years later from when he first turned his hand to treat the Kid's story would now have to be modified further, it will always be to Gene Cunningham's credit that he was willing to incorporate documented evidence when it was validly presented. Many have not been so willing.

Erna Fergusson's MURDER AND MYSTERY IN NEW MEXICO (Merle Armitage, 1948) is also unreliable in its historical construction of the Lincoln County War, but her account of the Kid's death, while it contains no new information, is valid.

On 12 May 1926, while he was doing preliminary research on THE REAL BILLY THE KID, Mrs. McSween Barber sent a letter to Miguel Otero denying emphatically that she had played the piano while the McSween home was burning. "Can you imagine any woman with a humane nature sitting at a piano playing national airs when the house was burning?" she asked.[141] THE GUNFIGHTERS (Time-Life, 1974), part of the TIME-LIFE series on the American West, goes every other account one better and in its account of the supposed incident has Mrs. McSween joined by her black servant at the violin to provide a piano/violin duet while the house burned to the ground! The date of the Kid's death is given as 13 July 1881—in short, a book to be avoided.

The account of the Kid provided in THE READER'S ENCYCLOPEDIA OF THE AMERICAN WEST (Crowell, 1977) edited by Howard Lamar is generally reliable, although I would question the statements that "there is some evidence that he was born William H. Bonney" and that, in the killings of Morton and Baker, "both men were killed, probably by Billy the Kid."[142] The Kid's date of birth is given as "1859?" and this, at least, is more probable than 1861.

There are hundreds of other books and articles which make reference to the Kid and, for the most part, these are to be found indexed in Dykes's bibliography or cited and corrected in Adams's books. With the exception of the last several titles, I have confined myself in this chapter to articles and books which will be helpful to a reader in seeking either to know more about the Kid that is factually reliable or which have played a central role in the development of the legend which has developed around the Kid's life and times. A further guide to archival collections of personal papers and various other documents relevant to a study of the Kid's life and the history of the Lincoln County War can be found in Appendix A.

In concluding this chapter, I feel compelled to comment that a new biography of Billy the Kid is not really needed unless something new is uncovered about his life or death. What *is* needed far more than another book about the Kid which either summarizes what is already known, or creates new fantasies about him, is a rigorously researched biography of Alexander A. McSween and Susan Hummer McSween Barber. When Reverend Ealy was living with the McSweens in Lincoln, McSween asked the minister/physician to write letters in German to potential Fritz relatives in Germany to see if they had any claim against the estate and if they would be willing to appoint McSween as their legal representative. Reverend Ealy noted that he did not think McSween had ever received a reply to any of these letters.

There are simply too many nagging questions about McSween's motives and intentions for this matter to be allowed to rest. What happened to the Fritz inheritance money? The heirs never received a penny. What happened to John H. Tunstall's considerable investments? His family in England never received a cent back. While I do not, naturally, incline to the Utley fantasy that Susan McSween was violent and homicidal—she never threatened violence or killed anyone—I do believe her subsequent financial success was paid for at least in part from money she managed to extort from Richard Brewer's family (through her claim on his ranch), from the Fritz estate, and from the Tunstall estate. By what legal instruments and financial arrangements did James J. Dolan take over ownership of the Tunstall store and his Rio Feliz ranch? Tunstall claimed to his father that he had McSween well within his control. Did he? How much influence did McSween exert on the youthful and relatively inexperienced Tunstall to get him to invest so heavily in Lincoln County and to dream of seizing the business domain of the House? Was McSween so foolish as to think that money alone could overcome political influence among the powerful legislative, judicial, and military leaders in the Territory, much less the Santa Fe Ring? Did McSween naïvely believe that faith in God alone would conquer the opposition, or was he more devious than that? What role might Tunstall's having contracted syphilis exerted on his business decisions and his grasp of events and circumstances? The truth of the matter is that we do not really know. McSween's origins, and those of his wife, are still obscured from us by the veil of time and Tunstall's many, many letters home show us only the persona he projected to his family and not the inner man.

It may be that the answers to some of these questions will alter our perspective on the Lincoln County War. If that is to happen, however, it will come about through means other than the fantasies created by Robert M. Utley or the partisanship displayed at times by Donald R. Lavash. It will come about through documents and research into areas and sources of information hitherto untapped and the existence of which may as yet be unsuspected. The folly of decades spent trying to locate the birth records of the Kid in New York City, prompted by an Upson fantasy and little else, might have been more fruitfully spent searching records in the state where he said he was born: Missouri. Why have otherwise competent historians preferred to believe Upson was telling the truth and the Kid lying when Upson was obviously compelled to fill in a life about which he knew very little and the Kid had no real reason to avoid the truth? It must be the same with the other personalities involved in this conflict. The proper questions have to be asked and researched before we are likely to make any significant progress toward an even more accurate construction of the historical reality than the one we now have. Lastly, before "politically correct" nomenclature banishes them totally into nonexistence through generic racism, what were the effects of the Lincoln County War on the Mexican-American population living there, those who sided McSween, those who sided Dolan, those who harbored and loved the Kid, and those who would have been as disenfranchised by a Tunstall-McSween combination as surely as they had been by the Murphy-Dolan ring? For me the stories of José Chávez y Chávez, Juan Patrón, Atanacio Martínez, Pablita [Paulita] Maxwell, Pedro [Pete] Maxwell, Bonifacia Brady, Martín Chávez, and Apolinaria Gutiérrez Garrett—among many others—hold answers for all of us which have been deliberately obfuscated by fabulists from Upson through Utley and, it must also be admitted, by historians from Fulton through Nolan—although to his credit Nolan did take great pains to restore some balance to our perspective. Notwithstanding, until someone conversant with Mexican culture and the milieu of native New Mexico writes a history from the *points of view* of these participants in the events, we have only half the history and—I strongly suspect—the less interesting half.

BIBLIOGRAPHY OF HISTORICAL SOURCES

Firsthand Accounts

Ball, Eve, MA'AM JONES OF THE PECOS (Tucson: University of Arizona Press, 1969).

Coe, George W., FRONTIER FIGHTER: THE AUTOBIOGRAPHY OF GEORGE W. COE WHO FOUGHT AND RODE WITH BILLY THE KID AS RELATED TO NAN HILLARY HARRISON (Boston: Houghton Mifflin, 1934).

Ealy, Ruth R., WATER IN A THIRSTY LAND (1955), a copy of which typescript is on deposit at the Wisconsin State Historical Society.

Ealy, Taylor F., MISSIONARIES, OUTLAWS, AND INDIANS: TAYLOR F. EALY AT LINCOLN AND ZUNI, 1878–1881 (University of New Mexico Press, 1984) edited and annotated by Norman J. Bender.

Garrett, Pat F. (pseud. Marshall Ashmun Upson), THE AUTHENTIC LIFE OF BILLY THE KID, etc., first published in 1882 was reissued (New York: Macmillan, 1927) edited and annotated by Colonel Maurice Garland Fulton and reissued again as part of The Western Frontier Library (Norman: University of Oklahoma Press, 1954) with an Introduction by J. C. Dykes. There have been other editions of this book—J .C. Dykes noted them in his Introduction—but the two listed are the most important.

Hoyt, Henry F., A FRONTIER DOCTOR (Boston: Houghton Mifflin, 1929).

Klasner, Lily, MY GIRLHOOD AMONG OUTLAWS (Tucson: University of Arizona Press, 1972) edited with an Introduction by Eve Ball.

Poe, John W., THE DEATH OF BILLY THE KID (Boston: Houghton Mifflin, 1933) edited with an Introduction by Col. Maurice Garland Fulton.

Poe, Sophie A., BUCKBOARD DAYS (Caldwell: Caxton Printers, 1936) edited by Eugene Cunningham; reissued (Albuquerque: University of New Mexico Press, 1981) with an Introduction by Sandra L. Myres.

Siringo, Charles A., A TEXAS COWBOY; OR FIFTEEN YEARS ON THE HURRI-CANE DECK OF A SPANISH PONY—TAKEN FROM REAL LIFE (1885); reissued (New York: William Sloane Associates, 1950) with an Introduction by J. Frank Dobie; this edition reprinted (Lincoln: University of Nebraska Press, 1966).

———, A LONE STAR COWBOY, privately printed (Santa Fe, 1919).

———, A HISTORY OF "BILLY THE KID," privately printed (Santa Fe, 1920).

———, RIATA AND SPURS (Boston: Houghton Mifflin, 1927).

Wallace, Lew, LEW WALLACE: AN AUTOBIOGRAPHY (New York: Harper's, 1906) published in two volumes.

Biographies

Burns, Walter Noble, THE SAGA OF BILLY THE KID (New York: Doubleday, 1926).

Cline, Donald, ALIAS BILLY THE KID: THE MAN BEHIND THE LEGEND (Santa Fe: Sunstone Press, 1986).

Hendron, J. W., THE STORY OF BILLY THE KID (Santa Fe: Rydal Press, 1948).

Hough, Emerson, THE STORY OF THE COWBOY (New York: D. Appleton, 1897).

———, "Billy the Kid, the True Story of a Western 'Bad Man,' " EVERYBODY'S MAGAZINE (Vol. 5, No. 25) September, 1901, pp. 302–310.

_____, THE STORY OF THE OUTLAW—A STUDY OF THE WESTERN DESPER-
ADO (New York: Outing, 1907).

Hunt, Frazier, THE TRAGIC DAYS OF BILLY THE KID (New York: Hastings House,
1956).

Kadlec, Robert F. (ed.), THEY "KNEW" BILLY THE KID: INTERVIEWS WITH OLD-
TIME NEW MEXICANS (Santa Fe: Ancient City Press, 1987) with an Afterword by J. C. Dykes.

Koop, W. A., "Billy the Kid: The Trail of a Kansas Legend," THE TRAIL GUIDE, Kansas
City: September, 1964.

Lavash, Donald R., SHERIFF WILLIAM BRADY: TRAGIC HERO OF THE LINCOLN
COUNTY WAR (Santa Fe: Sunstone Press, 1986).

Metz, Leon C., PAT GARRETT: THE STORY OF A WESTERN LAWMAN (Norman:
University of Oklahoma Press, 1974).

Mullin, Robert N., with Philip J. Rasch, "New Light on the Legend of Billy the Kid," NEW
MEXICO FOLKLORE RECORD (Vol. II), 1952–1953, pp. 1–5.

_____, "Pat Garrett: Two Forgotten Killings," PASSWORD (Vol. X, No. 2), published by
the El Paso Historical Society, Summer, 1965, pp. 57–63.

_____, A CHRONOLOGY OF THE LINCOLN COUNTY WAR (Santa Fe: Press of the
Territorian, 1966).

_____, THE BOYHOOD OF BILLY THE KID (El Paso: Texas Western Press, 1967),
Southwestern Studies Series (Vol. I, No. 1), Monograph 17.

_____, with W. H. Hutchinson, WHISKEY JIM AND A KID NAMED BILLIE (Claren-
don: Clarendon Press, 1967).

_____, THE STRANGE STORY OF WAYNE BRAZEL (Canyon: Palo Duro Press,
1969).

_____, "The Key to the Mystery of Pat Garrett," LOS ANGELES WESTERNERS
CORRAL (No. 92), June, 1969, pp. 1–5.

O'Connor, Richard, PAT GARRETT: A BIOGRAPHY OF THE FAMOUS MARSHAL
AND THE KILLER OF BILLY THE KID (New York: Doubleday, 1960).

Otero, Miguel Antonio, THE REAL BILLY THE KID WITH NEW LIGHT ON THE
LINCOLN COUNTY WAR (New York: Rufus Rockwell Wilson, 1936).

Rasch, Philip J., with Robert N. Mullin, "Dim Trails: The Pursuit of the McCarty Family,"
NEW MEXICO FOLKLORE RECORD (Vol. III), 1954, pp. 6–11.

_____, "The Twenty-One Men He Put Bullets Through," NEW MEXICO FOLKLORE
RECORD (Vol. IX), 1954–1955, pp. 8–14.

_____, "A Man Called Antrim," LOS ANGELES WESTERNERS BRAND BOOK (Vol.
VI), 1956, pp. 48–54.

_____, "More on the McCartys," ENGLISH WESTERNERS BRAND BOOK (Vol. III),
April, 1957, pp. 3–9.

_____, "John Kinney: King of the Rustlers," ENGLISH WESTERNERS BRAND BOOK
(Vol. IV), October, 1961, pp. 10–12.

_____, "War in Lincoln County," ENGLISH WESTERNERS BRAND BOOK (Vol. VI),
July, 1964, pp. 2–11.

_____, "The Trials of Lieutenant Colonel Dudley," ENGLISH WESTERNERS BRAND
BOOK (Vol. VIII), January, 1965, pp. 1–10.

_____, "The Hunting of Billy the Kid" [Part One], ENGLISH WESTERNERS BRAND
BOOK (Vol. XI), January, 1969, pp. 1–10.

———, "The Hunting of Billy the Kid" [Part Two], ENGLISH WESTERNERS BRAND BOOK (Vol. XI), April, 1969, pp. 1–10.

———, "Prelude to War: The Murder of John Henry Tunstall," ENGLISH WESTERN-ERS BRAND BOOK (Vol. XII), January, 1970, pp. 1–10.

———, "They Fought for the House," PORTRAITS IN GUNSMOKE (English Western-ers Society, 1971) edited by Jeff Burton, pp. 34–64.

———, "These Were the Regulators," HO! FOR THE GREAT WEST (English Western-ers Society, 1980) edited by Barry C. Johnson, pp. 50–69.

———, "Gus Gildea—An Arizone [sic] Pioneer," ENGLISH WESTERNERS BRAND BOOK (Summer, 1985), pp. 1–7.

———, "The Curious Case of Edward M. Kelly," NOLA QUARTERLY (Fall, 1987), pp. 8, 16–17.

Shirley, Glenn, SHOTGUN FOR HIRE: THE STORY OF "DEACON" JIM MILLER, KILLER OF PAT GARRETT (Norman: University of Oklahoma Press, 1970).

Utley, Robert M., BILLY THE KID: A SHORT AND VIOLENT LIFE (Lincoln: Univer-sity of Nebraska Press, 1991).

Weddle, Jerry, "Apprenticeship of an Outlaw: Billy the Kid in Arizona," JOURNAL OF ARIZONA HISTORY (Autumn, 1990), pp. 233–252.

General Books

Adams, Ramon F., A FITTING DEATH FOR BILLY THE KID (Norman: University of Oklahoma Press, 1960).

———, BURS UNDER THE SADDLE: A SECOND LOOK AT BOOKS AND HISTO-RIES OF THE WEST (Norman: University of Oklahoma Press, 1964).

———, SIX-GUNS AND SADDLE LEATHER: A BIBLIOGRAPHY OF BOOKS AND PAMPHLETS ON WESTERN OUTLAWS AND GUNMEN (Norman: Univer-sity of Oklahoma Press, 1954; enlarged and revised edition, 1969).

———, MORE BURS UNDER THE SADDLE: BOOKS AND HISTORIES OF THE WEST (Norman: University of Oklahoma Press, 1979).

Ballert, Marion, with Carl W. Breihan, BILLY THE KID: A DATE WITH DESTINY (Seattle: Hangman Press, 1970).

Breihan, Carl W., BADMEN OF THE FRONTIER DAYS (New York: McBride, 1957).

———, GREAT GUNFIGHTERS OF THE WEST (London: John Long, 1961).

Brown, Dee, with Martin F. Schmitt, TRAIL DRIVING DAYS (New York: Scribner's, 1952).

Coolidge, Dane, FIGHTING MEN OF THE WEST (New York: Dutton, 1932).

Cunningham, Eugene, TRIGGERNOMETRY (New York: Press of the Pioneers, 1934); reissued (Caldwell: Caxton Printers, 1941); British edition (London: Transworld Publishers, 1957).

Dykes, J. C., BILLY THE KID: A BIBLIOGRAPHY OF A LEGEND (Albuquerque: University of New Mexico Press, 1952).

Fergusson, Erna, MURDER AND MYSTERY IN NEW MEXICO (Albuquerque: Merle Armitage, 1948).

Fulton, Maurice Garland, HISTORY OF THE LINCOLN COUNTY WAR (Tucson: University of Arizona Press, 1968) edited by Robert N. Mullin.

Gibson, Arrell Morgan, THE LIFE AND DEATH OF COLONEL ALBERT JENNINGS FOUNTAIN (Norman: University of Oklahoma Press, 1965).

GUNFIGHTERS, THE (New York: Time-Life Books, 1974).

Keleher, William A., VIOLENCE IN LINCOLN COUNTY: 1869–1881 (Albuquerque: University of New Mexico Press, 1957).

———, THE FABULOUS FRONTIER: TWELVE NEW MEXICO ITEMS (Albuquerque: University of New Mexico Press, 1945; revised edition, 1962).

Lamar, Howard (ed.), THE READER'S ENCYCLOPEDIA OF THE AMERICAN WEST (New York: Crowell, 1977).

Morsberger, Robert E., with Katharine M., LEW WALLACE: MILITANT ROMANTIC (New York: McGraw-Hill, 1980).

Nolan, Frederick W., THE LIFE AND DEATH OF JOHN HENRY TUNSTALL: THE LETTERS, DIARIES, AND ADVENTURES OF A REMARKABLE YOUNG ENGLISHMAN WHO WAS MURDERED IN 1878 DURING NEW MEXICO'S LINCOLN COUNTY WAR (Albuquerque: University of New Mexico Press, 1965).

Nolan, Frederick, THE LINCOLN COUNTY WAR: A DOCUMENTARY HISTORY (Norman: University of Oklahoma Press, 1992).

O'Neal, Bill, ENCYCLOPEDIA OF WESTERN GUNFIGHTERS (Norman: University of Oklahoma Press, 1979).

Raine, William MacLeod, FAMOUS SHERIFFS AND WESTERN OUTLAWS (New York: Doubleday, 1929).

RIO GRANDE HISTORY (No. 9) published by New Mexico State University, 1978.

Utley, Robert M., FOUR FIGHTERS OF LINCOLN COUNTY (Albuquerque: University of New Mexico Press, 1986).

———, HIGH NOON IN LINCOLN: VIOLENCE ON THE WESTERN FRONTIER (Albuquerque: University of New Mexico Press, 1987).

3

BILLY THE KID
IN FICTION

Of the eight "cheap" novels featuring Billy the Kid which J. C. Dykes cited as appearing prior to the Garrett/Upson account in his Introduction to the reissue edition of THE AUTHENTIC LIFE OF BILLY THE KID, copies of three have yet to be located.[1] Chronologically the first to appear of the remaining five was BILLY LeROY, THE COLORADO BANDIT; or, THE KING OF AMERICAN HIGH-WAYMEN (Richard K. Fox, 1881). It was first advertised in the NATIONAL POLICE GAZETTE of 2 July 1881. When the Kid died, it was reissued under the title THE LIFE AND DEEDS OF BILLY LeROY, ALIAS THE KID, KING OF THE AMERICAN HIGHWAYMEN. In the early 1880s there actually was a highwayman named Arthur Pond who went by the alias of Billy LeRoy, but Thomas F. Daggett, who was listed as the author of this paper-covered book, may have had Billy the Kid in mind as well since he made reference in his text to members of the Kid's gang such as Dave Rudabaugh and Tom O'Phallier [O'Folliard] and narrated how Billy LeRoy was presumably on one occasion "hotly pursued and was obliged to take refuge in a house in Lincoln, which was surrounded by sixty colored soldiers. To the demand to surrender he only laughed and shot down a soldier to show that he was game. The house was set on fire, when the Kid, after loading his Winchester rifle, leaped from the burning building and made a dash for liberty."[2] The account was obviously influential insofar as it seems to have been the origin of the fantasy—repeated often subsequently by others—of how the Kid began to kill Chisum's cowboys to cancel a debt he felt Chisum owed him. At the end, he and his gang are hanged by a mob that breaks into the jail in Del Norte, Colorado, where they are being held.

Even more popular was THE TRUE LIFE OF BILLY THE KID (Frank Tousey, 1881) written by John Woodruff Lewis and published under the pseudonym Don Jernado. The Kid's real name is given as William McCarthy and his birthplace New

York state, and not New York City. The Kid has a brother and sister and the family emigrates to New Mexico where the Kid's father dies when he is thirteen years old. His mother then "married a man named Henry Antum [William H. Antrim]."[3] The Kid meets up with Tom O'Fallaher [O'Folliard] and the two launch a crime wave. The Kid's first killing is the result of a squabble with a rival over a Mexican-American girl. The Lincoln County War, according to this author, "started because of the determination of old John Chisum, the great cattle king, and his partner, Alex McSwain [McSween], to establish a monopoly in the cattle-grazing business."[4] This move forced all of the small ranchers to unite behind the Murphy/Dolan faction, fighting for their rights. Lewis, as was mentioned, first told of Mrs. McSween's playing her piano while her house burned, to keep up the spirits of its defenders, a tale which has since become endemic in the legend of Billy the Kid. The Kid escapes from the Lincoln jail by hitting Bell over the head with one of his handcuffs and then diving for his gun. Garrett kills the Kid by hiding with a cocked rifle behind Pete Maxwell's bed and plugging him when he enters the door.

John W. Morrison's THE LIFE OF BILLY THE KID, A JUVENILE OUTLAW (Morrison's Sensational Library, 1881) asserts that the Kid's real name was Michael McCarthy and he killed his first man, Tom Moore, in New York City on 9 September 1879, a year after John H. Tunstall was murdered, and then fled to the West. Morrison borrowed several incidents from Daggett's account of Billy LeRoy, including the killing of Chisum's cowboys—adding that the Kid allowed five dollars a head per man against the debt he claimed. Morrison also garbled Lewis's narrative of the Kid's escape and his death.

BILLY THE KID, THE NEW MEXICAN OUTLAW (Denver Publishing Company, 1881) by Edmund Fable, Jr., has a Preface dated 15 July 1881, the day after the Kid died. According to Fable, the Kid's father died in New York City whereupon his mother married Thomas [William H.] Antrim, "a well-to-do mechanic."[5] It was kids in New York who named him Billy the Kid because of "his daring and prowess."[6] The Kid goes West and tries the life of an honest cowhand, only to be cheated of his money by a saloon tart and accused of and jailed for a robbery when he was only attempting to prevent it. This circumstance inclines him toward a life of crime. When he escapes jail by climbing up a chimney, he goes to work for a brutal blacksmith who abuses him—he tries to hit him with a hammer—to the point where he must kill him. Going to work for a man named Tontsill [Tunstall], the Kid accompanies him with two other men to retrieve some stolen stock, only for them to be set upon by the Dolan/Riley party. Tontsill is killed in the fray. The Kid then joins Chisom's [Chisum] gang of rustlers, but a member of the gang, McCloskey, tips off the Kid that Chisom and the others are planning to double-cross him. The Kid determines to kill Chisom and his cowboys to satisfy his need for revenge. Unfortunately his scheme goes astray. He shoots McCloskey instead, in the back, and, to cover up his shame at this cowardly act, he also shoots down Morton and Baker, two of Chisom's riders and witnesses to McCloskey's death.

Brady and Hindman are pointed out to the Kid in a saloon and he hides behind a house in order to shoot both of them. After this double killing, the Kid sends for Tom O'Phaller [O'Folliard] and organizes a gang. When the Dolan gang steals a herd of cattle from the McSween gang, the Kid's gang joins forces with the McSween gang. In a shoot-out at McSween's home, the Kid himself is responsible for killing thirteen men on the opposing side. When, finally, the Kid is arrested and sentenced to hang, Olinger shows "a disposition to temper his official duties with as much kindness as he could permit."[7] The Kid hits Olinger over the head with his handcuffs, gets his revolver, kills him, and then is waiting at the jail house window with the revolver when Bell returns to the jail. He shoots down Bell. The Kid is dressed in this story in "a blue dragoon jacket of the finest broadcloth, heavily loaded down with gold embroidery, buckskin pants dyed jet black, with small tinkling bells sewed down the sides" and a hat "covered with gold and jewels until it sparkled and shone in a dazzling and blinding manner when one looked upon it."[8] In his subtitle for his book, Fable declared that this was A TRUE AND IMPARTIAL HISTORY OF THE GREATEST OF AMERICAN OUTLAWS . . . WHO KILLED A MAN FOR EVERY YEAR IN HIS LIFE.

Kent Ladd Steckmesser in his book THE WESTERN HERO IN HISTORY AND LEGEND (University of Oklahoma Press, 1965) demonstrated through a comparison of lines just how dependent Fable had been in his account on a newspaper article written by P. Donan which appeared in the *Chicago Tribune* on 7 August 1881, as was the author of THE COWBOY'S CAREER; or THE DARE DEVIL DEEDS OF BILLY THE KID (Belford & Clark Publishing Company, 1881) who signed his name as "One of the Kids."[9] However, the latter also drew on the accounts I have previously cited. In THE COWBOY'S CAREER, the Lincoln County War is said to have begun when John Chisum and Alex McSwain [McSween] attempted to monopolize the cattle business in New Mexico. The Kid kills McClusky [McCloskey] and then chains Morton and Baker together by the wrists. When they try to escape, the Kid kills both of them with a rifle. The author deviated from other accounts by having Brady and Hindman come to Chisum's ranch to arrest the Kid, only for the Kid to shoot both of them. Seeing that Hindman is still alive, the Kid walks over to where he is lying and tells him to " 'Give Baker my love' " as he places "the muzzle of his derringer at Hindman's right temple and finished the bloody work."[10] Following Lewis, Mrs. McSwain [McSween] plays the piano while the McSween house burns, but, in a notable addition, Tom O'Fallaher [O'Folliard] fights his way out using a sword!

The publication of the Garrett/Upson account, and its paraphrasing by Charles Siringo, did not really help matters, since they only perpetuated more fantasies about the Kid. Later dime novelists did not limit themselves to these fantasies, but as their predecessors spun their stories with a freewheeling flair. J. C. Cowdrick in SILVER MASK, THE MAN OF MYSTERY; or, THE CROSS OF THE GOLDEN KEYS (Beadle and Adams, 1884) made the Kid a highwayman who is continually trying to kidnap the heroine. Francis W. Doughty in OLD KING BRADY AND BILLY THE KID; or THE GREAT DETECTIVE'S CHASE (Frank Tousey, 1890) made the Kid a highwayman who kidnaps the heroine but only after killing her father. Pat Garrett, "hidden under Pete Maxwell's bed for the purpose,"[11] finally stops the Kid's outrages.

There is little or no effort to evoke the Janus-figure image of the Kid in these stories. According to both Dykes in his Kid bibliography and Steckmesser in THE WESTERN HERO IN HISTORY AND LEGEND, this did not occur until the appearance of the very popular and long-running stage play, BILLY THE KID (1903), written by Walter Woods, pseudonym for Walvin Woods. The plot of this play is somewhat significant. In it, Billy's father deserts his mother in New York before he is born. Some years later, Billy's mother remarries, to a New Mexico rancher named Stephen Wright, and the Kid grows up to be a fine rider, excellent shot, and an upstanding young man. However, his father, although presumed dead, is really very much alive and the leader of an outlaw gang. He appears on the scene, tricks Billy into robbing his stepfather's safe, and then himself kills Billy's mother and stepfather. He next frames Billy for the crime so he can get at Wright's estate. Forced into outlawry, the Kid organizes a gang, but he is known to have robbed the rich and aided the poor. After a number of confrontations with his father and his gang, his father being the true villain, the Kid captures him and learns the awful truth: he is the son of a murderer. He lets his father go, in a fit of compassion, giving him his clothes, only for his father to be killed and identified as the Kid. So the body cannot be examined, the Kid's father falls down a forty-foot well. The Kid, freed from the past, is able to say to the beautiful heroine, who has stood by him: " 'To the law I am dead. Today my life begins anew. Come Nellie—we'll wander down life's pathway together, where the sun shines always.' "[12]

It was perhaps this play which inspired O. Henry to write his famous short story about the Kid, "The Caballero's Way," which appeared in the collection HEART OF THE WEST (Doubleday, Page, 1904). O. Henry called him the Cisco Kid, known for short as merely "the Kid," whose real name was Goodall, a variation on Bonney. "It had been," O. Henry wrote, "one of the Kid's pastimes to shoot Mexicans 'to see them kick,' "[13] an obvious reference to Emerson Hough's THE STORY OF THE COWBOY (1897) in which he told of how Billy the Kid once shot down seven Mexicans at a waterhole "just to see them kick." It has to be noted in this context, since this particularly unfair accusation was carried forward for decades in fictional treatments of the Kid, that nothing could have been farther from the truth. " 'In all his career,' " as Martín Chávez told former Governor Miguel Otero, " 'Billy never killed a native citizen of New Mexico, which was one of the reasons we were all so fond of him.' "[14] "The Kid was twenty-five, looked twenty," according to O. Henry, and because of all the men he had killed or winged "therefore a woman loved him."[15] The woman is Tonia Perez. Lieutenant Sandridge of the state rangers is put on the Kid's trail. He learns about Tonia. He pays her a visit and the two fall in love. Sandridge's height impresses Tonia the most, since "even the Kid, in spite of his achievements, was a stripling no larger than herself, with black, straight hair and a cold, marble face that chilled the noonday sun."[16] Sandridge takes to visiting Tonia regularly, fully aware that he might encounter the Kid on any of these occasions. The Kid discovers their secret trysts. Tonia tells Sandridge that " 'the rattlesnake is not quicker to strike than is "El Chivato," as they call him, to send a ball from his *pistola*.' "[17] She will send a message to Sandridge through a trusted confederate when the Kid shows up. Sandridge, before riding off, promises he will come as soon as the message arrives, and will hide, killing the Kid from ambush. The Kid, however, switches clothing with Tonia (as early as BILLY LeROY, THE COLORADO BANDIT, the Kid was portrayed as a female impersonator), and it is Tonia, and not the Kid, whom Sandridge kills.

Emerson Hough included the Kid's capture at Stinking Springs as an incident in his novel, HEART'S DESIRE (Macmillan, 1905), albeit White Oaks is called Heart's Desire, Garrett is called Sheriff Ben Stillson, and Stinking Springs is called Piños Altos. The portrait adds nothing to the Kid's image. He is viewed as a hopeless reprobate. J. C. Dykes in his bibliography cited P. S. McGreeney's DOWN AT STEIN'S PASS (Angel Guardian Press, 1909) as the first novel in hard covers in which the Kid is a central character and he is, interestingly, as in Woods's play a tool of the real villain and his death at Garrett's hands is not altogether justified. Yet nowhere in his defense of the Kid was McGreeney as eloquent as was Eugene Manlove Rhodes.

I cited in the previous chapter the anecdote in Charles Siringo's A TEXAS COWBOY on which Rhodes based PASÓ POR AQUÍ. The short novel appeared first in THE SATURDAY EVENING POST and then was combined in book form with ONCE IN THE SADDLE (Houghton Mifflin, 1927) and published under the title of the latter only. In his article, "In Defense of Pat Garrett," also cited above, Rhodes claimed to be living "on Mrs. McSween's old ranch."[18] He felt that the Kid and Garrett had been on friendly terms during the Kid's rustling days and that Billy the Kid should not have been hanged, "not unless they hanged several others at the same time."[19] "My sympathies," he declared, "without reservation, are with the McSween-Tunstall-Chisum side."[20] "I wonder if you can believe," he commented with regard to the Kid, "that my deepest feeling for him is pity for his hard fate?"[21] In his short novel, considered his best effort by many, Rhodes appears to have combined the stories of Billy Bonney and Billie Wilson and wrote the Kid's story as he would have had it happen. Rhodes's hero, Ross McEwen, holds up a bank in a rather daring fashion and is pursued by a posse. He throws away the paper money rather than face capture. After changing horses, he rides a steer for several miles before the steer, too, plays out. He comes upon a Mexican family suffering from diphtheria and nurses them through the illness, even though it exposes him to arrest. Among those on his trail is Patrick Floyd Garrett, sheriff of Doña Ana County. Garrett is sufficiently impressed with McEwen's action—he was summoned to the old Mexican's rancho by means of McEwen's signal fire—that, although knowing McEwen's real identity, he manages at the end to provide him with a safe-conduct out of the Territory.

There is no romance in Rhodes's short novel, but Rhodes did introduce an Eastern girl, a nurse, Jay Hollister, who works at the Alamogordo Hospital and who hates the West. She is neither made to change her mind, through love for a cowboy, nor to alter her values. Instead her values remain intransigent against the Western values illustrated by McEwen, Garrett, and the Mexican, Monte, whose border English was thought so charming that he was imitated by many other Western writers. It is Monte's magnificent soliloquy to the nurse which closes the story. " 'And thees fellow, too, thees redhead,' " he says, " 'he pass this way, *pasó por aquí* . . . and he mek here good and not weeked. But, before that—I am not God!' " " 'And him the sheriff!' " the nurse objects to Garrett's having let McEwen go. " 'Why they could impeach him for that. They could throw him out of office.' " " 'But who weel tell?' " Monte responds. " 'We are all decent people.' "22

In early 1926 Zane Grey's novel, FORLORN RIVER (Harper, 1927), was serialized in THE LADIES HOME JOURNAL. It proved popular with readers and, in the sequel he wrote to it, carried in the same magazine near the end of 1928, Grey provided his own view of the Lincoln County War and interpreted Billy the Kid's role in it. The plot of the sequel which was titled "NEVADA" (Harper, 1928) will not, however, make complete sense without some mention of the first book. FORLORN RIVER is set in northern California. Ben Ide is a wild horse hunter, rejected by his family. He lives in a cabin on the edge of Clear Lake where Forlorn River begins with his two pards, Nevada, about whom he knows very little, and Modoc, an Indian. Les Setter is the principal villain and he has designs on the heroine, Ina Blaine, who has been in love with Ben since they were children. Nevada is drawn according to the prototype of Owen Wister's Virginian, "tall, slim, lithe, broad of shoulder, dark as an Indian, with black piercing eyes" and he drawls "in the cool easy tone of the Southerner."23 In the course of the novel, Nevada and Hettie Ide, Ben's sister, fall in love. It does not end in a clinch for them, as it does for Ben and Ina. Nevada shoots down Les Setter and his two henchmen and then rides off into the distance.

"NEVADA" takes up the story with Nevada's riding off after the shooting. He crosses the border into Nevada and arrives in Lineville, a town where he is known under his rightful name, Jim Lacy, a notorious gunfighter. Jim rooms at Mrs. Wood's boardinghouse and they talk about Billy the Kid and the Lincoln County War.

" 'Jim, I once saw Billy the Kid in New Mexico,' " she tells him. " 'You used to look like him, not in face or body or walk, but jest in some way, some look I can't describe. But now it's gone.'

" 'Ahuh. Wal, I don't know whether or not you're complimentin' me,' drawled Nevada. 'Billy the Kid was a pretty wild hombre, wasn't he?'

" 'Humph! You'd have thought so if you'd gone through that Lincoln County cattle war with me an' my husband. They killed three hundred men, and my Jack was one of them.'

" 'Lincoln County War,' mused Nevada. 'Shore I've heard of that, too. An' how many of the three hundred did Billy the Kid kill?'

" 'Lord only knows,' she returned fervently. 'Billy had twenty-one men to his gun before the war an' that wasn't countin' Greasers and Injuns. They said he was death on them . . . . Yes, Jim, you had the look of Billy, an' if you kept on you'd been another like him. But somethin' has happened to you.' "24

What has happened to Nevada is that he has fallen in love with Hettie Ide and this, according to the conventions of a Zane Grey formulary Western, has caused him to change his ways. Jim gets involved in a shooting scrape and heads toward Arizona where, under the name Texas Jack, he goes to work for Judge Franklidge.

In the meantime, Ben and Ina Ide, happily married in California, are now living with Hettie and Ben's widowed mother. Ben's mother suffers from a lung condition and they decide to move to Arizona for the sake of her health, selling out the home ranch to some investors.

Jim Lacy, as Texas Jack, proposes to Judge Franklidge and another rancher, Tom Day, that he work his way in with the rustler gang. He tells them his real identity. His intention is to kill rustlers, and that is just what he does. "The Lincoln County War in New Mexico had ended recently," Grey wrote. "It had been the blackest and bloodiest fight between rustlers and cattlemen and many others who had been drawn into the vortex, that had ever been recorded in the frontier history of the Southwest. . . . To be sure, Billy the Kid, the deadliest of all the real desperadoes of the Southwest, had fallen in the Lincoln fight, along with the worst of his gang. But they had not all bitten the bloody dust of New Mexico."[25] Jim forms his own rustling gang with an old acquaintance from Lineville, Cash Burridge, the man who sells Ben Ide his ranch when Ide arrives in Arizona. Jim learns that the leader of the rival rustling outfit, the Pine Tree gang, is in fact a desperado from the Lincoln County War, a "close pard of Billy the Kid,"[26] but at first he cannot find out the man's identity.

Hettie sees the man she knows as Nevada for the first time in Arizona in a gunfight in the center of the street in Winthrop. Ben's new foreman, Clan Dillon, tries to force his attentions on Hettie only, unbeknownst to Hettie, to be slugged down for it by Nevada. Hettie, after the gunfight and learning that Nevada is Jim Lacy, confides some of her concern to Judge Franklidge with whom she is staying while in town. Franklidge again conveys Grey's view of the Lincoln County War as a "rustler war" similar to what is currently happening in their community. " 'We will come out of it,' " he assures Hettie. " 'These outlaws destroy themselves. I've a hunch some hard-shootin' gunman will come along and do for the ringleaders. It's happened here before. It happened lately in New Mexico.' "[27] Although Hettie does not know it, the judge is referring to Jim Lacy.

Marvie Blaine, Ina's younger brother, has come to Arizona with Ben and falls in love with Rose Hatt, the only girl and youngest in the Hatt clan which is associated with the Pine Tree gang. Cedar Hatt, Rose's oldest and most vicious brother, discovers Marvie and Rose together, and there is a struggle which Jim witnesses. Jim shoots the gun out of Hatt's hand, but it is Marvie who picks up the gun and shoots down Hatt. From Rose, Jim learns that the ringleader is a man who was known in New Mexico as Campbell [Bill Campbell?], but whose real name is Ed Richardson and who is going by the name currently of Clan Dillon.

Jim shoots it out with Dillon, killing him. The judge and Tom Day are on hand to exonerate him. Then Judge Franklidge explains to Hettie Jim Lacy's role in the West, thereby evoking for the first time in this narrative spanning two novels the

Janus image of Billy the Kid. " 'I have lived most of my life on the frontier and I know what its wildness has been, and still is,' " Franklidge says. " 'There are bad men and bad men. It is a distinction with a vast difference. I have met or seen many of the noted killers. Wild Bill, Wess [*sic*] Hardin, Kingfisher, Billy the Kid, Pat Garrett, an' a host of others. These men are not bloody murderers. They are a product of the times. The West could never have been populated without them. They strike a balance between the hordes of ruffians, outlaws, strong evil characters like Dillon, and the wild life of a wild era. It is the West as any Westerner knows it now. And as such we could not be pioneers, we could not progress without this violence. Without the snuffing out of dissolute and desperate men such as Dillon, Cedar Hatt, Stillwell [another man Jim shot], and so on. The rub is that only hard iron-nerved youths like Billy the Kid, or Jim Lacy, can meet such men on their own ground.' "28 In the binate ending with which FORLORN RIVER could not conclude, Jim is united with Hettie and Marvie with Rose.

It wasn't until 1936 that Grey's fascination with the Kid caused him to introduce him physically into one of his novels. SHADOW ON THE TRAIL (Harper, 1946) was one of the novels Grey wrote during the last years of his life which was not purchased by any slick magazine (and he had been too long away from the pulps and the niggardly prices they paid to contemplate that as a market). The same reasons it is inferior among his novels—episodic, rambling, not effectively structured for drama or tension, and with most of the important action sequences occurring *in camera*, described after the fact rather than shown happening—probably made it also unattractive as the basis for a motion picture even though several studios had Zane Grey film series currently in production during this decade. In his Foreword, Grey claims to have been inspired to write this book because of the example set by a man named Henderson, one of Billy the Kid's outfit who vanished just prior to the Lincoln County War. Presumably in speculating about this disappearance—although no one by this name known to history was associated with the Kid—Grey came up with his tale of Wade Holden who has spent all his formative years riding with the notorious bandit Simm Bell, an obvious surrogate for Sam Bass since Bell's manner of death resembles that of the historical outlaw. Bell is mortally wounded during an attempted bank robbery where a trap has been laid by Texas Rangers. Pursued by the rangers, Bell confesses to Wade that Wade is really his son and holds the rangers off long enough for Wade to make a getaway. Among the various adventures which befall Wade on the way to Arizona where Grey will finally get down to the basic plot of the novel, he assists a cattleman in fighting off rustlers and joins the herd on its way to New Mexico where it will be sold to Jesse Chisum. This inattention to names—Wess Hardin is again the way that gunfighter's name is spelled in this novel—seems typical of Grey's rather cavalier approach to actual historical events in the West. Grey once more characterizes the Lincoln County War as a conflict between cattlemen. Billy the Kid, even before the reader meets him, is described as " 'all thet's bad on the frontier rolled into one boy of eighteen years' " and, it is further stated by one of the characters, that Chisum " 'had a lot to do with makin' Billy what he is today.' "29

Chisum is described as appearing "to be in the prime of a wonderful physical life, though rumor said he had some incurable disease. He was a short, square, extremely powerful man, with the cold blue eye of the Texan, a broad strong face, thin of lip and prominent of jaw."[30] Chisum puts Wade to work with one of his foremen, Jesse Evans. Grey evidently agreed with Dane Coolidge that Chisum as a cattleman was little better than a thief on a grand scale. Evans is a former friend of the Kid's in this story. They met when both were riding for Chisum. " 'Don't say nothin' agin my old pard,' " Jesse tells Wade. " 'I had to split with him 'cause he turned crooked. But I won't hear nothin' agin him.' "[31] Later Evans comments that it is " 'damn tough fer McSween's side. They'll get killed, the whole caboodle of them, even if they have Billy's outfit fightin' fer them.' "[32]

Thus is the stage set for Wade to meet the Kid. "It was the way he stood, the way he packed his gun. He wore it on the left side, in a reversed position. . . . Wade met and felt the clearest coldest eyes that it had ever been his fortune to gaze into. They seemed to search his very soul. Billy the Kid was not unprepossessing. But for a prominent tooth which he exposed when he laughed, he would have been handsome. It was a smooth, youthful face, singularly cold, as if carved out of stone. Wade's divination here recognized the spirit of the wildness of the West at its height. Billy the Kid was what the West had made him. He looked a boy, he had the freshness of a boy, but he was a man, and one in whom fear had never been born."[33] Billy and his outfit have just come from killing Sheriff Baker [Brady] and several of his deputies. The Kid tells Wade that the reason he split with Chisum is that the cattle king was against an " 'Englishman named Tunstan [Tunstall]. I've killed some of them. An' I'll kill Chisum before they kill me.' "[34] Grey describes the Kid's voice as "terrible in its ruthlessness" and Wade, in departing from New Mexico, finds Billy extending "that slim deadly little hand."[35]

Once he gets to Arizona and involved with fighting rustlers there for the father of the woman he loves, Wade hears now and then what has happened in New Mexico since he left. From a roving puncher he learns that there was a two-day fight in McSween's house with the other faction —Grey never does identify this faction—surrounding the place and setting it on fire. Billy with a gun in each hand spouting lead makes a successful break for it, although some of his own are downed in the rout. Final news about the Kid's death comes in the person of a ranger captain who had intended to arrest Wade, but doesn't, so impressed is he with the fine deeds Wade has done and charmed by Wade's wife and young daughter. The Kid was shot by Pat Garrit [Garrett]. Wade wants to know if it was a fair fight. " 'Wal, I should smile not. Garrit hadn't the nerve for thet. Billy would have beat him to a gun. . . . It happened at Pete Maxwell's in Lincoln. Garrit, the sheriff, an' his deputies were on Billy's track. They missed him. But at night when Garrit sat in the dark talkin' to Maxwell, Billy came to the door. Billy asked who the stranger was, instead of shootin' first. Pat recognized his voice and bored him.' "[36] One might almost forgive Grey for getting just about everything wrong in his reconstruction of events because he has the Kid taken utterly by surprise in the showdown by a man characterized as being too afraid of him to give him a chance to draw and fire (had he had a pistol on his person to do it). Since Grey's theme in SHADOW ON THE TRAIL is reclamation—in this case, Wade Holden's going straight only to end up prosperous, successful, and happily married—no doubt it was Burns's account which he had read some time before and, the passing years having dimmed memory, it was Billie Wilson's life which probably had inspired him to develop this theme in his own way. Grey seems to have been somewhat ambivalent about the Kid, at once seeing in him a man created by the wild West, a man for his time, an attitude that did not change from the period of the Nevada stories to that of SHADOW ON THE TRAIL, and admiring openly the way in which the Kid knew no fear, the way he was cold and imposing. Yet, he also felt he had to condemn him as a killer. Such men, he felt, the Hardins, the Billy the Kids, the Nevadas, or the Wade Holdens were necessary to combat lawlessness on the frontier because there was no one else capable of doing it. Yet, some, such as the Kid, were beyond reclamation while others, such as Holden, could still redeem themselves.

It was certainly as a consequence of the commercial interest generated by Burns's "saga" that a number of other authors of Western fiction besides Grey decided to incorporate incidents and characters based on the events of the Lincoln County War into novels which, notwithstanding, make no reference to any particular historical personality and in which characters are called by different names and may be regarded more as composite figures. William MacLeod Raine was fond of a picaresque structure primarily, I suppose, because he was somewhat inept at drawing characters with any kind of depth and this expediency permitted him to compensate for that deficiency through hectic action. THE FIGHTING TENDERFOOT (Doubleday, 1929) is such a novel. The hero, named Garrett O'Hara, would seem to be an amalgam of Pat Garrett, John W. Poe, and A. A. McSween, although of the three only McSween would qualify as having been a "tenderfoot." A character named Bob Quantrell is referred to as "the Kid," and some of the incidents in which he becomes involved are reminiscent of Billy the Kid's life, albeit they are highly stylized and shed no light whatsoever on his personality or his motivation. In fact, unlike Grey, Raine was not intent in the least in justifying the Kid's behavior, but rather in revealing him as one villain among many, albeit perhaps the most notable in terms of innate criminality, and the one most in need of being brought to the bar of justice.

Dane Coolidge's better formulary efforts do not employ a picaresque plot and, when he did resort to it as in WAR PAINT (Dutton, 1929), his first fictional adaptation of the Lincoln County War, the result tended to be disappointing. The hero of WAR PAINT is Curly Wells, a native Texan and obviously a combination of Garrett and Poe, albeit again highly stylized. Tuffy Malone is his surrogate for the Kid, a bucktoothed, amber-eyed youngster who smokes, drinks, wears a black hat, has a Mexican girl "in every jacal," and, at the opening of the novel, has killed "thirteen men, not counting Mexicans and Indians. Sure death—quick as lightning—either hand!"[37] Curly rides an Appaloosa named "War Paint" which Tuffy covets. He also covets the Anglo-American heroine, Melissa McCoy, the daughter of a beekeeper. It is a combination of these two yearnings that finally does in Tuffy.

Mike Broiles, a buyer of stolen cattle, seems to have been a combination of Major Murphy and Pat Coghlan. Judge Milligan, who presides at Tuffy's trial, is a law and order judge, sworn enemy to all cattle thieves, and based, apparently, on Colonel Fountain, since, although chronologically out of sequence, he disappears in the desert in this novel—an incident which occurred on 1 February 1896, or some sixteen years after the period in which WAR PAINT is set. Curly shoots Tuffy, but he is not aware of it when it happens, and Tuffy does have his gun drawn. Curly's promise to Melissa is that he will raise alfalfa and bees, as is the way among the McCoys, and he puts down his gun forever. With the reward money, he can afford to buy Melissa a ring.

Yet, whatever the problems with WAR PAINT, BLOODY HEAD (Dutton, 1940) is probably the worst novel Coolidge ever wrote. The time frame is 1867—because the Navajos and Apaches are still at Bosque Redondo—and the plot clumsily combines Colonel Charles Goodnight (to whose memory the novel is dedicated) and his efforts to bring cattle herds into New Mexico to supply beef for the Indians and the events of the Lincoln County War more than a decade in the future. Red Ryan is a cattle thief based on Billy the Kid. Captain Hightower is based on Colonel Goodnight. The hero is Beau McCutcheon who becomes known as Bloody Head fighting off Comanches. Martin Hockaday is based on John Chisum, embodying Coolidge's view in FIGHTING MEN OF THE WEST that he was basically a cattle thief. That Chisum was instead a deadbeat and crafty at legal maneuvering would have to wait until the next year in Nelson C. Nye's venture into the legend. Hightower and Hockaway have a falling out over the latter's dishonest business practices. The Haught family, a clan, also has come to New Mexico with a herd. Beau falls in love at first sight with Musette Haught and she with him. In fact they agree to marry upon their first encounter but this only prepares the stage for an invocation of the Romeo and Juliet theme when Musette's father opposes the match. Major O'Grady is based on Major Murphy. Jesse Mowbray is based on Jesse Evans. Sheriff Holey is based on Sheriff Brady. Rye Miles is a Texas Ranger whose horse Beau stole in Texas. He comes on the scene, allies himself with Beau in the service of Captain Hightower, and falls in love with Musette's sister, Odette (similarities to a Zane Grey formulary plot such as SHADOW ON THE TRAIL were not entirely coincidental since Coolidge was greatly influenced by Grey in his own fiction). Tunstall appears as J. Rogers Ismay. McSween appears as Bryan Sweeny. Colonel Dudley and Pat Garrett appear . . . as themselves! Just why all these other characters couldn't retain their rightful names is as unanswerable here as in Grey's case. Maybe Coolidge was trying to disguise palming off the same plot in 1940 as he had used, in many essentials, in 1929. Coolidge characterized the Garrett/Kid relationship in morally dubious terms: "Pat and Red had worked side by side in the old days and regarded each other as friends. Each man was a killer, as cold as a stone, but the cards said Garrett would win. He had the law behind him, had lived a hard life, and in every way he was *hard*."[38] Judge Bristol appears also by name and, rather incredibly, is portrayed as an honest justice! Notwithstanding all that he had previously written and presumably studied on the subject, Coolidge was so oblivious of conditions at the time that he makes the absurd assertion that "there wasn't a real prison in New Mexico."[39] Even the Kid would have had reason to disagree with that statement. Haught tries to frame Beau to get rid of him but in this he is foiled. Red has a gun in one hand *and* a knife in the other when Garrett shoots him. Beau and Musette as well as Rye and Odette are now free to marry. Yet, not surprisingly, two such hackneyed subplots cannot make an entertaining or memorable novel.

GAMBLIN' MAN (Morrow, 1934) by E. B. Mann is a fantasy insofar as the Kid survives and rides off at the end of the novel with his sweetheart, but a definite attempt is made to include many actual historical incidents, as well as a good many fantasies from the Garrett/Upson account, and an interpretation of Billy's motivation is made an integral part of the plot. Mann published the magazine version of this novel, titled "Outlaw Guns," under his Wes Fargo byline in BIG-BOOK WESTERN in August, 1934. The heroine, Kathie Haskel, is coming West with a wagon train led by wagonmaster Uncle Joe Flack. Flack has told Kathie a number of tales about Billy Bonney, who is already famous in the West despite the time period, September, 1877, a man born in New York who learned to gamble at an early age and who killed his first man when he was twelve because the man insulted his mother. The wagon train is attacked by Indians and Billy Bonney and his friend Jesse Evans come to the rescue. Kathie's brother is killed in the skirmish and the Kid takes her in her wagon to stay at the Chisum ranch, figuring Sallie Chisum, John's niece, will be a good companion to her in her grief. John Chisum asks Billy's help in his battle against the Murphy machine and Murphy's gang of Texans which includes Billy Morton, Frank Baker, and "Buckshot Bill" Roberts—indicating via this last that Mann had also read the Burns account. Chisum explains that he is president of the McSween/Tunstall bank. Billy responds that he will be of more help to Chisum by not working for him but keeping his eyes and ears open instead.

That fall, Billy stays with Frank Coe, not George, but he spends most of his time with John H. Tunstall, for whom he eventually goes to work. Kathie moves in to Lincoln to live with the McSweens and to start a school. Billy and Kathie fall in love. Although Billy likes McSween, he feels his belief in the "Golden Rule" is not going to work. At a Christmas party at the McSweens', Billy and Kathie are engaged. Pat Garrett shows up, and the point is made that, while he is from Texas, he is not "a Texas man," i.e., a hired gunfighter. Billy also hears that his friend Jesse Evans is running with a bad crowd. Major Murphy is the principal villain and he organizes the legal machinery against Tunstall and McSween. When Tunstall is on his way into Lincoln on 13 February 1878, accompanied only by Dick Brewer and Billy, the latter two ride off in pursuit of some wild turkeys and a Murphy posse sweeps down on Tunstall, killing him. Once Brewer and Billy reach town, Justice of the Peace Wilson makes Brewer a special constable and a posse is organized consisting of the Kid, McCloskey who is given the first name of Ike, and several others. Hunting down Tunstall's murderers, the posse encounters Tom O'Folliard. He claims he has just been ambushed by some men, narrowly escaping with his life. The Kid believes his story and Tom joins the posse. After a two-day siege,

Morton and Baker surrender to the posse. On the way to town, the two try to escape, killing McCloskey in the process, and the Kid alone downs them with his Mannlicher, a gift from Tunstall.

The shooting of Roberts, the shoot-out with Brady, Hindman, and Matthews [Mathews], and the siege in Lincoln all follow, based essentially on the Burns account. Dolan and a man named Hall set the McSween house on fire. At Billy's request, Mrs. McSween plays the piano and it is Billy who is the last one out of the house. Kathie gets a horse for Billy's escape. Then news comes, via Pat Garrett who now owns a restaurant at Fort Sumner, that the war is over because Major Murphy has died. Kathie comes to Fort Sumner to teach school. To his surprise, Billy learns from Pete Maxwell that there is a Billy Bonney look-alike somewhere in the area. Chisum arranges a meeting between Billy and the new governor, General Wallace, but Billy refuses to surrender his guns. This irritates Kathie. When Billy is accused of killing Bernstein, the clerk at the agency, Kathie refuses to see him. This action—rejection by the woman he loves—prompts Billy to join with O'Folliard and the others who are riding with Jesse Evans's rustlers. Once he kills James Carlyle, Billy begins to question the direction in which his life is going. He has banked most of the money he has made stealing cattle and has enough for a new start. He was given cattle instead of the $500 he demanded from Chisum for his help, and he does not steal from Chisum until Chisum backs Garrett in the election for sheriff. Billy goes to visit Kathie at Fort Sumner, splitting off from his gang. Kathie refuses to see him, only to regret it later. The gang is ambushed and O'Folliard is killed. Garrett is now in full pursuit. Billy is captured at Stinking Springs and, while in custody, he has a significant conversation with Garrett. " 'The law's a great thing, ain't it, Pat?' " he says. " 'I killed Morton and Baker and they made me an outlaw. You killed O'Folliard and Bowdre and you're the most famous fightin' sheriff in New Mexico! I killed Bob Beckwith, Ollinger's [Olinger] sidekick, in open fight—me alone, against not less than twenty killers churnin' lead at me. Ollinger, with twenty killers helpin' him, murdered Tunstall who never fired a shot. I must stand trial for my life, with Ollinger standin' guard over me with a gun. . . . It's sure a funny world.' "[40]

When Billy is under sentence to hang, Kathie goes to Governor Wallace, but he will not pardon him. Kathie then slips the Kid a gun with which he makes his escape. Garrett goes in pursuit and in Pete Maxwell's bedroom shoots a man who looks and sounds as the Kid, but it turns out to be the Billy Bonney look-alike. The Kid shows up and he and Kathie persuade Garrett to let him get away. Garrett cannot resist a pretty girl and warns Maxwell not to breathe a word of what happened. " 'I—I sort o' like the Kid, myself,' " Maxwell replies.[41] Killing the look-alike is justified because it was he, and not the Kid, who really killed Bernstein!

In a one-page article titled "Billy the Kid Alive?" in WESTERN YARNS in March, 1938, Eugene Cunningham, who had first dealt with the Kid in TRIGGER-NOMETRY in 1934, raised the question of the rumor which he said has persisted "that Governor Lew Wallace and Pat Garrett staged an act in Fort Sumner that moonlit July night of 1881, to give the Kid a chance to start life over again. By the claims of this faction, 'Billito' yet lives, a kindly old fiddler wandering over Arizona, New Mexico, West Texas, his real identity known by only a few close friends. If this were true, Billy the Kid would now (1938) be seventy-eight years old, very close to Trail's End. And if this (to me incredible) tale is true, Billy may yet be identified on his death bed. Or we may even see his own story—told to some reporter, in the fashion so popular today. But—most of us in the Southwest are confident that Garrett's bullet killed the Kid."[42] Cunningham was still alive when what he predicted somewhat ironically might happen did indeed happen and C. L. Sonnichsen and William V. Morrison published ALIAS BILLY THE KID, mentioned in the previous chapter. Cunningham did not comment on this book—as well he could have since he had Billy rightly near Trail's End almost two decades before its appearance—but Ramon F. Adams did. "Granted that the old man who claimed he was the Kid seemed to know a great deal about what happened, it was no more than a great many others knew. I still cannot help but believe that the friends who loved Billy and were saddened by his death, the people who prepared him for burial and sat up with his body in the carpenter shop that night, would have known without a doubt whether the corpse was Billy's. The authors themselves seem to have some doubt in their minds about the genuineness of the man's claim. I'm afraid it's another case of the six or seven Jesse Jameses who came to life at various times."[43] This alternative ending to the real events at Fort Sumner may have been assisted by such powerful stimuli as BILLY THE KID (M-G-M, 1930) and a novel such as GAMBLIN' MAN. That it represents a powerful impulse in the collective unconscious cannot, however, be denied, since even the most recent theatrical film about the Kid, YOUNG GUNS II (20th-Fox, 1990), shows him at the end in the guise of old Brushy Bill! Notwithstanding the endurance of this hope that the Kid did escape Garrett's bullet from ambush, it is a fantasy and as such belongs properly classed among the fictional "lives" of Billy the Kid.

Cunningham made fictional use of the Kid and certain of the events and personalities of the Lincoln County War in one of his best novels, DIAMOND RIVER MAN (Houghton Mifflin, 1934), which appeared as a five-part serial in LARIAT STORY MAGAZINE under the title "Burned Brands" running monthly from November, 1926 until March, 1927. Lit Taylor is the hero, stepson to Old Man Barbee, owner of the Bar-B ranch. He finds Frenchy Leonard's wild ways attractive, at least initially. Frenchy is the character based on the Kid, known as "*el francés*" instead of *el chivato*. He is introduced as a "handsome, deadly youngster."[44] The Texas town of Tom's Bluff is where the story opens and New Mexico is referred to simply as the Territory. Cunningham summarized conditions there more accurately in this novel than he had in TRIGGERNOMETRY: "Quite often, it was the honest man who found himself outside the law, while cow thieves and murderers sat in the saddle, riding roughshod, buying and selling county offices as suited them, issuing warrants for their rivals and competitors, shooting them down very legally on the pretense that they resisted arrest."[45] Frenchy rides with three cronies, "the huge, fearless, goodhumored Irish Tim Fenelon" based on Tom O'Folliard, the "rat-faced little first lieutenant" Art Brand possibly based on Charlie Bowdre, and the

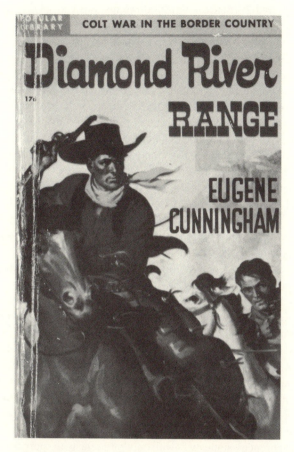

Popular Library's paperback edition of Eugene
Cunningham's Billy the Kid novel, DIAMOND RIVER
MAN (Houghton Mifflin, 1934).

"weak-faced cowboy, Hognose [Ott]" who might have been based on Dave Rudabaugh.[46] Cunningham notes in this scene that "the little outlaw's prominent
teeth—that showed always in the semblance of a grin, whether he danced or drank
or fought—flashed now in widening of the grin."[47] Frenchy wants to return to the
Territory and he wants Lit to accompany him. Lit is undecided but finally opts to
stay. After Frenchy and the others pull out, Lit finds a locket in the street, dropped
by Leonard, and in it a tintype of a blonde-haired girl with whom he falls in love
on first sight.

While helping to round up Bar-B strays in the Diamond River country, Lit
encounters Kate Quinn, a nester girl who isn't afraid to flash her "hogleg" at him.
When Lit tells her to act as a lady or " 'by Gemini! I'll turn you over my knee and
you'll collect the spanking of the year,' " she warns him that if he tries it she'll send

her Pap after Frenchy. " 'He's a sight more'n just a friend,' " she tells Lit. " 'Me an' Frenchy, we're goin' to be married!' "[48] Her only function in the story, as will be the case later with a Mexican girl who spits at Lit and brags of how she has lain in Frenchy's arms, is to illustrate his reputation as a hopeless womanizer and thus demonstrate his inadequacy as a suitor for the girl in the tintype. It becomes evident that Frenchy and his gang have run off most of the Bar-B strays and Lit goes into the Territory to get a line on what happened to them. He saves the girl in the tintype and learns her name is Sudie-May Connell [Sallie Chisum]. King Connell [John Chisum] instead of being her uncle is her father. Cunningham shared Coolidge's and Grey's view of Chisum as a man who pays no attention to brands and that this is how he has forged his empire. Frenchy is staying at King Connell's headquarters ranch, Los Alamos. The Pecos is renamed the Rowdy and there is said to be no law west of it. However, the law in Gurney is Smoky Cole [Sheriff Brady] and eventually he makes Lit a deputy. King Connell is described as "at least three inches over six feet" with "a round, red face" and "long mustaches of the same sorrel hue as his thinning hair." He also has about him a bit of Tunstall since "unlike most of the Old Country youngsters bringing pounds sterling into the American West, Connell had prospered amazingly."[49]

Wearing a badge makes it legal for Lit to run down the stolen Bar-B cattle Frenchy sold to King Connell and to compel Connell either to return them in comparable numbers or to pay their proper owner. This places Lit in the position Pat Garrett was reputed to have of a one-time friend and Frenchy, after lamenting their lost friendship, remarks to Lit: " 'You're wearin' a star an' you figger you got to play the game a certain way.' "[50] Governor Cuthbert [Lew Wallace] comes to Gurney and offers the men in the Territory a general amnesty if they'll put down their guns. Lit and a posse surrounded Frenchy and his gang in a hideout in a way similar to the capture at Stinking Springs and now Frenchy is in the jailhouse. Cuthbert offers Frenchy amnesty as well only for Frenchy to spurn the offer. " 'He's trash!' " Lit consoles the governor. " 'Plain trash! A sure-thing killer. I've heard about every killing he ever did. And if he ever gave a man an even break, the records don't show it.' "[51] Cunningham had titled his chapter on the Kid in TRIGGER-NOMETRY "The Sure-Thing Killer." Frenchy and his gang manage to break out of the jail house. Rather than leaving town at once, they hide in ambush and finish off Smoky Cole and his special town deputies. Afterwards, Frenchy heads for Los Alamos and that is where Lit finds him, demanding a thousand dollars from King Connell and telling Sudie-May and Connell both in the latter's office that he intends to take Sudie-May with him whether she likes it or not. Lit calls him out. " 'Why—why, he's faster'n me!' " Frenchy says as he falls, killed in a fair fight.[52] Connell, so grateful for Lit's intervention, makes good on what he owes for the Bar-B cattle and asks Lit to stay on as his ramrod, a proposition which suits both Sudie-May and Lit who intend to get married.

In late 1934 Popular Publications launched its new pulp Western magazine titled MAVERICKS. Each monthly issue (there were only to be four) had a novel featuring the Mavericks, a group of five owlhooters who, despite their reputations, go about setting right injustices where they find them. Each of the four issues also had a Billy the Kid novelette written by Ray Nafziger. Billy and his friend Jesse Smith, notwithstanding the Kid's notoriety, as the Mavericks help out those in distress. In "Guns of the Owlhoot Pack" in MAVERICKS from October, 1934 Luke Brodson, one of the villains, reacts this way when he encounters "the most feared gunman in New Mexico. But this slight rider with the big gold-banded white sombrero and neat black tie and white shirt, the smile that seemed perpetually grown on his face couldn't be that noted outlaw. Not even if he were balancing two six-shooters in his smallish hands."[53] Unfortunately, it really is the Kid and the villains don't have much chance against his prowess with a shooting iron. The other three novelettes are in the same vein, anticipating by a good six years the image of the Kid as a conventional Western hero which would characterize the Producers Releasing Corporation films of the early 1940s starring Bob Steele and then Buster Crabbe which will be discussed at further length in the next chapter.

In G. G. Price's DEATH COMES TO BILLY THE KID (Signal, 1940) the governor of New Mexico sends a youth, known as El Chivato, to find the Kid so he can return with him and receive a full pardon. The youth is shadowed by three gunfighters in the employ of the big cattlemen whose job it is to kill the Kid. One of the three physically resembles Pat Garrett, although his name is not given. The youth converts the Kid to Christianity, baptizing him in the Rio Pecos. When they arrive at Fort Sumner, the Kid is shot down by the hired killers. The "Spanish" people are praised for having sheltered the Kid and Price concluded on the hopeful note that "the bullet killing him, also pierced the vitals of the all powerful cattle association. It was dead, shot by the backfire of its own six-gun." The Kid is termed a "martyr for the oppressed."[54]

Such, however, was not the case with the Kid as portrayed the next year in Nelson C. Nye's PISTOLS FOR HIRE (Macmillan, 1941), perhaps more appropriately retitled for paperback reprint A BULLET FOR BILLY THE KID (Avon, 1950). Flick Farsom is the hero and he narrates the story, which ends after the "three-day" battle in Lincoln. "Dick Brewer and his bunch of Texas owl hooters were making it mighty hard for Murphy/Dolan to fill its government contracts; even Chisum, who had more cattle than he could keep tally of, was gobbling Murphy's beef. . . . McSween's blight was on the land, and all who had reason to fear it were looking to Murphy for protection."[55] Flick works for Chisum and has not been paid wages for eighteen months. He wants to quit but is convinced to stay on by Sally [Sallie] Chisum, to whom he is attracted. His sympathies are with Murphy and Dolan. However, his support of them is not blind. "Murphy was no saint, nor were his partners, Dolan and Riley. Few men *were*, in the Lincoln of that day, though some were trying to look like saints, and Tunstall, by the reported manner of his killing, had gotten a halo gratis."[56] Flick was with the posse that gunned Tunstall who was firing at them and he knows that the Kid swore over Tunstall's grave to kill " 'every sonofabitch who helped kill John.' "[57] Jesse Evans used to be Chisum's foreman, heading up Chisum's gang of rustlers which included Billy Bonney. Evans quit and now is a hunted man. Murphy asks Flick to get Jesse and his gang to throw in with

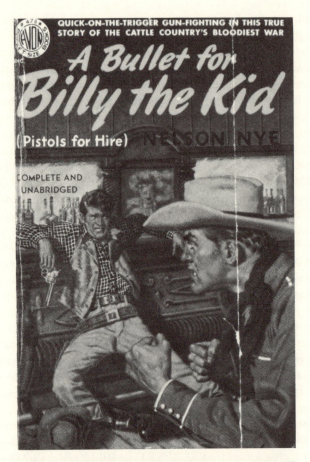

Avon Books's paperback edition of Nelson Nye's A BULLET FOR BILLY THE KID which appeared originally as PISTOLS FOR HIRE (Macmillan, 1941).

the Murphy forces. Flick rides out to Evans's camp. The next day they are raided by a gang of McSween's gunslicks, led by Dick Brewer. Morton and Baker dash away and are pursued. Later they are shot down by the gunslicks. McSween used the Fritz insurance money to set up Tunstall in the store and banking business. He now declares a reign of terror in response to the Tunstall killing, led by the Kid who is "the Dillinger of 1879."[58] Looking ahead, Flick tells of future events, such as the Kid's cold-blooded murder of James Carlyle. During the siege of the McSween house, the Murphy/Dolan forces are greatly outnumbered until, at the last desperate moment, the Army arrives under Colonel Dudley to save the day. Flick rejects the story of Mrs. McSween's playing the piano. Together with Dolan he helps set the McSween house on fire. Bonney escapes, but McSween and most of his hardcases are shot down by the forces of justice. Nye, in a brief Preface, noted that "no intentional liberties have been taken" when it comes to historical characters and the book in the Macmillan edition is subtitled: A TALE OF THE LINCOLN COUNTY WAR AND THE WEST'S MOST DESPERATE OUTLAW WILLIAM (BILLY THE KID) BONNEY. Since "Dad" Peppin emerges as one of the heroes of the battle in Lincoln and McSween as a master villain, it is also worth mentioning that in a Postscript Nye, in addition to many published sources, acknowledged assistance from Henry F. Fritz of Capitan, his daughter, Mrs. Wallace Ferguson, and C. W. Hyde, a one-time sheriff of Lincoln County, "for reminiscences and aid in arriving at a just conception of Sheriff Dad Peppin and his work."[59] Lastly he included John Sinclair of the Lincoln County Museum and it was to him that Nye dedicated the book. It is not significant that Nye here anticipated historian Frederick W. Nolan in viewing McSween as the principal cause of the turmoil in Lincoln County (since he rendered such a distorted portrait of the personality of the man and just about everyone else involved), but perhaps it is that the resentment in the Fritz family regarding McSween's admittedly high-handed method of dealing with the insurance money had been carried on through the succeeding generations and was still quite as strong sixty years later as it had been in 1879.

In a short novel titled "There's Hell Tonight in Lincoln County!" in STAR WESTERN in February, 1947 Harry F. Olmsted reprised the battle for the soul of Lincoln as seen through the eyes of Jeff Oglesby, a newspaper editor and publisher. The county is dominated by three crooks named Brophy [Murphy], Raney [Riley], and Dugan [Dolan]. They control the partisan Sheriff Jim Bradner [Brady] and Judge Aaron Van Dusen [Bristol]. Clay Chisum, the local cattle baron, has a beautiful niece named Sally [Sallie]. Chisum is allied with Alex McSween and Tunstall, an Englishman. It is Chisum's intention to fight fire with fire and so he has a monumental meeting at McSween's house in which he puts up the money for a store and a bank in which Tunstall also invests. "McSween, with less money to put into the company, was looked to for legal counsel."[60] Unfortunately for Brophy and his gang, Raney drops a notebook in McSween's living room with a list of all the rustlers in the district and how much they got for all the stolen cattle, brand by brand, which they sold to Murphy. A real plus for McSween is the loyalty of Billy the Kid, "the neatest thing with a gun in New Mexico."[61] Billy tampers with a villain's gun in a saloon. When he tries to shoot Jeff Oglesby, the hammer falls on an empty cartridge and the Kid fires into the man. When Tunstall is murdered by Brophy's men, Dick Brewer is appointed special constable and goes after the murderers. Baker and Morton are captured and, as the Kid tells it, " 'We took 'em to Agua Negra. One of our men tried to help 'em escape. McNab [MacNab] shot him an' I dropped Morton and Baker.' "[62] At Blazer's Mill, the Kid shoots "Buckshot Bill" [Andrew L.] Roberts "through the guts, but couldn't kill him."[63] McSween stands for law and order and for doing what is right. When the Kid and five of his gang assassinate Sheriff Bradner, McSween lowers the boom on the Kid: " 'Your cold-blooded crime deals me a body blow, Bonney,' he raged. 'You must answer for murder before God and man. I'll not defend you. Rather, I'll do all I can to convict you.' "[64]

The heroine is Celia McIver. Her father is putting out the corrupt Lincoln *Democrat* for the Brophy side. The story ends with the McSween home surrounded by the Brophy forces. It is set on fire and, as it burns, Jeff can hear "the faint notes of Susan McSween's beloved piano rising over the gunfire in 'Home Sweet Home' and her clear soprano: '*Be it ever so humble . . . there's no place like home.*' "[65] As the fire consumes all but the last room, Susan deserts her piano and flees to the home of a neighbor. "McSween came out, bareheaded and in his shirtsleeves, 'Here I am. I am McSween!' The Brophy men shot him to death."[66] The Kid is the last one out and he escapes without a bullet touching him. Jeff and Celia ride off. Her father is dead, a victim finally to Brophy whom he sought to expose at the last moment. "Those who had escaped the holocaust of Lincoln town had only vengeance to lean upon. He [Jeff] had earned the peace that was theirs."[67] It is obvious that Olmsted used Burns's "saga" as his sole source for the events and personalities. What is especially interesting, however, is that he ended the story with the villains triumphant and McSween dead. Occasionally in STAR WESTERN, which was published by Popular Publications, the point of view character might end up dead at the end, but I cannot think of another instance—and I have read virtually every issue from October, 1933, until September, 1954, when it ceased—where the story similarly concluded with the villains triumphant and without any resolution.

Edwin Corle in MOJAVE: A BOOK OF STORIES (Liveright, 1934) included a very short story titled "The Ghost of Billy the Kid." Despite its brevity, the tale has its share of fantasies. Corle asserted that when the Kid died there were "(twenty-one men sent to eternity by this youth not counting Mexicans and Indians)"; that the Kid was twenty-one when he died; and that "his legitimate name was William Bonney."[68] In ARIZONA HIGHWAYS (February, 1954) Corle published an article titled "Billy the Kid in Arizona" that was so riddled with errors—it purported to be factual—that Ramon F. Adams had to devote four pages to making corrections of its contents in A FITTING DEATH FOR BILLY THE KID. Between these two publications, Corle's novel BILLY THE KID (Duell, Sloan, and Pearce, 1953), appeared. In the novel, the Kid is born William Bonney in New York City, an only child. His mother is named Kathleen, married to a man named Bonney but no praenomen is provided. The Kid's first killing is a Chinese, after which Billy, rather stupidly, rides off with the hammer of his six-gun "down on the next bullet to go." Following the Burns account, only Brewer and the Kid accompany Tunstall on his ride into Lincoln. The usual rash of killings ensues: the Kid alone shoots Morton and Baker. He kills Bob Beckwith when fleeing from the burning McSween house after a three-day battle. He kills Bernstein casually, as if "he had merely swatted a fly."[69] The Kid in this novel is completely monogamous, having an affair with an Abrana Garcia who is married to an old man, Manuel Garcia. In an Afterword, Corle claimed to have known both Manuel and Abrana Garcia, albeit by internal evidence Manuel would have had to have been at least a hundred years old when they met. According to Corle, the Kid could "fire a six-shooter a split second sooner than any other man in the Southwest."[70] John Chisum believes that only violence can stop violence and in this he is opposed by Governor Wallace who believes in using peaceful means, if possible. A ridiculous conversation occurs between the Kid and Wallace in which the Chapman killing is not so much as mentioned. Corle has the Kid confess to killing Carlyle, claims that the Kid made no effort to contact Governor Wallace while he was in prison in Santa Fe, and shows him to be wondering if his mother is still alive in 1881 when she died in 1874. None of the characters, including the Kid, comes to life. "While the book is fiction and must be so designated," Corle wrote in his Afterword, "it contains many historical truths; I believe that it tells the story of Billy with veracity, and is removed from fact only in the exigencies of the technique of the novel."[71] Despite this preposterous contention, the actual purpose behind the novel would seem rather to have been to illustrate Corle's belief that "since they [the Kid and his gang] refused to be absorbed, they had to be eradicated"—a bald appeal for compliance by force to the values of one-settlement culture.[72] Corle also observed that Billy's killings had become "so matter-of-fact . . . that he didn't mention the two Mexicans."[73]

Paul Evan Lehman who tackled the Kid the same year in his novel PISTOLS ON THE PECOS (Avon, 1953) seems to have used as his basic sources the Garrett/Upson account, Burns's "saga," and Mann's GAMBLIN' MAN, although, unlike Mann, his intention, as was Corle's, was to show how much Billy "needed" killing. Cole Claiborne is bringing a herd of fifty horses to sell as remounts to Fort Stanton. On the way through the Sacramentos, Billy Bonney and Jesse Evans stop at Cole's camp. Bonney is described as "a young squirt not more than eighteen whom Evans called the Kid."[74] Cole's horses are driven off at night. Cole does manage to rip a coat pocket off one of the raiders. The next day he sets out in pursuit. On his way toward Lincoln, he overhears some shooting. Coming upon the scene, he finds a man who "had been shot several times" and whose "head had been crushed and battered by a stone."[75] Once in Lincoln, Cole goes to the Murphy store and meets L. G. Murphy who is entertaining at the bar some of the men Cole had seen riding away from the corpse. He is introduced to Sheriff Jim [William] Brady. Billy Morton who is present Cole recognizes as the leader of the gang and now he learns that Morton is Brady's deputy. They claim that Tunstall—the name of the man who was killed—was shot while trying to make a getaway, but Cole doubts what he hears since Tunstall was shot at close range and his skull was crushed. Cole turns down Murphy's offer to join his group in fighting McSween. It is Cole's hope to make good, for his own sake and for that of Susan Roberts, the woman with whom he is in love in Texas. It turns out that Susan is the niece of "Buckshot Bill" [Andrew J.] Roberts and she has herself just come to New Mexico with a wagon train that was attacked by Indians and was rescued by Billy Bonney and Jesse Evans. Susan is naturally grateful to Bonney and is attracted by his gray eyes and winning ways. Cole knows better, but Susan will not listen.

Searching for his horses, Cole comes upon Morton and Baker who are prisoners of the Brewer posse at Chisum's ranch. Baker's coat pocket is poorly sewed and he signs to Cole that he would like to talk to him, but Bonney prevents it. Cole is convinced that Baker was with the Kid and Evans in stealing his horses. The Kid shoots Morton and Baker, as much to silence Baker as for any other reason. Cole, regarding the Kid, reflects that "he found himself looking at a born killer."[76] Cole also discovers that the Kid is not the least concerned with the feud. He and his gang are only using it as an excuse to rustle stock from both sides with each side blaming the other. When Brady and Hindman are ambushed, Hindman manages to "fall just in front of the little church of San Juan."[77] The Kid strips off Brady's holster and six-gun and sends a bullet into his head for good measure. After this incident, Susan begins to agree with Cole about the Kid, " 'a bright coat of paint over a rotten interior.' "[78] Brewer, too, was in on rustling Cole's horses, but he is killed by Susan's uncle in the fight at Blazer's Mill. When Governor Wallace proclaims amnesty, Cole knows this act is worthless: "Bonney was the root of all evil; kill him and the feud would die."[79] Cole in a daring play holds up the Kid and gets the $5,000 which the Kid received for selling his horses. Cole then meets Pete Maxwell and his sister, Paulita. He arranges for Susan to teach school at Fort Sumner. After he gets paid $500 from John Chisum, the Kid, too, begins to hang around Fort Sumner, because he wants Susan, because "he had sworn that no man should have her before himself."[80] When Garrett is elected sheriff, Cole joins him in the manhunt for the Kid. While Garrett and his posse wait in ambush at Fort Sumner, the Kid cuts away from his gang so he can call on Susan. When O'Folliard is killed, the Kid comments: " 'That's his hard luck.' "[81] Captured finally and sentenced to hang, the Kid tricks Bell while they are playing monte. The reader is told he is left-handed. The Kid immediately heads for Fort Sumner where he plans to rape Susan and then to strangle her. Garrett guns him down, thus permitting Cole and Susan to marry and settle down on the Roberts spread.

Lehman made no pretentious claims for his novel, as Corle did, and in terms of literary quality neither work is more than mediocre. Yet it is to Lehman's credit that he tried to conceive some kind of framing story around the events of the Kid's life, rather than, as Corle, merely to rewrite blandly the fantasies of the Burns account with a few Garrett/Upson embellishments. Corle's work, by comparison with any of the others, is totally lacking in any imaginative originality whatsoever.

W. R. Burnett first wrote about the Kid in a magazine story, "Nobody's All Bad," which appeared in the 7 June 1930 issue of COLLIER'S. In this story the Kid's rightful name is given as William Bonney. McSween is the first out of the burning house, his Bible in his hands, the Kid is fourth. Billy is reputed to have rustled cattle in Old Mexico before the Lincoln County War which is being fought between the "Murphy boys" and the "McSween boys." The Kid goes on a drinking spree after shooting at a man he merely meets on the street. However, he and the narrator of the story get pinned down by Mescaleros and the Kid shoots two of them. When Billy says he has no use for Indians, this convinces the narrator that the Kid is not all bad. Pat Garrett is mentioned as the man who used to be the Kid's bosom friend. Burnett returned to the story of the Kid later in his career, basing his novel MI AMIGO (Knopf, 1959) on events from the Lincoln County War, although stylized considerably. Jamie Wiggan is the character known as the Kid in this novel, about whom it is murmured that " 'he's killed around twenty-odd, I hear,' " for all of his twenty-one years.[82] Burnett's hero is Sergeant John Desportes, better known as the

"Soldier." He is in his early forties when he meets the Kid whose horse is dead and whose ankle is sprained, calling himself Bud Smith. The Soldier saves his life and befriends him. The reader from the beginning suspects there is something wrong about Bud, but the Soldier for a long time is manipulated by him. About as far as Burnett probed into Jamie's psychology was to observe that "it was as if part of him had been forced into supernormal growth at the expense of the other parts. Yes, a very strange kid."[83] Bud goes to work for the Soldier as a scout at the post where the major's wife suspects that the daughter of their servant woman, a girl named Lolita, has been secretly carrying on an affair with him. The major's reaction (to himself) is that "virginity was at best a temporary state—it was hardly ever persisted in, and when it was, it was usually through lack of opportunity."[84] What this attitude gets for the major is that his wife, his servant, and Lolita all leave him to go East once the truth about Bud comes out, that he is the killer Jamie Wiggan who has also been carrying on a sexual relationship with Manuela, a young waitress in town. It is now said of the Kid that " 'he killed three men before he was sixteen years old' " and he is glad not to have to pretend any more, "no more lying and lollygagging around and being a good little boy."[85] He takes off with Manuela whose family comes to the Soldier and pleads for her return. " 'She's a minor,' " he says. " 'I'll get her back for you.' "[86]

The Soldier heads out after the Kid with two scouts. It is Blackpony, a former renegade Apache now a scout, who locates the Kid. Although the Kid could kill the Soldier, he does not. Instead, he agrees to release Manuela to him. To give the reader some reason other than his promiscuity to turn against the Kid at this point, Burnett had Jamie shoot a man, albeit a hardcase, in the back. There is a range war in the nearby city of La Paz. The major, now promoted to the rank of general, declares martial law and sends in a detail under the command of the Soldier to reestablish law and order. The Kid is on one side, the Mayhew/Caster group, whereas Judge Macfarlane and his foreman, Clayton Balfour, are on the other. Peace is negotiated. Natty Bugworth, the Soldier's best friend from the beginning of the novel, was responsible for helping to expose the Kid and even directed three killers to where the Kid was staying when he was a scout. The Kid humiliates Natty into a fight and shoots him down. The Soldier then offers a $1,000 reward for the Kid's capture, declaring him "beyond the law" which means "he will be hanged without a trial."[87] The Kid is trailed to old Fort Casa Grande where he is staying with a young Mexican girl named Juana. The reader learns that the Kid has become weary of sexuality. "Always the same old act, over and over! Was that all there was in the world?"[88] He straps on his gun to go out and cut off a beefsteak and is shot down by Blackpony. The Soldier sits with him as he dies in bed, while the Kid tells him how he wants his money divided among the women he has "known." Paquita, a woman the Kid knew at La Paz, perhaps a surrogate for Paulita Maxwell, becomes known as "Jamie Wiggan's one 'true love.' "[89] As for Blackpony, in the ideology of this story he comes to love the white man's road: "Blackpony came to hate the blanket Indians and their stinking wickiups. He'd learned his lesson. A man must obey. He has sworn duties; he must perform them. No exceptions."[90] The Soldier, who at the beginning of the story was spending a furlough with a whore, swears off women. Blackpony tells him at the end how Natty had called him "*mi amigo,*" and so had the Kid, and " 'Blackpony—now—he say "*mi amigo.*' "[91]

When Charles Neider's THE AUTHENTIC DEATH OF HENDRY JONES (Harper, 1956) was reissued in 1972 by Harrow Books, an Introduction by Wirt Williams made the rather exaggerated claim that it "may be the greatest 'western' ever written."[92] What might better be said of it would be that Neider's novel was a serious attempt to make truly literary use of the Billy the Kid legend and in this he succeeded better than virtually all of his predecessors. Wirt also asserted that Neider's title was derived from THE AUTHENTIC LIFE OF BILLY THE KID, which is no doubt accurate, but Wirt ran into a problem when he came to narrate the "facts" about Billy the Kid. "He was born William Bonney, in New York City, probably illegitimate," Wirt wrote.[93] He insisted that the Kid emerged from the Lincoln County War "as one of the conflict's 'heroes' " and that "subsequently, he and a band of young men lived off the land by rustling cattle, and a drinking companion, Pat Garrett, was hired by ranchers with the specific objective of killing Billy. He did so, in almost exactly the manner set forth in the novel."[94]

Neider's source for the killing of the Kid was the Garrett/Upson account, although he had obviously read Poe's account as well since Hendry Jones, approaching death, is seen "fumbling with the buttons of his trousers."[95] The Garrett surrogate is named Dad Longworth. The novel is narrated by Edward Richard Baker, called Doc Baker because he "had once assisted a traveling dentist back around Albuquerque."[96] It opens in the spring of 1881 and is set along the California coast, a region Neider apparently knew better than he did New Mexico and which, in at least one instance, allowed him to evoke an image from Robinson Jeffers's poetry. The Kid is described as having "red-rimmed slate-colored eyes," and the narrator recalls "the close-cropped small sandy head, the golden hair of his eyebrows and the golden hair that grew up from his chest to his throat."[97] In dress, save when out on the range, the Kid "always wore black except for his white shirts."[98] Doc Baker observes about the Kid's character that "you don't find many fellows like the Kid, who don't have nerves at all and who like to risk it for the hell of it and to test their luck."[99] For those versed in Jungian psychology, it is this characteristic of personality, the will to test one's luck, which will be immediately recognized as the mental state prior to possession by the shadow, that is, when the inferior, dark side of the personality usually projected from the unconscious becomes identified with the conscious ego. Perhaps in this way Neider hoped to make his image of the Kid archetypal in a psychological, as well as a literary, sense.

Neider made frequent use of foreshadowing in this novel. Dad Longworth is quoted early on as saying that the Kid " 'had a gun and a meat knife and I could see both of them glinting. Besides I'd have shot him anyway, just on the chance he had one.' " " 'I want to have an old age,' " Dad says at another point. " 'Times are changing.' "[100] When the Kid is under arrest and being held in the Monterey jail, he remarks to Dad Longworth: " 'About God. I hear he's fast but I'd like to see for myself.' "[101] These various lines of dialogue are used almost verbatim (with the exception of the comment about the Kid's being armed which is shown) in Sam Peckinpah's PAT GARRETT AND BILLY THE KID (M-G-M, 1973), a film discussed at some length in the next chapter.

Burns's image of Bob Olinger as a fiend in THE SAGA OF BILLY THE KID was even further intensified by Neider in drawing his Olinger surrogate, Lon Dedrick. Neider followed the Garret/Upson account in having the Kid sprint up the inside stairway ahead of Pablo Patron, the Bell surrogate, break into the armory, and get a gun with which to kill Pablo. The Kid's girlfriend is named Nika Machado, probably a derivation from the Abrana Garcia character in Edwin Corle's BILLY THE KID. Nika marries Miguel Gomez while the Kid is in jail, but the Kid does not know of it. Miguel is Nika's second cousin and Miguel marries her when he is so sick he believes he will die. The narrator has no use for Nika. "She was a fourflusher from way back," he comments, "and I'll give you ten to one that if she's still alive she's fourflushing right now. She was the kind of woman who could get hold of a peaceful man and in no time flat make a murderer out of him."[102] I do not know if this misogyny is to be given credence or not, but, if it is, then Nika must at least in part be blamed for what happens to the Kid after he escapes from jail. It is then that he becomes a Janus figure. "The Kid laughed," Doc recalls. "I glanced at him. He had changed all right, but it was hard to put your finger on it. Maybe the closeness of that noose had changed him—I don't know. He was more quiet than ever and there seemed to be something eating at him behind his eyes."[103] The Kid is described as a two-gun man, although he "never used both [revolvers] at the same time."[104] Heading down to Old Mexico with what is left of his gang, in El Segundo the Kid is riled by a lecherous old man and, while smiling at him, the Kid shoots him down. Neider evidently learned from Eugene Cunningham about the "border shift" since he wrote that with two-gun men "when the first gun went empty, they could make the border shift faster than your eye could spot it and then the second gun would come into play, but not before then."[105] I can readily believe, as it has been said, that Neider himself wore a six-gun the whole time he was writing this novel, since there is a little-boy-at-a-Saturday-matinee quality to much of the action. The Joe Grant encounter is treated as a walk-down, Grant called Smoky Hill, and the Kid lets Smoky empty his gun at him before firing only "one shot which hit Smoky Hill in the heart."[106]

The Kid turns on his own gang and kills a cohort named Bob, a killing that "affected him more than any other killing of his life."[107] The number of men the Kid killed prior to his escape from jail is set at sixteen—following the Garrett/Upson account—and it climbs to nineteen before the end. All of the sympathy generated for the Kid in the first half of the novel is dissipated by his wantonness during the second half and, coupled with his Janus-figure image, it becomes apparent to the reader, as it does even to Nika, that the Kid has not long to live. He is a fated man. Doc, it turns out, was sleeping with Nika while the Kid was in jail and, although she makes a token resistance, she resumes sleeping with the Kid when he returns after the short trip to Old Mexico. The Kid sends word to Dad Longworth that he is back, so there is no mistake: he wants to meet his fate. After romping in bed with Nika, the Kid decides he is hungry and armed with a knife and a .44 he goes to get some meat. The narrator points out the Kid's fatal mistake: he should not have "just loved that damned Nika and gotten up from sleep hungry and gone off in his stockinged feet for a chunk of meat."[108] The Kid is given some last words as he is dying: " 'Mother. Help me. I'm strangling.' "[109]

Will Henry in "A Bullet for Billy the Kid," a short story contained in his collection, SONS OF THE WESTERN FRONTIER (Chilton Books, 1966), told his version of the Kid's life, relying heavily on Walter Noble Burns's "saga." Here, the Kid's life is fated by a human embodiment of the devil named Asaph who is present at the Kid's birth, who follows him throughout his short life and the twenty-one men he kills, and who is there to collect his soul the night he is shot by Garrett.

The finest novel, in my opinion, inspired by the events of the Lincoln County War is Amelia Bean's TIME FOR OUTRAGE (Doubleday, 1967). Bean's novel, although long, covers only the period from the summer of 1877 to the five-day battle at Lincoln. In an Author's Note at the end, she tells what happened to many of the characters in the novel, articulating her view that Billy Bonney was "never at any time during the war a leader of any group or contingent."[110] Significantly, perhaps, in her encomia for such men as Juan Patrón who was assassinated in 1884 and whom she praised for "heroic leadership during the war," she avoided mention of the financial and political prosperity of men such as T. B. Catron and J. J. Dolan—no doubt because to have done so would have run counter to her feeling that the war was a "desperate struggle of decency and integrity" and, if that was what the struggle was about, then in history it was lost.[111] While there are a wide number of factual discrepancies in her narrative, there are also a number of genuine insights and for that reason her plot deserves to be dealt with at some length.

Bean's protagonist Luke Pendar is based on Sam Corbet. He is hired as a wrangler by Henry [John] Tunstall. Luke recognizes Billy Bonney as an old friend named Antrim who stole a horse when he quit cowboying in Texas. The Kid's front teeth became distended as a result of a fight with a blacksmith's helper named Swain. Luke had stepped in and saved the Kid, who was getting the worst of it due to his slight build. Later, Swain was found shot in the back and Luke was suspected. He now learns from the Kid that Billy shot Swain. Swain had met the Kid on a lonely road and challenged him to a fight and the Kid was compelled to use an equalizer. Billy claims his mother's maiden name was Bonney before she married a man named McCarty who died when he was very young. Antrim, his step-father, was supposedly shiftless and Billy's mother had to take in boarders to feed her children. Antrim also slapped frequently both Billy and his mother. His mother—so the doctor said—worked herself to death. After she died, Antrim drank heavily. The Kid got in some minor trouble and hit the trail. Billy is self-conscious about his stature. He confesses that he was involved in cattle rustling before Tunstall hired him, working at it with Fred Waite and George Robinson. Occasionally Charles Bowdre joined them. The Kid got Tunstall to hire Robinson, Waite, and Bowdre, and they have all gone straight. Tunstall pays off Dick Brewer's debt to Murphy and Brewer goes to work for him as his foreman. The Kid, it is rumored, also worked for Dolan at the latter's cow camp before joining Tunstall.

Major Murphy is very much in command of the opposition. Morris Bernstein, who formerly worked for T. B. Catron and then Murphy, as a clerk at the agency helps cover up the purchase of stolen stock and other irregularities. Murphy's chief method of coercion is through loans and mortgage-holding. Because peonage was abolished only ten years previously, the large landowners are still able to deliver large blocks of Mexican-American votes from voters who do not know the value of the ballot. Jesse Evans, Frank Baker, and Tom Hill are caught in the act of rustling Tunstall horses by Brewer, Luke, and the Kid. Tunstall takes them to town and puts them in jail. J. W. Bell is the jailer. That night, J. J. Dolan helps them to escape.

Luke changes jobs. He clerks in Tunstall's store. He finds himself attracted to Magdalena, an orphan adopted by Juan Patrón. McSween in the meantime holds off paying out the Fritz insurance money until Judge Bristol appoints a board of examiners to go over the Murphy House books to establish the extent of Fritz' equity. Dolan and Riley, who have bought out Murphy, object to this. Also, Spiegelberg Bros. of Santa Fe claims that Fritz signed over the insurance policy to them for what Charles Fritz insists was a corporate, not a personal, debt. Although Dolan is engaged to Charles Fritz' daughter, Caroline, Fritz wants her to wait until she is twenty-one before marrying. Two cattle rustlers, one of them Jesse Evans's brother, are caught by Frank McNab [MacNab]. With Tunstall's help, Squire Wilson had paid off his own debt to Murphy and so is free to prosecute these men. McSween also pays off his mortgage to Murphy and so can join in the prosecution, rejecting Murphy's request that he defend the thieves. One of them receives a lighter sentence because he is able to implicate Bernstein and the House of Murphy in crooked dealings. Juan Patrón, the court clerk, records the testimony in the court record.

The McSweens and John Chisum are arrested at Las Vegas. Chisum is sent on to Santa Fe. Tunstall views Colonel Fountain as an enemy of the Ring and gives him his tax fraud exposé to run in the *Mesilla Independent*. Bristol and Rynerson would have succeeded in controlling everything Tunstall and McSween owned with their attachments had George Robinson and Deputy Barrier not foiled Jesse Evans's play at Shedd's ranch. Robinson holds a shotgun on Dolan and Evans. Later, Barrier turns McSween over to Constable Martínez and Deputy U.S. Marshal Widenmann. The Murphy men are worried because a federal investigation has been started. Tunstall comes to Lincoln and repossesses his store, but he does accept Brady's attachment of his cattle, admitting that McSween has a small interest in them. Brady is portrayed sympathetically, a dupe of the ambitious Dolan in tax fraud and the murder of Tunstall. Luke accompanies Tunstall on the fateful ride into Lincoln. When Tunstall is shot, Bonney sinks "to his knees beside the body of the man. His hands reached out, shaking, touching, exploring desperately and he made muffled sounds that were unbearable to hear."[112] On the ride into town, Bonney holds "his mare far enough behind them so that the sound of his sobbing might be smothered in the night wind sighing through the trees."[113] Luke, too, cries in his sleep. What a sensitive contrast are these characters to all of the macho heroes and bravado from earlier male writers!

Dr. Ealy arrives with his family. He performs a postmortem with Dr. Appel. Mrs. McSween is out of town, visiting in Kansas. Miss Gates is not included in the Ealy party. The physicians report at the inquest that both bullet wounds were sustained while the deceased was mounted on his horse. There are no powder burns. Both bullets were fired from behind. Bonney is among those who testify at the inquest. Frank McNab [MacNab] is described as Chisum's foreman and Middleton works for McNab [MacNab]. Tunstall gave Bonney a Winchester '73, one of a thousand, and Brady confiscates this weapon when he arrests Bonney and Fred Waite, hitting Bonney when the Kid asks for the weapon back upon being released. Squire Wilson proposes the formation of the Regulators, based on an example set in North Carolina a hundred years before. Issac Ellis and Dr. Blazer agree to supply the Regulators and wages are committed from the Tunstall estate and *in absentia* from John Chisum. Bill McCloskey as a witness to Tunstall's murder [he was with the Dolan posse] is to go into hiding, as are McSween and Godfrey Gauss.

The shooting of Tom Hill and wounding of Jesse Evans come out of sequence before Morton and Baker are captured. Brady and some soldiers hunt for McSween. Fearful for his life, McCloskey joins the Brewer posse at Chisum's ranch—Chisum is ostensibly still in jail at Santa Fe—and helps take in Morton and Baker. When the Regulators get to Roswell, Upson has Axtell's proclamation posted in the post office, outlawing them. Widenmann, because of his naïveté, is often a victim of frontier hyperbole. Bonney has convinced him that he has killed a man for each year of his life and Widenmann now tells this to Upson. Dolan is cleared by Jesse Evans of involvement in the Tunstall murder in Bristol's court at Fort Stanton while Axtell is there. The shooting of Morton and Baker happens offstage: they are said to have made a break for it and McCloskey was also shot, accidentally, in the fracas.

Mrs. McSween returns and is accompanied by Chisum from Santa Fe to Chisum's South Spring ranch where she meets up with McSween. Rynerson sends George Peppin to be Brady's deputy and to keep an eye on Brady. Bristol and Rynerson deliberately do not show up for court so McSween will be caught in a trap to be sprung by Brady. Brady is on his way to the McSween house to arrest Bonney and the other Regulators there when, in desperation, they ambush him. The Kid gets back his Winchester but is wounded in the right buttock. There are only four ambushers—Bonney, Middleton, Waite, and George Robinson, although this last does no shooting. Luke hides the wounded Bonney under the floor in Tunstall's storeroom, but no search is made. Peppin and a military escort arrest McSween and several others and take them to the fort. Chisum, too, is arrested; but the point is made clear repeatedly that he is out strictly for himself. When Luke goes back to check on the Kid, he sees "Bonney lying with blanket stuffed in his mouth to smother sounds he might unconsciously make. His heavy lids lifted and he stared up at Luke like a sick child. His eyes were fever-bright and his face felt very hot. He whimpered with pain when Luke raised his head to help him drink."[114]

The Kid is taken to Dr. Blazer. He is still there some days later when Buckshot Roberts rides in. Roberts is hunting varmint pelts. He offers to switch sides for bounty money. He begins shooting when Brewer tries to arrest him and is shot by Bowdre and Luke. Chisum's money backs John Copeland as sheriff, with McNab [MacNab] as his chief deputy. Squire Wilson arranges for Luke to buy Brewer's spread and Bonney comes to help Luke out around the place. McNab [MacNab] is ambushed. Luke heads up a raid on stolen stock at the Dolan cow camp. Bonney, Waite, and Bowdre take the cattle they find, sell them, and split the proceeds among the Regulators. Peppin replaces Copeland as sheriff. Tom O'Folliard joins Bonney and George Robinson working for Luke. After McNab [MacNab] is killed, Chisum sells out, on paper at least, and drives his blooded stock to Texas. He refuses to pay the Regulators. Disgusted, McSween and the others decide to hold their ground in Lincoln. During the five-day battle, Luke is with the sharpshooters on the Montaño roof. Dolan has one of his men fire at Corporal Ben [Berry] Robinson, George's brother, and this is enough to give Colonel Dudley an excuse to interfere. Major Murphy is in Santa Fe, dying, even seeking death.

Luke trades places with Bowdre in the McSween house. Atanacio Martínez also joins this group and becomes their leader, not Bonney. Martínez guns down Bob Beckwith during the break from the burning house, and he helps carry the wounded Luke to safety. The day after the fight ends, Mrs. McSween vows to carry on resistance. A few days after that Martínez and the Regulators trace horses stolen from Luke's ranch to the agency and Bernstein is shot. Magdalena narrowly escapes being raped when John Kinney and his gang go on the rampage. Luke finally marries her by proxy—she is pregnant by him and in hiding—and Juan Patrón arranges for Luke to manage a sheep ranch he owns near Puerto de Luna until the trouble dies down enough for him to return with Magdalena to the Brewer ranch. Bonney and the others swear to carry on the fight.

Although TIME FOR OUTRAGE is no less a variety of historical romance than the other accounts featuring the Kid, I suspect that in more than one case Amelia Bean correctly interpreted and reconstructed what actually did happen.

JURY OF SIX (Pocket Books, 1980) by Matt Braun was the second in Braun's series of novels about Luke Starbuck, manhunter, who in the series becomes involved with actual historical events and historical personalities with occasional pornographic sequences. In JURY OF SIX, Billy the Kid kills Starbuck's good friend, Ben Langham, while stealing Langham's cattle and Starbuck, along with John Poe, heads into New Mexico representing the Panhandle Cattlemen's Association. The Kid is portrayed as a cold-blooded killer who enjoys killing for its own sake. "Of the eight men he'd killed," the reader is told, "at least seven had been gunned down with no chance."[115] On the other hand, Starbuck, the hero, is known to have killed eleven men, has a "reputation for steel nerves and suddenness with a gun," and over the past four years has "grown cold and hard, brutalized by the sight of death . . . outwardly he was stoic, somehow dispassionate . . . his thoughts [on] revenge."[116]

Sally [Sallie] is said to be Chisum's daughter. Dolan is called Jack Dobson. As for Garrett's association with the Kid, it is remarked, " 'Nothin' illegal, but they was real thick, and there ain't nobody knows the Kid better'n Pat Garrett.' "[117] Garrett confesses to Starbuck that he has a long way to go as a lawman and is glad to have Starbuck's help. The Kid is described as Garrett's "ticket to bigger things." [118]

After what is termed a three-day battle, "a lawyer who had supported Alexander McSween was callously murdered by two former members of the Murphy/Dobson [Dolan] faction. Upon learning that the Kid had witnessed the shooting, Governor Wallace promised immunity, and a full pardon, if he would testify. The Kid agreed, submitting to arrest, and gave testimony before a grand jury. Then, for no apparent reason, he escaped from jail and promptly returned to cattle rustling. . . . He was known to have murdered three men in cold blood, including the unarmed Indian agent on the Mescalero reservation."[119]

Starbuck's philosophy is this: "Violence was part of his trade. When words failed, he used his fists. Or in the last resort, he used a gun. Certain men, unpersuaded by reason, left him no alternative. Only a fool allowed the other man the first blow."[120] It is difficult sometimes to remember that this is the hero. Starbuck learns that the Kid was merely the tool of ambitious men, to wit the Santa Fe Ring.

In the Brady shooting, "leaving nothing to chance, the Kid had coolly walked into the street and fired a final shot into the sheriff's head."[121] For this reason, the jury at Mesilla finds the Kid guilty and nothing can be done about it by the Kid's attorney, Arthur [Albert] Fountain. Judge Walter [Warren] Bristol sentences the Kid to hang. The Kid somehow gets Bell's gun and escapes. The title of the book comes from Starbuck's method of dealing with the Kid: "Judge Colt and the jury of six. Verdict guaranteed."[122] Instead of McKinney, it is Starbuck on the porch with Poe when Garrett ambushes the Kid. The Kid has a cocked gun in his hand. Starbuck himself goes after Judge Hough, one of the men behind the Kid, and kills him when he is unarmed. It is said Hough's "sphincter voided in death."[123] Because Starbuck is the hero, he can kill in this fashion and is to be admired for it. As for the Kid, despite the many fictional variations in between, his image in Braun's novel is virtually the same as that projected in the dime novels of a century before.

This would also be the assessment of Braun's use of the Kid in the third volume of his tetralology about the Brannock family, RIO HONDO (New American Library, 1987). In this novel Billy is interviewed by Clint Brannock while in jail at Mesilla. The brief sketch Braun supplies of the factors and historical personalities involved in the Lincoln County War is a total misrepresentation. Alexander McSween is characterized as "a local storekeeper" and of the Kid it is written that "of the men he'd killed, at least seven had been gunned down with no chance to defend themselves."[124]

The most recent extended fictional treatment of the legend has been Larry McMurtry's ANYTHING FOR BILLY (Simon and Schuster, 1988). As far as sources for his inspiration, McMurtry seems to have confined himself to Alfred

Adler's view of human ambition being often a consequence of a person's physical stature. McMurtry's character, named Billy Bone, suffers from what Adler termed in Individual Psychology "perceived inferiority." This is posited as the motivating force behind the historical Billy the Kid in McMurtry's novel. The story is narrated by Benjamin J. Sippy. He is an author of dime novels who has deserted his wife and nine daughters in Philadelphia to roam about the real West. Sippy provides the Kid with epic dimensions: "The first time I saw Billy he came walking out of a cloud. He had a pistol in each hand and a scared look on his young face."[125] Billy has "buck teeth and both of them were chipped." The novel derives its title from Sippy's comment that "there was a time when I would have done anything for Billy."[126] Billy, we are told, "had been born on the Bowery in New York and brought West as a baby."[127] Sippy observes that Billy cannot read. Will Isinglass, owner of the Whiskey Glass ranch, is based loosely on John Chisum, very loosely since "his cowboys referred to him as Old Whiskey because of his habit of strapping a jar of whiskey to his saddle before he left his headquarters each morning."[128] Isinglass is also a far more sexual character than Chisum and has sired four half-witted sons by the widow of his deceased partner, an outlaw daughter by a Mexican woman, and a half-breed Apache son by a Mescalero woman. He has also started a couple of children in Lady Cecily Snow, daughter of his deceased partner Lord Snow, but she has managed successfully to abort them.

McMurtry knew so little about gunfighters that he has the Kid keep twelve loads in his two pistols, instead of carrying an empty shell beneath the hammer of each. However, it doesn't greatly matter because Billy cannot hit anything with his pistols and, finally, takes to carrying a shotgun with which to commit his gratuitous killings. Sippy claims that he is the one who first called Bone by the name Billy the Kid in his dime novel BILLY THE KID; or, THE WANDERING BOY'S DOOM, which he published shortly after the Kid's death. This title, mentioned early on, is consistent with the incessant foreshadowing so that the reader is ever aware that Billy is a marked man and that he will come to a violent end. "I just followed along with Billy as he rode the bloody trail—a wandering boy one step ahead of his doom."[129] Billy's first love is Katrina Garza. Katie is Isinglass's half-breed daughter and leader of the outlaw pack known as los Guajolotes [the Turkeys]. Isinglass's former partner Lord Snow is loosely based on John Tunstall. Lord Snow's faithful African retainer Mesty-Woolah rides a camel everywhere and is commonly referred to as the "tall nigger" by the other characters. He has transferred his loyalty to Isinglass. Sippy eventually writes a novel about him, THE NEGRO OF THE NILE; or, SON OF THE MAHDI. Sippy feels Governor Wallace is no better than he is since, in Sippy's opinion, "old Lew . . . is no more than an inferior dime novelist himself—for what was BEN HUR but a fat double-dimer set in Roman times?"[130]

It is Sippy who diagnoses Billy's perceived inferiority as the driving force behind his need to be violent in a sensational way. "He was an untried boy who had acquired a big reputation from doing little or nothing, and now no one could persuade him he didn't deserve the reputation."[131] Isinglass wants the band of gunfighters hanging around Greasy Corners off his range. He drives them out and he comes after them again when they set up camp in Puerta de Luna. Doc Holliday makes a brief appearance but he vanishes once Old Whiskey and his men come riding in—which may indicate that McMurtry was familiar with Howard Hughes's THE OUTLAW (RKO, 1943). The gunfighters are routed again, only to hole up in an adobe shack at Skunkwater Flat, an episode obviously based on the capture of the Kid at Stinking Springs. Billy shot a harmless horsebreaker, Elmer Fay, and his brother is with Isinglass's posse. The Kid suggests a parley with Jody Fay and when the man comes forward under a flag of truce Billy blasts him with his shotgun. When asked by one of the gunfighters why he shot Jody Fay, Billy responds: " 'It just seemed like fun at the time.' "[132] Billy's best friend, Joe Lovelady, makes a run for it wearing Billy's clothes and is chased by the "tall nigger" on the camel. The other gunfighters are finished off while Sippy is taken prisoner by Isinglass who returns with him to Winds' Hill, the location of the English castle built by Lord Snow. Now that her father and mother are dead, Cecily is Lady Snow. Although Isinglass regards her as his property, he sleeps in the bunkhouse. Lady Snow is a sketch artist, a botanist, and sexually promiscuous—if anyone doubted that ANY-THING FOR BILLY is a typical McMurtry novel rather than a serious effort at a historical reconstruction the presence of such McMurtry prototypes as Isinglass and Lady Snow make such a conclusion rather obvious. Cecily seduces Sippy but she loses all interest in him once she sees Billy. Mesty-Woolah arrives with Joe Lovelady. The latter spared Mesty-Woolah's life because at the end of the chase his camel was dead and he was exhausted. Notwithstanding, Joe is not to be spared. Mesty-Woolah decapitates Joe with his sword, an act which upsets Lady Snow because Lovelady's blood splashes her chicken coop and now it will have to be repainted.

Tully Roebuck is based on Pat Garrett. He arrests Billy in Lincoln for two gratuitous killings. Katie smuggles the Kid a gun and he shoots his way out of jail. However, if there is a real villain in this story, it is Lady Snow. It is she who induces Billy to kill the four half-witted half-brothers. She wants the Kid to elope with her but she stalls around so long it becomes evident that she wants Isinglass (who is intensely jealous) to catch up with them, as well as Bloody Feathers (Isinglass's half-breed son who is after Billy for shooting down a defenseless Indian boy) and Katie (who is jealous for her own reasons). If Isinglass and the others get killed, she will inherit everything. Such a plan is consistent with her cold-blooded temperament for she shoots Mesty-Woolah from ambush while he is praying. In the event it is Katie who plugs the Kid because she wanted him to die at the hand of one who loves him. Sippy reflects that perhaps the reason "Billy killed so easily, in such a conscienceless way" was that "he apprehended no future, neither his own nor his victims'. The present swallowed Billy as the whale swallowed Jonah."[133] The Kid does not die immediately but hangs on to talk briefly with Katie. Afterwards, legend attributes his death to Tully Roebuck because it would be inappropriate for a woman to have killed a man of his reputation. It is Tully who remarks to Sippy: " 'Ever notice how all these famous gunmen are no bigger than a pint?' "[134] There is probably no more basic way of stating the essential concept behind Adler's *Minderkomplex*—although in Billy's case, as Sippy has made clear from the beginning, his subjectively perceived inferiority caused as a reaction to his short stature is backed up by his persistent inferiority to his own reputation and he must be dead before the legend can come to have a life of its own.

Surveying the fiction from more than a century based on the legend of Billy the Kid and the Lincoln County War, there is no common thread. Almost as often as the character based on the historical Kid is called Billy the Kid, he is given a different name, although sufficient aspects of the Kid's physical appearance and the deeds he is reputed to have done are given to these characters to allow no question as to the source on which they are based. There is no evolution of the character. Inside the same decade, at times only a year or two apart, the Kid can be presented sympathetically or as a fiend. He can be killed, and "deserve" it, or he can be spared and given a second chance. One hundred years after the first dime novels appeared, Matt Braun can present a portrait of the Kid that might have stepped right out of their pages or out of the Garrett/Upson account. What is shown in the organization of events in these various treatments is an effort on the part of the particular authors to produce in the reader either empathy for the character or intense dislike (if not a stronger repulsion). Above all, it is perhaps most significant that the majority of writers who have stylized the Kid in their fiction were influenced by, or read, the same basic fantasies which for so long dominated most attempts to recreate an accurate historical construction of the Lincoln County War and the Kid's role in it.

I once thought it might be possible to write a reliable fictional account of the historical Billy the Kid and the Lincoln County War. I even had an outline worked out and tinkered with it for years before I realized that to make such an effort would be a waste of time. McMurtry was correct insofar as he recognized that what was of interest to a reader was not the truth about Billy but rather his legend. The truth could only disappoint, as Billy Bone disappoints everyone in his real life. Those who ought not to have won, according to the axiom that justice and fair play *should* win, did win and Billy while never a hero was not a villain, either. He was at best a victim of circumstances who has been made famous not by what he did or did not do, but by the legend others created about him. As far as a factual treatment goes, it is now available. If Billy's role in events is considerably diminished in accurate history, this has had no effect on the perpetuation of his legend nor will it prevent many new permutations to be created from it in the future.

BIBLIOGRAPHY OF FICTIONAL SOURCES

Bean, Amelia, TIME FOR OUTRAGE (New York: Doubleday, 1967).

Braun, Matt, JURY OF SIX (New York: Pocket Books, 1980).

Burnett, W. R., "Nobody's All Bad," COLLIER'S (Vol. 85, No. 23), 7 June 1930, pp. 20–21, 30.

———, MI AMIGO (New York: Knopf, 1959).

Coolidge, Dane, WAR PAINT (New York: Dutton, 1929).

———, BLOODY HEAD (New York: Dutton, 1940).

Corle, Edwin, "The Ghost of Billy the Kid" in MOJAVE: A BOOK OF STORIES (New York: Liveright, 1934).

———, BILLY THE KID (New York: Duell, Sloan, and Pearce, 1953); reissued (Albuquerque: University of New Mexico Press, 1979).

Cowdrick, J. C., SILVER MASK, THE MAN OF MYSTERY; or, THE CROSS OF THE GOLDEN KEYS (New York: Beadle and Adams, 1884).

Cunningham, Eugene, DIAMOND RIVER MAN (Boston: Houghton Mifflin, 1934).

Daggett, Thomas F., BILLY LeROY, THE COLORADO BANDIT; or, THE KING OF AMERICAN HIGHWAYMEN (New York: Richard K. Fox, 1881).

Doughty, Francis W., OLD KING BRADY AND BILLY THE KID; or, THE GREAT DETECTIVE'S CHASE (New York: Frank Tousey, 1890).

Fable, Edmund, Jr., BILLY THE KID, THE NEW MEXICAN OUTLAW (Denver: Denver Publishing Company, 1881).

Grey, Zane, FORLORN RIVER (New York: Harper, 1927).

———, "NEVADA" (New York: Harper, 1928).

———, SHADOW ON THE TRAIL (New York: Harper, 1946).

Henry, O., [pseud. William Sydney Porter], HEART OF THE WEST (New York: Doubleday, Page, 1904).

Henry, Will, [pseud. Henry Wilson Allen], "A Bullet for Billy the Kid" in SONS OF THE WESTERN FRONTIER (New York: Chilton Books, 1966).

Hough, Emerson, HEART'S DESIRE (New York: Macmillan, 1905).

Jernado, Don, [pseud. John Woodruff Lewis], THE TRUE LIFE OF BILLY THE KID (New York: Frank Tousey, 1881).

Lehman, Paul Evan, PISTOLS ON THE PECOS (New York: Avon, 1953).

McGreeney, P. S., DOWN AT STEIN'S PASS (Boston: Angel Guardian Press, 1909).

McMurtry, Larry, ANYTHING FOR BILLY (New York: Simon and Schuster, 1988).

Mann, E. B., GAMBLIN' MAN (New York: Morrow, 1934).

Morrison, John W., THE LIFE OF BILLY THE KID, A JUVENILE OUTLAW (New York: Morrison's Sensational Library, 1881).

Nafziger, Ray, "Hangman's Hostage," MAVERICKS (Vol. 1, No. 1) September, 1934, pp. 94–114.

———, "Guns of the Owlhoot Pack," MAVERICKS (Vol. 1, No. 2) October, 1934, pp. 120–140.

———, "Bullets for Breakfast," MAVERICKS (Vol. 1, No .3) November, 1934, pp. 120–141.

———, "Billy the Kid—Gun Friend," MAVERICKS (Vol. 1, No. 4) December, 1934, pp. 100–117.

Neider, Charles, THE AUTHENTIC DEATH OF HENDRY JONES (New York: Harper, 1956).

Nye, Nelson C., PISTOLS FOR HIRE (New York: Macmillan, 1941).

Olmsted, Harry F., "There's Hell Tonight in Lincoln County!," STAR WESTERN (Vol. 41, No. 1) February, 1947, pp. 8–25.

"One of the Kids," THE COWBOY'S CAREER; or, THE DARE DEVIL DEEDS OF BILLY THE KID (Chicago and St. Louis: Belford and Clark, 1881).

Price, G. G., DEATH COMES TO BILLY THE KID (Greensburg: Signal Publishing Company, 1940).

Raine, William MacLeod, THE FIGHTING TENDERFOOT (New York: Doubleday, 1929).

Rhodes, Eugene Manlove, PASÓ POR AQUÍ in ONCE IN THE SADDLE (Boston: Houghton Mifflin, 1927); reissued separately (Norman: University of Oklahoma Press, 1973).

Woods, Walter, [pseud. Walvin Woods], BILLY THE KID (1903) contained in THE GREAT DIAMOND ROBBERY AND OTHER RECENT MELODRAMAS (Princeton: Princeton University Press, 1940) edited by Garrett H. Leverton.

4

BILLY THE KID
IN FILM

Using Walter Noble Burns's THE SAGA OF BILLY THE KID as their basis, in 1930 Laurence Stallings and King Vidor decided to bring the life of Billy the Kid to the screen. They took a story outline to Irving Thalberg, then head of production at Metro-Goldwyn-Mayer, and described the whole thing to Thalberg in the tonneau of his limousine as Thalberg and his assistant, Eddie Mannix, were *en route* to Mabel Normand's funeral.

Vidor began the conference by saying that Billy shot his first victim because of an insult to his mother. Louis B. Mayer was vice president at M-G-M and he liked at least one reference to motherhood in every film the studio released. "This bit of historical half-truth was emphasized in the hope of convincing Thalberg that all of the Kid's murders were understandable, if not entirely excusable," Vidor later asserted in his autobiography. "Then I took Billy through scenes of murder in self-defense, and murders on the side of justice if not on the side of law."

"Too many murders," was Thalberg's whispered assessment as the four of them sat dutifully in a pew near the flower-draped coffin. On the way back to the studio lot in Culver City, Thalberg broke in with a question.

"Was Sheriff Pat Garrett his friend during the time of those last five murders?" he asked.

Stallings and Vidor gave their assent. They were both convinced that the screen was ready for what they termed a more truthful presentation of violence. Thalberg finally agreed with them.[1]

In his FROM HOPALONG TO HUD: THOUGHTS ON WESTERN FICTION (Texas A&M University Press, 1978), C. L. Sonnichsen told the following anecdote about Mrs. Sophie Poe, wife of John Poe and cited above as the author of BUCKBOARD DAYS. She had been hired as a consultant to King Vidor during the filming of BILLY THE KID (M-G-M, 1930). Disgusted by what she was seeing, she remarked to Vidor, "Sir, I knew that little buck-toothed killer, and he wasn't the way you are making him at all." "Mrs. Poe," Vidor responded, "I understand your feelings, but this is what the people want."[2] She was soon removed from her consulting position by the M-G-M publicity department and replaced by movie cowboy William S. Hart.

"One of the grips saw it first," Johnny Mack Brown, who had been cast in the role of the Kid, recalled for me once as we talked together. "A small cloud of swirling dust far off in the distance. It kept coming closer. We could make out that it was a rider. We were on location filming the cave scene on the desert where Billy gets starved out. The rider was nearer now. We could finally recognize him. It was William S. Hart."

"He acted as technical adviser on that picture, didn't he?" I asked.

"Yes," Brown agreed, "and I'm proud to say that we became friends afterward. You know, he wrote books and would give me autographed copies. He taught me a great many things. How to crouch, for instance, and to turn your left side away, to protect your heart. 'Diminish your target,' he told me. 'Diminish your target and keep your heart as far away as you can from an enemy's bullet.' I followed his advice when I had a gun battle in the picture. He even gave me one of Billy the Kid's guns. I still have it."

The presentation of the gun to Brown by Hart became part of the promotional campaign for the picture as did an open letter from then governor of New Mexico, R. C. Dillon. The letter appeared right after the credit crawl and endorsed the film. The scenario called for Billy to be portrayed as the victim of repeated injustice, Brown's warm characterization minimizing the terror that had once been attached to the person of the real-life Kid.

By way of addendum, I might mention that Wyatt Earp wanted to publish an accurate account of his life beginning in about 1905 and that a family friend, John J. Flood, Jr., collaborated with him to write it. However, no one would publish it, even with the effort in its behalf by William S. Hart, who was a personal friend of Earp's. "In 1926," Glenn G. Boyer noted in his Epilogue to I MARRIED WYATT EARP: THE RECOLLECTIONS OF JOSEPHINE SARAH MARCUS EARP, "shortly after the completion of the Flood manuscript, Wyatt was visited by Walter Noble Burns, author of the popular book THE SAGA OF BILLY THE KID. When Burns told the aging adventurer of his hope to be allowed to write the Earp story, Wyatt regretfully declined to help on the grounds that Hart was still trying to market the Flood work. Burns, however, smoothly persuaded Wyatt to aid him in constructing a biography of Doc Holliday. Wyatt helped considerably, but his suspicions were aroused when Burns's queries began to center around the old lawman's own activities rather than those of the homicidal Doc. Bill Hart gave Wyatt further cause for alarm when he wrote him that Burns's THE SAGA OF BILLY THE KID had been plagiarized in spots from an old story by the actor's cowboy friend Charles Siringo."[3]

Hart, of course, was only partly right. Burns did base some of his "saga" on Siringo's account, but only insofar as Siringo in turn based his account on the

Johnny Mack Brown, the screen's first Billy the Kid. *Photo courtesy of Johnny Mack Brown.*

Garrett/Upson account. It may be true that *"in bello non licet bis errare,"* but not in legendry. Indeed, in legendry the more often the same mistake is repeated the more acceptable it seems to become.

BILLY THE KID opens to a trail herd led by two Englishmen, Tunston [Tunstall] and McSween, played by Wyndham Standing and Russell Simpson. They want to settle in the Pecos. Donovan [Murphy], the local land baron played by James Marcus, tells them to push on. Donovan is the law in New Mexico. He is seen to seize a homesteader's ranch and has both the homesteader and his wife shot. The two Englishmen try to organize resistance to Donovan's rule. Factions develop, Donovan joined by Ballinger [Olinger], played by Warner Richmond, and Ballinger's gang on one side, Tunston and McSween and Billy the Kid and the Kid's supporters on the other side. After a shoot-out in town, Billy is offered amnesty if he will only make peace. Wallace Beery, cast as Pat Garrett, threatens to come after Billy if he will not agree. Billy rejects the offer. Garrett and a posse made up of Ballinger's men starve out Billy when he hides in a cave. Billy is taken to Lincoln and put in jail. Claire Randall, played by Kay Johnson, originally in love with Tunston until his death has now transferred her affections to the Kid. Billy is sentenced to hang and Ballinger is made his jailer.

The Kid gets hold of Garrett's gun and locks Pat in a closet. He shoots the gun which causes Ballinger, who is across the street, to run out into the street where the Kid guns him. Billy hides out at the home of Santiago, played by Chris-Pin Martin, where Claire joins him. Garrett sneaks up. The Kid and Claire ride off across the border, Garrett shooting after them, deliberately missing and smiling.

After this whitewash, the Kid was left alone until BILLY THE KID RETURNS (Republic, 1938) directed by Joseph Kane. The second entry in Republic's new Roy Rogers series, Rogers played a dual role, both the Kid in a prologue and himself during the rest of the film. The prologue shows the Kid is feared by the large cattle ranchers and that he is a friend of the nesters the ranchers are trying to drive off their land. Billy uses two guns and fights his way out of a siege led by Fred Kohler who plugs McSween as McSween's house burns. Wade Boteler, cast as Pat Garrett, shoots the Kid while he is asleep. The next morning Roy Rogers rides into town singing "Born to the Saddle" and is arrested because of his resemblance to the Kid. He proves he is Roy Rogers by singing a song. Smiley Burnette, as Frog Milhouse, also remembers going to school with Roy in Texas whereas the real Kid never had a day of schooling in his life. In due course, Roy is deputized to help the nesters by impersonating the Kid. Garrett is among those who want Roy to take on Kohler and his gang and Roy confesses he has always admired Garrett. Mary Hart is the heroine and her father opens a store in town to compete with Morgenson who is Kohler's boss. At one point Roy forces the gang members to buy all of the musical instruments Frog has for sale even though none of them can play the instruments. Roy and Garrett succeed in framing the gang for stealing Army horses and they are rounded up by the cavalry. Roy and Smiley in the course of the film sing seven songs.

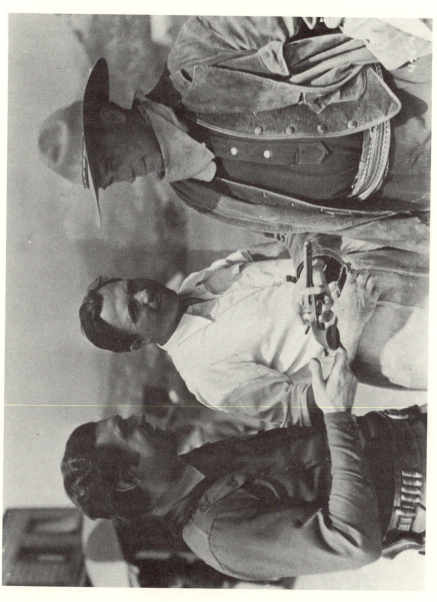

Johnny Mack Brown (l.), King Vidor (c.), and William S. Hart (r.) on the set of BILLY THE KID (M-G-M, 1930) as Hart presents Brown with a pistol that presumably once belonged to Billy the Kid. *Photo courtesy of Johnny Mack Brown.*

It was shortly thereafter that Producers Releasing Corporation began its Billy the Kid series. In the six films in the series released during the 1940–1941 season, Bob Steele was cast as the Kid. The first entry was titled BILLY THE KID OUTLAWED (PRC, 1940) and directed by Sam Newfield under a screen pseudonym, Peter Stewart, with a screenplay by Oliver Drake. Drake at least kept some semblance of the historical particulars insofar as the Kid avenges the murders of two friends by cleaning up Lincoln County which is dominated by two bad guys named Morgan [Murphy] and Daly [Dolan].

In BILLY THE KID IN TEXAS (PRC, 1940), again directed by Sam Newfield under the Peter Stewart byline, the screenplay was by Joseph O'Donnell. The Kid has a $5,000 reward on his head presumably for a holdup he committed back in New Mexico. Al "Fuzzy" St. John, who played the Kid's sidekick in the earlier film, was back, and he remained the "official" sidekick throughout the series. While in history, the Kid's brother, Joe Antrim, was reputed to be out to revenge Garrett's killing of the Kid until, as noted in a previous chapter, Antrim and Garrett met for a couple of hours' quiet conversation in the lobby of the Armijo Hotel in Trinidad, shaking hands afterward, in this film the Kid's brother is named Gil and is played by Carleton Young (misspelled on the credits as Carlton). Gil is in with a gang of thieves led by John Merton. In the first entry Young had been second lead cast as the Kid's pard, and here the two also form a triad hero of sorts with St. John. The Kid, after foiling a robbery by taking the loot from bad guy Charles King, gets himself appointed sheriff of Corral City (no matter if the town is Lincoln or Corral City, the town set was always Monogram City in the Bob Steele entries). Gil tells Merton that his brother was framed and that is why he is outlawed. Complications arise when Billy's identity is revealed, but Gil is essentially a good guy and joins forces with him to clean up the town and round up Merton, King, and the rest of the gang. Gil's reward is to be made sheriff as the Kid and Fuzzy ride on.

The trio—Steele, Young, and St. John—was back to round up a gang of murderous land profiteers in BILLY THE KID'S GUN JUSTICE (PRC, 1940) directed by Peter Stewart. Carleton Young, whose cast name had been changing from picture to picture with the character he was playing, was finally dubbed "Jeff" for this and the next two entries. Oliver Drake did the screenplay and, while the qualitative difference may be minimal, he could be relied upon to provide a less hackneyed plot than Joseph O'Donnell. However, neither was as wanting as William Lively who scripted BILLY THE KID'S RANGE WAR (PRC, 1941) directed by Peter Stewart. The gang is intent on preventing a stage road from being completed in order for the chief villain to get a government contract for his steamboat line. All the depredations the gang commits are blamed on Billy the Kid even though he is miles away from each incident when it occurs. Only the obligatory fist fights, gunplay, and occasional chase on horseback relieve the tedium of the plot which is moved to a swift resolution once the Kid comes on the scene to get to the bottom of who has been using his name and why.

BILLY THE KID'S FIGHTING PALS (PRC, 1941) was directed by Sam Newfield under yet another pseudonym, Sherman Scott. Newfield's brother Sig

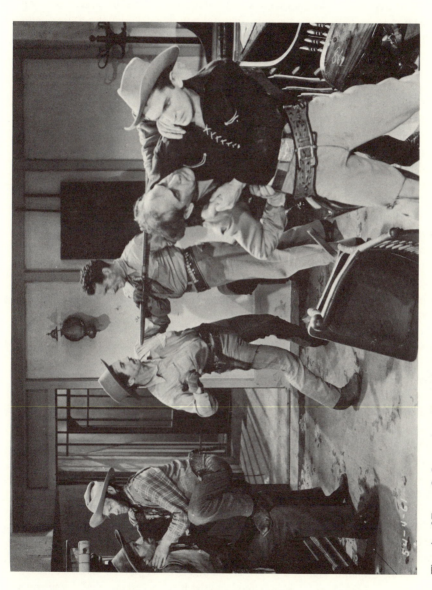

The trio of Fuzzy Q. Jones played by Al St. John (l.), Jeff played by Carleton Young (c.), and Bob Steele (r.) as the Kid with a headlock on Ted Adams as the sheriff in BILLY THE KID OUTLAWED (PRC, 1940). *Photo courtesy of Eddie Brandt's Saturday Matinee.*

Neufield produced the majority of PRC Westerns and Sam, it would appear, wanted to give the impression that the studio had more than a single contract director. Edward Peil, Sr., is a crooked banker who divides his time between forcing all the honest settlers into bankruptcy and having a tunnel dug across the border so he can engage in smuggling. Unfortunately, Peil did not anticipate having to deal with Billy and his pals. Since VARIETY singled out the direction in particular as deficient in pacing, it was just as well that Newfield used a different byline. George Plympton wrote the screenplay and it is difficult to decide if the awkward dialogue, the preposterous situations, or the pathetic attempts at comedy is sufficient compensation for the faulty direction!

In the meantime BILLY THE KID (M-G-M, 1941) directed by David Miller was released. One thing that Garrett, George Coe, and John Poe in their respective memoirs agreed upon was that the Kid was right-handed. The error about his being "left-handed" was derived from the manner of producing tintypes in which the sides can become transposed. The one full-length tintype we have of the Kid was (and still is) occasionally reversed in this way and, accordingly, when it is, the Kid appears to have been left-handed. It is perhaps a minor point—in view of the gross inaccuracies to be found in all the films about the Kid prior to Miller's film and after it—but it was added to the Kid's screen image in M-G-M's second attempt to film the Kid's life. Miller and screenwriter Gene Fowler saw the Kid's story as tragedy. Filmed in Monument Valley, the picture was given the benefit of Technicolor and, when Nature fell short, the M-G-M art department took over and painted in mesas and picturesque cloud formations.

Pat Garrett is not even in this version. Robert Taylor, cast as the Kid, is hired by Gene Lockhart to help his gang eliminate Ian Hunter, cast as an English cattle rancher. The Kid's boyhood chum, played by Brian Donlevy, works for Hunter. They meet again during a cattle stampede—and because Louis B. Mayer was still running the studio, Donlevy recalls how Billy loved Donlevy's mother's pies and had been wont to take them without asking. This was apparently the beginning of Billy's life of crime. Billy's first meeting with Ian Hunter is just as sentimental. Hunter plays the piano for him, tells him little parables about why it is better to be good than bad, and announces that he does not wear a gun because he is protected by the Kid's code never to shoot an unarmed man. It is, supposedly, a code upheld by all Western bad men.

When one of Hunter's wranglers dies, the Kid is so moved by the wrangler's sobbing wife that he quits Lockhart's gang and comes to work for Hunter. Lockhart's men then kill Billy's sidekick, Pedro, played by Frank Puglia, but Hunter persuades the Kid to hold off while he writes a letter to the governor. The governor responds by making Hunter a U.S. marshal and Billy is paroled into his custody. Hunter is shot down by Lockhart's men and the Kid, locked up in jail for his own good until Lockhart can stand trial, breaks out and takes off after Lockhart's hired killers. He shoots them down one by one before the posse, led by Donlevy, catches up with him. The Kid cannot resist the temptation of shooting Lockhart—who is with the posse—in the back. Knowing he deserves to be punished for this foul deed, the Kid reverses his holster to the right side, goes up against Donlevy, and, his draw slowed because of the switch, is gunned down. Taylor would make a number of exceptional Western films in his career, but this was not one of them.

Meanwhile, back at the PRC ranch, Bob Steele rode for the last time as Billy in BILLY THE KID IN SANTA FE (PRC, 1941) directed by Sherman Scott. What had saved him from continuing this depressing series was his signing a contract to join the roster at Republic Pictures. He was, in fact, busy working in Republic Westerns when the last entries in his Billy the Kid series went into release. Rex Lease replaced Young in the role of Jeff. Joseph O'Donnell did the screenplay and, almost as if he knew this was to be Steele's last picture as the Kid, was so uninspired that he dug out the screenplay he wrote for LIGHTNIN' BILL CARSON (Puritan, 1936), a low-budget Tim McCoy programmer. Marin Sais, a leading lady in "B" Westerns and married to silent movie cowboy Jack Hoxie, was cast as the heroine, but she had little enough to do. Tex, played by Dave O'Brien, works for heavy Charles King and frames Billy on a murder charge. Billy escapes jail and goes after the man who framed him. King, in turn, frames Tex into thinking he has committed a murder. Billy—whom Sais calls "Willie" Bonney—is turned loose on Santa Fe to clean up the town and get the goods on King and his gang. Dennis Moore works for Sais in her bank and is Tex's brother. When Tex is captured by a sheriff's posse and lynched, Moore goes berserk, killing off everyone in the posse, one by one. The one new element in this rehash of the earlier film's plot is that instead of having the character played by Moore shot down at the end by the hero, he is tried *in absentia* and found innocent. The Kid is having a walk-down with Moore when Fuzzy rides in with this news and Moore's life is spared.

Buster Crabbe replaced Bob Steele at the beginning of the 1941–1942 season and stayed with the series until it ended. His first entry was BILLY THE KID WANTED (PRC, 1941) and the press kit invited the public to meet the "new" Billy the Kid. Crabbe was joined by Dave O'Brien cast as second lead Jeff with Fuzzy included for comedy. This trio hears about some homesteaders who are having troubles with their water rights and, coming to their aid, so arranges things that one gang led by Glenn Strange starts to fight with the other gang led by Charles King. Sam Newfield as Sherman Scott directed and Fred Myton produced a vastly improved script—compared to the Bob Steele entries—with plenty of physical action. BILLY THE KID'S ROUND-UP (PRC, 1941), next in order of release, brought back Carleton Young as the second lead Jeff, but not even he could help the plot—the trio saves a town from an evil gang led by Glenn Strange and Charles King responsible for killing an honest newspaper publisher and father of the orphaned heroine played by Joan Barclay, making her second appearance in this series. Sherman Scott directed and Fred Myton did the screenplay, both obviously having had an off day.

BILLY THE KID TRAPPED (PRC, 1942) directed by Sherman Scott had a screenplay by Oliver Drake. Glenn Strange is the gang leader who has three of his men masquerade as Billy and his two pards, Bud McTaggart taking the second lead for this opus as Jeff. In order for the good trio to have an opportunity to commit the

Bob Steele as the Kid in BILLY THE KID IN SANTA FE (PRC, 1941) flanked by Marin Sais (r.) and Charles King (l.). *Photo courtesy of Eddie Brandt's Saturday Matinee.*

robberies perpetrated by the bad trio, Billy and his pards are broken out of jail and set free. The bad trio ambushes the sheriff but Billy nurses him back to health. Eventually, Billy and his pards joined by the recuperated sheriff bring peace to Mesa City by rounding up Strange and his gang and saving the day for Anne Jeffreys's stage line. The only parallel—and a loose one—with history is that Strange has the crooked judge in his power and gets a henchman appointed sheriff at Mesa City before they meet their reckoning. There are running inserts and good action throughout. By now it had become commonplace at PRC that Billy is constantly being framed by bad guys. At the end of this film, Fuzzy sells the outfits of the three masqueraders to another trio of men who are less than honest and again Billy, Jeff, and Fuzzy have to take off after this new group of impostors.

Dave O'Brien returned as the second lead Jeff in BILLY THE KID'S SMOKING GUNS (PRC, 1942) directed by Sherman Scott. It was another above average entry written by George Sayre and Milton Raison under the byline George Milton. The plot has Billy, accused of another crime he did not commit, escape across the border with his two pards, only for them to come upon a wounded rancher and find themselves arrested by the local sheriff. The actual leader of a crooked ranchers' protective association is the town doctor who is in league with the sheriff played by Karl Hackett. Joan Barclay is back as the heroine but this time without much to do. The Kid and his pals help the honest ranchers to wipe out the doctor's crooked association. Dave O'Brien stayed on for the next two entries as Jeff but billed on the credits as Tex O'Brien. BILLY THE KID IN LAW AND ORDER (PRC, 1942) directed by Sherman Scott is interesting because Crabbe was given a dual role, both as the Kid and his look-alike, an Army lieutenant. Charles King in an offbeat role is the local justice of the peace who has a scheme to cheat Sarah Padden as the lieutenant's rich and blind aunt out of her fortune by duping her into marrying a gang member pretending to be her old beau. The lieutenant is killed and the Kid takes his place, foiling King's scheme. Someone must have liked the idea of Crabbe's playing a dual role since in the next film, SHERIFF OF SAGE VALLEY (PRC, 1942) directed by Sherman Scott, Crabbe is cast both as the Kid and his twin brother, Kansas Ed. Billy and his two pards are hired, respectively, as sheriff and deputies and set about bringing Kansas Ed and his henchmen to justice notwithstanding the gang's efforts to get their own stooge elected sheriff. Kansas Ed, even though he is the Kid's brother, is killed in the fray.

While the Kid was riding for law and order at PRC, at Columbia Pictures it was a different story. In WEST OF TOMBSTONE (Columbia, 1942), an entry in the Charles Starrett Western series directed by Howard Bretherton, a prologue states that Billy the Kid was killed on 14 July 1881 at Fort Sumner. Who was he? the narrator asks. "The supposed killing was done by his lifelong friend, Sheriff Pat Garrett, and has long been disputed even by members of Billy's outlaw gang." Obviously, Maurice Geraghty who did the screenplay had read E. B. Mann's GAMBLIN' MAN. Russell Hayden, who had left the Hopalong Cassidy unit to free-lance, is the second lead. He and his sister, played by Marcella Martin, are son and daughter of the part-owner of a stage line played by George DeMain. Billy the

Kid is said to be leading his old gang again, holding up stagecoaches. Deputy U.S. Marshal Steve Langdon, played by Starrett, and his sidekick Cliff "Ukulele Ike" Edwards are sent to get to the bottom of the trouble. The two dig up the Kid's grave—with Edwards providing a song to help the work go faster—only to find out that it is empty. DeMain, it turns out, is actually the Kid. Pat Garrett let him go so he could find an honest life for himself. Confronted by his old gang in the final shoot-out, Starrett suggests DeMain shoot with his left hand, since he will be more accurate if he does. Starrett is wounded and DeMain killed in the fray but not before the latter tells his children the truth on his deathbed. DeMain's heavy French accent makes his portrayal of a middle-aged Billy the Kid slightly exotic by any standard.

When the PRC series went into its third season in 1942–1943, the idea of a second lead was dropped, primarily for budgetary considerations. In THE MYS-TERIOUS RIDER (PRC, 1942) directed by Sherman Scott, Billy and Fuzzy come upon a nearly deserted town and learn that the Kid is being blamed for the town's condition. The town is supposed to be Laramie although it is still Monogram City but without the added cost of extras to make it seem to be a thriving metropolis. The Kid sets matters aright in short order once he discovers John Merton and his gang are behind the depredations because they want a free hand to locate the rich gold vein running through the surrounding district. The next entry, THE KID RIDES AGAIN (PRC, 1943) directed by Sherman Scott with a script by Fred Myton, finds Billy and Fuzzy riding into a town where chief villain I. Stanford Jolley and his henchmen, Glenn Strange and Charles King, have been raiding ranches and rustling cattle in order to drive down land values so Jolley can buy up the land. Iris Meredith provides more than decoration as the heroine. The Kid is arrested after he shoots it out with Charles King, but Fuzzy lets him out and he is able to foil Jolley's attempt to stage a run on the local bank. Although he wasn't even in BILLY THE KID IN TEXAS, the dialogue establishes the fact that it was Jolley who originally had framed the Kid back in Texas. Jolley's career of crime is brought up short with lots of outdoor action and running inserts. It was as if Neufeld scrimped on some pictures so he could spend more on others.

Sam Newfield signed his own name as director of FUGITIVE OF THE PLAINS (PRC, 1943). I do not know if he did this because he felt it was a superior entry. If so, I don't think he was correct in his assessment of it. The budgets on these Billy the Kid pictures were set at $22,500. Crabbe was paid $3,000 apiece, Al St. John $1,000, and the rest of the cast was usually hired for less than $1,000 in the aggregate. Neufeld's salary was $1,200 and Sam Newfield was paid $1,250 a picture. The sets averaged about $1,500. FUGITIVE OF THE PLAINS has an offbeat plot insofar as Maxine Leslie is a gang leader who blames Billy the Kid for all the crimes she and her gang commit. Billy, in collusion with the local sheriff, joins her gang to get evidence against them. Jack Ingram, Leslie's right-hand man until the arrival of the Kid, tries to plug Billy in the final reel. Leslie, although herself wounded as a result of an abortive robbery (secretly foiled by the Kid), outdraws Ingram and shoots him before she collapses and dies in Billy's arms.

In WESTERN CYCLONE (PRC, 1943) directed by Sam Newfield with a screenplay by Patricia Harper, the Kid is framed for murder by Glenn Strange and his gang. Strange is the head of a political faction seeking to impeach the governor so that with the help of a state senator they can continue their reign of lawlessness. The Kid is tried and convicted, but he breaks jail with Fuzzy's help. Strange then kidnaps the governor's niece played by Marjorie Manners and threatens to kill her if the Kid does not turn himself in to be hanged on time. The Kid accedes but, back in jail, talks the governor into a twelve-hour leave in order to round up Strange and his gang, which he manages to do within the time limit, exonerating himself and the governor in the process.

THE RENEGADE (PRC, 1943) directed by Sam Newfield with a story by the team George Milton and a screenplay by Joseph O'Donnell finds a peaceful community preyed upon by a crooked mayor who knows that there is an oil deposit under all the ranchers' land. The local sheriff sends for the Kid and his sidekick to help out, but the Kid is framed for a robbery and the sheriff is forced to jail him. The crooked mayor then forces the sheriff to arrest honest rancher Karl Hackett on an embezzlement charge. However, before the fade, the Kid gets out, finds the missing loot, and exposes the mayor, clearing Hackett and himself of all charges.

The title—CATTLE STAMPEDE (PRC, 1943) directed by Sam Newfield— says it all . . . almost. Charles King and a henchman plan to stampede Hansel Werner's cattle and sell them. Recognizing the Kid, the gang offers to let him in on the deal, but it results in their own undoing. BLAZING FRONTIER (PRC, 1943), the initial entry in the series for the 1943–1944 season, was also the last. Directed, of course, by Sam Newfield, the plot has villains I. Stanford Jolley and Frank Hagney behind a crooked land company attempting to promote a real estate boom so that the railroad will have to pay inflated prices for the right-of-way. Among fantasies, what a fantasy this was! The villains hire Al St. John to work for them as a detective, but he helps the Kid instead to get the goods on them. Buster Crabbe once commented to me about this picture that it had such a low budget that in the chase sequence, after one of the villains rode his horse past the camera, he circled around behind the camera so that Crabbe could mount the same horse and then himself ride past the camera, supposedly chasing the villain. Yet, for all that, neither this nor any of the previous Crabbe entries in the Billy the Kid series became as static at times and deficient in action sequences as many subsequent entries in Crabbe's Billy Carson series which replaced it. The reason PRC felt impelled to alter the name of the character Crabbe was playing was due entirely to the unpleasant controversy which arose when Howard Hughes decided to release his version of the Kid's life.

Walter Woods's play BILLY THE KID (1903) is surely the earliest time in print, and well in advance of Vidor's film, that the Kid was permitted to slip across the border alive at the end of the story. Howard Hughes in directing his version which he titled THE OUTLAW (RKO, 1943) not only reverted to this ending, but he added Doc Holliday, played by Walter Huston, to the cast of characters. With the music of Tchaikovsky's "*Pathetique*" Symphony playing under the credits, the picture

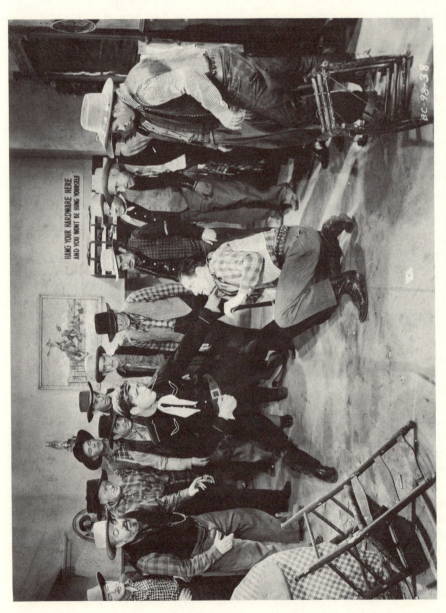

Buster Crabbe as the Kid in a barroom fight with Jack Ingram in WESTERN CYCLONE (PRC, 1943). *Photo courtesy of Eddie Brandt's Saturday Matinee.*

opens with Pat Garrett, played by Thomas Mitchell, declaring that Doc Holliday is his best friend. Doc and the Kid, ineptly played by Jack Beutel, get into a fight over Doc's horse which the Kid stole. When Garrett and Doc get the drop on the Kid, he gets out of his dilemma by telling Doc how much he has admired him ever since he was in short pants! Doc's mistress Rio, played by Jane Russell, takes a shot at the Kid. She bears him a grudge because he killed her brother in a gunfight. When Garrett tries to arrest the Kid, he bolts and Garrett wings him. Doc hides the Kid at his ranch where Russell is on hand to nurse him back to health. The Kid and Rio have sexual intercourse—according to the screen shorthand of the era.

"I'll give you your pick," the Kid says to Doc, referring to a choice between Rio and Doc's horse. Doc chooses the horse. "I like that horse!" the Kid sighs. "They're all alike," Doc advises the Kid about women. "There isn't anything they wouldn't do for you . . . or to you." The truth of these words is borne out when Garrett arrives on the scene and Doc and the Kid flee: Rio puts salt into their canteens. Garrett overtakes them in the desert and in an almost homosexual frenzy shoots Doc. The Kid gets away, kidnaps Rio, and then lets her go free. Garrett continues his pursuit of the Kid and the Kid again eludes him, this time Rio voluntarily joining up with the Kid as he rides for the border. An afterword implies that Garrett lived to be a worried old man because he had a reputation for having killed the Kid which he did not deserve.

According to Jane Russell, Hughes filmed two versions of her sex scene, one for commercial release and one for private viewing by himself and his close circle. The latter featured Russell naked from the waist up, whereas the commercial release version showed Russell's ample bosom piled into a "heaving" brassiere of Hughes' own design. It was Russell's erotic contribution to the film which caused the censors to rise up in arms and, certainly, not the distortions of history in the screen story. When the film was later reissued in 1946, to get it past the censors Hughes had a line dubbed in near the fade implying that Rio and the Kid were to be married.

If I am right in my supposition that Eugene Manlove Rhodes based the character of Ross McEwen on both Billy the Kid and Billie Wilson, then the same would have to apply for the film version of PASÓ POR AQUÍ titled FOUR FACES WEST (United Artists, 1948) directed by Alfred E. Green. The film actually follows the short novel rather faithfully in general with Joel McCrea cast as McEwen and Charles Bickford as Pat Garrett. The role of Fay Hollister is played by Frances Dee. The one significant difference between the film and the short novel is the fashion in which a romance between McEwen and Hollister, here a railroad nurse, is introduced. Hollister wants McEwen to return and face justice. Garrett catches him when McEwen stays behind to assist a Mexican-American family plagued by illness. The moral of this tale is that a sympathetic sheriff and the love of a good woman can change an outlaw's destiny, provided, of course, that outlaw also is *au fond* a humanitarian. It is actually an outstanding Western, notable for the depth of its characters, although Joseph Calleia as Monte is nowhere near as charming as the literary prototype. This film is notable also for the fact that not a single shot is fired and yet a viewer's interest never flags.

SON OF BILLY THE KID (Screen Guild, 1949) directed by Ray Taylor sought to answer the question as to what the Kid did after his death was falsified: in this case he changed his name and became an honest and successful banker. The Kid, played by George Baxter, also had a son in due course—Lash LaRue. When his bank is preyed upon by thieves, the Kid joined now by his son and his son's sidekick Fuzzy St. John bring the gang to justice.

Audie Murphy was cast as Billy in THE KID FROM TEXAS (Universal, 1950) directed by Kurt Neumann. New Mexico is in turmoil because of a range war with Dennis Hoey on one side, Albert Dekker and Shepperd Strudwick on the other. When four of Hoey's men raid the office of Dekker and Strudwick, the Kid saves the two men by disarming the attackers and routing them. Strudwick likes the Kid and gives him a job at the ranch. Dekker, on the other hand, does not like Billy —who wears two guns in the film—and particularly resents him once Gale Storm, cast as Dekker's wife, begins to take a romantic interest in him. When Hoey's men raid the ranch and kill Strudwick, Dekker sends the Kid and his other hands after them. The range war becomes so serious that Robert Barrat, military governor of the Territory, becomes alarmed. Dekker shifts all the blame onto the Kid and even offers a reward for his capture, dead or alive. The Kid decides to live the life of an outlaw and attracts a gang to follow him. When the Kid's gang pulls in at Dekker's ranch, Pat Garrett played by Frank Wilcox and his deputies have laid a trap, open up, and kill every member of the Kid's gang. Dekker, too, falls in the fight. The Kid alone escapes. He has gone to find Gale Storm. Coming up outside a window while she is playing the piano inside, the Kid stands there listening until Garrett discovers him. The Kid refuses to draw his gun and Garrett plugs him. It is a martyr's death.

Because of the success of the fanciful I SHOT JESSE JAMES (Lippert, 1949) directed by Sam Fuller, and perhaps encouraged by Universal's example with the Technicolor THE KID FROM TEXAS, Lippert released I SHOT BILLY THE KID (Lippert, 1950), a low-budget, black and white "quickie" directed by William Berke. Don Barry was cast as the Kid. The film opens with Pat Garrett played by Robert Lowery narrating the events of the Kid's life. The Kid saves Garrett's skin when Garrett is attacked by Indians. Once Garrett becomes sheriff, he is committed to bringing in the Kid. However, Garrett arranges for the Kid to talk with the local Army commander, played by Claude Stroud, who promises the Kid amnesty if he will give himself up. The Kid rejects this offer and continues his reign of crime. Garrett does capture the Kid and he is tried and found guilty. However, Garrett also makes good his promise for amnesty and he is on his way back to the jail with a pardon when the Kid kills a guard and breaks out. Locating the Kid through his girlfriend Francesca, played by Wendy Lee, Garrett shoots him down.

The Kid is nowhere in evidence in two films made by Republic despite their titles including a reference to him. In ALIAS BILLY THE KID (Republic, 1946) directed by Thomas Carr, the reference appears nowhere *but* in the title. When cowboy hero Sunset Carson joins Peggy Stewart's outlaw gang, he is asked by a gang member what he prefers to be called and replies: "Call me, alias the Kid." In

CAPTIVE OF BILLY THE KID (Republic, 1952) directed by Fred C. Bannon, the plot involves a quest for a treasure the Kid once buried, but he is at best a memory.

Scott Brady was on hand to play him, much too old for the part and wearing a typical 1950s-style haircut in THE LAW VS. BILLY THE KID (Columbia, 1954) directed by William Castle. Paul Cavanaugh was cast as Tunstall, a man who does not believe in violence and who treats Billy as a son. When he is shot by one of the crooked sheriff's posse, the Kid henceforth takes the law into his own hands. The Territorial governor appoints Pat Garrett, played by James Griffith, sheriff and offers amnesty to the Kid, but the Kid tells him: "You stick to legal, Governor, and I'll stick to right and wrong." The Kid—it is really inappropriate to refer to the aging Brady by this moniker—is in love with Tunstall's daughter, played by Betta St. John. Garrett tries to talk the Kid out of his vendetta against Tunstall's murderers, proves unsuccessful, and is forced to shoot him down. However, after the deed, he throws down his gun in disgust.

The character of Billy the Kid next made two cameo appearances in Westerns which were otherwise not concerned with him. In an effort to cash in on the popularity of Will Rogers, Jr., after he played the title role in the celluloid biography of his father, he was cast in a film titled THE BOY FROM OKLAHOMA (Warner, 1954) directed by Michael Curtiz. Anthony Caruso was cast as the principal villain controlling the lawless element in a town who hires Rogers to be sheriff because he thinks Rogers is stupid. When he realizes that Rogers is exceptionally competent, Caruso sends for his cousin, Billy the Kid played by Tyler MacDuff, and directs him to kill Rogers, only for Rogers to bluff the Kid in a confrontation in Caruso's saloon. In STRANGE LADY IN TOWN (Warner, 1955) directed by Mervyn LeRoy, Greer Garson plays a doctor from Boston who comes to New Mexico in 1880 to practice medicine. In a brief vignette, Billy the Kid played by Nick Adams comes to see her and establishes the fact that he is nineteen and has already killed nineteen men.

The decade also saw some old-timers try to resurrect the Kid's legend. To start off, Sig Neufeld produced and Sam Newfield directed LAST OF THE DESPERA-DOES (Associated, 1956). James Craig was cast as Pat Garrett, Jim Davis as John W. Poe. The plot is concerned with what happened to Garrett right after he shot down the Kid. Every gang leader wants a crack at Garrett, one of the foremost among them played by Bob Steele who had once played the Kid for Neufeld. After several innocent people lose their lives in shoot-outs, Garrett decides to resign and go into hiding. He finds work as a bartender for a saloon owner played by Margia Dean. Dean falls in love with Garrett and so swept away does she become that she begins talking about her first husband—Billy the Kid! At this point, Poe shows up and convinces Garrett to go back with him. They face the gang leaders and shoot down every one of them.

Next came THE PARSON AND THE OUTLAW (Columbia, 1957) directed by Oliver Drake who had scripted several films in the PRC series produced by Sig Neufeld. The story tells what happened to the Kid after Garrett let him escape across the border. Turning over his guns to Garrett at his gravesite, the Kid played by

Anthony Dexter promises to start homesteading. Later after he saves Jack Slade played by Sonny Tufts from Indians, he learns that Slade is on his way to find out if he can outdraw the Kid. Going by the name Bill Antrim, Billy tells Slade how the Kid was gunned by Garrett and the two of them team up. They come to where Bill's homestead is located and find the district dominated by Colonel Morgan played by Robert Lowery—a familiar face in Kid films—and another familiar face: Bill's homestead is being squatted on by one of Morgan's gang played by Bob Steele. Slade shoots down Steele and Steele's girl friend, played by Marie Windsor, transfers her affections to Bill. Buddy Rogers, cast as the parson in the title, recognizes the Kid and asks him for his help in wiping out Morgan and his gang so the community can be rightfully God-fearing. Slade goes to work for Morgan and the Kid rejects the parson's proposal. He changes his mind, however, when Slade shoots the parson who falls over a hitching rail and appears properly Christ-like. The Kid shoots down Slade, then shoots down Morgan and four of his men, suffering a minor injury in the process. At the fade, the Kid and Marie Windsor ride off together.

The next year saw two more additions to the cycle, both from the same company. In BADMAN'S COUNTRY (Warner, 1958) directed by Fred F. Sears, the Kid is already dead and Pat Garrett played by George Montgomery quits his job and wants to marry and lose his reputation. Neville Brand, as Butch Cassidy, has no intention of letting him do this and summons forty of the Wild Bunch to lay siege to the Territory. Wyatt Earp, played by Buster Crabbe, comes along to assist Garrett in battling against this crime wave. In THE LEFT-HANDED GUN (Warner, 1958)—guess *who* is left-handed?—directed by Arthur Penn, Paul Newman, who had played the Kid previously in the PHILCO PLAYHOUSE production of THE DEATH OF BILLY THE KID (NBC, 1955) by Gore Vidal, was again cast in the role for the film adaptation of the teleplay. The scenario, consistent with Vidal's interpretation of the Kid as a manic-depressive with an Oedipus complex, has the Kid befriended by a Scottish rancher named McSween, played by John Dierkes. When McSween is killed by four toughs, the Kid sets out to avenge him, killing not only the four responsible but three others as well. Given Vidal's sexual preoccupation, it is not surprising that the Kid's homosexuality comes very much into play in his rough-housing with his friends, James Congdon as Boudre [Bowdre] and James Best as Folliard [O'Folliard], and in his search for a father figure, a role which John Dehner, as Pat Garrett, seems best suited to fill. A huckster, played by Hurd Hatfield, disillusioned that the Kid is not more of a hero, turns him in to Garrett—who has become alienated from the Kid because the Kid disrupted his wedding—and Billy forces Garrett to draw when he has only an empty holster. The screenplay, to be sure, has the Kid unarmed, but the rest is nonsense. Penn's obvious interest was elsewhere. "The character of Hurd Hatfield," Penn said in his interview for THE DIRECTOR'S EVENT, "was constantly confronted with a myth he had formed in his own mind about Billy the Kid. His grave disappointment when he found out what Billy actually was, and his inability to reconcile these two, caused him to betray Billy. The need to have heroes be genuinely heroic seems to me to be an absurdity and a foolish intention, and when somebody like the Hatfield character is let down, his revenge has no limit."[4] Gore Vidal would eventually get a second chance at the Kid's story.

The reader may recall from the previous chapter that in Charles Neider's THE AUTHENTIC DEATH OF HENDRY JONES Dad Longworth kills Hendry Jones. When Marlon Brando brought his version of this novel to the screen in ONE-EYED JACKS (Paramount, 1961), Brando's director's cut ran almost five hours. The severely edited studio version that was released may or may not be an improvement on the original, but at the end Brando playing Rio, the character based on Hendry Jones, shoots Dad Longworth played by Karl Malden, and then rides off into the sunset. What is of even more interest about ONE-EYED JACKS when it comes to the Kid is that Sam Peckinpah worked for a time on the screenplay and had occasion to read Neider's novel. Nearly all of Peckinpah's own notions about the Kid were derived from Neider's novel, including in PAT GARRETT AND BILLY THE KID (M-G-M, 1973) the small, clean bullet hole in the Kid's chest and the yearning on Dad Longworth's part to make secure his old age by aligning himself with the law which is Garrett's basic refrain.

Chuck Courtney was cast as the Kid in BILLY THE KID VS. DRACULA (Embassy, 1966) directed by William Beaudine. A reformed outlaw, Billy is foreman of Melinda Plowman's ranch and engaged to her. When Dracula played by John Carradine shows up, he poses as Plowman's uncle. As Plowman falls increasingly under Dracula's spell, the Kid reads up on vampire lore. Finally, at the end, tracking Plowman and Dracula to a mine on her property where they are sequestered, the Kid finishes off the vampire. There are those, I suspect, who might say that a film such as this combines popular folklore from Europe with that of the United States. It may, but the combination proves preposterous and, ultimately, silly, and as a film the picture is a disappointment.

In CHISUM (Warner, 1970) directed by Andrew McLaglen, John Wayne was cast as John Chisum, Geoffrey Deuel as the Kid, and Glenn Corbett as Pat Garrett. At the outset Wayne and Ben Johnson as Wayne's close friend and employee, Mr. Pepper, talk about the West, their beginnings, and how the times are changing. "Well," says Chisum, surveying his land and cattle empire, "things generally change for the better." Forrest Tucker, cast as Murphy, is intent on taking over the town and Sheriff Brady, played by Bruce Cabot, is his right hand. The Indians on a nearby reservation are not Mescaleros, but Comanches. Wayne gets in his line from HONDO (Warner, 1953) about Indians—"It was a good way of life"—with the emphasis on the perfect tense. Chisum is paternalistic toward Indians as he is toward everybody. The Kid is supposed to have killed twelve men, his first at twelve. He works for the mild-mannered Tunstall who preaches the Bible to him and in one scene the Kid—significantly, very significantly—balances the Bible in one hand, his gun in the other. Both the Kid and Garrett fall in love with Chisum's niece. When Tunstall is killed, Chisum is deputized to bring back the killers and arrests Morton and Baker. On the way back to Lincoln, the Kid rides up and shoots them in cold blood. Next, also in cold blood, he guns down Sheriff Brady in the street. Garrett, at this point, presses his suit with Chisum's niece, instructing her that just as there is a difference between infatuation and love, so there is a difference between Chisum and the Kid: the Kid wants revenge, Chisum wants justice.

CHISUM, as a film, affirms that political structures are frequently inadequate, if not downright crooked, and in some cases gun law is the only way to invoke justice. However, it must be done in Chisum's way, and not the Kid's. When the Kid and his gang are cornered in McSween's store, Chisum and his men ride to town for a showdown. Stampeding a herd of cattle through a barricade, Chisum's wranglers rout Murphy's men, Chisum crashing through a window atop his horse in the best Tom Mix fashion, tackling Murphy, and fighting with him to the death. The Kid rides off alone at the end and Chisum has Garrett appointed sheriff. When Ben Johnson comments to Chisum's niece that there is no law west of Dodge and no God west of the Pecos, the line rings all the way back to a wry statement made by Gary Cooper as "Wild Bill" Hickok in THE PLAINSMAN (Paramount, 1936). Chisum, however, has a different answer than Hickok did: "Wherever there are people who come together, the law is not far behind and they'll find, if they look around, that God has already been there."

When DIRTY LITTLE BILLY (Columbia, 1972) directed by Stan Dragoti was first released, critics hailed it as the truth at last. In this opus, Billy Bonney played by Michael Pollard arrives in Kansas from New York with his mother and stepfather and the family takes up residence on an old, dilapidated farm. Billy does not like working in the fields, so he runs away and meets up with the wild Goldie, played by Richard Evans, and Goldie's trouble-making girl friend, a whore named Berle played by Lee Purcell. Very little happens in this film, except that the Kid loses his virginity and learns how to use a gun.

At the same time that Peckinpah was in Durango, Mexico filming his version of the Kid's life and death, John Wayne was about a mile away filming CAHILL, U.S. MARSHAL (Warner, 1973) directed by Andrew McLaglen. The cast and crew of both films mixed freely during their off hours—except for Wayne and Peckinpah. Wayne had such a personal antipathy for Peckinpah that he refused so much as to meet him. Dub Taylor, a character actor in the Peckinpah film whose part was cut from the initial release version, confided to me the morning I arrived: "I'll tell you this. After Sam gets through nobody will ever make a pitchur about Billy the Kid again. This is it! They'll never touch Billy again." Rudolph Wurlitzer provided Peckinpah with the screenplay and, in another example of the blind instructing the blind in how to see, Paul Seydor in PECKINPAH: THE WESTERN FILMS informed the reader that "Wurlitzer chose to confine his original screenplay to the last three months of Billy's life because they offered him the freest area for invention and imagination: no one knows what Billy did then, only that he was told to clear out of the Territory or face execution."[5] Who, ostensibly, told this to the Kid? In the Peckinpah/Wurlitzer version, Garrett himself! For Seydor, "one of the subtlest yet most impressive of Peckinpah's and Wurlitzer's achievements [was] the depiction of the casualness of frontier violence and of its ready acceptance by its perpetrators, victims, and spectators alike as a fact of their lives."[6] What incredible nonsense in terms of the historical reality, but I suppose this is more or less the covert intention of the film.

Peckinpah had been working out of an office on the Samuel Goldwyn lot and living in a house trailer on Malibu beach, supervising the editing of THE GET-AWAY (National General, 1972), when the deal was set for him to direct PAT GARRETT AND BILLY THE KID. He had watched Penn's THE LEFT-HANDED GUN three or four times and felt that now his opportunity had come to treat the Kid as the character in Penn's film and Neider's novel: a neurotic and a romantic victim. Once on location in Durango, using Chupaderos, a former Pancho Villa fort refurbished to look as Fort Sumner, New Mexico, Peckinpah was determined to tell the story of the clash between the Kid and Garrett as if it were a Bible story, where everyone knew how the story ended and the emphasis, therefore, could be placed on why it had to end that way. With Kris Kristofferson cast as the Kid and James Coburn as Garrett, Peckinpah wanted their story structured in tableaux, as stations of the cross in a medieval passion play, each scene bringing the Kid nearer his death and Garrett nearer his own self-crucifixion. Peckinpah originally wanted the film to open in 1908 with Garrett as an old man being shot down at the instigation of the same forces that had once hired him to murder the Kid and the Kid's gang, presumably in a dispute over the land which Chisum, played by Barry Sullivan, had given Garrett after he successfully dispatched the Kid. As the bullets tear into Garrett's body, there is a flashback to 1881, showing a chicken's head being shot off at Fort Sumner where the Kid and his gang are engaged in some target practice.

There is no celebration of capitalism in PAT GARRETT AND BILLY THE KID as there is in CHISUM, no new frontier as in so many Westerns, only a vast wasteland, a desert punctuated by silvery, surrealistic lakes and streams. Much of the film is photographed in shadow, at dusk, in hazy light, or after nightfall. There is a hopelessness in the terrain, an agonized loneliness in the principals, a frustrated quest for identity, a bitter confrontation with futility, and, moving through it all, desperately erupting, a sustaining violence, a lewd intimacy with death. Garrett comes to Fort Sumner to tell the Kid that Chisum and the others in the Santa Fe Ring, who had once hired the Kid to be sheriff of Lincoln County, have now hired Garrett. The Kid and Garrett have ridden together for years. Now Garrett wants the Kid out of the Territory.

"Why don't you kill him?" one of the Kid's henchmen asks Billy as Garrett leaves.

"Why?" the Kid returns, gulping whiskey. "He's my friend."

Cut to the Kid and two cronies—supposedly Bowdre, played by Charles Martin, and Tom O'Folliard, played by Rudolph Wurlitzer—in a shack at dawn surrounded by Garrett and a flock of deputies. The two cronies are shot to pieces, but the Kid surrenders, holding out his empty arms sacrificially. The Kid is sentenced to hang. He plays poker in a room above the jail with Garrett and Matt Clark, cast as J. W. Bell, while a scaffold is being erected outside. R. G. Armstrong is on hand to play Bob Olinger as a religious fanatic who, righteously holding a shotgun to the Kid's heart, demands, "Repent, you sonofabitch." Garrett leaves to collect some taxes,

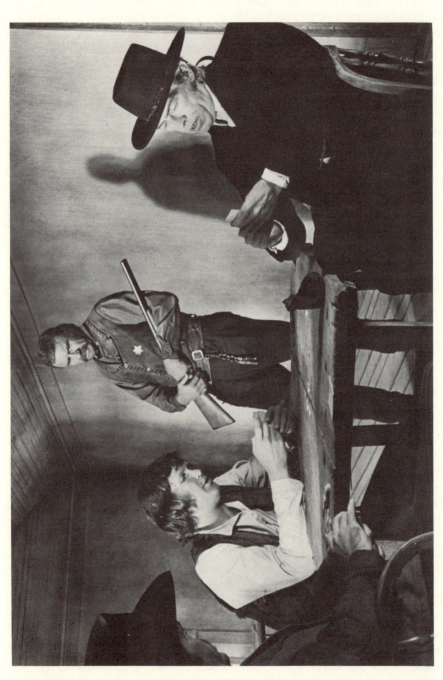

From left to right: Matt Clark as J. W. Bell, Kris Kristofferson as Billy the Kid, R. G. Armstrong as Bob Olinger, and James Coburn as Pat Garrett in PAT GARRETT AND BILLY THE KID (M-G-M, 1973). *Photo courtesy of M-G-M/Pathé.*

but, before he goes, he presumably places a gun in the outhouse so that the Kid can make an escape. Billy shoots Bell and Olinger —"How does Jesus look to you now, Bob?"—and rides off.

When Garrett gets back to Lincoln, he hires Jack Elam as a deputy to help him hunt for the Kid. Before he takes to the trail, Garrett stops briefly to see his Mexican wife. A parallel scene shows the Kid following after Marie, played by Rita Coolidge, a loose woman, if not an outright whore, at Fort Sumner, while a group of children heckle him. Stopping at the military governor's mansion, Garrett refuses an additional reward offered for the Kid's capture by two capitalist investors. Jason Robards, Jr., cast as Governor Wallace, is sympathetic with Garrett's position. The Kid, in the meantime, attempts to collect the twenty head of cattle Chisum supposedly owes him from when the Kid was sheriff. This move outrages Chisum and he has John Poe played by John Beck, who will eventually lure Garrett to his own death by ambush, assigned to ride with Garrett to insure that Garrett will capture the Kid. "This country's gettin' old," Garrett tells Poe, "an' I aim to get old with it. The Kid don't want it that way, an' maybe he's a better man for it."

This is Garrett's refrain throughout the picture. He says the same thing to Slim Pickens, cast as a deputy sheriff, when he wants to enlist Pickens to join him in killing some of the Kid's gang. Pickens is fatally shot in the attempt. When he is first seen, Pickens is building a boat—rather a clumsy symbol—behind the jail and intends to leave the Territory in it.

Garrett kills more of the Kid's gang. The Kid decides to go to Old Mexico to hide but, when Chisum's men kill his friend Paco played by Mexican film director Emilio Fernández and rape Paco's wife, the Kid decides to return to Fort Sumner to organize a showdown with Chisum. Garrett and Poe meet Chisum at Chisum's ranch and Chisum makes Garrett the offer of property which the viewer already knows will lead to Garrett's death at Poe's hands. Garrett accepts the offer and, after spending some time with the Kid's whore and three other hookers, Garrett, Poe, and Kip McKinney (played by Richard Jaeckel who was cast as Jesse Evans in CHISUM) ride out toward Fort Sumner. The Kid knows Garrett is coming, but he relaxes his vigilance to make love with Marie. On his way to Pete Maxwell's shack where the Kid and Marie are together in bed, Garrett happens upon Will, the coffin maker, played by Sam Peckinpah. Will is putting the finishing touches on a coffin and claims that when he is finished with it he will put his belongings in it and leave the Territory for good. "Finally figured it out, eh?" Will asks Garrett, turning down a drink. "Well, go get him. You don't even trust yourself any more, do you Garrett?"

Garrett shoots the Kid, who is barechested but armed with a gun he does not fire, pistol-whips Poe when he would cut off the Kid's trigger finger, and the next morning, in an ironic reference to the conclusion of SHANE (Paramount, 1953) where young Brandon DeWilde pursues Alan Ladd as Shane, calling for him to come back, Garrett rides off alone, a child following after him, throwing stones. Cut to Garrett riding in his buggy in 1908, an old man met on the trail by John Poe, and again the viewer is taken through Garrett's assassination. It was all a flashback in Garrett's last fleeting moments alive.[7]

Kris Kristofferson was drinking two quarts of whiskey a day while playing the Kid. Peckinpah, on location, was "pissed off" because gossip columnist Rona Barrett had said Sam had a drinking problem. Through every scene of PAT GARRETT AND BILLY THE KID, the drinking had been constant and intense, with at least Kristofferson preferring the real thing. In this way the film itself became a descent into alcoholic despair, in which life could be reduced to a state of permanent depression punctuated by sudden violence. James Aubrey, then head of M-G-M, had the film edited extensively before release, claiming that viewers could not follow the director's cut. The editing did not make the screen story any more accurate.

Dub Taylor proved a poor prognosticator. The decade had not ended before the Kid—or, at least, a search for him—was proposed as a theme for a weekly television series. GO WEST, YOUNG GIRL (1978) directed by Alan J. Levi and written and produced by George Yanok was a pilot for the proposed series made as a movie for television. Karen Valentine starred as Gilda. The story opens in Arizona Territory in 1886 and Gilda, who is the widow of a cavalry officer, is searching for the Kid whom she believes to be still alive. It is said that the Kid had already killed five men by the time he was seventeen. Gilda is joined in her quest by a young female reporter from the East played by Sandra Will. Gilda is good with a six-gun and the reporter is a card sharp. The Kid presumably is in jail at Yuma prison and the two help a gang break him out. The Kid, who is played by Richard Jaeckel, escapes and both the women and the gang go after him. The women are captured by Apaches. The Kid is supposed to meet the Indians at the border with rifles for them. The women escape and make off with a stagecoach. When they run into the Kid, Gilda announces that she is his sister—only to realize in her chagrin that Jacckel is not really the Kid. He has only been impersonating him! With that, they continue their search for the real Billy the Kid.

Between YOUNG GUNS (20th-Fox, 1988) and YOUNG GUNS II (20th-Fox, 1990), TNT produced and aired a television movie premiered on 10 May 1989 titled GORE VIDAL'S BILLY THE KID. Vidal himself introduced the film and, obviously, he had steeped himself in Burns's "saga." In his opening remarks Vidal asserted that in terms of literary prototypes Pat Garrett was Tom Sawyer to the Kid's Huckleberry Finn. Val Kilmer was cast as the Kid, Duncan Regehr as Garrett, Wilford Brimley (rather incredibly) as Governor Wallace, and Julie Carmen played Celsa Gutiérrez. Dolan, according to Vidal's plot, wants to lay claim to all of Tunstall's holdings. He has Sheriff Brady and Billy Morton alone when they gun down Tunstall who is unarmed and on his way to Santa Fe to have a word with the governor. Billy witnesses this murder and so Brady pursues him. The Kid and Tom O'Folliard ambush Brady and Morton on an open road. Outraged at this, Dolan posts a $500 reward for the capture of the Kid. On the way to Fort Sumner, Billy tells Tom that he expects they will all receive amnesty from the governor.

At Fort Sumner, Garrett is getting married. He refers jokingly to the Kid as Little Casino and himself as Big Casino. Celsa is Garrett's sister-in-law and in love with the Kid. While Garrett and the Kid share a drink, Garrett tells Billy he wants to settle down. "The country is changing, Little Casino," he says. Garrett owns a saloon and hires the Kid to deal monte for the house. Pete Maxwell informs the Kid, while in a card game, that the new governor wants to see him. All he has to do is testify against those who killed Tunstall. The fact that Brady and Morton are already dead and a trial would be senseless is overlooked. Joe Grant enters the saloon at this point and bets the Kid that he will kill a man that night before the Kid does. Garrett watches as the Kid turns back the chambers in Grant's gun and then plugs him. Pat declares it to have been a fair fight and he volunteers to ride to see the governor with the Kid. Bob Olinger collects their guns before the Kid enters the governor's office alone. Wallace wants the Kid to testify against Dolan so that he can bring the Santa Fe Ring to justice. The Kid doesn't think the Territory needs to become more civilized. The governor claims the Kid came from New York and promises to exonerate him of all charges once he gives evidence against Dolan. The Grand Jury wants to try the Kid after he presents his testimony. The Kid and the governor have a falling out after which Garrett goes to the governor and asks that he be appointed sheriff of Lincoln County now that Wallace has forced Sheriff Peppin to resign.

The Kid goes briefly to Old Mexico and then returns, intent on rustling Chisum's cattle. Billy runs into Garrett when he is having his picture taken and sees Pat's badge. Garrett tells the Kid to leave the Territory. Billy's response is to set up a cattle-rustling syndicate on a large scale. The governor chides Garrett and his deputy Poe for allowing these outrages. Garrett supposedly has already been sheriff for a year. Garrett rides into Fort Sumner with a posse to ambush the Kid. O'Folliard is killed during the ambush. Next Garrett and the posse surround the Kid and four others at Stinking Springs. Bowdre is plugged at night through a window and gets a couple of more bullets in him when he ventures outside. Billy is sentenced to hang and jailed in Lincoln. He finds a revolver in the outhouse and pulls it on Bell, telling the deputy to unlock his handcuffs. No sooner does Bell do this than he jumps the Kid and is shot. The Kid guns Olinger from the steps of the jail.

Returning to Fort Sumner, the Kid takes Celsa for a ride. She confides it was her father who put the revolver in the outhouse. Billy sits in a saloon, drinking and playing solitaire. Garrett and Poe ride in. Beaver Smith tells Garrett that the Kid is at Celsa's house. They go over to see Celsa but she tells them nothing. After they leave, the Kid climbs in a window. He comes across a dime novel narrating how he saved a gold mine for a widow. Celsa is angry and tells the Kid that he is waiting for Pat Garrett, not for her. Garrett goes to Maxwell's bedroom to catch some sleep in a chair. The Kid comes over to cut himself a steak with only a butcher knife in his hand. Garrett plugs him and Billy falls from the second-story porch.

YOUNG GUNS was directed by Christopher Cain and written by John Fusco. Harking back to the screenplay for THE TRUE STORY OF JESSE JAMES (20th-Fox, 1957) which depicted the James gang as made up of juvenile delinquents led by then teenage idol Robert Wagner, YOUNG GUNS cast the Kid and his gang with members of what was known as Hollywood's "brat pack," young actors popular at the box office. Emilio Estevez was cast as the Kid, Kiefer Sutherland as

Terence Stamp as John H. Tunstall smiles as Billy the Kid played by Emilio Estevez demonstrates his "triggernometry." *Photo courtesy of Twentieth Century-Fox Film Corporation.*

From left to right: Lou Diamond Phillips as Chávez y Chávez, Kiefer Sutherland as Doc Scurlock, Emilio Estevez as William H. Bonney, Casey Siemaszko as Charley Bowdre, Charlie Sheen as Dick Brewer, and Dermot Mulroney as "Dirty Steve" in YOUNG GUNS (20th-Fox, 1988). *Photo courtesy of Twentieth Century-Fox Film Corporation.*

Doc Scurlock, Lou Diamond Phillips as Chávez y Chávez, Charlie Sheen as Dick Brewer, Dermot Mulroney as "Dirty Steve" Stephens, and Casey Siemaszko as Charley Bowdre. Terence Stamp plays Tunstall. Jack Palance was cast as L. G. Murphy, Terry O'Quinn as Alex McSween, and Sharon Thomas as his wife Susan. In his deposition when Morgan Creek Productions was suing M-G-M/Pathé for copyright infringement on the basis of the latter's television series titled "The Young Riders," Fusco cited the first edition of this book as one of his sources for his screenplay. If it was so used, it certainly was not the chapter devoted to the Kid's biography.

In the film, Tunstall has a group of boys who are armed and dangerous out at his ranch. He and Doc save Billy in Lincoln one day as he is being pursued for a reason that is not clear. Tunstall has white hair and is middle-aged. He refers to Billy and the others as "flotsam and jetsam" and Dirty Steve seconds him, saying they're all "runaway, scud-bottom vagrants." Tunstall teaches the boys table manners and after dinner at night has them read aloud. Billy proves himself proficient at reading. Murphy, his sheriff, and men in his employ pay a visit to Tunstall's ranch. Murphy claims that Tunstall has been stealing his supplies and remarks slyly that he early on pegged Tunstall as a man who prefers "educating" young boys. When Tunstall protests, Murphy counters that he has the Santa Fe Ring behind him. "It's a family thing, John." J. McCloskey, having left Murphy, joins Tunstall's crew. They all head in to Lincoln for a New Year's Eve celebration. Billy, who has a crazy laugh whenever he does something outrageous, proves to be a good dancer. McSween informs Tunstall that Murphy now has the governor in his back pocket through a campaign contribution. Doc finds himself attracted to Murphy's young China girl, a concubine he was given by a Chinese laundry when a shirt of his was soiled.

On the way back to the ranch the next day, the young men chase a flock of turkeys while Murphy's gang rides up behind Tunstall and literally blasts him out of the buckboard he is driving. Brewer reads the service at Tunstall's funeral in Lincoln. McSween has Justice of the Peace Wilson deputize the young Regulators to bring in Tunstall's murderers. They track one man to a roadhouse. They have a warrant and it is given to the Kid to serve. Billy waits instead in the outhouse, plugs the man while he is urinating, and sticks the warrant in the mouth of the corpse. A newspaper report claims that the Kid has shot six men and is the captain of an organized gang. Doc, off on his own, encounters the China girl in the street and tells her that Murphy cannot own the Regulators the way he can some China girl, for the price of a shirt. However, Doc is with the group when they run down some Murphy men and take them prisoners. Billy insists McCloskey is a Murphy spy, goes berserk and plugs him, whereupon the Murphy men are shot down by the Regulators. Doc seems troubled by the bloodshed. A newspaper account attributes all the killings to just Billy and identifies a photograph of Brewer as the Kid.

Chávez now introduces the Regulators to peyote in which all partake but Brewer and they become crazy on the drug. After vomiting, Bowdre exclaims: "This is great!" Later, while Brewer is praying over the meal they are about to have at a wayside cafe, Buckshot Roberts played by Brian Keith rides up. When Roberts is confronted, he wounds Chávez and Doc and then hides in an outhouse. The Regulators shell it mercilessly but Roberts is still able to blast Brewer as he walks toward the door after the shelling. Billy now becomes the leader of the gang and they ride off to San Patricio so they can send a letter to Brewer's mother in Vermont. Billy wants them to settle with Sheriff Brady. Chávez tells how at Red Sand Creek 207 of his people were butchered in the snow with their stomachs empty. Murphy was responsible. Chávez says he is the last of his people. If he dies, the sacred hoop is broken (a Sioux reference although Chávez alleges he is a Navajo); but, no matter, since the Kid responds that if you have three or four good pals that is your tribe. They're Chávez' family now. "You walk away from us, you break our sacred hoop."

Doc slips again into town to see the China girl while the gang reads some of his poetry aloud at their camp. Doc tells the China girl he cannot live without her and he wants her to come with him when he breaks with the Kid. Murphy enters at this moment and Doc escapes. Feeling he has no choice, Doc rejoins the gang and they set up an ambush in Lincoln where Billy alone guns Brady. Riding out, Bowdre is fearful they will all be hanged. He wants to have a prostitute before that happens. When Bowdre is with the prostitute, saying he only wants to be held and being told it all costs the same, the Kid downstairs is confronted by Texas Joe Grant. Billy borrows Grant's pistol, empties it, and then blows him away. He asks Doc how many that makes and Doc says Billy has killed twenty-five men. Billy who wants to stay is outvoted by the gang. They go to Old Mexico. Once there, Bowdre courts a Mexican girl and marries her. At the ceremony, Pat Garrett played by Patrick Wayne (John Wayne's son) rides in to warn Billy that Murphy is planning to ambush McSween at his home in Lincoln. Pat assures Billy he is his friend. The gang heads back to Lincoln and busts into McSween's house only to learn that it is a trap. The Murphy men and Kinney and his gang blast away outside. McSween refuses to shoot back because, he says, it will invalidate his insurance policy. The next morning when the cavalry rides in Billy laughs gleefully, "I love these odds!" The China girl breaks through the lines and finds refuge in the house. When the house is set on fire, Bowdre overcomes his fear and starts firing crazily. Susan McSween leaves and physically attacks Colonel Dudley played by Gary Kanin. The China girl (she has no other character name) opts to stay with Doc. Billy is rolled off the second story of the McSween home in a trunk and, when it hits ground, comes out firing both guns. Chávez who has slipped away to get the horses is shot. Bowdre is shot. Doc is wounded but pulls the China girl onto a horse behind him. Bowdre finishes Kinney with his last bullet before he dies. McSween is ecstatic, but it is too early for celebration. The soldiers turn a Gatling gun on him and perforate his body with bullets. Billy rides out of town only to circle around so he can get a clear shot at Murphy. He drills the man through the forehead. Murphy dies in slow motion. "Now, it's over," Billy says. The narrative voice-over at the end claims Chávez lived and moved to California. Doc went east with the China girl, her mother, and her fourteen brothers and sisters. Mrs. McSween went on to see her husband's and Tunstall's dream realized by becoming the most prominent cattle woman of all time. Axtell is said to have resigned and with Murphy's death the Santa Fe Ring simply collapsed. On Billy's and Bowdre's headstone there would be one word: "Pals."

In preparing the case for the defense in the lawsuit, I analyzed YOUNG GUNS in terms of the seven basic modes of plot structure in Westerns and found it to be a combination of "The Outlaw Story" and "The Justice/Revenge Story." In terms of its inherent narrative structure, YOUNG GUNS loosely follows the historical events of the Lincoln County War from a time shortly before Tunstall's murder until the conclusion of the five-day siege in Lincoln. YOUNG GUNS is not a documentary. It is fiction. Therefore, those basic events have been deliberately distorted in order to advance the ideology invested in the film. To elucidate that ideology, it is best dissected in terms of the Purpose, Passion, and Perception embodied in the film's storyline. The Purpose of YOUNG GUNS is to explore the whirlwind of violence that can be unleashed where justice and law enforcement have been corrupted by power and money. The Passion of YOUNG GUNS is to show how step by violent step those seeking to correct injustice by revenge, although diminished in number and led by an unbalanced but charismatic leader, ultimately do triumph at the end. The Perception in YOUNG GUNS is embodied in the narrative overlay at the end: with the death of Major Murphy, the crooked machine of the Santa Fe Ring collapsed. In history, of course, this did not happen. The Ring flourished, its leader becoming the first U.S. senator from New Mexico after statehood in 1912. The reason history is distorted is that it *must be* in order to make the point clear in the Perception: no matter how much power and money are behind it, injustice will lose in the end. Whereas the theme intrinsic in "The Young Riders" television series (produced for the ABC network 1989–1991) is that of an extended, or surrogate, family (leaving to one side the absurdity of six or seven Pony Express riders being housed at a single station), the operative group dynamic in YOUNG GUNS is that of gang psychology. I suspect that the gangsterism in YOUNG GUNS, as opposed to the "family values" in "The Young Riders," is the ultimate reason the motion picture was so successful as to invite a sequel whereas the television series was canceled in the midst of its third season.

YOUNG GUNS II, notwithstanding the narrative voice-over at the conclusion of the previous film, finds Bonney, Scurlock, and Chávez together again, joined by Arkansas Dave Rudabaugh played by Christian Slater, Hendry French played by Alan Ruck, and Tom O'Folliard played by Balthazar Getty. John Fusco again did the screenplay, this time directed by Geoff Murphy. James Coburn provided a cameo appearance in the role of John Chisum and this time William Petersen played Pat Garrett. Framing the events is Estevez' appearance in the desert as an old man known as Brushy Bill Roberts. He has made himself known to a reporter because he wants to be pardoned for twenty-one murders before he dies. He tells of how, after the Lincoln County War, he took up with Dave Rudabaugh and Pat Garrett, killing and running wild. [One thing that GO WEST, YOUNG WOMAN, GORE VIDAL'S BILLY THE KID, YOUNG GUNS, and YOUNG GUNS II all have in common besides their subject matter is their locations: they were all filmed at the Old Tucson Western town set outside Tucson, Arizona.] General Lew Wallace, played by Scott Wilson, has ordered all those involved in the Lincoln County War to be rounded up. Doc Scurlock (without the China girl) is teaching school in New York when he is dragged off to Lincoln! Once there, he is thrown into a pit with Chávez and the others. The Murphy men are in the same pit. Garrett informs the Kid that the governor wants to make a treaty with him. The same structure as YOUNG GUNS is used here as well: a violent episode at least every ten minutes, but with even more bodies in the sequel than in the original. The Kid proposes a deal: his testimony in exchange for a full pardon. District Attorney Rynerson, played by R. D. Call, and the other Irish politicians have too much power to allow the governor to make good on his promise to the Kid. Billy escapes jail and comes back with Dave to break out Chávez and Doc. There is a shoot-out with a lynch mob. Scurlock wants out of the gang. Garrett feels the same way, but for a different

From left to right: Balthazar Getty as Tom O'Folliard, Alan Ruck as Hendry William French, Emilio Estevez as William H. Bonney, Kiefer Sutherland as Doc Scurlock, Lou Diamond Phillips as Chávez y Chávez, and Christian Slater as "Arkansas" Dave Rudabaugh in YOUNG GUNS II (20th-Fox, 1990). *Photo courtesy of Twentieth Century-Fox Film Corporation.*

reason: he wants to buy Beaver Smith's saloon. Billy goes to see Chisum and demands $500. Coburn as Chisum tells the Kid—as when he was playing Garrett he told two capitalist investors—to take his demand, shove it up his ass, and set fire to it. Chisum wants the Kid dead so he conspires with Wallace for Garrett to be hired to do the job. Garrett is offered a badge and $1,000 to "exterminate" Billy. Pat hires Ash Upson played by Jack Kehoe to ride with him on the hunt for the Kid and write a book about it. The killing of Carlyle is staged in a whorehouse in White Oaks. They dress Carlyle up to look as Chávez and he is blitzed when he is shoved outside in this getup. Garrett sets the whorehouse on fire and the madam in protest to this wanton action rides out of town stark naked. At Stinking Springs, Doc is slaughtered, Chávez and Dave make a getaway, and the Kid alone is captured. Jane Greathouse, the brothel madam from White Oaks played by Jenny Wright, smuggles the gun into the outhouse. The Kid escapes and Garrett fakes his death so Billy can find a new life. Brushy Bill Roberts doesn't get his pardon but he assures those who will listen that Billy did not die that fateful night at Fort Sumner. He does not enlighten us, however, whose body was buried in the Kid's grave. Since the ideology of this film is essentially the same as that in the original, it would not support the Perception if the forces of money and power overcame the legendary Billy as, in a sense, they killed the historical Billy, so he sustains, if not a resurrection, a continuance of sorts.

FILMOGRAPHY AND BIBLIOGRAPHY

Filmography

BILLY THE KID (M-G-M, 1930) [90 minutes] directed by King Vidor. Original Story: Walter Noble Burns. Continuity: Wanda Tuchock. Dialogue: Laurence Stallings. Additional Dialogue: Charles MacArthur. Cast: John Mack Brown, Wallace Beery, Kay Johnson, Karl Dane, Wyndham Standing, Russell Simpson, Blanche Frederici, Roscoe Ates, Warner Richmond, James Marcus, Nelson McDowell, Jack Carlyle, John Beck, Marguerita Padula, Aggie Herring, Soledad Jiminez, Don Coleman, Chris-Pin Martin, Lucille Powers, Hank Bell.

BILLY THE KID RETURNS (Republic, 1938) [58 minutes] directed by Joseph Kane. Screenplay: Jack Natteford. Cast: Roy Rogers, Smiley Burnette, Mary Hart (Lynne Roberts), Fred Kohler, Sr., Morgan Wallace, Wade Boteler, Edwin Stanley, Horace Murphy, Joseph Crehan, Robert Emmett Keane, Al Taylor, George Letz (later Montgomery), Chris-Pin Martin, Jim Corey, Lloyd Ingraham, Bob McKenzie, Oscar Gahan, Jack Kirk, Art Dillard, Fred Burns, Betty Roadman, Rudy Sooter, Betty Jane Haney, Patsy Lee Parsons, Ray Nichols, Ralph Dunn, "Trigger."

BILLY THE KID OUTLAWED (PRC, 1940) [52 minutes] directed by Peter Stewart (Sam Newfield). Screenplay: Oliver Drake. Cast: Bob Steele, Al St. John, Louise Currie, Carleton Young, John Merton, Joe McGuinn, Ted Adams, Walter McGrail, Hal Price, Kenne Duncan, Reed Howes, George Chesebro, Steve Clark, Budd Buster.

BILLY THE KID IN TEXAS (PRC, 1940) [52 minutes] directed by Peter Stewart (Sam Newfield). Screenplay: Joseph O'Donnell. Cast: Bob Steele, Al St. John, Terry Walker, Carleton Young, Charles King, John Merton, Frank LaRue, Slim Whitaker, Curley Dresden, Tex Palmer, Chick Hannon, Merrill McCormack, Denver Dixon, Bob Woodward, Sherry Tansey, Herman Hack, Pasquel Perry.

BILLY THE KID'S GUN JUSTICE (PRC, 1940) [57 minutes] directed by Peter Stewart (Sam Newfield). Screenplay: Oliver Drake. Cast: Bob Steele, Al St. John, Louise Currie, Carleton Young, Charles King, Rex Lease, Ted Adams, Kenne Duncan, Forrest Taylor, Al Ferguson, Karl Hackett, Edward Piel, Sr., Julian Rivero, Blanca Vischer.

BILLY THE KID'S RANGE WAR (PRC, 1941) [57 minutes] directed by Peter Stewart (Sam Newfield). Screenplay: William Lively. Cast: Bob Steele, Al St. John, Joan Barclay, Carleton Young, Rex Lease, Buddy Roosevelt, Milt Kibbee, Karl Hackett, Ted Adams, Julian Rivero, John Ince, Alden Chase, Howard Masters, Ralph Peters, Charles King, George Chesebro, Steve Clark, Tex Palmer.

BILLY THE KID'S FIGHTING PALS (PRC, 1941) [62 minutes] directed by Sherman Scott (Sam Newfield). Screenplay: George Plympton. Cast: Bob Steele, Al St. John, Phyllis Adair, Carleton Young, Charles King, Curley Dresden, Edward Piel, Sr., Hal Price, George Chesebro, Forrest Taylor, Budd Buster, Julian Rivero, Ray Henderson, Wally West, Art Dillard.

BILLY THE KID (M-G-M, 1941) [95 minutes/color] directed by David Miller. Original story: Walter Noble Burns. Screenplay: Gene Fowler. Cast: Robert Taylor, Brian Donlevy, Ian Hunter, Mary Howard, Gene Lockhart, Lon Chaney, Jr., Henry O'Neill, Guinn Williams, Cy Kendall, Ted Adams, Frank Conlan, Frank Puglia, Mitchell Lewis, Dick Curtis, Grant Withers, Joe Yule, Earl Gunn, Eddie Dunn, Carl Pitti, Kermit Maynard, Ethel Griffes, Chill Wills, Olive Blakeney.

BILLY THE KID IN SANTA FE (PRC, 1941) [66 minutes] directed by Sherman Scott (Sam Newfield). Screenplay: Joseph O'Donnell. Cast: Bob Steele, Al St. John, Rex Lease, Marin Sais, Dennis Moore, Karl Hackett, Steve Clark, Hal Price, Charles King, Frank Ellis, Dave O'Brien, Kenne Duncan, Curley Dresden.

BILLY THE KID WANTED (PRC, 1941) [64 minutes] directed by Sherman Scott (Sam Newfield). Screenplay: Fred Myton. Cast: Buster Crabbe, Al St. John, Dave O'Brien, Glenn Strange, Choti Sherwood, Charles King, Slim Whitaker, Howard Masters, Joe Newfield, Budd Buster, Frank Ellis, Curley Dresden, Wally West.

BILLY THE KID'S ROUND-UP (PRC, 1941) [58 minutes] directed by Sherman Scott (Sam Newfield). Screenplay: Fred Myton. Cast: Buster Crabbe, Al St. John, Carleton Young, Joan Barclay, Glenn Strange, Charles King, Slim Whitaker, John Elliott, Dennis Moore, Kenne Duncan, Curley Dresden, Dick Cramer, Wally West, Tex Palmer, Tex Cooper, Horace B. Carpenter, Jim Mason.

BILLY THE KID TRAPPED (PRC, 1942) [59 minutes] directed by Sherman Scott (Sam Newfield). Screenplay: Oliver Drake. Cast: Buster Crabbe, Al St. John, Bud McTaggart, Anne Jeffreys, Glenn Strange, Walter McGrail, Ted Adams, Jack Ingram, Milt Kibbee, Eddie Phillips, Budd Buster, Jack Kinney, Jimmy Aubrey, Wally West, Bert Dillard, Kenne Duncan, George Chesebro, Carl Mathews, Dick

Cramer, Ray Henderson, Curley Dresden, Augie Gomez, Horace B. Carpenter, Herman Hack, James Mason, Hank Bell, Oscar Gahan.

BILLY THE KID'S SMOKING GUNS (PRC, 1942) [58 minutes] directed by Sherman Scott (Sam Newfield). Screenplay: George Milton (George Sayre/Milton Raison). Cast: Buster Crabbe, Al St. John, Dave O'Brien, Joan Barclay, John Merton, Milt Kibbee, Ted Adams, Karl Hackett, Frank Ellis, Slim Whitaker, Budd Buster, Joe Newfield, Bert Dillard.

BILLY THE KID IN LAW AND ORDER (PRC, 1942) [56 minutes] directed by Sherman Scott (Sam Newfield). Screenplay: Sam Robins. Cast: Buster Crabbe, Al St. John, Tex (Dave) O'Brien, Sarah Padden, Wanda McKay, Charles King, Hal Price, John Merton, Kenne Duncan, Ted Adams, Budd Buster, Kermit Maynard.

SHERIFF OF SAGE VALLEY (PRC, 1942) [60 minutes] directed by Sherman Scott (Sam Newfield). Screenplay: Milton Raison and George W. Sayre. Cast: Buster Crabbe, Al St. John, Tex (Dave) O'Brien, Maxine Leslie, Charles King, John Merton, Kermit Maynard, Hal Price, Curley Dresden, Jack Kirk, Lynton Brent.

WEST OF TOMBSTONE (Columbia, 1942) [59 minutes] directed by Howard Bretherton. Screenplay: Maurice Geraghty. Cast: Charles Starrett, Russell Hayden, Cliff "Ukulele Ike" Edwards, Marcella Martin, Gordon DeMain, Clancy Cooper, Jack Kirk, Budd Buster, Tom London, Francis Walker, Ray Jones, Eddie Laughton, Lloyd Bridges, Ernie Adams, George Morrell.

THE MYSTERIOUS RIDER (PRC, 1942) [56 minutes] directed by Sherman Scott (Sam Newfield). Screenplay: Steve Braxton (Sam Robins). Cast: Buster Crabbe, Al St. John, Caroline Burke, John Merton, Kermit Maynard, Jack Ingram, Slim Whitaker, Ted Adams, Guy Wilkerson, Edwin Brien, Frank Ellis.

THE KID RIDES AGAIN (PRC, 1943) [60 minutes] directed by Sherman Scott (Sam Newfield). Screenplay: Fred Myton. Cast: Buster Crabbe, Al St. John, Iris Meredith, Glenn Strange, Charles King, I. Stanford Jolley, Edward Piel, Sr., Ted Adams, Karl Hackett, Kenne Duncan, Curley Dresden, Snub Pollard, John Merton, Slim Whitaker.

THE OUTLAW (RKO, 1943) directed by Howard Hughes. [Note: Howard Hawks was originally set to direct, but withdrew shortly after production began. Twentieth Century-Fox was slated to distribute, and even issued promotional materials on the film, but Hughes had a falling out with them. Hughes held the world premiere of the film at the Geary Theatre in San Francisco in February, 1943 and then withdrew it from distribution. United Artists released it henceforth, but was soon replaced by RKO. The original theatrical release ran 126 minutes; after withdrawal and reissue the running time was shortened to 117 minutes.] Screenplay: Jules Furthman. Cast: Jack Beutel, Jane Russell, Thomas Mitchell, Walter Huston, Mimi Aguglia, Joe Sawyer, Gene Rizzi, Frank Darien, Pat West, Carl Stockdale, Nena Quartaro, Dickie Jones, Frank Ward, Bobby Callahan, Ethan Laidlaw, Ed Brady, William Steele, Wally Reid, Jr., Edward Piel, Sr., Lee "Lasses" White, Ted Mapes, William Newell, Cecil Kellogg, Lee Shumway, Emory Parnell, Martin Garralaga, Julian Rivero, Arthur Loft, Dick Elliott, John Sheehan.

FUGITIVE OF THE PLAINS (PRC, 1943) [57 minutes] directed by Sam Newfield. Screenplay: George Sayre. Cast: Buster Crabbe, Al St. John, Maxine Leslie, Kermit Maynard, Jack Ingram, Karl Hackett, Hal Price, Budd Buster, Artie Ortego, Carl Sepulveda.

WESTERN CYCLONE (PRC, 1943) [56 minutes] directed by Sam Newfield. Screenplay: Patricia Harper. Cast: Buster Crabbe, Al St. John, Marjorie Manners, Karl Hackett, Milt Kibbee, Kermit Maynard, Glenn Strange, Charles King, Hal Price, Frank Ellis, Frank McCarroll, Artie Ortego, Herman Hack, Al Haskell.

THE RENEGADE (PRC, 1943) [58 minutes] directed by Sam Newfield. Screenplay: George Milton (George Sayre/Milton Raison). Cast: Buster Crabbe, Al St. John, Lois Ransom, Karl Hackett, Ray Bennett, Frank Hagney, Jack Rockwell, Tom London, George Chesebro, Jimmy Aubrey, Carl Sepulveda, Dan White, Wally West.

CATTLE STAMPEDE (PRC, 1943) [60 minutes] directed by Sam Newfield. Screenplay: Joseph O'Donnell. Cast: Buster Crabbe, Al St. John, Frances Gladwin, Charles King, Ed Cassidy, Hansel Werner, Ray Bennett, Frank Ellis, Steve Clark, Roy Brent, John Elliott, Budd Buster, Hank Bell, Tex Cooper, Ted Adams, Frank McCarroll, Ray Jones, Rose Plummer, George Morell.

BLAZING FRONTIER (PRC, 1943) [59 minutes] directed by Sam Newfield. Screenplay: Patricia Harper. Cast: Buster Crabbe, Al St. John, Marjorie Manners, Milt Kibbee, I. Stanford Jolley, Kermit Maynard, Frank Hagney, George Chesebro, Frank Ellis, Hank Bell.

FOUR FACES WEST (United Artists, 1948) [90 minutes] directed by Alfred E. Green. Original story: Eugene Manlove Rhodes. Adaptation: William and Milarde Brent. Screenplay: Graham Baker and Teddi Sherman. Cast: Joel McCrea, Frances Dee, Charles Bickford, Joseph Calleia, William Conrad, Martin Garralaga, Raymond Largay, John Parrish, Dan White, Davison Clark, Eve Novak, George McDonald, Sam Flint.

SON OF BILLY THE KID (Screen Guild, 1949) [65 minutes] directed by Ray Taylor. Screenplay: Ron Ormond and Ira Webb. Cast: Lash LaRue, Al St. John, Marion Colby, June Carr, George Baxter, Terry Frost, John James, House Peters, Jr., Clarke Stevens, Rob Duncan, Cliff Taylor, William Perrott, Felipe Turich, Rosa Turich, Jerry Riggio, Eileen Dixon, Fraser McMinn, I. Stanford Jolley, Bud Osborne.

THE KID FROM TEXAS (Universal, 1950) [78 minutes/color] directed by Kurt Neumann. Original story: Robert Hardy Andrews. Screenplay: Robert Hardy Andrews and Karl Lamb. Cast: Audie Murphy, Gale Storm, Albert Dekker, Shepperd Strudwick, Will Geer, William Talman, Martin Garralaga, Robert Barrat, Walter Sande, Frank Wilcox, Dennis Hoey, Ray Teal, Don Haggerty, Paul Ford, Zon Murray.

I SHOT BILLY THE KID (Lippert, 1950) [57 minutes] directed by William Berke. Screenplay: Ford Beebe and Orville Hampton. Cast: Don Barry, Robert Lowery, Wally Vernon, Tom Neal, Judith Allen, Wendy Lee, Barbara Woodell, Dick Lane, Sid Nelson, Archie Twitchell, John Merton, Claude Stroud, Henry Marud, Bill Kennedy.

THE LAW VS. BILLY THE KID (Columbia, 1954) [73 minutes/color] directed by William Castle. Screenplay: John T. Williams. Cast: Scott Brady, Betta St. John, James Griffith, Alan Hale, Jr., Paul Cavanaugh, William Phillips, Benny Rubin, Steve Darrell, George Berkeley, William Tannen, Martin Garralaga, Richard Cutting, John Cliff, Otis Garth, Frank Sully, William Fawcett, Robert Griffin.

THE BOY FROM OKLAHOMA (Warner, 1954) [88 minutes/color] directed by Michael Curtiz. Original story: Michael Fessier. Screenplay: Frank Davis and Winston Miller. Cast: Will Rogers, Jr., Nancy Olson, Lon Chaney, Jr., Anthony Caruso, Wallace Ford, Clem Bevins, Merv Griffin, Louis Jean Heydt, Sheb Wooley, Slim Pickens, Tyler MacDuff, Skippy Torgensen, James Griffith, Charles Watts.

STRANGE LADY IN TOWN (Warner, 1955) [112 minutes/color] directed by Mervyn LeRoy. Original Story and Screenplay: Frank Butler. Cast: Greer Garson, Dana Andrews, Cameron Mitchell, Lois Smith, Walter Hampden, Pedro Gonzales-Gonzales, Joan Camden, Jose Torvay, Adele Jergens, Bob Wilke, Frank de Kova, Russell Johnson, Gregory Walcott, Douglas Kennedy, Ralph Moody, Nick Adams, Jack Williams, The Trianas.

LAST OF THE DESPERADOES (Associated, 1956) [70 minutes] directed by Sam Newfield. Screenplay: Orville Hampton. Cast: James Craig, Jim Davis, Barton MacLane, Margia Dean, Donna Martell, Myrna Dell, Bob Steele, Stanley Clements.

THE PARSON AND THE OUTLAW (Columbia, 1957) [71 minutes/color] directed by Oliver Drake. Screenplay: Oliver Drake and John Mantley. Cast: Anthony Dexter, Sonny Tufts, Marie Windsor, Charles "Buddy" Rogers, Jean Parker, Robert Lowery, Madalyn Trahey, Bob Steele.

BADMAN'S COUNTRY (Warner, 1958) [68 minutes] directed by Fred F. Sears. Screenplay: Orville Hampton. Cast: George Montgomery, Neville Brand, Buster Crabbe, Karin Booth, Gregory Walcott, Malcolm Atterbury, Russell Johnson, Richard Devon, Morris Ankrum, Dan Riss, Lewis Martin, Steve Drexel, Fred Graham, John Harmon, Al Watt, Fred Krone, William Bryant, Jack Kinney, Tim Sullivan, LeRoy Johnson, Jack Carol.

THE LEFT-HANDED GUN (Warner, 1958) [102 minutes] directed by Arthur Penn. Original story: Gore Vidal. Screenplay: Leslie Stevens. Cast: Paul Newman, Lita Milan, John Dehner, Hurd Hatfield, James Congdon, James Best, Colin Keith-Johnston, John Dierkes, Bob Anderson, Wally Brown, Ainslie Pryor, Martin Garralaga, Denver Pyle, Paul Smith, Nestor Paiva, Jo Summers, Robert Foulk, Anne Barton.

ONE-EYED JACKS (Paramount, 1961) [141 minutes/color] directed by Marlon Brando. Original story: Charles Neider. Screenplay: Guy Trosper and Calder Willingham. Cast: Marlon Brando, Karl Malden, Pina Pellicer, Katy Jurado, Ben Johnson, Slim Pickens, Larry Duran, Sam Gilman, Timothy Carey, Miriam Colon, Elisha Cook, Jr., Rudolph Acosta, Ray Teal, John Dierkes, Margarita Cordova, Hank Worden, Nina Martinez, Snub Pollard.

BILLY THE KID VS. DRACULA (Embassy, 1966) [72 minutes/color] directed by William Beaudine. Original story and screenplay: Carl K. Hittleman. Cast: Chuck Courtney, John Carradine, Melinda Plowman, Virginia Christine, Walter

Janovitz, Bing Russell, Lennie Geer, Roy Barcoft, Olive Carey, Hannie Land-
man, Marjorie Bennen, William Forrest, George Cisar, Charlita, Harry Carey, Jr.,
Richard Reeves, Max Kleven, Jack Williams, William Chailee.

CHISUM (Warner, 1970) [111 minutes/color] directed by Andrew V. McLaglen. Screen-
play: Andrew V. McLaglen. Cast: John Wayne, Forrest Tucker, Christopher
George, Ben Johnson, Glenn Corbett, Andrew Prine, Bruce Cabot, Patric Knowles,
Richard Jaeckel, Lynda Day (George), Geoffrey Deuel, Pamela McMyler, John
Agar, Lloyd Battista, Ray Teal, Robert Donner, Edward Faulkner, Ron Soble,
John Mitchum, Alan Baxter, Glenn Langan, Alberto Morin, William Bryant, Pedro
Armendariz, Jr., Chuck Roberson, Hank Worden, Ralph Volkie.

DIRTY LITTLE BILLY (Columbia, 1972) [93 minutes/color] directed by Stan Dragoti.
Screenplay: Charles Moses and Stan Dragoti. Cast: Michael J. Pollard, Lee
Purcell, Richard Evans, Charles Aidman, Dran Hamilton, William Sage, Josip
Elic, Mills Watson, Alex Wilson.

PAT GARRETT AND BILLY THE KID (M-G-M, 1973) [106 minutes/color] directed by
Sam Peckinpah. Screenplay: Rudolph Wurlitzer. Cast: James Coburn, Kris Kris-
tofferson, Bob Dylan, Jason Robards, Jr., Richard Jaeckel, Katy Jurado, Slim
Pickens, Chill Wills, John Beck, Rita Coolidge, R. G. Armstrong, Luke Askew,
Richard Bright, Matt Clark, Jack Dodson, Jack Elam, Emilio Fernández, Paul
Fix, L. Q. Jones, Jorge Russek, Charlie Martin, Harry Dean Stanton, Claudia
Bryar, John Chandler, Mike Mikler, Aurora Clavel, Ruthie Lee, Rutanya Alda,
Walter Kelley, Rudolph Wurlitzer, Gene Evans, Donnie Fritts, Don Levy, Sam
Peckinpah.

GO WEST, YOUNG GIRL (1978) [74 minutes/color] directed by Alan J. Levi. Screenplay: George Yanok. Cast: Karen Valentine, Sandra Will, Stuart Whitman, Richard Jaeckel, David Dukes, John Payne.

YOUNG GUNS (20th-Fox, 1988) [107 minutes/color] directed by Christopher Cain.
Screenplay: John Fusco. Cast: Emilio Estevez, Kiefer Sutherland, Lou Diamond
Phillips, Charlie Sheen, Dermot Mulroney, Casey Siemaszko, Terence Stamp, Jack
Palance, Terry O'Quinn, Sharon Thomas, Brian Keith, Patrick Wayne, Gary Kanin.

GORE VIDAL'S BILLY THE KID (1989) [100 minutes/color] directed by William A.
Graham. Screenplay: Gore Vidal. Cast: Val Kilmer, Duncan Regehr, Wilford
Brimley, Julie Carmen, Michael Parks, Rene Auberjonois, Albert Salmi.

YOUNG GUNS II (20th-Fox, 1990) [105 minutes/color] directed by Geoff Murphy.
Screenplay: John Fusco. Cast: Emilio Estevez, Kiefer Sutherland, Lou Diamond
Phillips, Christian Slater, William Petersen, Alan Ruck, R. D. Call, James
Coburn, Balthanzar Getty, Jack Kehoe.

Bibliography

Boyer, Glenn G., (ed.), I MARRIED WYATT EARP: THE RECOLLECTIONS OF
JOSEPHINE SARAH MARCUS EARP (Tucson: University of Arizona Press,
1976).
Seydor, Paul, PECKINPAH: THE WESTERN FILMS (Urbana: University of Illinois
Press, 1980).

Sherman, Eric, and Martin Rubin, THE DIRECTOR'S EVENT (New York: Atheneum, 1970).
Sonnichsen, C. L., FROM HOPALONG TO HUD: THOUGHTS ON WESTERN FIC-TION (College Station: Texas A&M University Press, 1978).
Tuska, Jon, THE AMERICAN WEST IN FILM: CRITICAL APPROACHES TO THE WESTERN (Westport: Greenwood Press, 1985).
———, ENCOUNTERS WITH FILMMAKERS: EIGHT CAREER STUDIES (Westport: Greenwood Press, 1991).
Vidor, King, A TREE IS A TREE (New York: Harcourt, Brace, 1953).

5

THE LEGEND OF
BILLY THE KID

I

I have devised a methodology for approaching critically and classifying Western
fictional narratives, whether they are communicated via verbal or visual means,
that may be most helpful in understanding the legendry which has grown up around
Billy the Kid. Aristotle demonstrated long ago in the POETICS that the most viable
form of literary categories is that determined according to structure, then content,
and finally style. In dealing with Western fictional narratives, in order to circumvent
the ancient aesthetic debate between formalism and realism, I would opt for a
concept of historical reality as the basic standard of perspective and the content of
a Western fictional narrative would be distinguished on the basis of its deviation
(and the way in which it deviates) from this standard.

Historia scribitur ad narrandum non ad probandum, Quintilian wrote.[1] The
purpose of writing history is to provide a narrative, not give proof. Since historical
events cannot be recreated empirically, they must be recreated by means of a process
of inference according to logical principles, ideally taking into account all available
evidence. "The art of the historian," Morris R. Cohen wrote in THE MEANING
OF HUMAN HISTORY "is something that involves literary skill but, even more,
an imaginative capacity for seeing threads of connection between historic facts and
significant issues."[2] He devised a model for the historian: "The ideal of an
imaginative reconstruction of the past which is scientific in its determinations and
artistic in its formulations is the ideal to which the greatest historians have ever
aspired."[3] I would term such a model a historical construction. It is the re-creation,
as closely as possible, of a former reality in terms of what the reality was for those
who were then living and perceiving it. The questions to be asked at this stage of
historical inquiry are of this order: is all the available and pertinent evidence fully
taken into account? are the determinations such that they can be verified by the

BILLY THE KID ADVENTURE MAGAZINE, the most successful of the comic book versions of the legend of Billy the Kid.

known historical data? are the data themselves reliable? is the construction based on the documentary evidence logically consistent with all the documentary evidence and, internally, as a construction? how valid are the inferences and can they withstand logical scrutiny and are they consistent with all the documentary evidence? Finally, the historian must be willing to admit that his historical construction is at best only probable and provisional, capable of immediate revision in the light of any new evidence which becomes available.

Only once all this has been done ought ethics—which I define as the rational examination of human behavior patterns in terms of their effects—enter upon the scene. If a historian is going to evaluate a past reality in ethical terms, it must logically come after that reality has been recreated by means of a historical construction and the historian, in making such evaluations, is best advised to be straightforward as to just what ethical standard it is that is being used.

When it comes to Western fiction, I have found, employing this standard of historical reality, that there are three principal modes: the historical reconstruction, the historical romance, and the formulary Western. Now, it should go without saying that no critic is really qualified to evaluate historical fiction of any kind—including Western fiction—unless he knows enough about the historical period, the place, and the people involved to know the difference between historical reality and fantasy. Too much criticism of Western fiction—and Western films—has been written to date by critics who have not known the difference and the result has been confusion at worst and, at best, *jeux d'esprit*.

The difference between what I term a historical construction in Western American history and what I term a historical reconstruction in Western American fictional narrative consists in this: A historical construction, ideally, should contain no statement not necessitated or supported by the factual evidence whereas a historical reconstruction, because it is fiction and not history, can embellish the details based on the evidence *while it cannot at any point contradict the factual evidence*. It was acceptable for Leo Tolstoy in WAR AND PEACE (1862–1869) to "interpret" the personalities of Kutuzov and Napoleon—and those personalities did change as the novel passed through its several drafts—but he could not have Kutuzov win the battle at Borodino. No more and no less can an author of Western American fictional narrative write a historical reconstruction in which the known and documented facts of Western American history are deliberately distorted or violated.

Yet, although varying in degree and purpose, this is precisely what happens in the other two modes, the formulary Western and the historical romance. There are, in fact, two very powerful links between these two alternate modes. They both distort factual history and they both share a reliance on the structure of romance. Romance, as it was first developed by the Greeks, consists of an ἀγών [agon], or conflict, followed by a πάθος [pathos] in which the conflict is brought to its conclusion, and ends with an ἀναγνώρισις [anagnorisis], or a recognition. There is an optional middle term, a σπάραγμός [sparagmos], or a mangling. In the basic Perseus myth, the typical romance structure reveals a helpless community ruled by an old and ineffectual king. The community is threatened by a devouring sea-monster and, in order to propitiate the sea-monster, the community regularly offers up a human sacrifice. Perseus, the hero, comes upon the scene just as the king's beautiful daughter is about to be made the next sacrificial victim. Perseus defeats and slays the sea-monster in combat, winning, as his reward, both the princess and the kingdom. A sparagmos episode may be included, in which Perseus is mangled in the course of the combat. The anagnorisis, or recognition, in the Perseus myth, as is also the case in the formulary Western where the hero vanquishes the villain or villains, is—in Vergil's words—"*dabit deus his quoque finem*,"[4] a god, or in this case a hero, grants an end to such things.

The historical romance retains the structure of romance but, in addition, in the anagnorisis offers an ideological interpretation of human history. Whatever occurs in a historical romance occurs for ideological reasons and is never merely the result of the interaction with the land or between peoples, a consequence of character or different social values, as these phenomena have happened in history.

Just as for centuries Western literature has found its beginnings in the works of Homer, so it was long thought that historical fiction—what I have called the historical reconstruction—did as well; but we know now, through the combined efforts of archeology and anthropology, that there was no Trojan War as Homer described, and, if there was such a war at all, it did not happen even remotely as narrated in THE ILIAD. Rather, historical fiction, and in particular the idea of a historical reconstruction, first emerged in Western literature in the writings of Sir Walter Scott. "One would have to give Sir Walter Scott his due," Fritz Stern wrote in the Introduction to his collection of essays THE VARIETIES OF HISTORY "for every historian of the early Nineteenth century was stirred and inspired by Scott's bold reconstructions of the past, and admitted the deep effect of these fictions upon his own historical sense."[5] For some decades what Scott wrote has been classed as romance by literary critics and scholars and only recently has a reevaluation occurred which would tend to modify this view. "Although his materials are often those superficially thought of as 'romantic,' " Edgar Johnson observed, "fundamentally he is an unfaltering and clear-sighted realist. But his realism was deeply permeated with the sense of history; that is his revolutionary significance as a novelist. He saw history as more than causation, more than logic: it was the struggle between opposing schemes of values."[6] In Scott's best fiction, judged from the perspective of the historical reconstruction, his characters, while living and acting in the narrative present, have their passions excited by forces which have their roots in the past; in short, the values and viewpoints derived from nurture and the influence of historical forces in the past affect human behavior in the narrative present.

I think it should be evident at this point that really none of the narrative fictions inspired by Billy the Kid and the Lincoln County War, as surveyed in previous chapters, produced anything approaching a historical reconstruction as I have defined it. Yet, because these narrative fictions have employed actual historical personalities, they have to be regarded as varieties of the historical romance. Each is romantic because it attempts to prove something based on these characters and the events. Whether it is the fanciful Garret/Upson account of the Kid's life or Sam Peckinpah's film PAT GARRETT AND BILLY THE KID, there is an ideological purpose clearly discernible at the root of the fiction, as both the efficient cause and the primary mover of the action. In the instance of the Garrett/Upson account, the purpose was rather simplistic: to justify Garrett in his having to kill the Kid; in the instance of Peckinpah's film, it was to demonstrate that the "times are changing" and Garrett, in order to change with them and prosper, must kill the Kid and in so doing kill a part of his own soul. I am not questioning the right of such individuals to advance such notions, nor denying that their romantic, i.e., ideological motives, may have produced interesting and even enjoyable fictional narratives. I am rather calling attention to the ideologies which inspired their historical romances and, further, would suggest that we are best able to make this distinction by contrasting what they fancied as a historical reality with what, through a painstaking historical construction, we know to have been more nearly the historical reality.

The pitfall for the critic trying to evaluate a historical romance is the danger of writing all manner of absurdities precisely because the historical reality has been ignored. For example, in his Introduction to the reissue edition in 1979 by the University of New Mexico Press of Edwin Corle's BILLY THE KID, Professor William T. Pilkington wrote that "as to its historical reliability, Corle's book, like any book about Billy the Kid, is an interpretation of people and events from the past, and the author [was] perhaps simply being honest in saying that it is in some sense fiction. Ultimately, though, Corle's interpretation is no more fanciful or fictional than interpretations of the Kid advanced by professional historians, who must also deal with nebulous and conflicting evidence. We may agree or disagree with Corle's interpretation, but there is no way on earth we can absolutely validate or refute it."[7] To the contrary, there is a way we can validate or refute it, and that way is to contrast Corle's "interpretation" of the Kid with what can be documented about the Kid's life. By using historical reality as a standard of evaluation, it will be found that Corle deliberately violated historical documents 128 times in the course of his text. Further, by analyzing Corle's distortions of the historical reality, it will be found that his interpretation was scarcely his own, but rather it was his retelling of a number of the fantasies found in the Garrett/Upson account: the Kid was a savage killer who himself needed to be killed.

II

Several attempts, with varying degrees of success, have been made by psychologists, historians, and cultural critics to assess the nature and significance of the legend which has grown up around Billy the Kid. Perhaps the only complete failure among these attempts is also the most ambitious, Stephen Tatum's INVENTING BILLY THE KID: VISIONS OF THE OUTLAW IN AMERICA, 1881–1981 (University of New Mexico Press, 1982). In approaching the subject, Tatum began with a number of assumptions which apparently guided *a priori* all of his subsequent research, his most basic assumption being that of what I term the Henry Nash Smith thesis.

Smith and his book VIRGIN LAND: THE AMERICAN WEST AS MYTH AND SYMBOL are frequently cited by those who study what is called popular culture and it is to him that apparently is owed the notion that one can deduce the sentiments supposedly felt by a wide number of people by analyzing a sample of their popular fiction. Yet this is precisely what Smith's VIRGIN LAND does not do. In his "Preface to the Twentieth Anniversary Printing" issued by Harvard University Press, Smith confessed that "on rereading the book now I am forced to the chastening realization that I was guilty of the same kind of oversimplification I ascribed to others. Although I had gained some theoretical perspective on the nature of fictions from [Henri] Bergson, [Lucien] Levy-Bruhl, and [Hans] Vaihinger, my attitude toward popular beliefs about the West was often reductionistic. . . . The vestiges of dualism in my assumptions [between what he meant by symbol and myth] made it difficult for me to recognize that there was a continuous dialectic interplay between the mind and its environment, and that our perceptions of objects and events are no less a part of consciousness than are our fantasies."[8]

Smith, however, did spend two chapters analyzing the formulae of dime novels and he also tried to examine attitudes toward the American West to be found in fictional works by such authors as Timothy Flint, Emerson Bennett, and James Fenimore Cooper. His book was an experiment in perspective, an attempt to view the Westward movement through the propaganda and fictions inspired by it. Notwithstanding, Smith's premise in dealing with the dime novel, that "the individual writer abandons his own personality and identifies himself with the reveries of his readers,"[9] is farfetched to say the least. The reading public is too nebulous a concept to be measured with precision and, ultimately, its mood—to the extent that it is an entity and not a diversity of varied tastes and inclinations—is formed by such a confluence of factors as to be unknowable and incapable of measurement. Smith's methodology, while entertaining, cannot demonstrate by intuition any correlation between popular fiction and public sentiments that is meaningful, that can somehow be measured, or even verified negatively.

Beyond this premise, Tatum derived two of his other guiding notions from the writings of John G. Cawelti. These two notions are that of the "epic moment" and the feeling that somehow Zane Grey's Western fiction was significantly related to William S. Hart's films. The origin of Cawelti's notion of the "epic moment" is to be found in Frederick Jackson Turner's essay "The Significance of the Frontier in American History" (1893). "This perennial rebirth, this fluidity of American life, this expansion Westward with its new opportunities, its continuous touch with the simplicity of primitive society, furnish the forces dominating American character," Turner wrote. "The true point of view in the history of this nation is not the Atlantic coast, it is the Great West. . . . In this advance, the frontier is the outer edge of the wave—the meeting point between savagery and civilization."[10] At this "meeting point" who was savage, who civilized? Richard Drinnon answered that question in his book FACING WEST: THE METAPHYSICS OF INDIAN-HATING AND

EMPIRE-BUILDING. "In truth," Drinnon wrote, "Turner's 'meeting point between savagery and civilization'. . . was the supreme expression by an historian of all the other expressions before and since by novelists, poets, playwrights, pulp writers, painters, sculptors, and film directors. It separated the cowboys from the Indians by making the latter easily recognizable dark targets, especially if they had war paint on to boot. It unmistakably shaped national patterns of violence by establishing whom one could kill under propitious circumstances and thereby represented a prime source of the American way of inflicting death."[11] Yet for Cawelti in his book THE SIX-GUN MYSTIQUE and in Tatum's book on the Kid, Turner's racist ideology is posited to have been a historical fact! "The Western story," Cawelti insisted, "is set at a certain moment in the development of American civilization, namely at that point when savagery and lawlessness are in decline before the advancing wave of law and order, but are still strong enough to pose a local and momentarily significant challenge. In the actual history of the West, this moment was probably a relatively brief one in any particular area."[12]

More bluntly, without resorting to this brand of "newspeak"—to invoke George Orwell's term— this "epic moment" is merely occasion for "Two Minutes Hate"— as Orwell described this activity in NINETEEN EIGHTY-FOUR (Harcourt, Brace, 1949). In GREEN BERETS Robin Moore described the reaction of a South Vietnamese strike force during the showing of a Western at Nam Luong. It did not matter that the film was projected against the side of a building and probably was a cinemascope print so that the figures appeared elongated. "The strikers loved the action and identified themselves with it. When the Indians appeared the strikers screamed 'VC,' and when the soldiers or cowboys came to the rescue the Nam Luong irregulars vied with each other in shouting out the number of their own strike-force companies."[13]

In his book ADVENTURE, MYSTERY, AND ROMANCE: FORMULA STORIES AS ART AND POPULAR CULTURE, Cawelti asserted that Zane Grey and William S. Hart "produced what was unquestionably the most effective and successful work of the period 1910–25" and that "their works have so many points in common that it seems reasonable to view them as exponents of the same essential version of the formula."[14] Hart made sixty-two Western films. Cawelti cited two: HELL'S HINGES (Triangle, 1916), the plot of which he describes, and THE RETURN OF DRAW EGAN (Triangle, 1916) which is only mentioned by title. For Zane Grey, who wrote more than sixty novels with a Western setting over the years from 1910 to 1939, Cawelti cited only four of them. There is scarcely enough substance in such a limited sample to establish any kind of significant relationship between them. Hart was virtually finished as a leading box office attraction by the end of 1921. His sentimentality and pseudo-religious fervor were more typical of Harold Bell Wright than they were of Grey's fiction and Grey's philosophical naturalism. Indeed, the Western fiction Hart himself wrote most resembles that of Wright. This, of course, is not the place to probe deeply into this question of relationship, and I would not have brought it up at all if Tatum in his book on the Kid had not, in turn, tried to extend this significant relationship between Hart and

Grey to apply equally to visions of the Kid. In terms of the Western film, what is much more significant is that the Kid did not make his cinematic appearance until 1930 when Hart could no longer find screen work and when Zane Grey's popularity was definitely on the wane.

"This study's success," Professor Tatum wrote, invoking the Henry Nash Smith thesis, "rests on its demonstration that discovering, inventing, and understanding the Kid is in large measure discovering crucial aspects of ourselves and our cultural history."[15] For much of his book, Tatum then proceeded to carry through this thesis, although to do so he was required to declare that Walter Woods's stage play BILLY THE KID (1903), despite its initial success and subsequent twelve-year tour beginning in 1906, because of its image of the Kid as a hero, actually belonged in the period of the 1920s rather than chronologically where it occurred in American cultural history and that BILLY THE KID (M-G-M, 1941), because of its image of the Kid as a reprobate rather than a hero, also was an anomaly. He had to avoid mention of at least a third of the Kid's motion picture appearances for the same reason, whereas in Michael McClure's stage play, THE BEARD (Grove Press, 1965), the Kid's realization of his erotic fantasy of having oral sex with Jean Harlow paralleled "the ideological fragmentation of American society during the Vietnam and Watergate years' political and social upheavals."[16] The Kid was at first conceived as a reprobate because "as John Cawelti has stated, . . . the significant point about the Western formula is its dramatization of that epic historical moment in our national past when the opposing forces of civilization and wilderness confronted each other and shaped the course of American history."[17] What changed all this in the 1920s, so that the image of the Kid could become as something other than a misfit and murderer, were the "writings of Zane Grey and the films of William S. Hart."[18] According to Professor Tatum, who relied completely on Cawelti's text rather than reading Grey's novels or viewing Hart's films, "the Grey and Hart good-badman was typically domesticated by marriage, or was last seen in the heroine's company as the duo entered a secret, idyllic landscape in which violence had no place."[19] Almost as often as he ended up with the heroine, Hart did not—to cite WAGON TRACKS (Paramount, 1919), THE TOLL GATE (Paramount, 1920), O'MALLEY OF THE MOUNTED (Paramount, 1921), TRAVELIN' ON (Paramount, 1922), and WILD BILL HICKOK (Paramount, 1923) as only a few representative examples. Further, Zane Grey used the idea of a duo entering "a secret, idyllic landscape" in RIDERS OF THE PURPLE SAGE (Harper, 1912) filmed by Fox in 1918 starring William Farnum and again in 1925 starring Tom Mix (to stay within the same time frame) and not in his many other novels. Violence did have a place there, since we learn in the sequel, THE RAINBOW TRAIL (Harper, 1915), that the Mormons came to the "secret, idyllic landscape" and forcibly and brutally took young Fay Larkin away with them. This "decades" approach to Western fiction and film is never supportable when the total productions of a particular decade are studied in depth and only seems possible when they are not. As for films made during the time, presumably, of American "ideological fragmentation," such as DIRTY LITTLE BILLY which did so poorly at the box office that it has never been sold to network television for domestic showing, was never put into syndication, and never made it to the foreign television market, or PAT GARRETT AND BILLY THE KID which cost $4,345,000 to make and grossed $2,754,218, I find it altogether preposterous to assert, as Professor Tatum did, that these Billy the Kid pictures can somehow provide us with an insight into what most Americans were thinking and feeling during these years. Nor is it a meaningful statement to write that the Kid's exploits do not manage "to integrate him into society" in King Vidor's BILLY THE KID, "unlike earlier good-badman figures like William S. Hart's Draw Egan,"[20] and that therefore Vidor's film has something to tell us of special significance about how the feelings of Americans had changed by 1930 because Hart's exploits in his films of a decade or more prior to Vidor's film often do not result in his good-badman being integrated into society. What all this amounts to is trying to force Billy the Kid material into a thesis; it is not an observation that becomes self-evident after studying the history and development of the varying images of the Billy the Kid legend.

Professor Tatum devoted his second chapter to a brief account of the historical Billy the Kid. However, there are twelve errors of documented fact in it of varying seriousness, from having McSween "escape" from Deputy Sheriff Barrier's custody to having T. B. Catron appoint Garrett a deputy U.S. marshal prior to Garrett's assuming his duties as sheriff of Lincoln County, from going along with the fabrication that Poe got a "tip" on the Kid's whereabouts from a man in White Oaks to the Kid's being armed the night he was killed. But it would not bother Tatum greatly to have such errors pointed out to him. Firstly, this is true because, for Professor Tatum, the "Kid historian is a symbolic 'outlaw' when he delivers truthful visions that invalidate current beliefs, and when he complains that his vision is unacknowledged."[21] Secondly, this is so because Professor Tatum would have us "view myth and legend not as distortions or perversions of the truth—but rather as in fact different forms of reality and different forms of truth."[22] Now, I must confess that I am making an assumption in questioning this aspect of Professor Tatum's book: namely, that there is such a thing as past historical reality and that we, as human beings, are capable of constructing a comprehensible model of it which approximates what it once was. For Professor Tatum, "no historical narrative duplicates reality."[23] Also, as far as Professor Tatum was concerned, history can only be written in order to prove something, not just to narrate a sequence of events. "The point," he wrote, " is not that one explanation is more true, but that each explanation offers a different truth using the same data, that each, in short, distorts the field to tell a story."[24] Accordingly, since there is no such thing as an immutable historical reality, or even a close approximation to it, the question when it comes to Ramon F. Adams's style as opposed to Walter Noble Burns's style "is why, at that particular time, each author's stylistic techniques gained a following."[25] By means of this kind of reasoning, all we have, all we can ever have, is the Henry Nash Smith thesis: the historical past is whatever we wish at a given time to believe it to have been. All literary evaluations are also therefore in need of readjustment. If a play such as THE BEARD depicts the Kid's quest as a desire to learn the color of Jean Harlow's pubic hair or Michael Ondaatje's THE COLLECTED

WORKS OF BILLY THE KID (Wingbow Press, 1979) with its permise that life and death, love and violence, are "inextricably woven together,"[26] it is because Michael McClure and Michael Ondaatje wrote about the Kid in diverse albeit distinctly idiosyncratic ways that "they demand attention far greater than their obscurity would suggest we give to them, no matter how philosophically or aesthetically puerile some of their efforts are."[27] In terms of puerile efforts about the Kid, I wouldn't say Tatum's book was the worst offender, but it quite definitely holds the record for being the silliest.

Billy the Kid was one of four frontier personalities Kent Ladd Steckmesser undertook to focus upon in his book THE WESTERN HERO IN HISTORY AND LEGEND. I heartily agree with Professor Steckmesser's sentiment that "people . . . have a right to know whether they are reading fact or fiction, and the historian has a responsibility to draw the line which separates the two."[28] His modus operandi was to provide first an accurate, albeit brief, historical account of the subject—Kit Carson, "Wild Bill" Hickok, and General Custer were selected for study in addition to the Kid—and then to trace the growth and diversification of the subject's legend. Sadly, Professor Steckmesser, too, was lured by the attractions of the Henry Nash Smith thesis. In treating of Kit Carson, for example, he proposed that 19th-Century "mountain-man biographies reveal less about frontier life than they do about the literary techniques and moral ideas of the period in which they were written."[29] In his favor, Professor Steckmesser did not use this notion to promote a belief in historical solipsism; but I think it is more to the point to understand that the legends about frontier historical personalities reveal very little about the "period" in which they were composed and a great deal about the "moral ideas" of those who worked in manufacturing the legends. What is ultimately wrong with the Henry Nash Smith thesis is the emphasis it mistakenly places on the public receiving the media action. Presumably, so the thesis goes, the public gets only what it wants and what it wants is to be reassured of what it already believes, that the most successful "popular" notions are always those which reflect and reinforce what the public wants. This is too static a concept for an interchange as essentially dynamic and interactive as the relationship between media and the public. A better concept, one that is more workable, is that the media, in the 19th Century as in the 20th, tend most of the time to be prescriptive, not reflective. The "moral ideas" embodied in media projections of frontier legends are moral ideas prescribed for the receiving public. Popular literature, newspaper editorials, and, in this century, radio, films, and television are all components of emotional media, that is, media seeking to persuade through the manipulation of the emotions. In these terms, 19th-Century mountain man biographies, as fictions about the Kid, while they may reveal little about actual frontier life, do act as indicators of what certain individuals, namely their authors, wanted the public to believe concerning certain moral ideas.

"There are two Billy the Kids in legend," Steckmesser observed, I believe correctly. "The first is a tough little thug, a coward, a thief, and a cold-blooded murderer. The second is a romantic and sentimental hero, the brave and likable leader of an outnumbered band fighting for justice."[30] These two images of the Kid have, in fact, persisted almost from the beginning, although the latter has been made more feasible in the years since the turn of the century by the efforts historians have made to represent more accurately the forces involved in the Lincoln County War. The same year, in fact, can witness appearances of the Kid in accordance with both of these legends, as is the case with DIRTY LITTLE BILLY and PAT GARRETT AND BILLY THE KID which were released almost within a year of each other. Yet, what I have defined above as the historical reconstruction as opposed to the other two modes does not divide characters into either heroes or villains; indeed, this dichotomy is wholly alien to its perspective. But the dichotomy does point up the two possibilities within the historical romance. Whereas in the formulary Western, the hero must triumph, in the historical romance, as is more consistent with the ideological potentialities of this mode, Billy can be either a villain whose death stresses the ultimate victory of the forces of good against evil or he can be a "tragic" hero whose death emphasizes the injustice of society, of fate, of circumstances.

There are eight serious errors in Professor Steckmesser's historical construction of the life of the historical Billy the Kid, but many of these are the product of when he wrote and published his book. Steckmesser was the first, to my knowledge, to recognize that "the first tentative step toward a heroic interpretation [of the Kid] occurred when newspaperman Ash Upson in 1882 wrote a biography of the Kid under Pat Garrett's name."[31] Another issue which Steckmesser stressed was that to be an outlaw hero the story of the Kid must be told in such a fashion that his outlawry is seen to "result from social injustice rather than from any defect of character."[32] This principle is certainly borne out in those novels and films about the Kid which do attempt to depict him in the role of a hero. Steckmesser cited Walter Woods's play BILLY THE KID, in which the Kid survives the end and leaves to wander with his sweetheart, as the first full statement of the heroic image, and in this I would have to agree with him. "From being a symbol of malicious criminality," Steckmesser said of this play, "the Kid now is viewed as a victim of circumstances who deserved a better life."[33] He saw a direct line in this tradition from Woods's melodrama through Harvey Fergusson's article "Billy the Kid" in AMERICAN MERCURY (May, 1925) in which Fergusson compared the Kid to Robin Hood in that "he befriended the poor" and characterized him as a "quixotic romantic, who cared nothing for money. He lived and died an idealist."[34] The Kid in this view, according to Steckmesser, as one whose side loses, "endows his career with the same fascination that surrounds the Confederates at Gettysburg, the Texans at the Alamo, and Custer's troopers at the Little Big Horn."[35] Steckmesser further developed this notion until, he felt, the Kid in the heroic aspect of his legend could be compared to the tragic hero in Greek drama "moving inexorably toward death by treachery."[36] This strikes me as too much of an abstraction because I cannot find among the fictional narrative structures about the Kid one that actually follows this course, although there are many parallels with a medieval passion play which would portray the Kid's death as a variety of martyrdom. It is a subtle distinction, perhaps, but nonetheless an essential difference between the classical Greek point of view and that of the ancient Hebrews and the Judaeo-Christian tradition. In Greek tragedy, a human being is reconciled to the nature of the universe through what Aristotle called the πραχις [praxis], i.e., the progress, the movement, the action of the drama, whereas in the other tradition one's death can be a form of protest against the injustice of a social order and an appeal to a higher, divine order. Those fictions which present the Kid as a victim and a hero belong to the latter tradition, it seems to me. The meaning of his death is not reconciliation but protest. Steckmesser also left no allowance for the Kid as a Janus figure, an image which occurs frequently in the fiction inspiring the legend, with the Kid being presented as both a hero and villain within the context of a single narrative structure. Walter Noble Burns may have been the first to advance this Janus-figure image of the Kid, but it became a commonplace after him.

Marshall Fishwick attempted to explain the enduring popularity of Billy the Kid in his article "Billy the Kid: Faust in America" in THE SATURDAY REVIEW of 11 October 1952, later included in his book AMERICAN HEROES: MYTHS AND REALITY (Public Affairs Press, 1954). As the title of the article implies, Professor Fishwick's contention was that Billy the Kid is the American equivalent of the Faust legend in Europe. "This elusive phantom rider lived a full life before he was old enough to vote," Fishwick wrote, "and died just as he should have: with his boots on and his gun roaring." Ramon F. Adams cited Professor Fishwick's book in BURS UNDER THE SADDLE and remarked, concerning this image, that "we know that the Kid was in his sock feet and unarmed when he was killed; therefore, he did no shooting."[37]

When Fishwick sought to provide the factual history of Billy the Kid, he resorted to the Garrett/Upson account, with the Kid being born on 23 November 1859 in New York City of William H. and Kathleen Bonney, and so on. He also asserted that the Kid definitely picked off "Sheriff James A. [William] Brady and a deputy, and refused to accept amnesty when urged to do so by Governor Lew Wallace."[38] For Professor Fishwick the Kid was endowed, as was the Faust legend, with the traits of earlier folk heroes. The four major influences in so endowing the Kid's legend were identified by Professor Fishwick as Ash Upson, Charles Siringo, Emerson Hough, and, finally, Walter Noble Burns. In presenting brief vignettes of their respective careers, his information was occasionally erroneous, as, for example, his claim that Siringo "stopped writing about 1920."[39] Fishwick summed up his view: "The Kid had a lurking devil in him, sometimes debonair and impish, sometimes bloodthirsty and fiendish, as circumstances prompted. History favored the worser angel, and the Kid fell. His damnable life ended with a deserved death. Since God condemned, Americans have been content to forgive. May God have mercy on his soul."[40] To be quite honest, I do not know how seriously Professor Fishwick expected a reader to take this final image of the Kid. Personally I have the impression that, just as Professor Tatum used the Kid to give credence to the Henry Nash Smith thesis, Professor Fishwick tried to merge his popular image with that of the Faust legend, and about as unsuccessfully.

It may well be that Alfred Adler's essay, "Billy the Kid: A Case Study in Epic Origins," which appeared in WESTERN FOLKLORE a year before Professor Fishwick's analysis, came nearer the mark in concluding that "the case of Billy the Kid leads us to formulate an hypothesis: created at a certain time, a legend is not a reflection of that time, but an indication that the time needed a legend."[41] I find it worth remarking that this author, with the same name as the founder of Individual Psychology, did not mention once, with regard to the Kid, either organ inferiority or the *Minderkomplex,* albeit some of those who have portrayed the Kid in fiction have stressed his diminutive stature as his prime motivation. What Adler did do in his essay was to draw parallels between the traits assigned to the Kid by those who helped create his legend. He even mentioned C. G. Jung by name and, in fact, his hypothesis is very close to what in Jungian psychology is referred to as archetypal patterns.

There is one point I would like to make about another line of inquiry which I do not follow below but which might bear some attention. Alfred Adler in this article remarked that it is perhaps of importance that the Kid was identified with a name which embodied the image of an animal, namely *el chivato,* colloquial Mexican Spanish for a young goat, or kid, between six months and a year. The Janus-figure image of the Kid lends itself not only to his use as a scapegoat in the sense of Leviticus XVI:21—" . . . and confess over him all the iniquities of the children of Israel, and all their transgressions in all their sins, putting them upon the head of a goat, and send *him* away by the hand of a fit man into the wilderness . . . "—but also to what in primitive Greek religion was called φαρμακος [pharmakos], that poison which would destroy what was feared and yet could bring about a renewal. Such a renewal might require a human or animal sacrifice, but it might also imply a savior, what Gilbert Murray in FIVE STAGES OF GREEK RELIGION (Anchor Books, 1955) conjectured to be the meaning of τριτος σοτερ [tritos soter], or "the third savior." Such an inquiry into the psychological depths of the meaning of the legend of Billy the Kid, already indicated in part by Alder's suggestion, could produce some significant psychological interpretations well beyond the superficial conscious psychology employed by virtually all of the historians who have tackled the Kid's biography or the history of the Lincoln County War.

I will confess that initially I was attracted by the possibilities afforded by an archetypal approach. As should be evident from the examples cited in previous chapters, fictions featuring the Kid by name are historical romances and the structure of the romance is the keystone of this mode. Indeed, I am indebted to Northrop Frye's ANATOMY OF CRITICISM: FOUR ESSAYS in arriving at my definition of what constitutes a romance and I agree with him that "the central form of romance is dialectical: everything is focused on a conflict between the hero and his enemy, and all the reader's values are bound up with the hero. Hence the hero of romance is analogous to the mythical Messiah or deliverer who comes from an upper world, and his enemy is analogous to the demonic power of a lower world."[42] For Professor Frye, "the romancer does not attempt to create 'real people' so much as stylized figures which expand into psychological archetypes. It is in the romance that we find Jung's libido, anima, and shadow reflected in the hero, heroine, and villain respectively."[43] I might have been inclined to pursue this line of inquiry had I not in the end had to bow to the caution expressed by Marie-Louise von Franz in SHADOW AND EVIL IN FAIRYTALES. "I would like to warn you against taking Jungian concepts and pinning them on to mythological figures," she remarked, "saying this is the ego, this the shadow, and this the anima, because you will see that this works only for a time and that then there come contradictions—and finally distortions as people try to force the figures in the story into a definite form."[44] This, I believe, is the fault of both the popular culture and psychological approaches to the legend of Billy the Kid. Both attempt to force the Kid's legend into some external framework, be it the Henry Nash Smith thesis or the theory of archetypal patterns. The Kid's legend may resemble the Faust legend in some particulars, but not in all, and the resemblance is probably more superficial than significant.

"To write history is so difficult that most historians are forced to make concessions to the technique of legend," Erich Auerbach wrote.[45] This is not only true for fabulists and filmmakers but equally so for *soi-disant* Kid historians from Upson to Utley. "Legend," as Auerbach defined it, "arranges its material in a simple and straightforward way; it detaches it from its contemporary historical context, so that the latter will not confuse it; it knows only clearly outlined men who act from few and simple motives and the continuity of whose feelings and actions remains uninterrupted."[46]

Such observations are useful as generalities, but they do not address the Kid's legend specifically nor explain its hold on the public. J. Frank Dobie tried to account for the popularity of the Kid in his essay "Billy the Kid" in the SOUTHWEST REVIEW which was later expanded for inclusion in his book, A VAQUERO OF THE BRUSH COUNTRY (Southwest Press, 1929). "What was there about this killer of men," Dobie asked, "this pariah of society, this product of Bowery slum and Western lawlessness that has made him the object of such wide and undimming interest?"[47] Dobie's answer seems to have been that because the Kid possessed "the art of daring" and "because his daring apotheosized youth—youth in the saddle— youth with a flaming gun—and because his daring kept him running and balancing on the edge of a frightful precipice, as it were, for an unprecedented length of time, Billy the Kid will always be interesting, will always appeal to the popular imagination."[48]

Mody Boatright, as Dobie, approached the Kid's legend from the point of view of a folklorist in "The Western Bad Man as Hero." He suggested that there are certain common ingredients in the folklore efforts to transform Western bad men into heroes. His initial requirement is that the outlaw/hero "belong to the dominant Anglo-American majority. Indians and half-breeds and Latins are excluded. A Joaquin Murieta might become a hero to the Latin-American in California and elsewhere, and even to Joaquin Miller, who appropriated his name; but never to a considerable number of Argonauts or their descendants. The chief repository of the Murieta saga and myth is Chile."[49] This requirement overlooks the tremendous popular success of the Cisco Kid, who was, after all, based in the original O. Henry story on Billy the Kid and on a variation of the Joaquin Murieta saga, not merely in the early films, but throughout the entire film series and the television series that followed.

Boatright's other requirements have perhaps more validity. Such an outlaw/hero must come from "a respectable but not wealthy family."[50] This is true for the most part of those narrative structures of the legend which show the Kid's family, but there is a minor tradition which characterizes the Kid as a New York tough let loose in the Wild West and even Dobie referred to him as a "product of Bowery slum." Another requirement "is an unfortunate childhood."[51] This would hold true for the Kid only half the time, since a powerful tradition in the legend stresses the Kid's closeness to his mother. There is, however, almost no exception to the next requirement, that "the youth from a respectable but unfortunate family . . . commits his first crime under extreme provocation."[52] Yet, even here, there are components to the legend, such as Will Henry's short story, which depict the Kid as possessed by the devil from the moment of his birth. Another requirement "is that the bad-man hero fight the enemies of the people. This does not mean that the people wholly approve the methods of warfare."[53] Curiously, in effect, this requirement finds the Kid in a film such as CHISUM siding with Chisum and in a film such as PAT GARRETT AND BILLY THE KID fighting against Chisum—in both he is a pawn in the film's ideology. A final requirement "is that during the career of outlawry, the hero performs acts of tenderness and generosity."[54] This has been true of the Kid of the legend only about half the time.

"The outlaw," Boatright concluded, "must, of course, atone for his misdeeds. For the lesser ones like Frank James and Emmett Dalton a penitentiary sentence followed by a quiet, law-abiding life is sufficient." However, in Frank James's case, historically, he was acquitted; Emmett Dalton served fourteen years of a life sentence. For others, such as Jesse James, Joaquin Murieta, and Billy the Kid, "the outlaw can attain the highest heroic stature only by an atoning death. That death must be a result of treachery and must have in it an element of martyrdom."[55]

It is with this conclusion that I am most in sympathy. Yet, even here, the Kid of legend sometimes survives and rides off across the border with his sweetheart. At base I do not believe that the legend of Billy the Kid can be reduced to any one legendry structure. Over the years his life has served to illustrate too many very different moral parables for a single one ever to suffice; nor have these moral parables been so much a manifestation of the times in which they were created as simply indicators of what meaning the creator of a particular fiction wanted to convey. The legend of Billy the Kid is not simple, but complex, not uniform, but a polyglot.

III

"We were told, for instance," Mark Twain wrote in ROUGHING IT, "that the dreadful 'Mountain Meadows Massacre' was the work of the Indians entirely, and that the Gentiles had meanly tried to fasten it upon the Mormons; we were told, likewise, that the Indians were to blame, partly, and partly the Mormons; and we were told, likewise, and just as positively, that the Mormons were almost if not wholly and completely responsible for that most treacherous and pitiless butchery. We got the story in all these different shapes, but it was not till several years afterward that Mrs. Waite's book, THE MORMON PROPHET, came out with Judge Cradlebaugh's trial of the accused parties in it and revealed the truth that the latter version was the correct one and that the Mormons were the assassins. All our 'information' had three sides to it, and so I gave up the idea that I could settle the 'Mormon question' in two days. Still, I have seen newspaper correspondents do it in one."[56]

What, in my opinion, a legend about an American frontier outlaw must have about it is three sides. In addition to the inherently dramatic ingredients in the Lincoln County War and the Kid's life, what has enabled him to be made into a legendary character is that his image had from the beginning the potentiality of a Janus figure. He can be portrayed as all bad, as all good, or as part good and part bad. This flexibility is a vital first step in the legendry process. One need only survey the various novels and stories inspired by the Kid, or the films which have featured him as a character, to recognize this Janus-figure quality: that he can be portrayed as all bad, all good, or something of both.

The spectrum of the historical romance is sufficiently broad to encompass all manifestations of such a Janus figure. At one side of the spectrum a particular Billy the Kid story can closely resemble the narrative structure of the formulary Western, be it a novel such as E. B. Mann's GAMBLIN' MAN which places the legendary Kid into a typical formulary ranch romance setting, or Paul Evan Lehman's PISTOLS ON THE PECOS which makes the Kid the arch villain but includes a formulary ranch romance between the hero and the heroine. At the other side of the spectrum, a Kid story can be closer to the historical romance, such as Amelia Bean's TIME FOR OUTRAGE which has many of the historical details accurately depicted and yet distorted for the purpose of revealing the Kid as a minor player and never a leader. It may seem curious at first that no true historical reconstruction has been inspired by the Kid's life, but this is due to the fact that the Kid in such a historical reconstruction must necessarily be shorn of all legendary aspects, must be presented in his historical context as he actually was, and in these terms he can never occupy the center of the stage since, as John H. Tunstall and A. A. McSween and all the others, he was only a participant in a historical process. In short, the Kid's life and death are of no significant historical importance. He was only one element among many in a vicious mercantile war and a struggle for power and wealth. It is difficult to resist the temptation to write historical fiction in order to prove something; and, when one sets out to prove something by means of historical events, one is writing historical fiction not as history but as a variety of romance.

Depending to what end the legend is employed, that is, who dies and why, the legend is being used to tell us who must die. Maud Bodkin in ARCHETYPAL PATTERNS IN POETRY: PSYCHOLOGICAL STUDIES OF IMAGINATION noted that "the experience of tragic drama both gives in the figure of the hero an objective form to the self of imaginative aspiration, or to the power-craving, and also, through the hero's death, satisfies the counter movement of feeling toward the surrender of personal claims and the merging of the ego within a greater power—the 'community consciousness.' Thus the archetypal pattern corresponding to tragedy may be said to be a certain organization of the tendencies of self-assertion and submission."[57] It is my feeling that "the experience of tragic drama" is entirely alien to the legend of Billy the Kid in any of its manifestations, but not the tension of self-assertion versus the demands of one-settlement culture. Even historically, the Lincoln County War was a struggle between forces which would define the character of life in the community. In very much simplified terms it was a struggle between the system that was being imposed on the community and the right for individual initiative, competition, and enterprise. This struggle has been variously characterized in accordance with how the polarities have been defined. If the "system" that was being imposed is viewed as the coming of civilization, or law and order, or community values, then the McSween/Tunstall faction and the Kid himself must be viewed as disruptive, contrary, or chaotic. If sympathy is expressed toward the McSween/Tunstall faction, the Kid can be variously interpreted as a victim or as a good man gone bad in the aftermath. What remains consistent in all the many variations of the legend is that those who die do so for one or another ideological reason. A fictional death is usually prescriptive, but the kind of prescription depends entirely on the author who is making use of the legend.

It is because there has been such a plethora of variations on the legend that there has continued a controversy about the biographical facts of the Kid's life and the events of the Lincoln County War. This phenomenon, of course, is not unique to the Kid. It has been duplicated with regard to virtually all of those historical personalities about whom legends have been created for the purpose of proving some contention or another, whether it be "Buffalo Bill" Cody, "Wild Bill" Hickok, General George Armstrong Custer, Davy Crockett, Jesse James, et al. But this is not to say that at any given time the research and findings of historical evidence will exert a significant influence on the uses to which a specific legend is put. Such uses are not determined by historical truth, but instead by the intention of the fabulist.

However, by providing a historical construction of a given past reality and contrasting with that construction the various fantasies and legends which have sprung up, we are in a position to evaluate the meaning and aim of each use of the legend. I disagree with Professor Tatum's notion that the legendary Billy the Kid was invented. I believe rather that the historical Billy the Kid was variously endowed with certain characteristics, depending on what effect was intended. What, instead of the Henry Nash Smith thesis, I would have hoped Professor Tatum would have done with his book was to define the historical reality and then show the growth, variation, and development of the various legendary components. This kind of study is very much needed and I attempted, in a small way, to make a beginning for it by isolating the specific fantasies in the Garrett/Upson account, the Burns account, and now in Utley's accounts. Could a comprehensive catalogue of fantasies about the Kid be drawn up, it would be possible to trace the persistence of each of them through the ever-expanding Billy the Kid bibliography. What I am calling for, in short, is a concordance to accompany the Billy the Kid bibliography. Until there is such a concordance, however, I have at least provided a historical construction with which the distortions of the legend may be contrasted and a description of the modes of Western fictional narrative which can be used in classifying those distortions in order to isolate the ideologies that they embody.

I am reminded of words Joseph Ernest Renan wrote, hard on a century ago. "*Voir le passé tel qu'il fut est la premiere jouissance de l'homme et la plus noble de ses curiosités.*"[58] Surely his advice is nowhere more relevant than in studying the legends of the American West.

BIBLIOGRAPHY OF CRITICAL SOURCES

Adler, Alfred, "Billy the Kid: A Case Study in Epic Origins," WESTERN FOLKLORE (Vol. 10), April, 1951, pp. 143–152.

ADVENTURE, MYSTERY, AND ROMANCE: FORMULA STORIES AS ART AND POPULAR CULTURE (Chicago: University of Chicago Press, 1976).

Auerbach, Erich, MIMESIS: THE REPRESENTATION OF REALITY IN WESTERN LITERATURE (Princeton: Princeton University Press, 1953).

Boatright, Mody C., MESQUITE AND WILLOW (Dallas: Southern Methodist University Press, 1957).

Bodkin, Maud, ARCHETYPAL PATTERNS IN POETRY: PSYCHOLOGICAL STUDIES OF IMAGINATION (New York: Oxford University Press, 1963).

Cawelti, John G., THE SIX-GUN MYSTIQUE (Bowling Green: Bowling Green University Popular Press, 1975).

Cohen, Morris R., THE MEANING OF HUMAN HISTORY (LaSalle: Open Court, 1947).

Dobie, J. Frank, A VAQUERO OF THE BRUSH COUNTRY (Dallas: Southwest Press, 1929).

Drinnon, Richard, FACING WEST: THE METAPHYSICS OF INDIAN-HATING AND EMPIRE-BUILDING (New York: New American Library, 1980).

Fergusson, Harvey, "Billy the Kid," AMERICAN MERCURY (Vol. 5), May, 1925, pp. 224–231.

Fishwick, Marshall, AMERICAN HEROES: MYTHS AND REALITY (Washington, D.C.: Public Affairs Press, 1954).

Franz, Marie-Louise von, SHADOW AND EVIL IN FAIRYTALES (Dallas: University of Dallas Press, 1980).

Frye, Northrop, ANATOMY OF CRITICISM: FOUR ESSAYS (Princeton: Princeton University Press, 1957).

Johnson, Edgar, SIR WALTER SCOTT: THE GREAT UNKNOWN (New York: Macmillan, 1970) published in two volumes.

McClure, Michael, THE BEARD: A PLAY (New York: Grove Press, 1965).

Moore, Robin, GREEN BERETS (New York: Crown, 1965).

Ondaatje, Michael, THE COLLECTED WORKS OF BILLY THE KID (Berkeley: Wingbow Press, 1979).

Orwell, George, NINETEEN EIGHTY-FOUR (New York: Harcourt, Brace, 1949).

Smith, Henry Nash, VIRGIN LAND: THE AMERICAN WEST AS MYTH AND SYMBOL (Cambridge: Harvard University Press, 1950).

Steckmesser, Kent Ladd, THE WESTERN HERO IN HISTORY AND LEGEND (Norman: University of Oklahoma Press, 1965).

Stern, Fritz (ed.), THE VARIETIES OF HISTORY (New York: Meridian Books, 1956; revised edition, 1972).

Tatum, Stephen, INVENTING BILLY THE KID: VISIONS OF THE OUTLAW IN AMERICA, 1881–1981 (Albuquerque: University of New Mexico Press, 1982).

Turner, Frederick Jackson, "The Significance of the Frontier in American History" in FRONTIER AND SECTION: SELECTED ESSAYS OF FREDERICK JACKSON TURNER (Englewood Cliffs: Prentice-Hall, 1961) selected with an Introduction by Ray Allen Billington.

Twain, Mark [pseud. Samuel L. Clemens], ROUGHING IT (1872; New York: New American Library, 1962).

APPENDIX A

A BILLY THE KID MISCELLANY

In the chapters of this book I have appraised the significant appearances of Billy the Kid in fiction and in film and have both assessed the basic sources for the legend of Billy the Kid and provided a survey of the more reliable books on the historical Billy the Kid and the Lincoln County War. I have not dealt with appearances on radio or in television productions other than TV movies because these have contributed nothing new to the legend, much less to the historical reality—e.g., the appearance of the Kid as part of a story for THE NEW MAVERICK (NBC, 1982)—and can be safely passed over. The same is true for appearances in comic books, various obscure stage plays, and avant-garde poetry. One possible exception that might be mentioned is THE COLLECTED WORKS OF BILLY THE KID (House of Anansi Press, 1970; reissued by Wingbow Press, 1979) by Michael Ondaatje. This collection of verse, falsified newspaper interviews, and dime novel adventures, photographs, and quotations from various sources follows, as concerns the Kid's life, the Garrett/Upson account and Burns's "saga." There is no new information in it as such, but it does attempt to conceive of the Kid as an artist with a six-gun. Michael McClure's stage play THE BEARD, while it adds nothing to any understanding of the historical Billy Bonney, does provide the legendary Kid with a motive in life: his desire to see the color of Jean Harlow's pubic hair. Presumably as sexual fluids are exchanged orally by these two legendary figures, one legend does merge into the other in a prophylactic eroticism that can only enhance the legends of the participants. The comic book BILLY THE KID was formerly THE MASKED RAIDER and succeeded the earlier comic with the ninth issue in November, 1957. It continued until No. 153 in March, 1983, a significant run when compared to BILLY THE KID ADVENTURE MAGAZINE which lasted from October, 1950, until No. 30 in 1955 which was not given a month. BILLY

THE KID AND OSCAR appeared for three issues, beginning in Winter, 1945, and concluding in Summer, 1946.

As part of the promotional campaign for Burns's "saga," when it became a selection of the Book-of-the-Month Club, the Reverend Andrew Jenkins composed "The Ballad of Billy the Kid" which was first recorded by tenor Vernon Dalhart (Brunswick, 100) in 1929 and which was recorded subsequently by Woody Guthrie in the 1930s, Tex Ritter in the 1940s, Tex Ritter again in the 1950s, and, more recently, by Ry Cooder in the 1970s. Also on 9 February 1968 Tex Ritter recorded another ballad about the Kid, titled "The Governor and the Kid" (Capitol, ST-2974). Bob Dylan recorded his sound track for Sam Peckinpah's motion picture PAT GARRETT & BILLY THE KID (Columbia, PC-32460). J. Frank Dobie in A VAQUERO OF THE BRUSH COUNTRY (Southwest Press, 1929) quoted Jenkins's "The Ballad of Billy the Kid" and it was from Dobie—under whom he once studied at the University of Texas—that Tex Ritter first heard of the ballad. The text is as follows:

> I'll sing you a true song of Billy the Kid
> I'll sing of the desperate deeds that he did,
> Way out in New Mexico, long ago
> When a man's only chance was his own fo'ty-fo'.
>
> When Billy the Kid was a very young lad
> In old Silver City he went to the bad;
> Way out in the West with a gun in his hand
> At the age of twelve he killed his first man.
>
> Fair Mexican maidens play guitars and sing
> A song about Billy, their boy bandit king,
> How ere his young manhood had reached its bad end
> He had a notch on his pistol for twenty-one men.
>
> 'Twas on the same night that poor Billy died,
> He said to his friends: "I'm not satisfied
> There are twenty-one men I have put bullets through
> And Sheriff Pat Garrett must make twenty-two."
>
> Now, this is how Billy the Kid met his fate:
> The bright moon was shining, the hour was late.
> Shot down by Pat Garrett, who once was his friend,
> The young outlaw's life had now come to its end.
>
> There's many a man with a face fine and fair
> Who starts out in life with a chance to be square,
> But just like poor Billy he wanders astray
> And loses his life in the very same way.

In 1938 Aaron Copland composed his ballet, BILLY THE KID, which has been recorded numerous times, perhaps the first most complete version being that with the Ballet Theatre Orchestra conducted by Joseph Levine (Capitol, P-8238), recorded under Copland's supervision; even Copland's own recordings of this work are only of the suite from the ballet. The most recent complete recording has featured Leonard Slatkin and the St. Louis Symphony Orchestra (EMI CDC-7473822). The ballet opens to Garrett's leading a group of settlers into the Southwest. Riding through a town, Garrett is cheered. Among the onlookers are the Kid and his mother. She is shot by a townsman named Alias, whom then the Kid knifes. Garrett speaks kindly to the Kid, but the Kid rejects his advice and refuses to curb his impulse to kill. When Billy is next seen, he has grown to manhood. He plays cards with a crooked land agent, portrayed by the same dancer who played Alias. He shoots him when the land agent objects to Billy's cheating. Then the Kid plays cards with Garrett, who has been elected sheriff. Garrett, too, objects to the Kid's cheating and rides off, angry. Garrett returns with a posse, the men shooting. Billy is arrested and put in jail, the townspeople dancing to celebrate his capture. Alias is now Billy's jailer. The Kid kills him and escapes. An Indian guide leads the Kid to the hiding place selected by the Kid's girl. The Kid rests and has a dream in which he dances a pas de deux with his girl. She is portrayed by the same dancer as played his mother. Garrett, guided by the Indian, creeps up on the Kid. Billy lights a cigarette, making a target for himself. Garrett kills him. The action then fades again to Garrett leading the settlers onward.

Every year during the first week in August, Lincoln in New Mexico has its Billy the Kid Days and celebrates a three-day pageant during which "The Last Escape of Billy the Kid," an outdoor drama, is reenacted. Also, in 1981, celebrating the centennial of the Kid's death, Fort Sumner put on a nine-day celebration at which Jarvis Garrett appeared, son of Pat Garrett, and he displayed the gun with which his father killed the Kid. An anthology of newspaper accounts concerned with the Kid has been published, BILLY THE KID: LAS VEGAS NEWSPAPER ACCOUNTS OF HIS CAREER, 1880–1881 (W. M. Morrison Books, 1958), but those included are far from exhaustive. A complete listing of relevant newspapers to be studied for the years 1877 through 1882 would have to include the following:

Alamogordo News (New Mexico)
Albuquerque Review (New Mexico)
Carrizozo News (New Mexico)
Cimarron News and Press (New Mexico)
Denver Tribune (Colorado)
El Paso Daily Herald (Texas)
El Paso Daily Times (Texas)
El Paso Evening News (Texas)
El Paso Herald-Post (Texas)
El Paso Lone Star (Texas)
El Paso Times (Texas)
Grant County Herald (New Mexico)
Las Cruces Rio Grande Republican (New Mexico)
Las Cruces Semi-Weekly (New Mexico)
Las Cruces Thirty-Four (New Mexico)

Las Vegas Daily Optic (New Mexico)
Las Vegas Gazette (New Mexico)
Lincoln County Leader (New Mexico)
Mesilla Valley Independent (New Mexico)
Rocky Mountain Sentinel (Colorado)
Roswell Daily Record (New Mexico)
Roswell Register (New Mexico)
Santa Fe New Mexican (New Mexico)
Santa Fe Weekly New Mexican (New Mexico)

Beyond this, important archival papers and documents which have a direct relevance on the Kid's life and the Lincoln County War include:

Thomas B. Catron Papers. University of New Mexico Library, Albuquerque.
James H. East Papers. University of Texas at Austin Archives.
Albert J. Fountain Papers. University of Oklahoma Library Archives.
Colonel Maurice Garland Fulton Papers. University of Arizona Library, Tucson.
Robert N. Mullin Papers and Evetts Haley Interviews. Evetts Haley Library, Midland, Texas.
National Archives at Washington, D.C., and New York:
Azariah F. Wild, special Treasury agent, investigating counterfeiting in New Mexico, 1880, Record Group 56.
N.A.M. Dudley to Acting Assistant Adjutant General, 8–9 November 1905, AGO, 1878.
New Mexico State Records Center and Archives, Santa Fe: Corporation Records; Court Records for Bernalillo County (Albuquerque); Territorial Papers and Sheriffs' Accounts; WPA New Mexico Writers' Program.
Panhandle-Plains Historical Museum, Canyon, Texas. Oral and written interviews with early settlers relating to Texas and New Mexico history.
C. L. Sonnichsen Papers. University of Texas at El Paso Archives.
Lew Wallace Papers. William Henry Smith Memorial Library, Indianapolis, Indiana.

There are also the various courthouse records at Roswell, New Mexico for Chaves County; Fort Sumner, New Mexico, for DeBaca County; Las Cruces, New Mexico, for Doña Ana County; and Carrizozo, New Mexico for Lincoln County.

Pulp magazines featuring stories about the Kid, copies of books in which he is a central character, or BILLY THE KID comic books can most readily be obtained from two sources:

Arthur W. Hackathorn	David T. Alexander
230 West 6th Avenue	P.O. Box 273086
Denver, Colorado 80204	Tampa, Florida 33618

APPENDIX B

A BILLY THE KID CHRONOLOGY

1824	15 August: John Simpson Chisum born in Madison County, Tennessee.
1829	Catherine McCarty born?
1831	Lawrence Gustave Murphy born, Wexford County, Ireland. [In the 1870 census his age is listed as fifty-three. If true, he could have been born as early as 1817. At Fort Canby, N.M. Territory his age was given as thirty. If true, then he could have been born as late as 1834.]
1840	6 October: Thomas Benton Catron born, near Lexington, Missouri.
1842	William Henry Harrison Antrim born, near Huntsville, Indiana.
	Alexander A. McSween born in Charlotte Town, Prince Edward Island, the Dominion of Canada.
1845	30 December: Susan Hummer born in Adams County, Pennsylvania.
1848	2 February: New Mexico Territory ceded to the United States of America by the Treaty of Guadalupe Hidalgo.
	22 April: James Joseph Dolan born in Laughrea, Galway County, Ireland.
1850	19 February: Richard M. Brewer born in St. Albans, Vermont.
	12 May: John Henry Riley born Valentia Island, Ireland.
	5 June: Patrick Floyd Garrett born, Chambers County, Alabama.
1851	José Chávez y Chávez born.
1853	Jesse Evans born (rightful name perhaps Davis).
	6 March: John Henry Tunstall born, at No. 14 Liscombes Cottages, Dalston, District of Hackney, Middlesex County, England.
1855	Joseph McCarty born.
	Martín Chávez born.
	5 May: Fort Stanton founded.
1856	Henry McCarty born?

1861	27 July: L. G. Murphy joins the New Mexico Volunteers in Santa Fe as a First Lieutenant, having had previous military service as a Sergeant Major with the regular U.S. Army.
1862	Summer: General James Henry Carleton and his California Column enter New Mexico Territory to liberate it from the Confederate States of America.
	26 September: William H. Antrim honorably discharged from Company "I" of the 54th Regiment of the Indiana Volunteer Infantry.
	31 October: Fort Sumner established at the Bosque Redondo.
1863	L. G. Murphy promoted to the rank of Captain, thereafter brevetted Major.
1866	Murphy, Colonel Emil Fritz, and former drummer James J. Dolan mustered out of the U.S. Army. Fritz and Murphy establish a store adjacent to Fort Stanton.
	T. B. Catron arrives in New Mexico.
	Mrs. Catherine McCarty living with her sons Joseph and Henry in Marion County, Indiana.
1868	John Chisum arrives in New Mexico Territory and establishes a ranch at Bosque Grande.
	Lucien B. Maxwell purchases Fort Sumner.
1869	16 January: Lincoln County established.
	14 September: Mrs. Catherine McCarty purchases a town lot in her own name in Wichita, Kansas.
1870	Roswell Smith and his son, Van C. Smith, quitclaim 160 acres, including the later town site of Roswell, to T. B. Catron.
	10 August: Mrs. Catherine McCarty files on a quarter-section near Wichita.
1871	August: Mrs. Catherine McCarty sells out her holdings in Kansas.
1872	U.S. Post Office established at Rio Hondo [later changed to Roswell].
1873	1 March: Mrs. Catherine McCarty and William H. Antrim are married at Santa Fe.
	Summer: L. G. Murphy & Co. is evicted from Fort Stanton. The store is moved to the quarters which will eventually be sold to Alexander A. McSween while a new, much larger store building is erected across the main street of Lincoln. J. J. Dolan attempts to kill Captain James F. Randlett, responsible for the eviction, and is detained for a time in jail.
1874	26 June: Colonel Emil Fritz dies in Stuttgart, Germany.
	16 September: Mrs. Catherine McCarty dies in Silver City.
1875	John Chisum transfers his New Mexico holdings to Hunter & Evans of St. Louis, Missouri.
	3–15 March: Alexander A. and Susan McSween arrive in Lincoln.
	2 April: The Murphy/Dolan party is defeated at the Lincoln County nominating meeting at Lincoln.
	15 September: Juan B. Patrón is shot in the back by John H. Riley of L. G. Murphy & Co., but recovers.
	23 September: Henry McCarty is arrested in Silver City in connection with a clothes theft.
	25 September: Henry McCarty escapes from jail in Silver City.

November: Alexander A. McSween becomes attorney for John Chisum.

1876   6 November: John Henry Tunstall arrives in Lincoln.

21 November: John H. Riley able to purchase a junior partnership in J. J. Dolan & Co.

1877   9 February: A. A. McSween buys the former site of the Murphy store to be his home from L. G. Murphy.

March: James J. Dolan and John H. Riley buy out controlling interest in L. G. Murphy & Co. from Major Murphy.

April: Godfrey Gauss enters the employ of J. H. Tunstall.

3 May: J. J. Dolan kills Hiraldo Jaramillo and is acquitted.

1 August: A. A. McSween, who was retained by Emil Fritz' brother and sister to represent them in claiming the proceeds of a $10,000 life insurance policy, is notified that the sum, less collection fees, has been deposited in his account in St. Louis.

17 August: Kid Antrim kills Frank P. Cahill near Camp Grant, Arizona.

August: J. H. Tunstall establishes the Lincoln County Bank and in a goodwill gesture McSween approves a loan to J. J. Dolan for $1,000.

18 September: Horses belonging to Tunstall, McSween, and Dick Brewer are stolen from Brewer's ranch by the Jesse Evans gang.

Fall: A young man calling himself William H. Bonney enters Lincoln County and stays for a while with the Heiskell Jones family at their homestead near Roswell.

21 September: Brewer, Doc Scurlock, and Charles Bowdre reach Las Cruces where they have warrants sworn out for the arrest of the members of the Jesse Evans gang.

20 October: Jesse Evans and Frank Baker are arrested by Lincoln County Sheriff Brady and placed in the Lincoln County jail out of which they walked and left town shortly thereafter.

18 December: The McSweens and John Chisum leave on a trip for St. Louis to take care of individual and mutual business interests.

21 December: J. J. Dolan presents District Attorney Rynerson with an affidavit in order to have a warrant issued for A. A. McSween on a charge of embezzlement. Dolan claimed the insurance money as part of a debt owed to L. G. Murphy & Co. of which he was the principal owner.

24 December: A. A. McSween and John Chisum are held at Las Vegas on the basis of a telegram from T. B. Catron, the charges and warrants to follow.

26 December: The charges and warrants not arriving in forty-eight hours, Chisum and A. A. McSween are released from custody only to be rearrested. Chisum chooses to be confined in the Las Vegas jail. McSween is to be kept in custody and transported to Mesilla to appear before Judge Bristol.

1878   4 January: McSween leaves Las Vegas for Mesilla accompanied by two deputies.

January: Arriving in Lincoln on the way to Mesilla, McSween learns that Judge Bristol will not hold court for two or three weeks. Deputy Sheriff Barrier agrees to remain with McSween in Lincoln until court convenes.

January: William H. Bonney is hired by J. H. Tunstall.

26 January: The McSween party, now including his brother-in-law, David P. Shield, Squire Wilson, J. H. Tunstall, and Deputy Sheriff Barrier arrive at Mesilla.

2 February: Judge Bristol begins the McSween hearing.

4 February: McSween and Shield ask for a continuance of the case until a grand jury can be called during the regular court session in Lincoln in April. Judge Bristol agrees to the request and sets bail at $8,000, leaving it up to District Attorney Rynerson to approve the sureties.

5 February: At Shedd's ranch, on the way to Lincoln, J. H. Tunstall is threatened by J. J. Dolan, Jesse Evans, Frank Baker, and John Long for having accused J. J. Dolan & Company of tax fraud.

11 February: J. H. Tunstall arrives in Lincoln to find his store in Lincoln has been attached by Sheriff Brady. Sheriff Brady agrees to allow Tunstall to retain possession of six horses and two mules and this livestock is herded back to Tunstall's Rio Feliz ranch, accompanied by John Middleton, Godfrey Gauss, William McCloskey, Rob Widenmann, Fred Waite, and Billy Bonney. Tunstall remains in Lincoln to assist McSween in raising bond and lifting the attachment from his store. McSween is still in the custody of Deputy Sheriff Barrier who refuses to surrender his prisoner to Sheriff Brady.

13 February: Widenmann, Waite, and Bonney return to Lincoln to inform Tunstall that a sheriff's posse led by Billy Mathews and including Jesse Evans and Frank Baker proposes to attach the Tunstall cattle in which McSween has no financial interest.

16 February: Tunstall rides to Chisum's ranch to seek his counsel but finds that Chisum is still in jail in Las Vegas.

17 February: Tunstall arrives at his Rio Feliz ranch. He learns that the Mathews posse is eight miles distant and is intent on driving off his cattle and fighting any armed resistance. Tunstall sends McCloskey to see Mathews to inform him that the posse can take possession of the cattle provided they do not remove them from the ranch.

18 February: Tunstall with the six horses and two mules begins a journey to Lincoln, accompanied by Dick Brewer, Middleton, Widenmann, and Bonney. On the way, Brewer and Widenmann espy some turkeys and take off in pursuit of them. A sub-posse led by William Morton, Jesse Evans, and Tom Hill swoops down on Tunstall and kills him. The others are driven off. Late that night, the men who were with Tunstall arrive in Lincoln and tell of what happened. A notebook obtained from John Riley implicates the House in rustling activities.

19 February: McSween sends for Tunstall's body to be brought into town. Bonney and Brewer swear affidavits before Justice of the Peace Wilson who issues warrants for the men in the sub-posse and gives them to Atanacio Martínez, constable of Lincoln, for service.

Dr. Taylor F. Ealy, a physician and minister, arrives in Lincoln with his wife and two children and a schoolteacher. He and his party stay with the McSweens. In the late afternoon with the arrival of Tunstall's body, Squire Wilson impanels a coroner's jury to take testimony and it is determined that Tunstall was killed by a sub-posse in which Jesse Evans, Frank Baker, George Hindman, Tom Hill, William Morton, and J. J. Dolan could be identified.

20 February: Sheriff Brady asks Dr. D.M. Appel, the Fort Stanton post surgeon, to perform a postmortem and two different written statements result. Dr. Ealy assists in the embalming and records the truth as does Appel in a report he gives to Widenmann to be sent to Tunstall's family in London. Constable Martínez with Bonney and Waite try to serve the warrants on Dolan and others at the Dolan store, now protected by soldiers from Fort Stanton, only themselves to be arrested by Sheriff Brady and charged with disturbing the peace. Martínez is released by nightfall, but Waite and Bonney are kept in custody.

22 February: Tunstall is buried. Bonney and Waite are still in jail. Robert Widenmann, who was appointed a deputy U.S. marshal during the search for Evans and Baker who were also charged with stealing stock from the Mescalero agency, a federal offense, is able to garner troops from Fort Stanton to search Lincoln for the two; in the process he repossesses the Tunstall store.

25 February: A. A. McSween makes out his will.

26 February: McSween and Deputy Sheriff Barrier leave Lincoln and hide outside of town. Mrs. McSween prepares to depart on a trip back to Kansas.

6 March: The Regulators—Bonney, Waite, Middleton, Frank MacNab, a stock detective for Hunter & Evans, Doc Scurlock, Charles Bowdre, Henry Brown, Sam Smith, and Jim French under the leadership of Dick Brewer—chase and arrest William Morton and Frank Baker.

9 March: After spending the previous night at Chisum's South Spring River ranch, Morton, Baker, and William McCloskey, who had joined the Regulators probably at Chisum's, are shot down at Agua Negra.

Governor Axtell issues his proclamation declaring Judge Wilson's appointment illegal and outlawing the Regulators.

McSween returns to Lincoln to see the governor and leaves again, still in the company of Deputy Sheriff Barrier.

Tom Hill is killed and Jesse Evans wounded in a raid on the John Wagner camp. Evans rides to Fort Stanton and turns himself in, receiving treatment at the post hospital.

1 April: McSween had moved to Chisum's South Spring River ranch and would be coming to Lincoln with Chisum for a court hearing. Sheriff Brady and deputies Hindman, Mathews, John Long, and George Peppin may well have been preparing to ambush McSween when they themselves were ambushed by MacNab, French, Waite, Middleton, Brown, and Bonney. Bonney, who was shooting at Mathews in the fracas, may have been himself wounded by Mathews when he tried to retrieve his rifle impounded by Brady when he was arrested. Brady with eight bullet wounds and Hindman with one are killed. The Regulators ride out of town except for the wounded Bonney who is treated by Dr. Ealy and hidden from searchers by Sam Corbet, a clerk in the Tunstall store. Mrs. McSween, back from Kansas, meets her husband when he arrives in Lincoln. [Robert N. Mullin's research indicated that Susan McSween was at Fort Stanton on 29 March and at Chisum's ranch on 31 March. Montague R. Leverson's letter puts Susan McSween at Chisum's on 29 March.]

3 April: McSween is in military custody and transported to Fort Stanton accompanied by his wife who returns alone to Lincoln.

Circa 3 April: Billy Bonney meets Tom O'Folliard at San Patricio and enlists him in the McSween cause.

4 April: The Regulators put in at Blazer's Mill and have a shoot-out with Andrew J. "Buckshot" Roberts, a bounty hunter working for Dolan. Middleton is seriously wounded; George Coe has his trigger finger shot off; Bonney is grazed; and Dick Brewer is killed by Roberts who is fatally wounded by a shot fired by Charles Bowdre. George Coe later claimed that earlier in the week Roberts had attempted to dry-gulch the Kid and Bowdre.

13 April: McSween is tried before a grand jury impaneled by Judge Bristol.

18–22 April: The grand jury exonerates McSween but brings in a massive number of indictments, including indictments for Dolan, Evans, and Mathews as well as others for the murder of Tunstall and against Bonney, Middleton, Waite, and Brown for the deaths of Brady and Hindman. Bowdre is indicted for the death of Roberts.

23 April: J. J. Dolan & Co. suspends business.

24 April: A mass meeting of Lincoln citizens requests the members of "the Irish firm" to leave Lincoln permanently.

27 April: John S. Copeland, first appointed by Judge Bristol to serve the warrants Brady had when he died, is confirmed as interim sheriff by the Board of Commissioners of Lincoln County. Dolan, who regards Copeland as a McSween sympathizer, rides to Santa Fe to have Governor Axtell reverse this appointment.

28–29 April: The Seven Rivers gang under Marion Turner and John Jones is organized into a posse and rides toward Lincoln to assist Dolan in fighting Chisum. On the way they encounter Frank MacNab, Ab Saunders, and Frank Coe. They kill MacNab, wound Saunders, and capture Frank Coe.

28–30 May: John S. Copeland is removed from office and replaced by George Peppin, a stonemason who once worked on the Tunstall store and a man now in Dolan's employ. John Kinney and his gang join Peppin as special deputies to hunt Regulators. McSween again becomes a fugitive.

4 July: A portion of the Seven Rivers gang lays siege of McSween and several Regulators, including Bonney, at Chisum's South Spring River ranch, but their forces are insufficient.

11 July: A large posse under command of Dolan and Peppin terrorizes San Patricio.

14 July: McSween and an expanded group of followers numbering fifty or sixty ride into Lincoln and take up defensive positions. McSween reoccupies his home with his bodyguard—French, Bonney, Tom Cullins, O'Folliard, Joseph J. Smith, José Chávez y Chávez, Francisco Zamora, Eugenio Salazar, Vicente Romero, Ignacio Gonzalez, and his law clerk, Harvey Morris. Sheriff Peppin deploys a few men in the "Indian tower" to take potshots and sends for Dolan and his forces, still in San Patricio.

15 July: The first day of what would prove a five-day battle. McSween tries to clear the Indian tower by serving an eviction notice on Saturnino Baca, a retired

cavalry captain renting from him the land on which the *torreón* is located. Baca appeals to Colonel Dudley at the fort and Dudley dispatches Dr. Appel to act as mediator. Dr. Appel is confronted with an *impasse*. Dolan arrives with his forces, including the Doña Ana bunch under John Kinney, still a deputy sheriff, and the Seven Rivers gang. The only casualties this day are a horse and a mule, although around midnight a Murphy man named Daniel Huff dies, presumably from poison.

16 July: Sharpshooters from both sides assume strategic positions. Sheriff Peppin sends to the fort a request for a cannon. Dudley turns him down and dispatches a note to this effect carried by a black enlisted man who is fired upon, probably by accident. Peppin sends a note back to Dudley declaring that Private Robinson was shot at by one of the McSween faction.

17 July: Charlie Crawford, one of the Dolan sharpshooters, is severely wounded by Fernando Herrera of the McSween faction and no one from the Dolan forces is willing to chance being shot at to rescue the wounded man. Colonel Dudley dispatches a board of inquiry to determine who fired the shot at Private Robinson and, predictably, since only the Dolan forces are interviewed, the McSween faction is blamed. Dr. Appel and other soldiers retrieve Crawford and he is taken to the fort hospital where, five weeks later, he will die.

18 July: Matters in Lincoln remain at a stalemate. Colonel Dudley succeeds in getting his officers to agree to intervene. Tom Cullins of the McSween side is killed and George Bowers, a Murphy man, is seriously wounded.

19 July: Dolan, aware that Colonel Dudley and the troops are on the way, deploys his forces in a tight net around the McSween house. Dudley arrives with all of his officers, thirty-five enlisted men, a mountain howitzer, and a Gatling gun. On the way into town, Dudley compels Judge Wilson to swear out a warrant against A. A. McSween personally for firing on Private Robinson. The cannon is so situated that the McSween faction is forced to abandon their positions and leave town, only McSween and his personal bodyguard remaining in his fortified home. Dudley refuses to grant McSween military protection despite an exchange of two notes with McSween and two visits from Mrs. McSween. Andrew Boyle of the Dolan forces successfully sets fire to the McSween house, possibly with rifle cover from Dudley's troopers. Mrs. McSween and the other noncombatants are allowed to leave the McSween house. Billy Bonney assumes leadership of what is left of the McSween faction and proposes to lead an exodus after dark to draw the fire of the besiegers so that McSween and others can escape. The Kid, Tom O'Folliard, and Jim French make it through the firing line, Harvey Morris does not. McSween, hesitant through fear, tries to surrender. Bob Beckwith agrees to accept his surrender but loses his life trying to stop John Jones from shooting McSween. The shot prompts a fusillade in which McSween is killed and with him Francisco Zamora and Vicente Romero. Eugenio Salazar is badly wounded, but survives. McSween's body is ignited and the Dolan forces go on a rampage through Lincoln.

20 July: A coroner's jury, appointed by Peppin, determines that McSween and the others lost their lives resisting arrest.

5 August: Billy Bonney and two other outlawed Regulators, George Coe and Henry Brown, meet up with a posse led by Atanacio Martínez *en route* to repossess some Tunstall cattle. Near Blazer's Mill, Martínez shoots agency clerk Morris J. Bernstein, a death sometimes attributed to the Kid. Colonel Dudley so interprets the action and dispatches a detail from Fort Stanton to hunt for the Kid.

Late Summer: John Kinney's Doña Ana bunch is loosed on Lincoln County, rustling, raiding, raping women, and shooting down children in the fields. Kinney is no longer a deputy, but he will be again once the Kid is captured.

13 August: Billy Bonney, having eluded the soldiers, shows up at Chisum's Bosque Grande ranch with some fellow Regulators. Perhaps the Kid first learns that it is Chisum's intention to pull out of the Territory.

Late August: Billy confronts Chisum at Fort Sumner and demands $500 in pay for the Regulators. Chisum turns him down. George and Frank Coe leave the Regulators.

1 September: The Kid helps Doc Scurlock move from Lincoln to Fort Sumner with his family.

4 September: President Hayes replaces Governor Axtell with General Lew Wallace.

Mid-September through October: Bonney, Middleton, Brown, Waite, O'Folliard, and French stage a concerted raid on J. J. Dolan's livestock, stealing fifteen horses and 150 cattle. French leaves the gang when the cattle are sold. The others proceed to Tascosa. After selling the horses, the gang splits up. Only Bonney and O'Folliard return to Fort Sumner.

20 October: L. G. Murphy dies in Santa Fe. T. B. Catron is assigned controlling interest in J. J. Dolan & Co. and he appoints his brother-in- law, Edgar Walz, to manage the store in Lincoln. T. B. Catron's resignation as U.S. district attorney becomes effective during this time but he remains in office until the first of the year.

13 November: Governor Wallace's amnesty proclamation is issued.

5 December: Colonel Dudley's efforts to cover up Catron's use of stolen stock to fill federal contracts is exposed by the *Cimarron News and Press*.

22 December: John Kimbrell, who replaced George Peppin as sheriff of Lincoln County when Peppin resigned due to lack of pay, arrests Billy Bonney and jails him in Lincoln. Bonney escapes.

Circa 28 December: The Kid meets Jesse James at Las Vegas.

1879   18 February: The Kid, O'Folliard, Jesse Evans, and J. J. Dolan hold a peace parley in Lincoln. Dolan and a follower named Bill Campbell murder Mrs. McSween's attorney, Houston I. Chapman, in Lincoln.

5 March: The citizens of Lincoln hold a ball in honor of Colonel Dudley as part of a goodwill gesture. At the same time Governor Wallace arrives in Lincoln and is shocked to learn that Jesse Evans, Billy Mathews, and Bill Campbell, implicated in the Chapman killing, are staying at the old Murphy ranch and that no effort has been made to arrest them. He offers a reward for Billy Bonney, hoping to use him as a witness against Chapman's assailants.

Circa 12 March: Billy Bonney writes a letter to Governor Wallace.

15 March: Governor Wallace writes a note to Billy Bonney suggesting a meeting between them in Lincoln.

18 March: Jesse Evans and Bill Campbell escape their confinement at Fort Stanton.

21 March: Bonney and Tom O'Folliard are arrested by arrangement by Sheriff Kimbrell.

14 April: At Governor Wallace's insistence, a grand jury is convened. Bonney is not permitted to testify by Colonel Rynerson who instead changes the venue of Bonney's trial to Doña Ana County where he will be tried for the murder of Sheriff Brady.

25 May: A court of inquiry investigates charges against Colonel Dudley from which, eventually, in a travesty of procedure he is exonerated.

Late June: Bonney rides off from his loose captivity at Lincoln, suspecting that Governor Wallace is unable to effect his pardon and he is unwilling, under these circumstances, to stand trial.

2 July: Jesse Evans is arrested and charged with murder and robbery by Texas Rangers near Alamito Creek, Texas.

August: All charges against J. J. Dolan are dismissed by Judge Bristol.

October: Bonney with Scurlock, O'Folliard, Bowdre, and two Mexican-Americans crosses into the Texas Panhandle and rustles a hundred head of cattle from Chisum. Chisum sends his brother James and some picked men after the cattle. Doc Scurlock quits the gang.

6 December: All civil charges against Colonel Dudley brought by Mrs. McSween are dismissed by Judge Bristol.

1880   10 January: Joe Grant, a hardcase, perhaps hired by the Chisums to kill the Kid, is shot by Bonney at Fort Sumner.

The Kid makes his living stealing horses occasionally and gambling.

October: John Chisum, Captain Lea, and J. J. Dolan nominate Pat Garrett for sheriff of Lincoln County.

2 November: Pat Garrett is elected sheriff. He is appointed a deputy to Sheriff Kimbrell until his term of office is to begin officially.

November: Pat Garrett begins his pursuit of Billy the Kid.

27 November: The citizens of White Oaks form a posse under Deputy James Carlyle and lay siege to the Kid, Dave Rudabaugh, and Billie Wilson at the Greathouse trading post. Carlyle is shot by members of his own posse and his death is blamed on the Kid.

12 December: Bonney writes a letter to Governor Wallace explaining his side of Carlyle's death.

15 December: Governor Wallace offers a $500 reward for the "delivery" of Bonney to the sheriff of Lincoln County.

19 December: Tom O'Folliard is shot from ambush by Garrett and posse at Fort Sumner.

23 December: Charles Bowdre is killed and Billy Bonney and others are captured by the Garrett posse at Stinking Springs.

24 December: Bonney is put in chains at Fort Sumner and Paulita Maxwell has a romantic meeting with him.

26 December: Bonney is jailed at Las Vegas. He is to be transported to Santa Fe.

1881   1 January: From jail in Santa Fe, Bonney writes a letter to Governor Wallace, but the governor is in the East.

28 February: An attempt to burrow out of the jail is discovered in Santa Fe and Bonney is placed in solitary confinement.

2 March: Bonney writes again to the governor, who has since returned.

4 March: Again Bonney writes to Governor Wallace.

18 March: The San Miguel County grand jury indicts Bonney on a charge of cattle stealing.

27 March: Bonney writes to Governor Wallace for the last time.

28 March: Bonney is transported to Mesilla for trial.

9 April: Bonney is convicted for murder of Sheriff Brady in Judge Bristol's court.

15 April: Judge Bristol orders that Bonney be executed by hanging on 13 May.

15 April: Bonney starts out under heavy guard to Lincoln where he will be hanged.

21 April: Bonney arrives in Lincoln.

28 April: Bonney escapes from jail at Lincoln, killing his two guards, J. W. Bell and Robert Olinger.

14 July: Bonney is shot in the dark in Pete Maxwell's bedroom at Fort Sumner by Pat Garrett. He is unarmed except for a butcher knife.

1882   January: Paulita Maxwell marries José Jaramillo shortly before she gives birth to a male child.

18 February: Pat Garrett is finally paid the $500 reward by the Territorial legislature.

2 November: John Poe is elected sheriff of Lincoln County, replacing Garrett.

1884   20 December: John Chisum dies at Eureka Springs, Arkansas.

1898   26 February: J. J. Dolan dies.

1908   28 February: Pat Garrett is shot to death while urinating by Wayne Brazel.

NOTES

Preface to the Second Edition

1. Ranke, Leopold von, *"Vorrede zur ersten Ausgabe,"* GESCHICHTEN DER RO-MANISCHEN UND GERMANISCHEN VÖLKER VON 1492 BIS 1514, (Leipzig, 1888), p. vii.

2. Adams, Ramon F., A FITTING DEATH FOR BILLY THE KID (University of Oklahoma Press, 1960), pp. 297–298.

Acknowledgments

1. Turner, Frederick Jackson, "The Significance of the Frontier" in FRONTIER AND SECTION: SELECTED ESSAYS OF FREDERICK JACKSON TURNER (Prentice-Hall, 1961), p. 17.

Chapter One: The Life and Death of Billy the Kid

N.B. Many of the documents quoted in the various works cited below are accessible to the public and location for them can be found in Appendix A. Since for many readers the published sources will be more readily available than the original documents in various archives, as a convenience the published sources are cited below.

1. SANTA FE COUNTY BOOK OF MARRIAGES ("A" pp. 37–38). *Vide* Appendix A.

2. Mrs. W. C. Totty of Silver City, N.M., WPA File, New Mexico Historical Society, Santa Fe, New Mexico. *Vide* Appendix A.

3. Information confirmed in a letter from Frederick Nolan to Jon Tuska dated 8 December 1992.

4. Mrs. W. C. Totty, op. cit.

5. Quoted in Mullin, Robert N., op.cit., p. 12.

6. Ibid., p. 12.

7. Ibid., p. 12.

8. Ibid., p. 13.

9. *Silver City Enterprise* on 3 January 1902.

10. In reconstructing the details of the Kid's early life in Silver City and later in Arizona, I am indebted as all henceforth must be to Frederick Nolan's THE LINCOLN COUNTY WAR: A DOCUMENTARY HISTORY (University of Oklahoma Press, 1992), pp. 56–59 and pp. 148–149 and Jerry Weddle's article "Apprenticeship of an Outlaw: Billy the Kid in Arizona" in JOURNAL OF ARIZONA HISTORY (Autumn, 1990), pp. 233–252.

11. Quoted in Rasch, Philip J., and Robert N. Mullin, "New Light on the Legend of Billy the Kid" in NEW MEXICO FOLKLORE RECORD 7 (1952–53), p. 4.

12. Mullin, Robert N., op.cit., pp. 14–15. Mullin added as an afterthought that "Gildea's friendship here with Billy may have been responsible for saving the Kid's life later when the two were enlisted on opposing sides in the Lincoln County War. Gildea told Col. Fulton that at the end of the five-day battle at Lincoln he had 'a perfect bead' on one of the men escaping from the burning house, but recognized Kid Antrim, and held his fire." Original interview is in the Fulton Papers. *Vide* Appendix A.

13. Quoted in ibid., p. 16. If the Kid was telling the truth about his age in 1880, he was actually at least nineteen by this time. It is possible, even probable, that appearing so many years younger than he actually was made him choose an age that would perhaps be more believable.

14. Denton, J. Fred, "Billy the Kid's Friend Tells for First Time of Thrilling Incidents" in Tucson *Daily Citizen* dated 28 March 1931.

15. Quoted in Nolan, Frederick, THE LINCOLN COUNTY WAR: A DOCUMENTARY HISTORY, op. cit., pp. 58–59.

16. Nolan, Frederick, op. cit., p. 59.

17. Quoted in Mullin, Robert N., op. cit., p. 16.

18. Keleher, William A., VIOLENCE IN LINCOLN COUNTY (1957; University of New Mexico Press, 1982), pp. 310–311.

19. Cline, Donald, ALIAS BILLY THE KID: THE MAN BEHIND THE LEGEND (Sunstone Press, 1986), p. 51.

20. Ball, Eve, MA'AM JONES OF THE PECOS (University of Arizona Press, 1969), p. 117.

21. Ibid., p. 120.

22. Quoted in Keleher, William A., op. cit., p. 3.

23. Sabin, Edwin L., KIT CARSON DAYS (Pioneer Press, 1935) in two volumes, in Vol. II, p. 702. Sabin reproduced a number of documents pertaining to the New Mexico campaign.

24. Ibid., pp. 702–703.

25. Sonnichsen, C. L., THE MESCALERO APACHES (University of Oklahoma Press, 1972), p. 116.

26. Quoted by Fulton, Maurice Garland, HISTORY OF THE LINCOLN COUNTY WAR (University of Arizona Press, 1968) edited by Robert N. Mullin, p. 33.

27. Klasner, Lily, MY GIRLHOOD AMONG OUTLAWS (University of Arizona Press, 1972), p. 94.

28. Quoted in Fulton, Maurice Garland, op. cit., p. 47.

29. Quoted in Fulton, Maurice Garland, op. cit., p. 50.

30. Quoted in Nolan, Frederick, op. cit., pp. 17–18.

31. Quoted in Fulton, Maurice Garland, op. cit., p. 55.

32. Quoted in Nolan, Frederick, op. cit., p. 127.

33. Quoted in Fulton, Maurice Garland, op. cit., p. 59.

34. Quoted in Nolan, Frederick, THE LIFE AND DEATH OF JOHN HENRY TUN-STALL (University of New Mexico Press, 1965).

35. Fulton, Maurice Garland, op. cit., p. 60.

36. Quoted in Hunt, Frazier, THE TRAGIC DAYS OF BILLY THE KID (Hastings House, 1956), p. 21.

37. Quoted in Otero, Miguel Antonio, THE REAL BILLY THE KID WITH NEW LIGHT ON THE LINCOLN COUNTY WAR (Rufus Rockwell Wilson, 1936), p. 114.

38. Quoted in ibid., p. 121.

39. Keleher, William A., THE FABULOUS FRONTIER: TWELVE NEW MEXICO ITEMS (University of New Mexico Press, 1962), pp. 151–152.

40. Quoted by Keleher, William A., VIOLENCE IN LINCOLN COUNTY: 1869–1881, op. cit., pp. 42–43.

41. Quoted in Fulton, Maurice Garland, op. cit., pp. 105–106.

42. Quoted in ibid., p. 104.

43. Quoted in ibid., p. 110.

44. Quoted in ibid., p. 110.

45. Quoted in ibid., p. 110.

46. Quoted in ibid., p. 113.

47. Quoted in ibid., p. 113.

48. Quoted in ibid., p. 114.

49. Quoted in ibid., p. 114.

50. Quoted in ibid., p. 114.

51. Quoted in ibid., p. 115.

52. Quoted in ibid., p. 120.

53. Quoted in ibid., p. 116.

54. Quoted in ibid., p. 120.

55. Quoted in ibid., p. 120.

56. Quoted in Fulton, Maurice Garland, op. cit., p. 124. Also see Ruth R. Ealy's unpublished memoir WATER IN A THIRSTY LAND, unpublished manuscript on deposit at the Wisconsin State Historical Society, pp. 64–65 and pp. 76–77.

57. Quoted from the affidavit of David M. Appel, July, 1878 in the Angel Report and available also in the Westphall Collection of the New Mexico State Records Center and Archive.

58. Quoted in Nolan, Frederick, THE LINCOLN COUNTY WAR: A DOCUMEN-TARY HISTORY, op. cit., pp. 286–287. The [illegible] is from Nolan's text. I have suggested [sphenoid] because there is one os sphenoidale in the human skull but nothing called "ephinoid" and "cribuform" is clearly a typographical error for the cribriform plate which is the thin, perforated medial portion of the horizontal plate of the ethmoid bone or os ethmoidale. "Acromian" can only be the acromial process, the acromion being the lateral, triangular projection of the spine of the scapula which forms the point of the shoulder and articulates with the clavicle.

59. Ealy, Ruth R., WATER IN A THIRSTY LAND, op. cit., p. 76.

60. Quoted in Fulton, Maurice Garland, op. cit., p. 127.

61. Quoted in ibid., p. 128.

62. Quoted in ibid., p. 138 and corroborated by the copy of Morton's letter of 8 March 1878 in the Fulton papers.

63. Quoted in ibid., pp. 139–140. While Morton does not identify the trigger-happy Regulator by name, the consensus has it that it was the Kid and I have followed that interpretation in my account.

64. Quoted in ibid., p. 144.

65. Nolan, Frederick, THE LINCOLN COUNTY WAR: A DOCUMENTARY HISTORY, op. cit., pp. 247–249.

66. Ealy, Ruth R., op. cit., p. 66.

67. Ealy, Taylor F., MISSIONARIES, OUTLAWS, AND INDIANS: TAYLOR F. EALY AT LINCOLN AND ZUNI, 1878–1881 (University of New Mexico Press, 1984) edited and annotated by Norman J. Bender, p. 31.

68. Ealy, Ruth R., op. cit., pp. 85–86.

69. Quoted in Fulton, Maurice Garland, op. cit., p. 163.

70. This excerpt of the letter Leverson addressed to President Rutherford B. Hayes on 1 April 1878 is quoted in Hunt, Frazier, op. cit., p. 54, and Nolan, Frederick, THE LINCOLN COUNTY WAR: A DOCUMENTARY HISTORY, op. cit., cites other parts of this letter, pp. 250–251, using as his source the copy on deposit at the British Foreign Office File 05–1965.

71. Coe, George W., FRONTIER FIGHTER: THE AUTOBIOGRAPHY OF GEORGE W. COE WHO FOUGHT AND RODE WITH BILLY THE KID AS RELATED TO NAN HILLARY HARRISON (Houghton Mifflin, 1934), p. 64.

72. Ibid., pp. 66–67.

73. Fulton, Maurice Garland, op. cit., p. 177 and p. 179.

74. Quoted in full in ibid., pp. 196–199.

75. Document signed by J. H. Blazer quoted in full in ibid., pp. 199–201.

76. Trial transcript reproduced in part in Keleher, William A., VIOLENCE IN LINCOLN COUNTY: 1869–1881, op. cit., pp. 101–102.

77. Interview with J. Evetts Haley, 20 March 1927, at Haley History Center, Midland, Texas.

78. Conversation quoted in Fulton, Maurice Garland, op. cit., p. 204.

79. Quoted in full in ibid., pp. 210–212.

80. Conversation quoted in ibid., p. 215.

81. Document quoted in full in ibid., pp. 226–227.

82. The Angel Report remains a key document in any effort to reconstruct the events of the Lincoln County War. Angel, Frank W., "In the Matter of the Cause and Circumstances of the Death of J. H. Tunstall, a British Subject," 44–4–8–3, RG 60, National Archives.

83. Quoted in Hunt, Frazier, op. cit., p. 76.

84. Quoted in full in Fulton, Maurice Garland, op. cit., pp. 246–247.

85. Otero, Miguel Antonio, op. cit., p. 167.

86. Based on an interview with Susan McSween Barber in the Fulton Papers and quoted in Fulton, Maurice Garland, op. cit., p. 267.

87. Document in the Records relating to the Dudley Court of Inquiry RG 153, CQ 1284 at the National Archives. Quoted in ibid., p. 255.

88. Document in the Records relating to the Dudley Court of Inquiry, see above. Quoted in ibid., p. 256.

89. Document in the Records relating to the Dudley Court of Inquiry, see above. Quoted in ibid., p. 262.

90. Letter quoted in ibid., p. 265.

91. Based on interview transcripts of Susan McSween Barber in the Fulton Papers. Quoted in ibid., p. 267.

92. Ibid., p. 268.

93. Letter from Susan McSween to John Tunstall's father date 19 July 1878, a copy of which is in the Fulton Papers. It is quoted only in part in ibid., p. 270.

94. Document in the Records relating to the Dudley Court of Inquiry, see above.

95. Based on the interview transcripts between Colonel Fulton and Susan McSween Barber. Quoted in Fulton, Maurice Garland, op. cit., p. 273.

96. Angel Report, see footnote 82 above.

97. Document quoted in full in ibid., p. 274.

98. Coe, George W., op. cit., p. 77.

99. Otero, Miguel Antonio, op. cit., pp. 114–115.

100. Quoted by Hunt, Frazier, op. cit., p. 117.

101. Conversation cited by Fulton, Maurice Garland, op. cit., p. 379, but quoted out of chronological sequence, a point discussed in the next chapter.

102. Coe, George W., op. cit., p. 139.

103. Quoted in Hunt, Frazier, op. cit., p. 112.

104. Hoyt, Henry F., A FRONTIER DOCTOR (Houghton Mifflin, 1929), pp. 91 and 94.

105. Document quoted in part in Fulton, Maurice Garland, op. cit., pp. 299–301.

106. Quoted in Keleher, William A., VIOLENCE IN LINCOLN COUNTY: 1869–1881, op. cit., p. 204.

107. This reconstruction is based on testimony at the Dudley Inquiry. The conversation appears in Fulton, Maurice Garland, op. cit., p. 326, and Nolan, Frederick, THE LINCOLN COUNTY WAR: A DOCUMENTARY HISTORY, op. cit., pp. 375–376. It is sometimes stated that the muzzle flash from Campbell's pistol set Chapman's clothes on fire. The condition of the body, and the thoroughness with which virtually all his clothing was burned off him when he was found, makes this an unlikely explanation.

108. Letter reproduced in Morsberger, Robert E. and Katharine M., LEW WALLACE: MILITANT ROMANTIC (McGraw-Hill, 1980), p. 274. All the correspondence between them is in the Wallace Papers, see Appendix A.

109. Reproduced in ibid., p. 274.

110. Letter reproduced in Keleher, William A., VIOLENCE IN LINCOLN COUNTY: 1869–1881, op. cit., p. 214.

111. Wallace Papers. Letter reproduced in its entirety in Keleher and excerpted in Morsberger.

112. Letter quoted in Keleher, William A., VIOLENCE IN LINCOLN COUNTY: 1869–1881, op. cit., p. 216.

113. Nolan, Frederick, THE LINCOLN COUNTY WAR: A DOCUMENTARY HISTORY, op. cit., p. 383.

114. Morsberger, Robert E. and Katharine M., op. cit., p. 216.

115. Wallace Papers. Reproduced in Keleher, William A., VIOLENCE IN LINCOLN COUNTY: 1869–1881, op. cit., p. 239.

116. Wallace Papers for Pope letter. For Swaine report and recommendation JAG, Washington, to AAG Department of Missouri, 29 September 1879 and JAG to Secretary of

War G. W. McCrary 22 October 1879, File 1405, Adjutant General's Office, at National Archives.

117. Conversation cited by Fulton, Maurice Garland, op. cit., p. 349.

118. Letter from Godfrey Gauss to John P. Tunstall dated 22 November 1879. A copy of it is to be found in the Fulton Papers.

119. Conversation quoted in its entirety in Otero, Miguel Antonio, op. cit., pp. 84–86.

120. Entire letter reproduced in Metz, Leon C., PAT GARRETT: THE STORY OF LAWMAN (University of Oklahoma Press, 1974), pp. 38–39.

121. Comment quoted by O'Connor, Richard, PAT GARRETT: A BIOGRAPHY OF THE FAMOUS MARSHAL AND THE KILLER OF BILLY THE KID (Doubleday, 1960), p. 19.

122. Metz, Leon C., op. cit., p. 37.

123. Curry, George, AN AUTOBIOGRAPHY (University of New Mexico Press, 1958), p. 218.

124. Keleher, William A., THE FABULOUS FRONTIER, op. cit., pp. 72–73.

125. Quoted in Otero, Miguel Antonio, op. cit., pp. 158–159.

126. Metz, Leon C., op. cit., p. 44.

127. Conversation quoted by Eve Ball, op. cit., pp. 174–175.

128. Conversation quoted in ibid., p. 179.

129. The entire affidavit is reproduced in Adams, Ramon F., A FITTING DEATH FOR BILLY THE KID, op. cit., pp. 160–166.

130. Document reproduced in Keleher, William A., VIOLENCE IN LINCOLN COUNTY: 1869–1881, op. cit., pp. 288–289, and with closing salutation, Hunt, Frazier, op. cit., pp. 230–231.

131. The reward was offered on 13 December 1880 and recorded in the Executive Record Book No. 2, 1867–1882, pp. 507–508.

132. Document reproduced in Keleher, William A., VIOLENCE IN LINCOLN COUNTY: 1869–1881, op. cit., pp. 232–233.

133. Quoted in Hutchinson, W. H., A BAR CROSS MAN: THE LIFE AND PERSONAL WRITINGS OF EUGENE MANLOVE RHODES (University of Oklahoma Press, 1956), pp. 264–265. The letter is now in the Rhodes Collection at the Henry E. Huntington Library.

134. Siringo, Charles A., A TEXAS COWBOY; OR FIFTEEN YEARS ON THE HURRICANE DECK OF A SPANISH PONY—TAKEN FROM REAL LIFE (1885; University of Nebraska Press, 1966), p. 129.

135. Document reproduced partially in Otero, Miguel Antonio, op. cit., pp. 93–94. See Note 139 below for the origin of this letter.

136. Quoted in Hutchinson, W. H., op. cit., p. 264. Harrison Leussler was the West Coast representative for Houghton Mifflin.

137. Garrett, Pat F. (pseud. Ash Upson), THE AUTHENTIC LIFE OF BILLY THE KID (1882; University of Oklahoma Press, 1954) with an Introduction by J. C. Dykes, p. 123.

138. Otero quoted this portion of East's letter [written not to him but to Charles A. Siringo] separately in Otero, Miguel Antonio, op. cit., p. 99.

139. James East's letter to Judge William H. Burges dated 20 May 1926 in the Mullin Collection.

140. Otero, Miguel Antonio, op. cit., p. 178.

141. Hoyt, Henry F., op. cit., pp. 170–171.

142. Both Frazier Hunt and William A. Keleher in VIOLENCE IN LINCOLN COUNTY: 1869–1881 reproduce the Kid's correspondence in its entirety. As the more accessible account, my page references are to Keleher, p. 300. The correspondence itself is in the Wallace Papers.

143. Ibid., p. 300.

144. Ibid., p. 301.

145. Ibid., p. 302.

146. Hoyt, Henry F., op. cit., p. 160.

147. Criminal Cases 531 and 532, Territory v. William Bonney alias Kid: murder; and Doña Ana County, District Court Journal: 384–91, 406–07, 411, at the New Mexico State Records Center and Archives.

148. Utley, Robert M., BILLY THE KID: A SHORT AND VIOLENT LIFE (University of Nebraska Press, 1989), p. 173.

149. Ibid., p. 172.

150. Document in Fulton Papers. It is quoted in Fulton, Maurice Garland, op. cit., p. 391.

151. Quoted in Poe, Sophie A., BUCKBOARD DAYS (Caxton Printers, 1936) edited by Eugene Cunningham, p. 102.

152. Reminiscence quoted in Hunt, Frazier, op. cit., pp. 300–301.

153. Metz, Leon C., op. cit., p. 133.

154. Macrobius, Book II, c. 5.

155. Reminiscence quoted in Otero, Miguel Antonio, op. cit., p. 155.

156. Poe, John W., THE DEATH OF BILLY THE KID (Houghton Mifflin, 1933) edited with an Introduction by Col. Maurice Garland Fulton, p. 32.

157. On unnumbered pages between p. 304 and p. 305 in VIOLENCE IN LINCOLN COUNTY: 1869–1881 by William A. Keleher, the author reproduces a photostat of the coroner's jury from 15 July 1881. It is completely in Spanish except for the words "Who is it?" which are in English. Garrett in the Garrett/Upson account has Pete say: "That's him."

158. From a conversation quoted in Otero, Miguel Antonio, op. cit., pp. 156–158.

159. Poe, John W., op. cit., pp. 37–38.

160. Conversation quoted in ibid., pp. 156–158.

161. J. Evetts Haley's interview with Deluvina Maxwell at Fort Sumner 24 June 1927 contradicts slightly when this was said, now on deposit at the Haley History Center, Midland, Texas. Most accounts, however, have her saying it the night the Kid was killed.

162. Interview reproduced in Otero, Miguel Antonio, op. cit., p. 154.

163. Adams, Ramon F., op. cit., p. 142.

164. Otero, Miguel Antonio, op. cit., p. xii.

165. Note 157. Col. Fulton also reproduced the entire document in his Epilogue to Poe's THE DEATH OF BILLY THE KID, op. cit., pp. 54–56.

166. Quoted in Metz, Leon C., op. cit., p. 240.

167. Quoted in Otero, Miguel Antonio, op. cit., p. 119.

Chapter Two: Billy and the Historians

1. Garrett, Pat F. (pseud. Ash Upson), op. cit., p. xxvii.

2. Ibid., p. 7.

3. Ibid., p. 8.

4. Ibid., p. 9.

5. Ibid., p. 9.

6. Ibid., p. 9.

7. Ibid., p. 10.

8. Ibid., p. 22.

9. Ibid., p. 23.

10. Ibid., p. 27.

11. Ibid., p. 31.

12. Ibid., p. 49.

13. Ibid., p. 49.

14. Ibid., p. 51.

15. Ibid., pp. 52–53.

16. Ibid., pp. 60–61.

17. Ibid., p. 83.

18. "Verando" was probably a reference to La Berrenda, or Berrendo, a settlement northwest of Roswell.

19. Ibid., p. 109.

20. Ibid., p. 125.

21. Ibid., p. 134.

22. Ibid., p. 137.

23. Ibid., p. 138. However, one of the Lincoln jail trusties with whom the Kid had words during his escape was named Alexander Nunnelly.

24. Ibid., p. 142.

25. Ibid., p. 145.

26. Ibid., p. 147.

27. Ibid., p. 147.

28. Ibid., p. 148.

29. Ibid., p. 149.

30. Ibid., p. xxvii.

31. Garrett, Pat F., THE AUTHENTIC LIFE OF BILLY THE KID (Macmillan, 1927) edited by Maurice Garland Fulton, p. 81.

32. Quoted in Adams, Ramon F., A FITTING DEATH FOR BILLY THE KID, op. cit., p. 34.

33. Siringo, Charles A., A TEXAS COWBOY; OR, FIFTEEN YEARS ON THE HURRICANE DECK OF A SPANISH PONY—TAKEN FROM REAL LIFE, op. cit., p. 170. Orlan Sawey in an article "Charlie Siringo, Reluctant Propagandist" in WESTERN AMERICAN LITERATURE (Fall, 1972) explores the reasons behind Siringo's fascination with the Kid. Siringo's biographer Ben E. Pingenot in SIRINGO (College Station: Texas A&M University Press, 1989) notes that however popular the Kid may have been with readers, Siringo's frequent return to him as a subject proved to be financially unrewarding and that somehow Siringo "could not regenerate the éclat of his first book, A TEXAS COWBOY," p. 95.

34. Siringo, Charles A., op. cit., p. 177.

35. Quoted in Dykes, J.C., BILLY THE KID: THE BIBLIOGRAPHY OF A LEGEND, op. cit., p. 46.

36. Quoted in Adams, Ramon F., A FITTING DEATH FOR BILLY THE KID, op. cit., p. 171.

37. Garrett, Pat F., THE AUTHENTIC LIFE OF BILLY THE KID, op. cit., p. 5.

38. Siringo, Charles A., A TEXAS COWBOY, op. cit., pp. 171–172.

39. Ibid., p. 172.

40. Quoted in Adams, Ramon F., A FITTING DEATH FOR BILLY THE KID, op. cit., p. 215.

41. This subject is explored in greater depth in Richard Patterson's article "Jesse James Meets Billy the Kid—Fact or Fantasy" in TRUE WEST (10/92) pp. 39–43. Although Patterson seems to embrace several of the Utley fantasies, his conclusion based on documents and testimony is that "the evidence supporting the encounter is fairly strong," p. 43.

42. Quoted by Adams, Ramon F., BURS UNDER THE SADDLE: A SECOND LOOK AT BOOKS AND HISTORIES OF THE WEST (University of Oklahoma Press, 1964), p. 266.

43. Ibid., p. 266.

44. Quoted in ibid., p. 269.

45. Hough, Emerson, THE STORY OF THE OUTLAW (Outing, 1907), pp. 311–312.

46. Adams, Ramon F., SIX-GUNS AND SADDLE LEATHER: A BIBLIOGRAPHY OF BOOKS AND PAMPHLETS ON WESTERN OUTLAWS AND GUNMEN (University of Oklahoma Press, 1969), p. 186.

47. Burns, Walter Noble, THE SAGA OF BILLY THE KID (Doubleday, 1927), p. 135.

48. Ibid., p. 184. The Burns letter to Judge Burges was collected by Robert N. Mullin and is now to be found among his papers at the Haley Historical Center in Midland, Texas.

49. Ibid., pp. 196–197.

50. Ibid., p. 265.

51. Ibid., p. 283.

52. Hunt, Frazier, op. cit., p. 314.

53. Nolan, Frederick, THE LINCOLN COUNTY WAR: A DOCUMENTARY HISTORY, op. cit., p. 424.

54. Poe, John W., THE DEATH OF BILLY THE KID, op. cit., p. 36.

55. Garrett, Pat F., op. cit, p. 147.

56. Ibid., p. 50.

57. Ibid., p. 174.

58. Ibid., p. 175.

59. Ibid., p. 159.

60. Ibid., p. 231.

61. Ibid., pp. 321–322.

62. Ibid., p. 310.

63. Ibid., p. 301.

64. Ibid., p. 280.

65. Ibid., p. 200.

66. Ibid., p. 19.

67. Ibid., pp. 177–178.

68. Ibid., pp. 184–185.

69. Ibid., p. 195.

70. Hersey, Harold, SINGIN' RAWHIDE (Doran, 1926), p. 128.

71. Burns, Walter Noble, op. cit., pp. 180–181.

72. Letter reproduced in Nolan, Frederick W., THE LIFE AND DEATH OF JOHN H. TUNSTALL, op. cit., p. 174.

73. Utley, Robert M., HIGH NOON IN LINCOLN: VIOLENCE ON THE WEST-
ERN FRONTIER (University of New Mexico Press, 1987), p. 6.

74. Ibid., p. 175.

75. Ibid., p. 193.

76. Ibid., p. 193.

77. Francisco Trujillo interview in THEY "KNEW" BILLY THE KID: INTER-
VIEWS WITH OLD-TIME NEW MEXICANS (Ancient City Press, 1987) edited by
Robert F. Kadlec, p. 68.

78. Ibid., p. 71.

79. Ibid., pp. 72–73.

80. Ibid., p. 74.

81. Ibid., p. 74.

82. Ibid., p. 75.

83. Ibid., p. 75.

84. Ibid., p. 76.

85. Ibid., p. 68.

86. Ibid., p. 69.

87. Ibid., p. 109.

88. Utley, Robert M., HIGH NOON IN LINCOLN, op. cit., p. 7.

89. Ibid., p. 6.

90. Ibid., p. 33 and in BILLY THE KID: A SHORT AND VIOLENT LIFE, op. cit., p. 22.

91. Ibid., p. 35 and in BILLY THE KID, p. 30.

92. Ibid., p. 49 and in BILLY THE KID, p. 46.

93. Ibid., p. 50 and in BILLY THE KID, p. 46.

94. Ibid., p. 52 and in BILLY THE KID, p. 46.

95. Ibid., p. 53 and in FOUR FIGHTERS OF LINCOLN COUNTY (University of
New Mexico Press, 1986), p. 91.

96. Ibid., p. 53.

97. Ibid., p. 54 and in BILLY THE KID, p. 52.

98. Ibid., p. 60 and in BILLY THE KID, p. 64.

99. Ibid., p. 60 and in BILLY THE KID, p. 64.

100. Ibid., p. 61 and in BILLY THE KID, p. 65.

101. Nolan, Frederick, THE LINCOLN COUNTY WAR: A DOCUMENTARY HIS-
TORY, p. 247. Nolan in this section discusses all of the theories advanced so far as to why
Brady was walking past the Tunstall store and having eliminated all of them but one,
namely that he knew McSween was on his way into town and wanted to be in position to
arrest him, that one must be closest to the truth.

102. Utley, Robert M., HIGH NOON IN LINCOLN, op. cit., p. 61 and in BILLY THE
KID, pp. 65–66.

103. Ealy, Taylor F., MISSIONARIES, OUTLAWS AND INDIANS: TAYLOR F.
EALY AT LINCOLN AND ZUNI, 1878–1881, op. cit., p. 31. However, Bender is incorrect in claiming the Kid was already known as "Billy the Kid." That happened first in 1881
when Koogler of the Las Vegas Optic gave him that moniker for the first time.

104. Utley, Robert M., HIGH NOON IN LINCOLN, op. cit., p. 75 and in BILLY THE
KID, p. 81.

105. Ibid., p. 82.

106. Ibid., p. 92 and in BILLY THE KID, p. 92. In FOUR FIGHTERS OF LINCOLN
COUNTY, p. 45.

107. Fulton, Maurice Garland, op. cit., p. 255.

108. Utley, Robert M., HIGH NOON IN LINCOLN, op. cit., p. 94 and in BILLY THE KID, p. 92.

109. Ibid., p. 91 and in BILLY THE KID, p. 93.

110. Ibid., p. 104 and in BILLY THE KID. p. 242, n.23.

111. Ibid., p. 133 and in BILLY THE KID, p. 114.

112. Utley, Robert M., FOUR FIGHTERS OF LINCOLN COUNTY, op. cit., p. 35.

113. Nolan, Frederick, THE LINCOLN COUNTY WAR: A DOCUMENTARY HISTORY, op. cit., p. 392.

114. Utley, Robert M., HIGH NOON IN LINCOLN, op. cit., p. 153.

115. Ibid., p. 164 and in BILLY THE KID, p. 83.

116. Ibid., p. 156 and in BILLY THE KID, p. 175.

117. In BILLY THE KID, p. 172.

118. Fulton, Maurice Garland, op. cit., p. 389 and Keleher, William A., VIOLENCE IN LINCOLN COUNTY: 1869–1881, op. cit., p. 315.

119. Keleher, William A., op. cit., p. 329.

120. Utley, Robert M. BILLY THE KID, op. cit., p. 173.

121. Ibid., p. 180.

122. Ibid., p. 194.

123. Utley, Robert M., HIGH NOON IN LINCOLN, p. 165.

124. Metz, Leon C., op. cit., pp. 80–81. The quotation is from the Garrett/Upson account, p. 125.

125. Utley, Robert M., BILLY THE KID, p. 195.

126. Document in the Sonnichsen Papers, see Appendix A. Quoted in part in Metz, Leon C., op. cit., p. 91.

127. Utley, Robert M., HIGH NOON IN LINCOLN, op. cit., p. ix.

128. Cline, Donald, op. cit., p. 103.

129. Ibid., p. 65.

130. Ibid., p. 118.

131. Poe, John W., op. cit., p. 41.

132. Adams, Ramon F., SIX-GUNS AND SADDLE LEATHER, op. cit., pp. 324–325.

133. Metz, Leon C., "The Lincoln County War: A Bibliographic Essay," in RIO GRANDE HISTORY No. 9 (1978), p. 18.

134. Lavash, Donald R., SHERIFF WILLIAM BRADY: TRAGIC HERO OF THE LINCOLN COUNTY WAR (Sunstone Press, 1986), p. 75.

135. Ibid., p. 9.

136. Nolan, Frederick, THE LINCOLN COUNTY WAR: A DOCUMENTARY HISTORY, op. cit., p. 439.

137. Ibid., p. 440.

138. Raine, William MacLeod, FAMOUS SHERIFFS AND WESTERN OUTLAWS (Doubleday, 1929), p. 125.

139. Cunningham, Eugene, TRIGGERNOMETRY (Caxton Printers, 1941), p. 169.

140. Cunningham, Eugene, TRIGGERNOMETRY (London: Transworld Publishers, 1957), pp. 169–170.

141. Otero, Miguel Antonio, op. cit., p. 70.

142. Lamar, Howard R., ed., THE READER'S ENCYCLOPEDIA OF THE AMERICAN WEST (Crowell, 1977), p. 95.

Chapter Three: Billy the Kid in Fiction

1. Garrett, Pat F., THE AUTHENTIC LIFE OF BILLY THE KID, op. cit., p. xviii.

2. Quoted by Adams, Ramon F., A FITTING DEATH FOR BILLY THE KID, op. cit., p. 32.

3. Quoted in ibid., p. 33.

4. Quoted in ibid., p. 33.

5. Quoted in ibid., p. 37.

6. Ibid., p. 37.

7. Ibid., p. 43.

8. Ibid., p. 45.

9. Steckmesser, Kent Ladd, THE WESTERN HERO IN HISTORY AND LEGEND (University of Oklahoma Press, 1965), p. 75.

10. Quoted in Adams, Ramon F., A FITTING DEATH FOR BILLY THE KID, op. cit., p. 46.

11. Ibid., p. 47.

12. Steckmesser, Kent Ladd, op. cit., p. 84.

13. Henry, O. (pseud. William Sydney Porter), HEART OF THE WEST (Doubleday Page, 1904), p. 189.

14. Otero, Miguel Antonio, op. cit., p. 172.

15. Henry, O., op. cit., p. 187.

16. Ibid., p. 190.

17. Ibid., p. 196.

18. Rhodes, Eugene Manlove, "In Defense of Pat Garrett," in THE RHODES READER: STORIES OF VIRGINS, VILLAINS AND VARMINTS (University of Oklahoma Press, 1975, second edition) selected by W. H. Hutchinson, p. 307.

19. Ibid., p. 314.

20. Ibid., p. 307.

21. Ibid., p. 316.

22. Rhodes, Eugene Manlove, PASÓ POR AQUÍ (1927; University of Oklahoma Press, 1976), p. 128.

23. Grey, Zane, FORLORN RIVER (Harper, 1927), pp. 180–181.

24. Grey, Zane, "NEVADA" (Harper, 1928), p. 197.

25. Ibid., pp. 177–178.

26. Ibid., p. 197.

27. Ibid., p. 206.

28. Ibid., p. 362.

29. Grey, Zane, SHADOW ON THE TRAIL (Harper, 1946), p. 76.

30. Ibid., p. 77.

31. Ibid., p. 81.

32. Ibid., p. 84.

33. Ibid., pp. 86–87.

34. Ibid., p. 88.

35. Ibid., p. 89.

36. Ibid., p. 275.

37. Coolidge, Dane, WAR PAINT (Dutton, 1929), p. 13.

38. Coolidge, Dane, BLOODY HEAD (Dutton, 1940), p. 174.

39. Ibid., p. 186. Italics in original.

40. Mann, E. B., GAMBLIN' MAN (Morrow, 1934), p. 267.

41. *Ibid.*, p. 314.

42. Cunningham, Eugene, "Billy the Kid Alive?" in WESTERN YARNS (Vol. 1, No. 2) March, 1938, p. 98.

43. Adams, Ramon F., A FITTING DEATH FOR BILLY THE KID, op. cit., p. 289.

44. Cunningham, Eugene, DIAMOND RIVER MAN (Houghton Mifflin, 1934), p. 5.

45. Ibid., p. 6.

46. Ibid., p. 15.

47. Ibid., p. 19.

48. Ibid., pp. 38 and 39.

49. Ibid., p. 125.

50. Ibid., p. 154.

51. Ibid., p. 214.

52. Ibid., p. 265.

53. Nafziger, Ray, "Guns of the Owlhoot Pack" in MAVERICKS (October, 1934), p. 127.

54. Quoted by Adams, Ramon F., in A FITTING DEATH FOR BILLY THE KID, op. cit., p. 196. Dykes in BILLY THE KID, THE BIBLIOGRAPHY OF A LEGEND indicated that this sixteen-page chapbook was very scarce already in 1952.

55. Nye, Nelson C., A BULLET FOR BILLY THE KID (1941; Avon, 1950), p. 8.

56. Ibid., p. 7.

57. Ibid., p. 10.

58. Ibid., p. 50.

59. Ibid., p. 155.

60. Olmsted, Harry F., "There's Hell Tonight in Lincoln County!," STAR WESTERN (February, 1947), p. 17.

61. Ibid., p. 13.

62. Ibid., p. 21.

63. Ibid., p. 21.

64. Ibid., p. 21.

65. Ibid., p. 25.

66. Ibid., p. 25.

67. Ibid., p. 25.

68. Corle, Edwin, "The Ghost of Billy the Kid," reprinted in WESTERN STORY OMNIBUS (World Publishing, 1945) edited by William Targ, pp. 140 and 141.

69. Corle, Edwin, BILLY THE KID (Duell, Sloan, and Pearce, 1953), p. 85.

70. Ibid., p. 102.

71. Ibid., p. 290.

72. Ibid., p. 188.

73. Ibid., pp. 43–44.

74. Lehman, Paul Evan, PISTOLS ON THE PECOS (Avon, 1953), p. 5.

75. Ibid., p. 14.

76. Ibid., p. 37.

77. Ibid., p. 67.

78. Ibid., p. 70.

79. Ibid., p. 97.

80. Ibid., p. 107.

81. Ibid., p. 108.

82. Burnett, W. R., MI AMIGO (1959; Bantam, 1963), p. 117.

83. Ibid., p. 63.

84. Ibid., p. 69.

85. Ibid., pp. 101 and 100.

86. Ibid., p. 107.

87. Ibid., p. 139.

88. Ibid., p. 148.

89. Ibid., p. 151.

90. Ibid., p. 153.

91. Ibid., p. 153.

92. Neider, Charles, THE AUTHENTIC DEATH OF HENDRY JONES (1956; Harrow Books, 1972) with an Introduction by Wirt Williams, p. vii.

93. Ibid., p. x.

94. Ibid., pp. x–xi.

95. Ibid., p. 219.

96. Ibid., p. 21.

97. Ibid., p. 21.

98. Ibid., p. 26.

99. Ibid., p. 49.

100. Ibid., pp. 50 and 52.

101. Ibid., p. 69.

102. Ibid., p. 161.

103. Ibid., p. 112.

104. Ibid., p. 115.

105. Ibid., p. 116.

106. Ibid., p. 117. The "border shift" is the throwing of a gun from one hand to the other and catching it, cocking it, even firing it in the other hand without pause. Eugene Cunningham illustrated it in TRIGGERNOMETRY, op. cit., p. 423.

107. Ibid., p. 122.

108. Ibid., p. 218.

109. Ibid., p. 222.

110. Bean, Amelia, TIME FOR OUTRAGE (Doubleday, 1967), p. 443.

111. Ibid., p. 445.

112. Ibid., p. 178.

113. Ibid., p. 181.

114. Ibid., p. 265.

115. Braun, Matt, JURY OF SIX (Pocket Books, 1980), p. 60.

116. Ibid., p. 19.

117. Ibid., p. 34.

118. Ibid., p. 53.

119. Ibid., p. 59.

120. Ibid., p. 97.

121. Ibid., p. 111.

122. Ibid., p. 175.

123. Ibid., p. 197.

124. Braun, Matt, RIO HONDO (New American Library, 1987), p. 9.

125. McMurtry, Larry, ANYTHING FOR BILLY (1988; Pocket Books, 1989), p. 3.

126. Ibid., p. 4.
127. Ibid., p. 9.
128. Ibid., p. 34.
129. Ibid., p. 87.
130. Ibid., p. 141.
131. Ibid., p. 162.
132. Ibid., p. 221.
133. Ibid., p. 383.
134. Ibid., p. 394.

Chapter Four: Billy the Kid in Film

1. Vidor, King, A TREE IS A TREE (Harcourt, Brace, 1953), p. 189.

2. Sonnichsen, C. L., FROM HOPALONG TO HUD: THOUGHTS ON WESTERN FICTION (Texas A&M University Press, 1978), p. 19.

3. Boyer, Glenn G., ed., I MARRIED WYATT EARP: THE RECOLLECTIONS OF JOSEPHINE SARAH MARCUS EARP (University of Arizona Press, 1976), p. 248.

4. Sherman, Eric, and Martin Rubin, THE DIRECTOR'S EVENT (Atheneum, 1970), p. 105.

5. Seydor, Paul, PECKINPAH: THE WESTERN FILMS (University of Illinois Press, 1980), p. 188.

6. Ibid., p. 202.

7. Much more discussion of this film can be found in my books THE AMERICAN WEST IN FILM: CRITICAL APPROACHES TO THE WESTERN (Greenwood Press, 1985) and ENCOUNTERS WITH FILMMAKERS: EIGHT CAREER STUDIES (Greenwood Press, 1991). There are actually four different versions of the Peckinpah film. The one narrated above is based on Peckinpah's original director's cut, a print of which survives in possession of Matthew Peckinpah, the director's only son.

Chapter Five: The Legend of Billy the Kid

1. Quintilian, Book X, i.3.

2. Cohen, Morris R., THE MEANING OF HUMAN HISTORY (Open Court, 1947), p. 33.

3. Ibid., p. 34.

4. Vergil, ÆNEID, I.199.

5. Stern, Fritz, ed., THE VARIETIES OF HISTORY: VOLTAIRE TO THE PRESENT (Meridian Books, 1972), p. 17.

6. Johnson, Edgar, SIR WALTER SCOTT: THE GREAT UNKNOWN in Two Volumes (Macmillan, 1970), Vol. I, p. 530.

7. Corle, Edwin, BILLY THE KID: A NOVEL (1953; University of New Mexico Press, 1979) with an Introduction by William T. Pilkington, p. xi.

8. Smith, Henry Nash, VIRGIN LAND: THE AMERICAN WEST AS MYTH AND SYMBOL (1950; Harvard University Press, 1970), pp. vii–viii.

9. Ibid., p. 91.

10. Turner, Henry Jackson, op. cit., p. 38.

11. Drinnon, Richard, FACING WEST: THE METAPHYSICS OF INDIAN-HATING AND EMPIRE-BUILDING (Meridian Books, 1980), p. 463.

12. Cawelti, John G., THE SIX-GUN MYSTIQUE (Bowling Green Popular Press, 1975), p. 38.

13. Moore, Robin, GREEN BERETS (Crown, 1965), p. 122.

14. Cawelti, John G., ADVENTURE, MYSTERY, AND ROMANCE: FORMULA STORIES AS ART AND POPULAR CULTURE (University of Chicago Press, 1976), pp. 232–233.

15. Tatum, Stephen, INVENTING BILLY THE KID: VISIONS OF THE OUTLAW IN AMERICA, 1881–1981 (University of New Mexico Press, 1982), p. x.

16. Ibid., p. 153.

17. Ibid., pp. 41–42.

18. Ibid., p. 94.

19. Ibid., p. 95.

20. Ibid., p. 111.

21. Ibid., p. 140.

22. Ibid., p. 175.

23. Ibid., p. 174.

24. Ibid., pp. 175–176.

25. Ibid., p. 176.

26. Ibid., p. 140.

27. Ibid., p. 151.

28. Steckmesser, Kent Ladd, op. cit., p. 250.

29. Ibid., p. 32.

30. Ibid., p. 57.

31. Ibid., pp. 76–77.

32. Ibid., p. 77.

33. Ibid., p. 85.

34. Quoted in ibid., p. 85.

35. Ibid., p. 100.

36. Ibid., p. 100.

37. Adams, Ramon F., BURS UNDER THE SADDLE (University of Oklahoma Press, 1964), p. 175. Fishwick's prose is slightly different in the article than in the later book version. Adams quotes the book version in his entry. The image, however, is the same.

38. Fishwick, Marshall, "Billy the Kid: Faust in America," THE SATURDAY REVIEW (11 October 1952), p. 12.

39. Ibid., p. 35.

40. Ibid., p. 36.

41. Adler, Alfred, "Billy the Kid: A Case Study in Epic Origins," WESTERN FOLKLORE (April, 1951), p. 152.

42. Frye, Northrop, ANATOMY OF CRITICISM: FOUR ESSAYS (Princeton University Press, 1957), p. 187.

43. Ibid., p. 304.

44. Franz, Marie-Louise von, SHADOW AND EVIL IN FAIRYTALES (University of Dallas Press, 1980), p. 20.

45. Auerbach, Erich, MIMESIS: THE REPRESENTATION OF REALITY IN WESTERN LITERATURE (1953; Anchor Books, 1957) translated from the German by Willard Trask, p. 17.

46. Ibid., p. 16.

47. Dobie, J. Frank, "Billy the Kid," SOUTHWEST REVIEW (Spring, 1929), p. 314.

48. Ibid., p. 320.

49. Boatright, Mody C., "The Western Bad Man as Hero," MESQUITE AND WIL-LOW (Southern Methodist University Press, 1957), p. 97.

50. Ibid., p. 97.

51. Ibid., p. 98.

52. Ibid., p. 98.

53. Ibid., p. 99.

54. Ibid., p. 100.

55. Ibid., p. 101.

56. Twain, Mark, ROUGHING IT (1872; Signet Classics, 1962), p. 111.

57. Bodkin, Maud, ARCHETYPAL PATTERNS IN POETRY: PSYCHOLOGICAL STUDIES OF IMAGINATION (1934; Oxford University Press, 1963), p. 23.

58. Quoted on the frontispiece of Lucas, F. L. and Prudence, FROM OLYMPUS TO THE STYX (London: Cassell, 1934).

INDEX